THE COMMUNISM OF LOVE

AK PRESS

THE COMMUNISM OF LOVE

An Inquiry into the Poverty of Exchange Value

by
Richard Gilman-Opalsky

The Communism of Love: An Inquiry into the Poverty of Exchange Value

© 2020 Richard Gilman-Opalsky
This edition © 2020 AK Press

ISBN: 978-1-84935-391-5
E-ISBN: 978-1-84935-392-2
Library of Congress Control Number: 2020933409

AK Press
370 Ryan Ave. #100
Chico, CA 95973
www.akpress.org
akpress@akpress.org

AK Press
33 Tower St.
Edinburgh EH6 7BN
Scotland
www.akuk.com
ak@akedin.demon.co.uk

Please contact us to request the latest AK Press distribution catalog, which features books, pamphlets, zines, and stylish apparel published and/or distributed by AK Press. Alternatively, visit our websites for the complete catalog, latest news, and secure ordering.

Printed in the United States on acid-free, recycled paper

For my children
and the pleasure of participating in their becoming

And once again, for Robyn,
who isn't with me for the money

CONTENTS

Introduction

"*I love you. —So do I ... So-do-I* inaugurates a mutation: the old rules fall away, everything is possible—even, then, this: that I give up possessing you. A revolution, in short—not so far, perhaps, from the political kind: for in both cases, what I hallucinate is the absolute New: (amorous) reform has no appeal for me."

–Roland Barthes, *A Lover's Discourse*

"People who talk about revolution and class struggle without referring explicitly to everyday life, without understanding what is subversive about love and what is positive in the refusal of constraints—such people have a corpse in their mouth."

–Raoul Vaneigem, *The Revolution of Everyday Life*

This book is about the communism of love. It is, in other words, about the necessarily and irreducibly communist form and content of love. The chapters of this book travel far, but are held together by an overarching argument about love as a communist power. At the same time, this book is an inquiry into the poverty of exchange value. By "poverty of exchange value" I mean that the capitalist mode of assessing value is incapable of appreciating what human beings—everywhere on earth—value the most. For all of its multifarious meanings, love reveals the limits of capital to appropriately value the experiences and relationships that human beings treasure most. Yet *most* human life is subordinated to exchange relations. In recent decades, the logic of capital has been increasingly extended to the administration of love in ways previously unimaginable. But capital only succeeds in commodifying love by destroying it, by converting it into an impoverished "false form" (that is, a spectacle) of itself. We will have to say what is specifically meant by love, a task that defines the first three chapters.

The Communism of Love moves from a cautious exploration of love as a political concept to the argument that love is a practice of relationality incommensurate with capitalist exchange relations. Human relationality is formed in our worldly intersubjectivity, and what shapes our relationships with others can be (and often is) far more valuable than those relationships established by capitalist exchange relations. The nature of a social relationship is and can be variegated and emotionally and constitutively diverse. However, Harry Cleaver observes: "Capitalists, unfortunately, try to organize this kind of relationship in ways that give them power over us. They seek to impose our relationship to them to such a degree that we come to define ourselves, and are defined by others, primarily in terms

3

of our jobs.... In actuality, of course, we may *do* and *be* a great many things, but within capitalism the expectation is that we will identify with our work."[1] Whatever else we are and whatever else we do, besides and beyond our work, is best seen, appreciated, and understood in relations of love. People usually do not want their entire identity determined by what they do for money. In contrast to the global power of capital, global aspirations for love challenge and displace relations of life governed by the logic of capital.

Because the present book draws on a vast bibliography including not only philosophy and political theory but also psychoanalysis, social psychology, theology, and sociological theory, readers may expect a full sweep or promise of exhaustive understanding. Such readers should be disabused of that expectation from the start. I am offering a critical and substantial development of Erich Fromm's old theory of love in the light of more contemporary social, political, technological, and psychoanalytic research—and, perhaps most importantly, in the context of present currents in twenty-first-century Marxist philosophy. However, aspects of this work aim at a longer historical view and broader context, which can be seen for example in chapter 2 on Plato's *Symposium*.

But, in what ways will we think about love beyond what has already been said by philosophers from Plato to Fromm, bell hooks, Alain Badiou, and so many others who have produced a veritable library on love? There are four basic distinguishing features of the present study, and far more in the particularities.

First, I bring together interdisciplinary sources on love *that have never been synthesized in a single study*. Such a synthesis will be contextualized and proven necessary for both appreciating and moving beyond the tendencies and deficits prominent in the literature's history. Too many theories of love (*indeed all of them*) ignore the other major studies of love to their own detriment.

Second, I claim that love is a practice that socializes a unique polyamory beyond the structure of romantic relationship. This polyamory is not about having multiple partners, and is not primarily sexual or romantic, but is instead the polyamory of a communist affection for others. I argue that the human aspiration to love expresses a longing for a form of communist relationality. This can be demonstrated whether or not one recognizes the communism of their own relationships. In this way, I shall

---

1. Harry Cleaver, *Rupturing the Dialectic: The Struggle against Work, Money, and Financialization* (Oakland: AK Press, 2017), 110–11.

muster the courage to speak of the universality of at least one communist tendency (the communist tendency of love).

Third, I argue for the desirability and practicality of a logic of human relations that is irreducibly antagonistic to capitalist exchange relations. If everyone who aspires to love aims, through that peculiar aspiration, to separate and defend their most cherished relationships from the exigencies of capital, then no capitalist totality can be fully realized. Capitalism, as both an ideological position and as an actual power that organizes life, cannot satisfactorily encompass the psychosocial and emotional needs of everyday people.

Fourth, I argue that revolts and other disruptive social and political movements are always, at least to some extent, concerned with the creation or restoration of relations of love against a monetized life of exchange relations. In such movements—and indeed, in a wide range of global uprisings—love is often wielded as a nonmilitaristic weapon, or, rather, as a *threatening sensibility*. Love activates a sensibility about being with other people that is antithetical to capitalist reasons for being-with-others.

Of course, all of this and more will need to be substantiated. But the conclusions of *The Communism of Love* are far from obvious and far from common understanding. Take the example of a major rival in the philosophy of love, Martha Nussbaum, one of the most influential philosophers in the world. Nussbaum wrote a philosophy of love in *Political Emotions: Why Love Matters for Justice* (2013). Remarkably, in her 450-page study, Nussbaum is silent on the tensions between love and capitalist exchange relations, and she thinks that Marx has nothing to contribute to her inquiry, mentioning him only once in passing. Nussbaum assumes we can pursue a politics of love that will lead to increasing justice, the latter being fully compatible with capitalism. In contrast to Nussbaum, the present study offers a refutation and rejection of both liberal *and* conservative conceptions of love as a force of justice within existing capitalist societies, and argues instead that love is either a communist power or it is not in fact love. We shall also explore major disagreements with Erich Fromm, Axel Honneth, bell hooks, Eva Illouz, Alain Badiou, and Hannah Arendt, among others.

There is a way in which this book attempts to address one of the concluding questions posed by Kathi Weeks at the end of her book *Constituting Feminist Subjects*. There, Weeks asks:

[W]hat are some of the different ways to conceive a collective subject, ways that move beyond the liberal model, according to which the individual is primary and authentic, the group is a "mere" secondary construction, and a legitimate group is posed as a consensual aggregation of individuals? Given the pervasiveness of liberal individualism and its stubborn grip on our thinking in late capitalist societies, this remains a difficult task indeed. What are some of the possible ways of regarding collectivities not only as determined subject positions but also as active subjects—how can these subject positions be transformed into relatively autonomous agents capable of social change?[2]

We are trying to understand the possibility of a real collective subject that is *not* secondary to the individual because—among other reasons—the individual's personality is realized only in dialectical relations with others around her. The individual is developed within that sociality, and does not precede it. But, since so many of our social relations are determined by the capitalist mode of life and work, we cannot answer the question of the collectivity with a simple sociological observation. We are not looking for a collectivity that is the determined subject position of capitalist society, but, rather, we are looking for a collectivity formed in our noncapitalist being-in-the-world, our relations to other human beings that maintain a sociality beyond and against exchange relations. We address Weeks's open question by looking at the collective subject positions of possible and already-existing love relations in the world.

Chapter 1 outlines the basic theorization of love as a communist power. We begin by thinking about regard for other people and exploring the meaning of love following the insights of Simone Weil and Emmanuel Levinas. Weil and Levinas think about love from the vantage points of two very different religiously inflected philosophies, yet they are both always also concerned with the social and political significance of our intersubjectivity. We connect these general theories of human relationality to a discussion of the *Gemeinwesen* (that is, community, or communal being) as a communist idea. To connect this basic theorization of love and human relationality to the *Gemeinwesen*, we move from Levinas to his friend and colleague, Maurice Blanchot. Blanchot specifically considered the relationship of Levinas's thought to key questions about community, politics, uprisings, and even to communism in books such as *The Unavowable Community* and *Friendship*. While these authors are not committed to a communist theory of love, they think about human relations in accordance

---

2. Kathi Weeks, *Constituting Feminist Subjects* (London: Verso Books, 2018), 159.

with Marx's concept of the *Gemeinwesen*. I bear this out by substantiating the clear resonance between their thinking and that of Jacques Camatte, who argued that the heart of communism is nothing other than a form of human relations that both he and Marx call the *Gemeinwesen*. This chapter provides the initial theorization for the book's thematic chapters to follow.

Having set the stage for our inquiry, chapter 2 revisits the famous ancient text of Plato on the subject of love in order to retrieve and critically consider some of the contested meanings of love in the history of philosophy. In the many speeches given in praise of love in Plato's *Symposium*, an understanding of love as a peculiar great power emerges, although there is much disagreement about everything else, including the kind of power love is. Chapter 2 is an effort to work toward a preliminary definition of love relating points in the ancient discussion to the general theory outlined in the first chapter. In a subsection of this chapter titled "Too Many Aphrodites," I assess the many disagreements in Plato's text and identify which understandings have survived to the present, which ones are dead and buried, and why any of it matters. I touch on the ancient relationship of love to war through the examples of Socrates and Spartacus in the Peloponnesian War and the Third Servile War, respectively, in order to show how thinking about the other, and about loving the other, has long been linked to friendship in war. Although Spartacus arrives long after Socrates, they both lived, thought, and fought before the life and times of Christ, and for them, love was a power that could be seen and tested in warfare and rebellion. This chapter is not a historical piece. Rather, it is an effort to reclaim certain understandings of love that have been abandoned. Most contemporary theorists of love gloss over the ancient discussion as if there is nothing to learn from it. They are wrong.

While the first two chapters think about love in variegated historical and philosophical contexts, chapter 3 focuses on the love of communists— or, more precisely, the particular loves of a communist conception. Here we explore how the best of previous accounts of love makes its way into a communist concept of love. This chapter undertakes a close reading of Karl Marx's *Grundrisse* to show his concern with the capitalist disfiguration of the *Gemeinwesen*. Marx analyzes how capital organizes and establishes a community of alienation. I show that the heart of Marx's communist theory, from the *Economic and Philosophic Manuscripts of 1844* to *Capital*, is ultimately about unacceptable forms of life necessitated by capitalism. All of this, I claim, can be studied best in *Grundrisse*, where Marx radically rethinks and updates his insights on alienation from 1844 and builds the bridge to his major multivolume study of capital. This reading of Marx is followed by a consideration of what I call "revolutionary affection"—namely, a feeling for others that breaks with capitalist exchange relations—which can best be seen in the lives and writings of communist women such as Jenny Marx, Rosa Luxemburg, and Alexandra Kollontai. Communist women, I observe, were less inhibited than communist men in addressing the role of affection in revolutionary politics. Culminating and concluding a discussion of the revolutionary philosophies and affections of Jenny Marx and Rosa Luxemburg is a section devoted to Alexandra Kollontai's theory of love, which unifies the relevant insights of both of the Marxes and Luxemburg.

We therefore enter chapter 4 with a good understanding of the communism of love. But, the middle of the twentieth century, the historical period following Kollontai's writings on love, saw the emergence of new theories of love informed by psychoanalysis and interdisciplinary critical theory. Chapter 4 critically assesses the major contributions in this milieu beginning with the work of Erich Fromm. Fromm was concerned that an increasingly proprietary individualism within culture and psychology would make healthy human relations impossible, and he thus defended and extended Marx's concerns with the help of psychoanalytic research. Fromm diagnosed a certain pathology, which he regarded as "insanity," in the growth of a brazen disregard for others than one's self. What is especially important about Fromm is his focus on the specific fate of love in contemporary capitalist society. He insists on love as a form of praxis and being-in-the-world, and not as a modality of "having." While Fromm's critique of love under capital is integral to my own study, his concept of communism is a rather anemic social democratic notion far from the radicalism of Marx's original view. Current critical theory with different ideas of socialism, mainly that of Axel Honneth, is also discussed in this chapter. However, Honneth's attention to love is fleeting, and he glosses over Fromm where he should be learning from him. Chapter 4 moves beyond the analysis of critical theory from Fromm to Honneth with supplementary discussions of psychologist John Cacioppo (on loneliness), psychoanalytic theorist Julia Kristeva (on narcissism and alienation), media theorist Dominic Pettman (on technology and love), and philosopher Bernard Stiegler (on contemporary disaffection). All in all, chapter 4 examines the contemporary psychosocial context in which people look for love.

Most studies of love risk (and are guilty of) dangerous overgeneralization, and because they tend to be so general and abstract, they are especially prone to overlooking real stratifications in social life. This book does not make that mistake. Chapter 5 considers the conditions of life within which love is defined, practiced, or problematized across lines of race, class, gender, and sexuality, singling out the different roles that love plays, or *must* play, in communities of color, for women, and among impoverished people and those at the margins of society. The chapter considers stratifications of love from various feminist, Black radical, and communal points of view.

And, unlike most academic studies of love, we do not ignore the extensive body of work by bell hooks on the subject of love. Further enhancing our analysis of race and racism, we engage with Cornel West and Tommy J. Curry, and we consider marginalities of class and gender with the help of the foremost scholar of love today, Eva Illouz (who is here subjected to sustained criticism for her lopsided fixation on the romantic love of heterosexuals). With Curry, we consider attention to the love of Black men in the United States within the current contexts of police brutality and mass incarceration. Finally, we consider Valerie Solanas's thinking about love in order to take seriously the position of a misfit, impoverished, radical woman at the fringes of lesbian feminism. Overall, chapter 5 provides a focused account of particular challenges to love in contexts of marginalization and exclusion.

Chapter 6 focuses predominantly on the works of Zygmunt Bauman and Ulrich Beck and Elisabeth Beck-Gernsheim. We take up Bauman's theory of "liquid love" and Beck and Beck-Gernsheim's theory of "the normal chaos of love." Our aim is to consider the relationship of love to growing global insecurity. For these theorists, the ties that bind people together are more important now than ever, and yet they have never been more threatened by the increasing mobility of peoples, globalization, and growing precarity. People who are more and more dispersed globally, living lives of flexible labor and cellular connection, fraught with financial insecurity, held together by high-speed connections, and inundated with growing flows of information, are in need of new ways of securing relationships in a chaotic world and a liquid life. The liquid life of the twenty-first century is technologically facilitated and mediated, and is physically unfixed to both human bodies and geography. In this chapter, I introduce and explore the notion of "little precarious communes," which we still manage to establish as spaces of refuge for love and community in a liquid, chaotic world. My notion of the precarious commune as an existential asylum and sanctuary is developed with the help of Franco Berardi and others.

Chapter 7 focuses on activities that counteract alienation in the world today. I begin by exploring several social, political, and cultural movements that bring people together and rest on some conception of what love demands. We consider the "eventuality" of love with the help of Alain Badiou, and think through love as a form of radical politics with Michael Hardt and Antonio Negri. In short, we go to the theorists who write about love while thinking about contemporary movements with some hope and optimism. And we draw also on writers who happen to be concerned with the post–Cold War fate of communism. In chapter 7, we think about the place of love in insurgent politics, including in global uprisings and revolts. I use the works of Raya Dunayevskaya, John Holloway, and George Katsiaficas, all of whom theorize a dialectics of revolution in terms of a juxtaposition of different forms of life. For example, following Herbert Marcuse, Katsiaficas speaks of "the eros effect," by which he refers to the ways that love travels through insurgent social movements and animates and inspires other uprisings, as could be seen in many examples from 1968 to the present. I aim in this chapter to develop the idea of love as a practice of "unalienation." But I do so with special attention to the limitations of such a politics of love. In a critical engagement with the sources, I caution against any romanticization of the power of Eros.

Chapter 8, which concludes the book, synthesizes what love is *for* and *against*. I assess what love is against (and what is against love) by extracting and extrapolating the conclusions and major insights of each chapter. Then, in the second and final part of chapter 8, we consider what love is for (and what is for love), following the same method of extraction and extrapolation. This concluding chapter builds on the conclusions of the previous chapters and presents the full synthesis in a new theory of love as a communist power. Chapter 8 aims to unify and clarify the overarching argument of the book, with reference to key examples and further engagement with Hannah Arendt, Oskar Negt and Alexander Kluge, Simone Weil, Maurice Blanchot, Raya Dunayevskaya, Alain Badiou, Michael Hardt and Antonio Negri, Martin Luther King, Jr., Huey P. Newton, Karl Marx, Martha Nussbaum, and Maurice Merleau-Ponty.

Books on love either avoid treating love as a political concept altogether or fail to recognize and explicitly unpack its communist content. Sociological studies of love, such as the many works of Eva Illouz (1997, 2007, 2012) and Ulrich Beck and Elisabeth Beck-Gernsheim (2004), focus too much on the concept of love as a romantic, sexual, and mainly monogamous relationship. This is even true—somewhat surprisingly— in the works of Alain Badiou (2012) and Srećko Horvat (2016), both of whom are connected to Marxian theory. Badiou denies any political philosophy of love, and while Horvat does not, he is focused mainly on dating and on romantic and sexual relationships. Other theorists of love who are directly interested in transromantic and political concepts of love, mainly bell hooks (2000, 2001, 2002, 2004), Zygmunt Bauman (2017), and Dominic Pettman (2006), refuse to seriously consider the irreducible communism of love, the question around which this book is thematized. Simply put, most philosophies of love are neither communist nor seriously consider the communism of love.

This book was written on the premise that we need a study that takes up the communism of love as its sustained focus. Those who have come closest would be Alexandra Kollontai (see Alix Holt's edited volume, 1980), Erich Fromm (1955, 1956), and, in a series of fragmentary passages from their larger coauthored works, Michael Hardt and Antonio Negri (2004, 2011, 2017). However, Kollontai's and Fromm's studies are in various ways markedly outdated and wholly unaware of the issues of the twenty-first century. Kollontai's theory of love is too bound up with statist initiatives for family planning and the hopes of the early decades of the Soviet Union. Fromm's concept of socialism has been long outstripped in the years after the Cold War and is no longer useful to communist philosophy. As for Hardt and Negri, none of the books in which they allude to what I call "the communism of love" are in fact about that subject. They have only made more or less fragmentary and fleeting commentaries on the communism of love, which are nowhere developed into a full and rigorous study.

The Communism of Love is conceived of and written—like all of my other books and articles—as a contribution to new autonomist Marxist theory for the twenty-first century. Thus, I want to contribute to our understanding of the present limits and catastrophes of capitalism, the necessary abolition of capitalist society, and why we must abolish it without resuscitating the statist and otherwise failed so-called "communist experiments" and movements of the twentieth century. This means the exact opposite of ignoring the many triumphs and failures of the radical struggles of the twentieth century; instead, it means a commitment to learning from them.

I do not speak of the anarchism of love because of an insistence on (a) the most systematic and total critique of capitalism (which is grounded in Marx and Marxism) and (b) the communist concept of the *Gemeinwesen*. Readers will nonetheless note a thoroughgoing connection or affinity to anarchism here (and in all of my work), as I have always found anarchist insights about power indispensable to any good analysis of society and politics. Still, it makes more sense to speak of the communism of love, and also for etymological reasons: anarchy—from the French *anarchie*, from the Latin *anarchia*, from the Greek *anarkhia*—defines itself negatively by a lack or absence of an objectionable power (that is, a ruling class, government, or state power). In contrast, we are interested primarily in the positivity and establishment of a certain power: the communist power of love. In any case, the compatibilities of autonomist Marxism with anarchism are far more interesting than their oppositions, and I offer this book as a bridge, not a wall.

Harry Cleaver is correct to point out that

> capitalists seek *totalization*, the imposition of their way of organizing society everywhere. They seek to convert all elements of human life—both things and relationships into commodities and, in the process, to convert all human activities into commodity-producing work. Making things becomes waged factory labor and salaried engineering labor. Growing things becomes hired field labor. Cooking for and feeding each other becomes waged labor in the processed food industry and that of cooks, dishwashers, and waitpersons in restaurants. Taking care of each other becomes the paid work of nurses, doctors, psychiatrists, day-care monitors, and prostitutes working for brothel owners. Helping our children learn becomes teaching jobs in schools, colleges, and universities. Figuring out how to live together with all our differences is reserved to professional politicians.... [T]here is no theoretical limit to capitalist expansion. Capitalist totalization is, therefore, at least potentially, *infinite*.[3]

But these tendencies of totalization have not made—and cannot make—a totality.

Children make things to play with out of cardboard boxes that adults would throw away. They make imaginary spaceships and cardboard arcades that don't run on money. So many people and communities with gardens tend to them for their produce, for fruits and vegetables that are eaten and shared but never converted into commodities. Kitchens of all kinds everywhere on earth are full of families cooking for and feeding one another because they want to and need to, and washing the dishes in order to have clean ones tomorrow. The processed-food industry will never make the best and freshest foods. Those are made by people who prepare them with love and thoughtful consideration. If the industry were to commodify such meals for grocery stores, we would know they were of lesser quality than the ones they simulate. There are always people everywhere

---

3. Cleaver, *Rupturing the Dialectic*, 121–22.

taking care of others, doing the best by the ones that they love, and for many such caregivers, being paid is not their motivation, though it may be helpful. And children are of course taught by everything and everyone they interact with, very often learning more important lessons outside of schools than in them. While politicians may try to figure out how so many different people could live together on a grand scale, we are busy figuring out how to live with others—both those we love and those we do not love—in the smaller circles of our actual lives every single day. There remain countless no-go zones for capitalist totalization in so many of the precarious little communes of everyday life, and those zones are often the most precious and important.

Because we live in a society ruled by money, governed by the logic of capital, it may appear to make sense to demand payment for all of the unpaid work done every day around the world. But only the most fundamental ignorance of capital would demand that capital pay for anything it isn't profiting from. Capitalism has never paid people for their work. Rather, it pays only for units of time measurably disconnected from the actual quantity and quality of people's labor, and from the real value of their work. We may get paid for commodity-producing work, yes, but a demand to commodify everything we do *is not even a demand worth making*. It is the defining demand of capitalist totalization, and we must beware its deceptive allure.

What if instead we could identify the communism of love in the relationships that matter most to us, in the relationships (or in our longing for the relationships) that make our lives worth living, that help us realize our personalities and gifts? The aspiration and practice of love relations with other people point to (conceptually) and materialize (in our lived experience) a collective subject position beyond the liberal model and, critically, beyond capitalist logics and monetary valuations. Inasmuch as the communism of love is both necessary and actual, it is only carried out by and for active subjects in pursuit of a sociality greater than that manifested by exchange relations. It is perhaps the experience and practice of love—more than anything else in a human life—that reveals the inestimable extent to which the best things under capitalism are the least capitalist things. There resides, in the irreducible communism of love, a rival logic of life that defends real people against commodification and that can only be expanded to the displacement of exchange value.

When love is acted out within the boundaries of our precarious little communes—if we are fortunate enough to have those—it constitutes a little collectivity called "home." But beyond those lamentably tiny boundaries, love constitutes a collective subject with a more threatening sensibility, a collectivity capable of a defiance and creativity that capital cannot bear.

CHAPTER 1

THE LOGIC OF LOVE
AS A COMMUNIST POWER

"The sea is not less beautiful in our eyes because we know that sometimes ships are wrecked. On the contrary this adds to its beauty."

–Simone Weil, *Waiting on God*

"Loving and perishing may indeed, as Nietzsche claims, always go together, but when what is to be destroyed is the world that makes us possible, the world in which we can exist as legible subjects, the task of creating a new world can be a frightening, even dystopian, prospect."

–Kathi Weeks, *The Problem with Work*

One day, I will die. So will you. Perhaps I am already dead. You are definitely not yet. The human body only takes us so far, and only for so long, and I suspect that there is nothing further. Perhaps I am wrong and you will somehow live on after your body expires, or I will live on whenever this book is read. Perhaps, after I am dead, I will be surprised by the fact that I'm still invisibly here and watching you read these lines. I do not think so. But even if I am wrong, what needs to be said and done needs to be said and done in the here and now, in the lifetime in which the saying and the doing of things is certain and available. This book is fundamentally about what to do with a life, what a life is for.

Death is inevitable; love is not. Most people do not want a life without love. Love may mean very different things to different people, but everyone wants a life of love. Those who have lived a life full of love can even be reconciled with death, for they have had the best of what a life enables. Perhaps we should say that the aspiration for love, however love is defined, *is inevitable*—as inevitable as death—even if the experience of love is less certain. Love is neither life nor death, and many live without it. But here already our questions begin, because to "have love" seems to make love into an object, into a kind of property that one does or does not possess. Yet most would readily agree that love is not a commodity, not a private property. Questions such as these can be so daunting that they alone may stop further questioning. Indeed, many don't question love. Instead, they feel around for love, and speak of it without thinking much about what it really means, largely following the supposed ineffability and mystery of its experience. Love is not ineffable. While it is hard to say anything about love, given its power and appeal, we should try to know what it means.

Must a poet or philosopher or anyone be deeply religious in order to write about love? From much of the literature, it may seem that one should first be willing and able to write about God in order to say something about love, as if they were comparable subjects. I do not think so. Nonetheless, in the history of philosophy (and not only in Western philosophy), thinking about God and love swirls together. Perhaps those willing to write about God and the human soul would approach love with more confidence, whereas the rest of us are only comfortable with smaller or less overwhelming metaphysical questions. And even for those willing to speak of love, God, or both, connecting these with power and politics can seem dangerous, undesirable, or impossible. If God is too mysterious or ineffable for political inquiry, then so too is love. I intend to reverse such sensibilities with regard to love as the sole property of some mysterious, ineffable, or metaphysical black hole. To the contrary, I explore love's material and social signification, love as a concept, an experience, and a practice that helps us understand a rich field of human relations beyond the rules and realities of exchange relations.

If we want to speak of forms of human relationality that are not governed by money, not organized by the logic of capital, we will have to speak about love. When we speak of communism, ears may burn and bad feelings bristle, whereas when we speak of love, we speak of a common aspiration that, for all of its difficulties, may be easier to take up than communism. Suffice it to say, we will take up more than one topic of difficult conversation. Indeed, this is a book of difficult subjects that we must have the courage to theorize together. So let us step off the precipice now.

1.1 Basic Theorization:
Simone Weil and Emmanuel Levinas

Simone Weil was one of the most complex thinkers of the twentieth century. Her philosophical range was too big for any one category, even for the categories she selected for investigation. When Weil was a Marxist, Marxism could not contain her unruly criticism; when she was a revolutionary, revolution seemed too small of a notion for the transformations she wanted to see; and when she was a Christian, religion was only a straitjacket on her spiritual thought. These assertions could be substantiated in a different reading of her work, but my aim is to do something else. I begin with the observation that when Weil spoke of God, she spoke of love. And although she proclaimed her love for God, she also insisted that "we must love something other than God."[1] But what, for Weil, does love mean?

Weil's definition of love was maddeningly short and deceptively simple: "Belief in the existence of other human beings as such is *love*."[2] As in the work of Emmanuel Levinas and other philosophers who have written about love, Weil's definition of love is tied to one's relation with others. We could say that love only makes sense with relation to other people. Love is not the private property of an isolated individual, although it may be something that one acts out *for* another. Even when you *have* love for another human being, that love emerges from and depends on a relation to the other being, and is in no simple way more your property than theirs. Notice that Weil specifies belief in the existence of other human beings as such, meaning that it is not enough to merely recognize other human beings; love demands that we *believe* in them such as they are. Belief implies a certain faith or trust in their being. When Weil says "as such," she means to specify *as they really are.* "Love needs reality. What is more terrible than the discovery that through a bodily appearance we have been loving an imaginary being? It is much more terrible than death, for death does not prevent the beloved from having lived. That is the punishment for having fed love on imagination.... If there are grounds for wishing to be understood, it is not for ourselves but for the other, in order that we may exist for him."[3]

This point about reality and the love of imaginary beings is crucial to understanding Weil's basic idea. When we claim to love a person for whom we imagine they could possibly be, we do not love them *as such*. We do not even love them, but rather we love an idea of an imagined possible version of them. We do not see the other if what we see is a different being than they really are. To see a human body and to be drawn to it, sexually or otherwise, is not love. It is an attraction, and with enough desire and imagination, that human body could be made into a whole being we may want to love, and may even attempt to love on the basis of a hope that the being we imagine will become a reality. But rarely does a person become the person whom you wish her or him to be. Every human person is an open field of possibility. There are many potential becomings, so one must love who and what the other is at the actual stage of development. The love can grow with the person. There is always the risk that the beloved

---

1. Simone Weil, *Gravity and Grace*, trans. Emma Crawford and Mario von der Ruhr (London: Routledge Classics, 2002), 63.
2. Ibid., 64.
3. Ibid., 65.

will no longer be loved in the future. People do not want to confess this because they want to believe that if they love a person deeply, they will love that person no matter who or what they become. But there is always the possibility that the other will become a being for whom your love is not possible. Commitment can keep people together, and often by means other than love. Sometimes when one says to the other "I love you," what they really mean is "I am committed to you." But commitment does not make love superfluous. People want something more than a contractual obligation, more than a dispassionate loyalty or business transaction.

In politics, as in love, imagination cannot simply be celebrated as good news. Political imagination can lead to dangerous plans and endless justifications of violence. In politics, one cannot trust that the political imagination will always be in accordance with one's *own* imagination. Some of the ways that others are imagined lead to illusion, delusion, or fatal misunderstanding. When Weil goes so far as to say that loving an imaginary being is worse than death, she means that death is the end of an actual life, whereas one who is never seen for who they are, who is never understood as such, is denied before death, killed in the imagination of another who sees them as something they are not. Wanting to be understood and seen as you really are, as opposed to how you are imagined by the other, is not only for you. It is also for the other, for the other to know you as you are, and not to be misguided by imagination. I think of this with regard to a family in which a child feels chronically misunderstood by the people who have always been closest to her. As she grows and develops her personality, she wants to be seen by a brother or a mother or a father for who she has become. There is an unusual pain in being seen only through the inaccurate imagination of a person who should know you better than anyone. I think that most young people experience this at some point, and it feels like a kind of injustice. The expression, "How can you of all people think of me that way?" carries the sentiment of an impossible misrecognition, and it can be a real injury, a real wound.

In a letter to philosopher Gustave Thibon, a friend of hers, Weil wrote: "Human existence is so fragile a thing and exposed to such dangers that I cannot love without trembling."[4] The context in which Weil lived and thought was a context of world war, mass carnage, widespread propagandistic manipulation, authoritarianism, and tenuous revolutions. In her context of life, to believe in other human beings as such took courage and faith. People often have to try hard to avoid seeing certain others, usually

---

4. Ibid., xiii.

racialized, scapegoated, and vilified others, as enemies, evil, threatening, and so forth. Sometimes, to see the other as human just like you is a political act. We know this from many examples in history and politics where people (individually and collectively) grapple with overcoming their own racism. Love is a power capable of helping us to see others as they are, and not as they are vilified. As Weil suggests, love demands looking upon the other with the generosity of real attention.

This is not a bad starting point for thinking about love. Love generates a belief in other people, an attention to them and to their real human existence and being. Generous attention to another person generates feeling for the person, a feeling upon which certain actions become possible. But Weil's considerations on love are still too thin to be called a theory. They are only gestures that we can further develop. Matters are complicated when Weil claims that love can draw us toward suffering, not always toward joy. For her, the happy person can be moved to suffering by way of love, by way of wishing to share the suffering of the other. The other side is also true. Weil claims that the unhappy person can, by way of love for another, "be filled with joy by the mere knowledge that his beloved is happy without sharing in this happiness or even wishing to do so."[5] In this way, the beloved's suffering and joy are also unlocked from the status of private property and become the suffering and joy of those who love them. If I love you, I am moved by your victories and disappointments, not as if they were my own victories or disappointments, but as if I could deeply appreciate the real feeling of your accomplishments and failures. I may see the joy on your face, and I can feel it too. The same goes for sadness.

Love entails, among other things, a sharing of miseries and joys, a sharing that *deprivatizes* pain and happiness, making each of them into a shared concern of two or more, of a small collectivity. However, this does *not* mean that, if I am unhappy, I will want or expect my children or my lover to be unhappy too. From Weil's perspective, I should know that if my children or my lover see me suffering, it must be an experience of suffering for them too. I do not want my child to experience sadness, but if he knows I am sad and suffering and if he loves me, he will experience some of that pain. It is not that he should or should not feel one way or the other. That is not the point. This is not a moral position but rather an observation of what love does, how it works on the level of feeling for others. Here love functions as a connective tissue between beings, and, of course,

---

5. Ibid., 63.

it is a connective tissue that is not always there. The absence of love makes possible a total separation of the other person's joy and misery from your own. The absence of love is not, however, hatred. The absence of love cultivates indifference and separation, but not necessarily any hateful feeling for the other. Love is therefore capable of drawing us toward pain, and where it is absent, indifference is more likely than hatred. This is what is meant by love as a connective tissue, although for Weil, love also connects us to something else: *justice*. When we begin to think of love in relation to justice, we begin to think of a political dimension to love.

Weil observes that to feel real gratitude, "I have to think that it is not out of pity, sympathy or caprice that I am being treated well, it is not as a favour or privilege, nor as a natural result of temperament, but from a desire to do what justice demands."[6] This complicates the pain-joy-sharing aspect of love. It is not enough to feel badly for a suffering person. That may be useful, but if it comes from pity, sympathy, or privilege, it is not love. A person does not want to be pitied, and least of all by the ones who love her. She reacts against that feeling by declaring, "Don't pity me!" To be treated well as a favor—as in, "I will do this for you as a favor"—is no better than pity. This is not to say that favors or pity are bad things. So what is the problem? I can feel pity or sympathy over the misfortunes of a total stranger yet be guilty of no injustice for doing nothing to address those misfortunes. When doing someone a favor, I am saying that I will do something that is wholly for that person. As a favor, it is in no way a benefit to me. Love, however, is not a favor; it compels some activity, some active engagement that moves us past a position of passive, voyeuristic pity. If I help my beloved in a time of need, the active assistance I give moves beyond pity. I am not doing a favor—I am doing justice, no matter how microscopic that justice may be.

But to say that being treated well comes from a desire for justice is distinct from the question of love for two reasons: First, the presence and practice of love does not depend on justice in any social, political, or legal sense. Love may function somewhat independently, and certainly without any necessary regard for the question of justice. Most of us probably have some experience with love that is unconcerned with justice. Second, and more importantly, we are not accustomed to thinking that love has any connection to justice in the world. While love and justice are not synonyms, and while each can exist independently of the other, I think (in agreement here with Weil, Martin Luther King, Jr., and Martha

---

6. Ibid., 68.

Nussbaum) we need to correct the idea that they have no meaningful relationship, and we should try to think about what forms of justice are mobilized by love.

Indeed, Weil suggests that doing what justice demands is connected with the practice of love, the latter of which is primarily concerned with the being and well-being of other people. Without attention to the other, and without serious regard for the other's well-being, what kind of justice is possible? Justice without love would be a formal and legalistic justice, but one that only emerged from some original deliberation about how other people should be regarded and attended to. When we think of justice from love, we think of a justice that moves beyond formal and legalistic resolutions—the latter of which can be dilapidated and grossly inadequate—and we start to think instead of justice movements animated by real feeling for others. This real feeling may itself be motivated and mobilized by the dilapidation and inadequacy of laws.

Weil wrote extensively on the concept of attention. In many ways, the concept of attention was at the very heart of her philosophy. In *Correspondance*, which contains Weil's letters to Joë Bousquet, Weil writes, "Attention is the rarest and purist form of generosity."[7] And, in her *First and Last Notebooks*, she argues: "Compassion consists in paying attention to an afflicted man and identifying oneself with him in thought."[8] And, in *Gravity and Grace*, Weil writes: "We have to try to cure our faults by attention and not by will."[9]

To develop Weil's gestural theory of love, we must unpack this notion of attention, which is more important today than ever. Your attention—and mine, and ours—has become the pathological concern of highly competitive capitalist interests. Everything everywhere demands the limited resource of our attention. We cannot pay attention to everything and everyone that clamors for attention, and we must be careful about what we give our attention to. We enlarge the power of everything we attend to, even the power of those things we despise. Because our attention has been increasingly targeted and sold, and because it is colonized by every moneyed interest, we must carefully consider what gets the energy of our precious attention—and, of even greater political importance,

7. Simone Weil and Joë Bousquet, *Correspondance* (Paris: Editions L'Age d'Homme, 1982), 18. In the original French: "L'attention est la forme la plus rare et la plus pure de la générosité."

8. Simone Weil, *First and Last Notebooks*, trans. Richard Rees (Eugene, OR: Wipf and Stock, 2015), 327.

9. Weil, *Gravity and Grace*, 116.

what is refused and denied our attention. If we manage our attention with love, we will not invest it in the capitalist scattershot of "clickbait" culture, a president's social media, or other screens, schemes, and scandals that would exploit our time and attention, laying them ultimately to waste. But we are getting ahead of ourselves. What does Weil mean by attention?

It is hard to pay attention to others. If we cannot see ourselves and our own interests in other people—in a self-interested and narcissistic culture of individuation and constantly expanding privatization—how can we be expected to pay attention to others? In many instances, other humans appear to us as alien beings. At the same time, however, if we have had the good fortune to feel well-attended to, to have been actively at the center of another's attention, we know the importance of another person to the self. Genuine attention—that is, based in real concern and interest—is rare, according to Weil, and expresses a profound generosity. But that attention *to you* is no less for the other than it is for you. Paying attention to other people, particularly to those with afflictions for whom your attention may be of urgent importance, brings you closer to them, closer to an understanding of their situation in life. As a result, attention to other people increases the compassion of the one who attends. What is most stunning in Weil's thinking is that our problems and faults are better addressed by attention than by will. This contrasts with an old concern in political science and philosophy over the will to solve problems. In psychology, we may speak of the will of the patient to do something difficult yet necessary for their health. *One has to really want it to make it happen.* But Weil argues against such a discourse on the will and argues for attention instead. Most problems—personal, social, political, economic— require attention; the political will to solve problems is never sufficient. One of the things that comes through attention—and not from will—is understanding. What would become of problems like poverty and white supremacy if they were deeply attended to with serious concern?

Even though Weil was inclined to radicality in politics, her thinking about love tends too much toward a liberal ethic of caretaking. Despite her efforts to posit the simultaneous subject-object position of both the lover and the beloved, her theory does not grasp the subversive power of love. While Weil writes about the tumultuous sides of love and attention, the subject is for her entirely cut off from any revolutionary politics. In later writings where Weil writes more about the subject of love, she does so mainly to rein it in to the service of her distinctive theology. As Weil approached the topics of love and God, she traveled further from the problems of capital and exploitation and the question of revolution. She came ultimately to conclude that revolution was a problem for which religion was the solution.

Weil argued, "It is not religion but revolution which is the opium of the people."[10] While this may well have been true for a time in the 1930s and 1940s, in the late 1800s and early 1900s, or in the 1950s or 1960s, revolution is certainly no popular opiate today. Revolution is largely regarded as an old-fashioned or impossible idea. Weil worried that revolution would absorb and waste human energies and faith that would be better invested in spiritual and religious practices, in different kinds of devotion. But Weil never forgot the problems of capitalist society, particularly the commodification of everything. She maintained a critique of capitalist exchange relations and the way that capitalism replaces meaningful things with marketable significations that can be branded and sold. "The relation of the sign to the thing signified is being destroyed, the game of exchanges between signs is being multiplied of itself and for itself."[11] Yet the more she spoke of God and love, the more she adopted a resolute mysticism of transcending the world instead of transforming it. The same basic social and political problems remain as those she diagnosed and discussed in the early 1930s in *Oppression and Liberty*, but by the late 1930s and early 1940s (just before her death in 1943), the solutions were different.[12] While it is true that Weil remained politically radical after her conversion to Catholicism and mysticism in the late 1930s, she ultimately sought to transcend the existing state of affairs, not to abolish it.[13] Unfortunately, we cannot deal with the problems of the world by way of their mystical transcendence. Or at least I do not think so; and if you think so, you may be reading the wrong book.

Within a different mystical-philosophical trajectory, also concerned with human relationality, love, and politics, we find Emmanuel Levinas's major study, *Totality and Infinity* (1979). Some professional intellectuals may bristle at the thought, but I find it accurate to describe Levinas's *Totality and Infinity* as a philosophical long-form love poem. Levinas is mainly focused on the ways in which forms of human relation are related to

---

10. Ibid., 181.

11. Ibid., 152.

12. Simone Weil, *Oppression and Liberty*, trans. Arthur Wills and John Petrie (London: Routledge, 1958).

13. For one example of her postconversion politics, see Simone Weil, *On the Abolition of All Political Parties*, trans. Simon Leys (New York: New York Review of Books, 2013), originally written in 1943, the last year of her life.

experiences of transcendence and infinity, in both materialist and spiritual contexts. As with Weil, the concept of love is not Levinas's main focus, but unsurprisingly (as also with Weil), it is the subject of recurring attention throughout his work. For Levinas, love must never be understood as some "sublime hunger" to be satisfied, for it is really about human becoming and transformation.[14]

Levinas begins with one's individual subjectivity as a human person in the world. There is the person, and then there are other people. The other is always another subject who "remains transcendent with respect to me."[15] Each of us confronts the other as a being beyond herself. The other is a being-beyond-me, and through connection with the other, I connect with a *reality* of being-beyond. This designates a materialist form of transcendence. But Levinas is ultimately more interested in the question of infinity.

Before we touch infinity, however, I should note a particular challenge in reading Levinas today that derives from the fact that, for him, face-to-face relations are optimal and irreplaceable. "The face to face remains an ultimate situation."[16] Levinas sees embodied and face-to-face relationality as ideal, while today, human relationality has moved into cyberspace and other highly mediated discursive realms. For Ulrich Beck and Elisabeth Beck-Gernsheim, to take one example, the physical and geographic demands of the face-to-face relation are negotiable.[17] In the twenty-first century so much of human relationality is technologically mediated; faces are often masks, avatars, or strategic performances on a screen. And globalization seems to require that we find ways of staying connected while apart, that we stay connected in the absence of face-to-face relations. Reading Levinas today, one either despairs at the dilapidated state of face-to-face relationality or looks optimistically at transgeographic and metatopical forms of life. Any present-day engagement with *Totality and Infinity* raises this crucial question right away: Does human relationality need the proximity and presence of human bodies?

Even in the present world of mediated relationality, the face-to-face may remain the ultimate situation. Consider the example of the MTV television show, *Catfish*, where individuals try to cultivate relationships without face-to-face interaction, but there always remains the ultimate

---

14. Emmanuel Levinas, *Totality and Infinity: An Essay on Exteriority*, trans. Alphonso Lingis (The Hague: Martinus Nijhoff, 1979), 34.

15. Ibid., 52.

16. Ibid., 81.

17. We discuss Beck and Beck-Gernsheim in chapter 6.

situation of the face-to-face somewhere on the horizon. Within the context of the show *Catfish*, people mostly agree with Levinas about the ultimate situation, but the most deceptive or least confident person in each pair always tries to avoid it. The possibility of the other person standing before you, face-to-face, represents a moment of terror, a moment of truth, and a possible transformation of the relationship (even its end). Levinas insists on the face-to-face because it presents the other as a reality "effectuated in the non-postponable urgency with which he requires a response."[18] When the other appears through a distant communiqué, through an old physical letter, an email, or some technological mediation, the other waits for a response but lacks the presence to demand it. The body is in this way a force, sometimes a necessary one, and not a dispensable or superficial feature of human relations.

This is why we often need to go places, with and in our physical bodies, not only in friendship but also in politics and protest. The presence of the body—or bodies—demands a response. Governments and their militaries, for example, may learn through screens how much they are hated by their people, but they need not respond until bodies confront them face-to-face, in the square, in the streets, as obstructions to commerce and normal business. In this political example, if we were to conclude that the face-to-face is an old-fashioned ultimate situation, we would imply that the power of our bodies is also old-fashioned. But don't our bodies remain fundamental to our being-in-the-world? Why not meet the lover only through a screen? Why not attend every conference only at home by video calls? The answer is that we want to bring our bodies to places and people because bodies are part of the indispensable apparatus of human relationality, even today where connections are more disembodied and cellular than ever. Even if we do not need to be at the conference physically or to go to the family's house in a distant city because we can talk by video calls, we still want to go there because we recognize that as the ultimate situation. Similarly, in politics, if we really want to stop them, we will eventually need to place our bodies on the line. Speaking of a strike is not the same thing as materializing one in picket lines.

This concern about the other and her body was central to the French phenomenology and existentialism of Levinas's generation, perhaps most notably in the work of Maurice Merleau-Ponty.[19] The face-to-face can be catastrophic, of course, which is perhaps why we are so motivated to

---

18. Levinas, *Totality and Infinity*, 212.
19. See, for example, Maurice Merleau-Ponty's *Phenomenology of Perception*, trans. Colin Smith (London: Routledge, 1962).

relate without it. But I think the potential for catastrophe is not so much because of the face-to-face as it is because of the cultivation of expectations before the ultimate situation. This is exactly the dangerous situation Weil describes, where one claims to love—not the other as they really are—but only as one hopefully imagines the other to be. Wherever bodies are kept apart, it is much easier to present one's self as something other than the reality and, likewise, to avoid seeing the other. With face-to-face relationality, it is more difficult (although not impossible) to preserve the delusion one favors.

In this regard, both Levinas and Weil occupy a shared position, despite other differences. For Weil, what matters is the reality of the other, and the wishful thinking of a desirous imagination can be dangerous. For Levinas, the reality of the other demands the ultimate situation of the face-to-face. For both, human relationality and love are also always about possibility and becoming. Levinas thinks about love and life in terms of moving "beyond being," which is the title of one of his conclusions to *Totality and Infinity*.[20] The key in Levinas's theory is always the other and other people more broadly. Everything about one's self and one's world is to be found in relation to others. But as in Weil's later mystical writings on love and human relations, Levinas does not directly confront questions about how capital and capitalism affect social relations. Both authors are concerned with social, political, and economic questions, but they bring different sensibilities to the discussion of relationality, love, and spiritual transcendence. The problems of capitalist reality appear as smaller and highly contingent concerns, having to do with historically and politically specific phenomena, whereas spirituality, love, and friendship appear as transhistorical, universal, or metaphysical phenomena. Yet there are certain tendencies in Levinas's work that suggest the application I am pursuing here, even though Levinas himself did not embark on the journey. Let's consider his more fruitful recommendations.

Levinas writes: "Society must be a fraternal community to be commensurate with the straightforwardness, the primary proximity, in which the face presents itself to my welcome."[21] There is a simple idea within this complex statement. When the face of another person is before you, that other both demands and implicates a certain sociality. If your eyes meet and you do not or cannot simply race past one another, what you want to find in the face of the other is a welcome. Sometimes, it is easy to totally

---

20. Levinas, *Totality and Infinity*, 301.
21. Ibid., 214.

ignore the other, but wherever that is neither possible nor desirable, welcome is the ideal disposition. As always with Levinas, this has to do with proximity, because it is more difficult to be inhospitable to those who are right before you. There is something very simple about these observations, about what Levinas calls straightforwardness. But the implication is profound: the only social disposition appropriate to this encounter is that of a fraternal community, a community of brothers and sisters, where each one is a member of a social family, a sociality. It is at this juncture that we may see a clear link between relationality—a brotherly or sisterly love, for example—and a welcoming social regard for other people in general.

It is perhaps more important to observe, however, that the concept of a fraternal community is antithetical to the privatization of social life, to the competitive individuation prized as the virtue of capitalist ideology. The concept of fraternal community is opposite to privatization of social life, and is more cooperative than competitive. Fraternal community opposes hostility to others elsewhere; it opposes the hatred of strangers who are easy to perceive as enemies, villains, or thieves. We cannot simply establish a fraternal community within society, especially when the basic sensibility for such community is lacking. Even though Levinas claims that fraternal community is the position commensurate with face-to-face social relations, generating such community and its basic sensibility would require a confrontation of the disposition of love against that of the existing society, of healthy social relations against capitalist exchange relations.

Levinas defines love somewhat ambiguously: "Has love no other term than a person? The person here enjoys a privilege—the loving intention goes unto the Other, unto the friend, the child, the brother, the beloved, the parents. But a thing, an abstraction, a book can likewise be objects of love.... Love remains a relation with the Other that turns into need, and this need still presupposes the total, transcendent exteriority of the other, of the beloved. But love also goes beyond the beloved."[22] This is as close as we get in *Totality and Infinity* to a definition of love, although Levinas has more to say about its practice.

Levinas understands that love is not always romantic or erotic. Romantic or erotic love are forms of loving, yet different forms of love apply to the child, parent, friend, or sibling. Nonetheless, human persons have a special privilege as "objects" of love, more so than beloved films, music, or books. This is because the beloved, in the case of a human being, participates in a reciprocal intersubjective relation. The beloved book is

---

22. Ibid., 254.

unchanged by the love, for it is entirely oblivious to those who read and love it. Levinas is always ultimately interested in the movement of human beings becoming and not in the valuation of static material artifacts. This is expressed in Levinas's phrase above, "transcendent exteriority of the other." The other indicates possibility outside of and beyond one's self. And love is necessarily beyond *both* the lover and the beloved. This is why, for Levinas, love is important. It is beyond each of us alone, and yet it depends on us and our active relationality; love is an experience of totality and infinity through human relationality. This means that the totality of humanity can be experienced and appreciated in our love for others, and when we move beyond the scene of two lovers, we approach the concept of an infinite affection, at least in principle. For Levinas, love points to the necessity of transcendence, of moving beyond our being.

We have to acknowledge in Levinas's idea of love yet another trajectory toward the immaterial and spiritual, as we also touched on in Weil's metaphysical thinking. But the central concern of my book is in the embodied earthly practice of love within (and against) the existing reality. What does love do here in the world? How is it practiced?

Levinas is not taking up the same particular questions as I am taking up here, yet he makes a useful contribution to our project. Levinas writes: "Love aims at the Other; it aims at him in his frailty [faiblesse].... To love is to fear for another, to come to the assistance of his frailty."[23] Here it is essential to stipulate that frailty is not, according to Levinas, a weakness. It is rather a universality of the human being, although the kinds of frailty differ and thus the forms of assistance most appropriate will differ.

There are at least two ways of deciphering this action of love. First, we may regard it as acting *on behalf of* the other's frailty, as in a practice of care or caregiving, solidarity, or support. Second, we may regard it as acting *against the causes of* frailty in the beloved person. The two are not mutually exclusive. Take the love of a parent, for example. The parent may comport herself to her child in the following way: *My love will look after you, fear for you, and be available for assistance where and when needed. The nature of your frailty will suggest the nature of my care.* But also, a parent might work to counteract forms of exclusion, insecurity, sexism, discrimination, or other harmful dimensions of social life so as to attend to frailty at its social nexuses: *My love, I will fight against your exclusion and against the cruelty that takes aim at you in school, at work, and elsewhere in this hurtful world.* Wherever one's beloved is injured by the cruelty of the

---

23. Ibid., 256.

world, we must attend to that human frailty, at least in part, in a confrontation with the conditions of life.

To his credit, Levinas also appreciates a more radical or transformative dimension of love. "Eros is not accomplished as a subject that fixes an object, nor as a projection toward a possible. Its movement consists in going beyond the possible."[24] This is what Levinas refers to as "being not yet."[25] We do not love the other merely to assist with his or her frailty such as it is, but to participate in a movement toward a being to come. Love is a peculiar power in that it does not seek to preserve or hold the beloved at a point of fixity, but rather to participate in others becoming something that they are not yet. This point is perhaps best clarified in the example of the child.

With my own young children, presently twelve and five years old, it is not controversial to say that they are *not yet* the *beings* they are becoming. Certainly, some becomings will be impossible, but it is very difficult to know what those are right now, so very little can be ruled out at this stage. It is also likely that what I may think is possible will not include everything that is in fact possible. Many things that a person becomes are things that those who love them could not have predicted and, moreover, would have declared impossible. (To take but one example, fifty years ago it would have struck most any parent as impossible that their son might become a daughter.) But what do I want my love for my children to do in the world? Do I want to ossify my children just as they are, making them into static objects of my love? This is in no way an ultimate hope or aim, in no way the interest or orientation of love. What I really want to do is participate in their becoming what they are not yet but could be and desire to be—a future being that I cannot yet specify, a being to be determined. How does one participate in a person becoming what they ought to be when neither the lover nor the beloved knows yet what that is? How can I assist my beloved children in becoming what they are not yet, beyond my own limited sense of possibility? This is precisely what I want to do with my love for my children. And participating in this way necessarily employs Levinas's conception of assistance for frailty and Weil's conception of attention.

Levinas claims that love works "toward a future which *is not yet* and which I will not merely grasp, but I *will be*—it no longer has the structure of the subject which from every adventure returns to its island, like

---

24. Ibid., 261.
25. Ibid., 257.

Ulysses."[26] Love is not an adventure that enriches us, from which we bring back memories, stories, and knowledge. Love is a creative power that changes us in deep and meaningful ways, a transformative process of becoming that affects our identity. But I want to ask about more than what love does to singular subjects and subject positions in the world. I want to think through the possibility for a love that participates in society becoming something that it is *not yet*, in processes of collective becoming. How can we help society with its being not yet, and particularly with its becoming something beyond its capitalist being in the present time?

To address this question, we can begin where Levinas ends: "Nothing is further from *Eros* than possession. In the possession of the Other I possess the Other inasmuch as he possesses me; I am both slave and master."[27] For Levinas, love does not look on other people as properties to possess, for the other is not a possession. If the expression of erotic or romantic love takes the form of each lover possessing the other, then it is *not* an expression of love but rather a relation that is closer to a logic of slavery. Each side asserts himself or herself as master over the other, and, inasmuch as that holds, the relationship assumes a master-slave relational logic. Human relationality is *never governed by the logic of love* when it is compatible with master-slave relations. Moreover, all systems of ownership and possession of other human beings—from slavery to patriarchy to capitalism—are irreducibly antagonistic to love. Love is an opposite logic to the various logics of possession and private property, and can be understood and enacted as an antidote to privatization, isolation, and frailty.

1.2 *Gemeinwesen* as Communist Logic

Maurice Blanchot was a friend of Emmanuel Levinas. Some of Blanchot's major works, including *Friendship* (1971) and *The Writing of the Disaster* (1980), take up Levinas's philosophy directly, and elsewhere in Blanchot's writings the influence of Levinas is clear. Blanchot also read and referenced Simone Weil in various texts, including in *The Writing of the Disaster*. Yet Blanchot was often thinking of and writing about communism, about communist writers and philosophers, social upheaval, revolt, and the political dimensions of community. Nevertheless, Blanchot does none of this as a communist himself. Indeed, Blanchot often criticizes Marx and

---

26. Ibid., 271.
27. Ibid., 265.

Marxist thinkers like Henri Lefebvre, and he reliably points out the errors of Marxism.[28] At the same time, however, Blanchot was able to discern and appreciate the communist logic of love. Nowhere is this clearer than in his profound little treasure of a book, *The Unavowable Community* (1988). For me, the question of whether the communism of love was too obvious to deny from even resolutely noncommunist perspectives was first raised and answered in my reading of Blanchot.

My book *Specters of Revolt* (2016) had just recently been published when I began to reread Blanchot's *The Unavowable Community*. I went to Blanchot only to clear my head, and not to initiate a new stream of research (with Blanchot, one is always certain to journey in many directions). Any of Blanchot's books would suffice to change the subject, to clear and then joyfully clutter the mind, and I had given no thought as to what to study next. Part 2 of *The Unavowable Community* is titled "The Community of Lovers." Flipping to that section, I was seized by Blanchot's first entry: "May '68." For Blanchot, to think about love and community was, *in the very first instance*, to think about revolt. So be it, I thought at the moment, I suppose I will stay on the subject of revolt a little longer.

What do revolt and love have in common? A cursory reflection reveals a few interesting commonalities: First, both love and revolt go in search of others with whom to make common cause. Both love and revolt throw people together with feeling and purpose. Second, both love and revolt disrupt the present state of affairs. They discombobulate everyday life, usual composure, and the interpersonal order, yet their upheavals always suggest something hopeful on the horizon. One is provoked by both love and revolt to wonder about hopeful possibilities. Possible does not mean inexorable. Franco Berardi uses the term "futurability" to think about possible futures that may or may not become realities, saying that "the possible is immanent, but it's unable to develop into a process of actualization."[29] Love and revolt both propose actualizations from possibility, yet they are largely experienced as immanence. Finally, both love and revolt counteract alienation, isolation, and privatization inasmuch as both tend to create new arrangements of sociality. With both love and revolt, we may speak of a new generation of the *Gemeinwesen*, meaning community, communal being, communal sensibility, or commonwealth, and of the *Gemeingeist* as a common, collective spirit capable of expressing itself in the world.

---

28. All of this could be seen in Maurice Blanchot, *Friendship*, trans. Elizabeth Rottenberg (Stanford: Stanford University Press, 1997).

29. Franco "Bifo" Berardi, *Futurability: The Age of Impotence and the Horizon of Possibility* (London: Verso, 2017), 21.

The first chapter in part 1 of *The Unavowable Community* is titled "Communism, Community." Blanchot thus begins his book on community with the concept of communism because he understands the irreducible intimacy between the ideas of community and communism. Quoting Edgar Morin, Blanchot associates communism with aspirations for "the possibility of another society and another humanity."[30] I accept that same basic sentiment.

Blanchot is deeply attentive to Georges Bataille and follows Bataille in his basic theorization of community. Blanchot considers the necessity of community on the grounds of a "basic insufficiency" in each individual being.[31] Each individual person needs another—or others—at precisely those moments when he or she becomes aware of his or her insufficiency alone. Insufficient here means "not enough" in more of an existential than a biological sense. From this sense of our own insufficiency comes a tendency for community, which in human affairs appears as an inevitable or natural development. Eventually, the "existence of every being thus summons the other or a plurality of others.... It therefore summons a community."[32] This is a rather old supposition. Many philosophers, going back at least to Aristotle, have spoken of the human being as a social or political animal by nature. Yet in *The Unavowable Community*, the human being appears as a kind of "communist animal" because of its inevitable beckoning of the human community. In a different book, *Friendship*, Blanchot goes so far as to speak of "real freedom, the achievement of the human community, reason as principle of unity, in other words, a totality that must be called—in the full sense—communist."[33] This means that communism, for Blanchot, is—at least in the first instance—less about politics and political economy than it is about a common human aspiration for an ideal community.

It does not take long for Blanchot to begin connecting the concept of community to the concept of social movement. He discusses the protest activity of the group Contre-Attaque, which he positions as a prelude to the French uprisings of May 1968. Blanchot observes that Contre-Attaque "could subsist only through struggle rather than through its non-active existence. It exists, in a way, only in the streets.... outside."[34] This formulation is reminiscent of the agonistic notion of public space in Hannah

30. Maurice Blanchot, *The Unavowable Community*, trans. Pierre Joris (New York: Station Hill, 1988), 2.

31. Ibid., 5.

32. Ibid., 6.

33. Blanchot, *Friendship*, 107.

34. Blanchot, *Unavowable Community*, 13.

Arendt's *The Human Condition*.[35] One cannot declare that an inert and disparate constellation of bodies is an active community any more than one could declare that an empty public park is an active public sphere. Like the public sphere, love and community are not actualized outside of their activity, a point I make throughout this book as well. But we will not conflate love with community. The two ideas are clear and distinct, although linked in various essential ways. In order to understand love it is necessary to understand a certain instance of community with another or with others, and in order to understand community, we will have to explore different logics of human association, only one of which is the logic of love. Nonetheless, both love and community are active practices, and they both are—*in very different ways*—collective actions. The understanding of love and community as actualized by human activity is essential to our theory. There is nothing communist about this fundamental point, since even capitalist production and exchange relations are only actualized by human activity. Human activity only takes a communist turn when it moves against the existing social order.

In *The Unavowable Community*, Blanchot brings love and community together in part 2, titled "The Community of Lovers." Blanchot begins to think about the community of lovers through the example of the French revolts of May 1968. He refers to the upheaval as "a happy meeting" of "*explosive communication*."[36] Each person who arrived in the streets was received in the streets as "an already loved being, precisely because he was the unknown-familiar."[37] This characterization of the general and open affection of people participating in social upheaval is not new. A large part of the significance of each revolt to its individual participants—as well as to a passive society looking on at what is happening—derives from the presence and collective activity of others, veritable strangers acting out together. Only the presence and activity of others made May 1968 into a major event in French social and political history. And, for Blanchot, the meeting of bodies for an explosive communication in the streets is a happy meeting. It is happy in that it amplifies what the individuals inside of the activity would like to say but could not audibly or visibly say without the combined effort of the group. To speak of participants as "unknown-familiars" makes sense. You do not know most of the others in the uprising personally, you do not know their names, who

35. See chapters 1 and 2 in Hannah Arendt, *The Human Condition* (Chicago and London: The University of Chicago Press, 1958).

36. Blanchot, *Unavowable Community*, 29.

37. Ibid., 30.

they are, what they did in the days before. Yet there is an instantaneous familiarity because you are all there, a familiarity forged through the collective expression of disaffection in the existing society. It is precisely in that familiarity and affection that participants find common cause, a community, and the feeling of communal force or being—in short, the *Gemeinwesen*.

If there is something communist inside the revolt, it is not a collective vision for establishing a new society. Rather, it is an explosive and antagonistic form of a being-together. Blanchot describes it as follows:

> Contrary to "traditional revolutions," it was not a question of simply taking power to replace it with some other power, nor of taking the Bastille or the Winter Palace, or the Elysée or the National Assembly, all objectives of no importance. It was not even a question of overthrowing an old world; what mattered was to let a possibility manifest itself, the possibility—beyond any utilitarian gain—of a *being-together* that gave back to all the right to equality in fraternity through a freedom of speech that elated everyone.... [O]ne could have the presentiment that with authority overthrown or, rather, neglected, a sort of *communism* declared itself, a communism of a kind never experienced before and which no ideology was able to recuperate or claim as its own.[38]

In order to understand the purposes of this book, and to understand the idea of love as a communist power, it is essential to fully unpack this passage. Our theoretical argument will take significant steps forward in so doing.

Again, Blanchot is not writing about the revolt as a Marxist or a communist, for he is neither. His early political affiliations were rather far to the right, in fact. He did eventually come to abandon his earlier right-wing politics, years after meeting and befriending Levinas at the University of Strasbourg, and, indeed, there would be little trace of his right-wing views by the time of his later works (the works after his books of fiction, that is, from the late 1960s until his death in 2003). It is true that the later works are the ones I am consulting here, but Blanchot never traded his more conservative thinking for a committed Marxian or radical left-wing position. It is clear that he supported the student uprisings of 1968, and he even came out of relative obscurity to say so. Over time, his

---

38. Ibid., 30.

politics became more like those of Jacques Derrida: they could be clearly discerned and applied in certain cases, but only from beneath a certain political ambiguity, which was essential to both of their philosophical dispositions.

Blanchot understands the revolt as first of all concerned with being-in-the-world, and not motivated by any pretensions of taking political power. This was not only true of May 1968. It is a no-less-apt description of more recent global revolts in the decades following 1968. From the Stonewall uprising of 1969 to the Attica prison revolt of 1971, the Egyptian bread riots of 1977, the 1981 and 1985 Brixton uprisings in the UK, the Tunisian food riot of 1984, the 1989 riots in Argentina, the Zapatista rebellion in Mexico in 1994, and on up to the more recent wave of uprisings in the Arab Spring, Occupy Wall Street, Black Lives Matter, Hong Kong: we see a turn in *all of this* (and this list leaves out many other major examples of global revolt) toward experimental searching for possibility, creating space for conversation, defiance, critique, and art, and all for something other than the existing reality, for new forms of life, new ways of being together, of being in the world. Blanchot refers to this activity as a sort of communism, and I find his description to be fitting in all of the above-mentioned cases, and in many others unmentioned. We are talking about a sort of communism that is not immediately recognizable as communist or as any other political ideology.

The revolts break with and move beyond political ideology, which is what, for Blanchot, makes them politically powerful: "That is what makes them formidable for the holders of a power that does not acknowledge them: not letting themselves be grasped, being as much the dissolution of the social fact as the stubborn obstinacy to reinvent the latter in a sovereignty the law cannot circumscribe, as it challenges it while maintaining itself at its foundation."[39] The power of the revolt lies precisely in the fact that the revolt is illegible from the perspective of those who hold offices of political power. The revolt questions and challenges established legal and political power, and even confuses that power by refusing to want it. The revolt expresses and proposes an entirely different concept of power using a language that, because of its form and content, cannot be governed by legal power such as it is. Essential to our hypothesis is the possibility that this powerful challenge is the active formation of a community of lovers that does not and cannot abide by the rules and values of existing political power.

---

39. Ibid., 33.

In *Friendship*, Blanchot writes "communism" in quotation marks and explains his intended meaning in an important footnote.[40] He says: "*Communism* here is necessarily in quotation marks: one does not belong to communism, and communism does not let itself be designated by what names it."[41] Communism exceeds what it describes. So if we call a certain revolt or a particular community "communist," this naming does *not* mean that communism is only defined by the revolt or community we have named. Some other thing may emerge as communist in the future, just as it has in the past. Moreover, communism does not belong to a particular group of self-proclaimed communists as their own theory, nor to anticommunists as the caricature of a dangerous villain. Communism is no one's private property, which is fitting, of course. Like Georg Lukács, Blanchot understands communism as a movement with a changing function throughout history, defined dialectically in conflict with the enemy's position—defined, in other words, by what needs to be confronted and abolished in the present time.

There is also an accidental and ephemeral dimension to Blanchot's theory of communism. He says that in the 1968 revolts, "a form of community happened then, different from the one whose character we had thought to have defined, one of those moments when communism and community meet up and ignore that they have realized themselves by losing themselves immediately. It must not last, it must have no part in any kind of duration. That was understood on that exceptional day: nobody had to give the order to disband. Dispersal happened out of the same necessity that had gathered the innumerable."[42] Both communism and community appear on the scene together, realizing themselves momentarily in an activity or an event. The communism and community of the revolt happen because they are necessary, not because they are following a plan of implementation. The revolt is not a permanent condition. It takes place in the communist and communal activity of the uprising, but then it settles down and goes away after what had to be said has been spoken out loud in an explosive communication. Everyone—especially the communists—will want to know the practical or political use of such an amorphous kind of communism. If this is what communism looks like, is it not bad news for communism? These are questions that will be answered before the end of this book, and, indeed, there is much practical and political significance here, and much good news, in the kinds of communism we are talking

---

40. Blanchot, *Friendship*, 86.
41. Ibid., 295.
42. Blanchot, *Unavowable Community*, 32.

about. (We will have to keep in mind Blanchot's important point that communism exceeds what it names.)

Thinking about revolt elsewhere, in a short piece originally published in 1958, shortly after Charles de Gaulle's return to power, Blanchot asserts that there are moments when "in the face of public events, we know that we must refuse. The refusal is absolute, categorical. It does not argue, nor does it voice its reasons.... Men who refuse and who are tied by the force of refusal know that they are not yet together. The time of joint affirmation is precisely that of which they have been deprived. What they are left with is the irreducible refusal, the friendship of this certain, unshakable, rigorous No that keeps them unified and bound by solidarity."[43] No doubt, this passage, and the short essay from which it comes (titled "Refusal," chapter 13 of *Friendship*), foreshadows Blanchot's support of the uprising in France ten years later. What I want to focus on in this passage is the notion of the refusal coming out of an unformed community, a not-yet-togetherness. Those who rise up are not yet together, and their active and public refusal is an insurgence of community, no matter how temporary. But the categorical refusal of saying "No" together is an activity that asserts a possibility of real community, a fraternal "being not yet," to return to Levinas's term. A collective action of refusal implies a certain unity and human solidarity. This active refusal of the existing reality is indispensable to Blanchot's association of revolt with community, and to his association of both revolt and community with communism.

But why does Blanchot speak of the communism of revolt in relation to the idea of love? For Blanchot, the connection to the subject of love has to do with the subversion of rules, an opposition to the established order, and an aspiration for community. Blanchot quotes Georges Bizet's claim that "love has never known any law," and recalls how close love was to the concept of chaos in Phaedrus's speech in Plato's *Symposium*.[44] Much like revolt, love is a constructive disruption. Love breaks laws (consider the history of human sexuality, for example) and interrupts psychosocial life, yet it tends toward the generation of new modalities of being-together. When we think about a queer politics of love, for example, we must think also about the law and subversion. It is necessary to think of intersections of love and politics there. Also, when we think of recent Black revolt in Ferguson or Baltimore in the United States, we have to think about disruption and about affirmations and assertions of community.

---

43. Blanchot, *Friendship*, 111.
44. Blanchot, *Unavowable Community*, 40.

For Blanchot, the community of lovers is an elective community. The community of lovers is not the kind of community that is an accident of birth, such as when one is born Jewish or German or Brown or Black. There are those communities that one simply finds oneself in, regardless of any activity of the will, but then there are other communities that one may join by way of some commitment, voluntary activity, or participation. Blanchot asks if the latter kind of community "attracts the beings in order to throw them towards each other (two by two or more, collectively), according to their body or according to their heart and thought, by tearing them from ordinary society?"[45] Yes, the community of lovers forms when people come together in and by a movement away from their normal positions—into other gatherings than those assigned by family at birth, in their jobs, and established in everyday life.

Toward the end of his short study, Blanchot concludes that the community of lovers "has as its ultimate goal the destruction of society."[46] This may have a negative connotation, and indeed, for Blanchot, a community of lovers in a state of revolt is neither simply good news nor simply bad. It can be catastrophic and transformative, much like love. It can be happy and victorious or sad and tragic. But it is critical to remember that Marx also spoke about the destruction of existing society, and the destruction he preferred was called communism. This can be seen in many places, and with crystal clarity in the famous line of *The German Ideology* where Marx declares: "We call communism the *real* movement which abolishes the present state of things."[47] Blanchot, oddly enough, presents a formulation similar to Marx's: "'Radical change' might be conveyed if it were specified in the following manner: from what comes to pass, the present is excluded."[48] Did Blanchot know how close he was to Marx's formulation? Did he understand that the peculiar kind of communism he wrote of was quite like Marx's original conception? *Is it possible that a community of lovers in action is part of the communism Marx spoke of?*[49]

But my interest is also in identifying a different logic of human relationality than that of exchange relations. Blanchot, who (like Levinas) was interested in relationality for very different reasons than mine,

---

45. Ibid., 47.

46. Ibid., 48.

47. Karl Marx, *The German Ideology* in *The Portable Marx*, ed. Eugene Kamenka (New York: Viking Penguin, 1983), 179.

48. Maurice Blanchot, *The Writing of the Disaster: New Edition*, trans. Ann Smock (Lincoln: University of Nebraska Press, 1995), 114.

49. Jacques Camatte, to whom I shall turn next, helps us understand Marx's basic theory of communism in accordance with this possibility.

nonetheless understood the problem well: In economic terms, "men have a market value for one another, are things and can be exchanged as such; thus, should men be hired, bought, employed by other men, they become instruments and tools. This toolness, this relation of use between men, gives men the value of things; this is as clear for the slave as it is for any man who hires out his work—his time—to another, but it is also clear for the master."[50] This means that, from top to bottom, capitalist exchange relations—within the relations of production and socioeconomic class relations—require the toolness of people, that is, their conversion into things to be used. The relationship of such tools, not only to those who use them but to one another, is a relation governed by capitalist exchange. The logic of this capitalist relationality is of course pervasive and dominant today, in a world that is still (and no less) governed by money, governed by the logic of capital. We are together in this book right now, however, because we are interested in love as a different logic of relationality, one that humanizes instead of instrumentalizes individual persons, that views people as beings not things.

In *Friendship*, Blanchot provides a straightforward definition of communism, which he calls "the incommensurable communication where everything that is public—and then everything is public—ties us to the other (others) through what is closest to us."[51] Although I would not accept this definition (and would reject it on the grounds of its claim that communism means everything is public), it does contain an interesting Levinasian inflection about the other. Incommensurable means having no common measure, so to define communism as an incommensurable communication is to define it as a kind of human relationality and communicative interaction that cannot be measured. Communism, for Blanchot, is also defined by our ties to others through what we hold closest, through a concern for our nearest and dearest. But our intimate ties to our nearest may not be the dearest. Later, we will explore how family and other close face-to-face relationships should not be mistaken as spaces of mutual care and love. Notice, however, that Blanchot's idea of communism once again connects communism to a *new* (and incommensurable) community with others.

Communism, community, love, and revolt. In Blanchot's writing, this quartet comprises an ensemble. Nothing synonymous here, but something like an improvising jazz quartet. The four can interact in such a way as to

---

50. Blanchot, *Friendship*, 93.
51. Ibid., 149.

make something beautiful or ugly, or even to make something that is ugly to one person and beautiful to another.

Yet, revolt is regarded as an ethical activity. "The awareness at each moment of what is intolerable in the world (tortures, oppression, unhappiness, hunger, the camps) is not tolerable: it bends, sinks, and he who exposes himself to it sinks with it."[52] This is why many prefer, consciously or not, to remain unaware of intolerable conditions. Real awareness of the intolerable may be too much to bear for anyone with an untroubled moral sensibility. To remain willfully ignorant of the intolerable, to avoid thinking of it and what it means for the lives of real people, is one of the oldest and most common ways of dealing (or not dealing) with intolerable reality. Ample evidence for this tendency can be found in the Nuremburg trials or truth and reconciliation commissions, for example. Ignorance is especially seductive when one knows that awareness of the intolerable brings with it a dangerous culpability. This is one of the reasons Blanchot is drawn to revolt, even though he worries about it in other ways: "An initial remark: revolt, yes, if revolt is understood as the demand of a turning point where time changes, where the extreme of patience is linked in a relation with the extreme of responsibility. But one cannot, then, assimilate revolt and rebellion. Rebellion only reintroduces war, which is to say the struggle for mastery and domination."[53]

Patience is an extremist position in a world of intolerable conditions. It is no virtue to be patient in the face of torture, oppression, unhappiness, widespread trauma, hunger, death, concentration camps, detention centers, deportations, ecological catastrophe, and other human suffering. Indeed, such patience demands justification. There are times when we need to invert the old saying that patience is a virtue. Revolts happen when the extreme of patience is linked with and broken by an extreme sense of urgency or responsibility, something like, "We have been waiting, but we can wait no longer now." Had we not been so patient, perhaps something gentler than a revolt would occur. And yet, the "normal" reality of extreme patience, whence responsibility can wait no longer, is likely to be interrupted in the most explosive and disruptive ways. Blanchot is clear to distinguish revolt from rebellion: he sees rebellion as more to do with the struggle for taking over the existing power, whereas revolt is about refusing that power and working out new forms of being-together. The revolt is about changing time and relations, giving rise to new forms of

---

52. Maurice Blanchot, *The Step Not Beyond*, trans. Lycette Nelson (New York: State University of New York Press, 1992), 114.

53. Blanchot, *Writing of the Disaster*, 138.

being-together; the rebellion is about contesting or replacing the personnel of the already-existing power while preserving its tempo and basic structure. Blanchot's anxieties about communism likely derive from his suspicions about the latter, from his very sensible fear that the communists may only wish to place the old form of power into new hands. It seems to me that the revolt, and not rebellion, is closer to what is best in the communist idea.

Blanchot's notion of communism as incommensurable communication helps us to further engage what I have said about exchange relations and what Blanchot has said about the reduction of human beings to tools. A communication without any common measure is a communication outside of legible discursive norms. It is hard to know how to respond to a communication that is outside the normal range of discursive exchange. For example, if I am walking past a colleague and say, "Hi, how's it going?" the communication is immediately legible as a passing greeting, not a genuine question. The response is ready at hand: "Good, how are you?" But if I were to walk up to a colleague and say one simple word—"pain," for example—this would be a perplexing communication, a normative failure. Blanchot touches on this in *The Writing of the Disaster*: "The simplest words convey the inexchangeable; they switch back and forth with each other all around it; it appears not."[54] Only the presence of the other words surrounding a word like "pain" make a communication about pain successful.

However, people in a more intimate relationality, friends, lovers, or family, can sometimes communicate with fewer words, or even no words at all, through an incommensurable communication that succeeds only within the space of an intimate little commune. To think of Levinas, about whom Blanchot was also often thinking in his own writing, we can imagine physical bodies in proximity, face-to-face. There, a communication transpires that is gestural, physical, nonverbal, inaudible, yet expressive. In sexual activity, this is also often the case. A lot can be said without words because the communication is "all around," and not measurable as a logical exchange of words or phrases. Of course, one often has something to say and says it in order to communicate something but not in order to acquire something of equal worth in exchange for the communication. If my partner can help me come to terms with some problem in life by blanketing me in a series of thoughtful monologues before we fall asleep, I will neither have to pay her for the communication nor repay her

---

54. Ibid., 86.

with a similarly effective set of monologues tomorrow. All of this is to say that exchangeability is not the sole logic of communication. Blanchot observes as well that exchange pretends to be about mutuality and equality when, in fact, it generates unsharable, disproportionate burdens.[55] Blanchot is right, yet he does not tie these observations to a critique of capitalism. But we *will* do that.

Whereas "capital" and "capitalism" are scarce words in Blanchot's writing, they are the enduring focus of another obscure French theorist, Jacques Camatte. I have been writing about Camatte for over ten years, assigning his work in my classes for more than twenty, and it turns out that he needs our attention here as well. No other serious thinker of the postwar period has done more than Camatte to theorize the relationships between capitalism and community, on the one hand, and communism and community, on the other. The actualized human community, or the *Gemeinwesen*, is the centerpiece of Camatte's theory of communism, and Camatte extends Blanchot's communist gestures fully in the direction of a Marxian critique of capitalist society. Camatte, like many of the postmodern French philosophers of his generation, claimed to have made a break with Marx. Such claims were not always as accurate as they appeared, and especially not in the case of Camatte, who always remained far more recognizably Marxist than figures like Jean Baudrillard, Michel Foucault, Jacques Derrida, Gilles Deleuze, Jean-François Lyotard, and Guy Debord. Camatte even writes as a Marxicologist of sorts, cataloguing and explaining Marx's original writings (including neglected and long-lost materials) in both chronological and painstaking exegesis and textual analysis, almost all of which clearly express his appreciation and defense of Marx's work against the most common misinterpretations. Essential to our present task is Camatte's major study, *Capital and Community*.

Camatte locates Marx's idea of communism, above all else, in the notion of community. A communist is concerned with the position and well-being of human community, above the interests of money or capital, above the concerns of any one individual or nation. Camatte observes that the concept of community in Marx's work is the *Gemeinwesen*, which always indicates a being-together with others. *Gemeinwesen* may refer either to (a) an ideal-typical communal being, a community of shared human aspiration, or to (b) community such as it is. Therefore, there is the *Gemeinwesen* as it is, and then there is the ideal *Gemeinwesen* we may discuss as possible and desirable. When Camatte thinks about the possible

---

55. Ibid., 87.

and desirable *Gemeinwesen*, he does not think about the *Gemeinwesen* of capital. Camatte reads Marx's *Capital, Vol. 1*, as "the study of the domestication of men by capital; the birth of the workers' subordination to capital."[56] Capitalism is destructive and corrosive to the healthy *Gemeinwesen* since it instrumentalizes community, positioning community in the service of capital. Camatte therefore declares that "the human community is only realizable if men and women abandon the world of capital.... This will allow them to undertake a different dynamic."[57] This reflects Camatte's contention that a *real* human community cannot exist within and according to a world organized by the logic of capital and that a healthy sociality—the *Gemeinwesen*—will need reasons for being other than reasons of money and capital.

A basic premise of sociology: no human person exists as an isolated individual, for each person is developed individually only in relation to other human beings in a shared social world. This common social world includes many things, such as language, cultural-valuational norms, customs and practices, and complex systems of interaction (for example, various divisions of labor observable in the family). Against this premise, individualist capitalist thinking interprets reality as if each individual is personally responsible for who she is and for her lived reality, as if each person is her own private property. The mythology of spectacular capitalism casts all forms of interdependence as evidence of weak-willed parasitic or lazy dependency, and all forms of cooperation as insufficiently ambitious or competitive. This is one of the ways that the communist *Gemeinwesen* is devalued already at the level of prepolitical sensibilities in capitalist society. The *Gemeinwesen* of a healthy human community would be, in practice, a constraint on capital and is therefore intolerable to it. Capital has long sought total autonomy from the real needs of human community.

This problem is exacerbated by the actual liberation of the economy from real needs. Guy Debord wrote well about this historic liberation in *The Society of the Spectacle*. Debord analyzed the "autonomous economy" as follows: "The economy's triumph as an independent power inevitably also spells its doom, for it has unleashed forces that must eventually destroy the *economic necessity* that was the unchanging basis of earlier societies. Replacing that necessity by the necessity of boundless economic development can only mean replacing the satisfaction of primary human

---

56. Jacques Camatte, *Capital and Community*, trans. David Brown (New York: Prism Key, 2011), 82.

57. Ibid., 10.

needs, now met in the most summary manner, by a ceaseless manufacture of pseudo-needs, all of which ultimately come down in the end to just one—namely, the pseudo-need for the reign of an autonomous economy to continue."[58]

Here, Debord observes that the capitalist economy's greatest victory in the twentieth century was its liberation from the historic purposes of all preceding economic activity. Throughout history, economics encompassed the organization of human activity for the satisfaction of human needs. In any earlier epoch, if you wanted to explain the primary organization and activity of the people within any community, you would find that people do what they do largely (not wholly) in order to satisfy the primary needs of community members. That was, at least, the fundamental historic purpose of economic activity. But that orientation has been mutated by capital, which viewed the old economic concern about satisfying human needs as a fetter on accumulation. According to Debord, twentieth-century capitalist societies were able to realize a growth and accumulation beyond and indifferent to the satisfaction of human needs. This economy is autonomous by way of its independence from real human needs, but, for Debord, this autonomy also dooms the economy because it abandons the historic justification for economic activity. Now, the capitalist economy primarily manufactures pseudo-needs, apparent needs that are not real human needs at all, and capitalist societies perpetuate the myth that freedom consists in the total freedom of an autonomous economy. Today, if one enters the field of politics and asserts that the economy must be made subordinate by the force of coercive laws to primary human needs, there is an outcry as if any restriction of the autonomous economy were a restriction of human freedom writ large. In short, the greatest triumph of the autonomous economy is that we come to accept the freedom of capital as human freedom. In this, Debord brilliantly summarized and predicted the coming neoliberalism of his day, whose ascendancy in the 1970s and 1980s has brought us to the current juncture in global political economy.

What Debord is talking about is none other than the capitalist abandonment of the human community and the retooling of human beings into instruments of capital. Camatte agrees with Debord to a certain point. Camatte concurs that "the objects which are proposed for human consumption become decreasingly necessary for the species as they are

---

58. Guy Debord, *The Society of the Spectacle*, trans. Donald Nicholson-Smith (New York: Zone Books, 1994), Thesis 51, 33–34.

artificial or dangerous, while those which are really necessary become increasingly expensive. Capitalism abandons the sphere of the satisfaction of man's material needs."[59] However, the reader should notice in Debord's analysis that the horizon is economic doom. Camatte does not see economic doom as the horizonal destination; he sees, rather, that the autonomous economy has still to triumph over the human being. Inasmuch as the human being cannot be fully converted into an instrument of capital, the human being remains an impediment to capital. Camatte argues that capital ultimately "only wants consuming slaves," such that the whole of society is comprised of "classes of slaves condemned to consume capital."[60] From this point of view, the human being is an impediment because humans can only consume so much. We are limited vessels. Even if the normalization of permanent debt means that we do not actually need capital to consume, capital wants more consumption than the human community can furnish. Instead of dooming the economy, however, this dooms the human community, which is almost nonexistent outside of the capitalist *Gemeinwesen* but has no chance of developing within the limits of capital. Camatte proclaims: "Society has become capital."[61] This means that our social being, our daily lives, our experiences of community, work, and even leisure time, are constructed to support the logic and interests of capital. In this way, our experience in the world is a direct experience with capital, even outside of school or work.

The total subsumption—and elimination—of human life on earth is the dark heart of Camatte's dystopian thesis. This is a thesis that I challenge, even in the face of more recent ecological catastrophe. Yet Camatte captures the despair of his vision well:

Capital incorporates the human brain; appropriates it to itself, with the development of cybernetics; with computing, it creates its own language, on which human language must model itself, etc. Now it is not only the proletarians—those who produce surplus-value—who are subsumed under capital, but all men.... It is the real domination over society, a domination in which all men become the slaves of capital.... Capital's process of incarnation (*Einverleibung*) which began in the West about five centuries ago, is complete. Capital is now the common being, oppressor of man.[62]

---

59. Camatte, *Capital and Community*, 179.
60. Ibid., 77.
61. Ibid., 145.
62. Ibid., 156.

These lines, published originally in 1972, are impressively prescient when one considers cybernetics and developments in computer and cellular technology since they were written. When one considers what I refer to in *Precarious Communism* as "technontology," we see that cognitive activity is now, more than ever, an elusive "producer" of constant content.[63] (Many others, such as Manuel Castells, Paul Virilio, and Franco Berardi, have written well about this phenomenon.) Camatte's overarching idea, and his novel reading of Marx, recasts capital chiefly as a power of totalitarian domination and assimilation, not only of class exploitation and oppression. For Camatte, following the logic of capital can, in the end, only convert humanity into an accessory of autonomous global capitalist functioning.

Camatte speaks of force in the realm of consumption. People who do not wish to consume cannot opt out of consumption without punishment. He discusses the example of construction to show how people who build homes and buildings, and who have the technical capabilities to build their own habitations, are nonetheless forced to spend part of their wages on rent, and then to give back the rest of the wages they earn to the capitalists who sell them other things they need, such as food and transportation. Thus, it is not really possible to opt out of the circulation of capital back to capital. If one stops the flow of capital to capital at one nexus, other flows of capital to capital will remain. Consider the consumer who works at one supermarket yet buys her groceries elsewhere because she hates her employer. The consumer nonetheless returns her wage, but only to the less offensive vendor. The consumer's wage, paid by a capitalist today, is returned to one capitalist or another tomorrow. There is nothing new in this account. It goes back to the earliest political economy, to Adam Smith before Marx. But Camatte's defining interest is in looking at the transposition of these relations into broader social relations throughout capitalist society, changing the ways that people relate to one another, destroying the prospects for the healthy *Gemeinwesen* and preserving the *Gemeinwesen* of capital. In other words, our forceful subordination to capital is at the same time a violent reduction of human relations to the exchangeability of work and consumption. Community in Camatte's sense, or in Marx's concept of community, is antithetical to the community of capital; it's always one *Gemeinwesen* versus another.

The "versus" relationship between capital and community is not a

---

63. See Richard Gilman-Opalsky, *Precarious Communism: Manifest Mutations, Manifesto Detourned* (Wivenhoe, UK: Autonomedia, 2014), 21–29.

hard, categorical logic of displacement. When we talk about capital and community we are not talking about the on and off positions of a light switch. In capitalist society, community is not totally abolished. Human community, and specifically love relations, still function and even thrive in various ways and places, and for different periods of time. Camatte is, however, a theorist of totality, which is to say that he always follows the most terrible theses to their worst imaginable ends. I argue instead that while community is indeed antithetical to capital, and vice versa, they press against each other in the actual practice of human affairs. Therefore, we must think of them in terms of "more or less" and not "on or off." Recognizing the oppositional logics of capital and community requires demystifying a whole lot about existing capitalist social relations. Capitalist social relations—essentially, exchange relations extended throughout the whole social body—are obscured by a capitalist mythology that presents this society as the optimal space for human flourishing and public health. Camatte understands Marx's work as essential to any project of the demystification of capitalist mythology.[64]

What is the form of community at work? What is the form of community in a household? What is a community of friends? Camatte claims that "man was separated from his community, or more precisely, the latter was destroyed.... The different communities had tried to marginalize money from the social relations.... With capitalism, a stage now completed by the autonomization of exchange-value, the last residues of the communities were destroyed."[65] So at work, where most of our wakeful life is invested (for those of us who have jobs), we are taken out of our community and thrown into the competitive navigation of other workers. It is difficult to establish *real* community at work, although it is not impossible. The difficulty lies in the fact that the other workers, like you, are only at the workplace because they have to be; they are compelled to be there by the demands of life in a capitalist society. Moreover, there is always some comparative measurement of the different workers. Even if workers wear a mask of comradery and collegiality, someone—if not the workers themselves—is counting, measuring, and comparing their relative worth, assessing their exchange value.

One might assume that a refuge awaits every worker in the community of the household. But even in the household, money often colonizes family life, as Camatte rightly grasps. Leopoldina Fortunati's radical

---

64. Camatte, *Capital and Community*, 196.
65. Ibid., 209.

analysis perhaps stands out most sharply among studies of the problems of the family.[66] In her book *The Arcane of Production*, in a chapter titled "The Family as a Form of Capital's Development," Fortunati writes:

> Within capitalism this structure—the family—has always had the crucial function of producing and reproducing labor-power.... It is common knowledge that family relations are alienated and alienating, that the "love" we have for our fathers, mothers, children and siblings has to be expressed through the work we do for them.... *All family members—even within the "love" of the family—are not protected from but remain subject to capital's will and discipline.* Children "must" go to school whether they want to or not, for example, and everyone is aware that *the family is in reality the pool of labor on which capital draws.* It appears as a place of "love," but is in reality a place of alienation, of commoditization, of non-communication.[67]

Suffice it to say for now (although we shall return to this later) that loving community at home is often impossible, and thus many seek the refuge of real community from *both* work and family life.

Indeed, an assembled and well-nourished community of friends remains a real possibility, though it may be less a refuge from the capitalist organization of life than a casualty of it. Friendship requires what is often called (problematically) "leisure time," the time left over after obligations of work and home life are satisfied. Leisure time has, for many billions of people, been all but abolished. There is often so little common time and space left over for a community of friends to take shape that friendship migrates to social media, where it takes on a technologically facilitated metaphorical existence. These remain merely skeletal interactions on which the real body of full friendship never grows. Many friendships today are like some scaffolding in New York City, where the scaffolding itself appears to have become the permanent structure. This effectively destroys what Camatte refers to as the possible and desirable *Gemeinwesen*. The time and space of our togetherness is mostly mediated through

---

66. For some of the other critical studies of the family that I have in mind, see Susan Moller Okin, *Justice, Gender, and the Family* (New York: Basic Books,1989); bell hooks, *All about Love: New Visions* (New York: Harper Perennial, 2000); and Angela Mitropoulos, *Contract and Contagion: From Biopolitics to Oikonomia* (Wivenhoe, UK: Autonomedia, 2012).

67. Leopoldina Fortunati, *The Arcane of Reproduction: Housework, Prostitution, Labor and Capital*, trans. Hilary Creek (New York: Autonomedia, 1995), 125–26.

activities of production and consumption, which Camatte calls "the total parcelization of men" where it "is no longer the association of men, but rather their division, which leads to the socialization of their products."[68] This means that our division and individuation are now presupposed, even required, as premises on which our lives depend.

The community that we know is not the only kind possible. It is to be expected that our experience of what we call community in our daily lives is what we think community means. But Camatte wants us to think about "men's alienated community" in which capitalist society is only and always "presenting antagonistic forms as forms of association."[69] What happens, then, is that we come to see our separateness, our antagonistic and competitive individualism, as if it were just a "natural" feature of the human community. Community comes to mean, therefore, an agonistic collectivity of antagonistic persons. One of the key aspects of alienation discussed in Marx's *Economic and Philosophic Manuscripts of 1844* is the estrangement of each individual from the human community (estrangement from *species-being*), and Camatte singles out and focuses on this form of alienation with sustained attention. Camatte analyzes how capitalism destroys not only the human community but also the human being who can only be fully human within the real (that is, desirable, healthy, possible) human community (*Gemeinwesen*), a claim with which Marx concurs.

What kind of community can alienated persons comprise? According to Marx, alienation is one of the necessary and distinguishing features of life in capitalist society, and according to Camatte, alienation is extinguished by real community. "The question of alienation can only be treated exhaustively if linked with the question of the *Gemeinwesen*.... There is no alienation except when the human being has been separated from his natural *Gemeinwesen*."[70] Let's put these points together: Alienated persons cannot comprise the *Gemeinwesen* because in so doing they cease to be alienated. Thus, where alienation reigns, community recedes, dissipates, or disappears. For Marx, as discussed in his 1844 manuscripts and in the 1848 manifesto, this is a problem of capital because capitalism exacerbates all earlier forms of alienation by multiplying processes of estrangement in work and society. For Camatte, the establishment of the *Gemeinwesen* would be an antithetical and oppositional movement because *real community* always counteracts alienation. Thus, a dialectical relationship between community, capital, and alienation can come into focus.

---

68. Camatte, *Capital and Community*, 216–17.
69. Ibid., 232–33.
70. Ibid., 240.

The problem is that capitalism promises human flourishing while necessitating forms of dehumanization. Following Camatte, growing alienation and dehumanization can be observed in the state of the *Gemeinwesen* at each period in human history. In subverting and degrading the human community, capitalism subverts and degrades the human person too, as the individual is best situated—from the perspective of capital—as a tool, as an instrument. This makes humanism into a radical proposition. That was the contention of many of the Marxist-humanists (although Camatte was not one) who focused on the subject of alienation in Marx's early writings (such as Erich Fromm, Raya Dunayevskaya, Herbert Marcuse, Jean-Paul Sartre, and others). As the Marxist-humanist Maurice Merleau-Ponty put it: "Any serious discussion of communism must therefore pose the problem in communist terms, that is to say, not on the ground of principles but on the ground of human relations. It will not brandish liberal principles in order to topple communism; it will examine whether it is doing anything to resolve the problem rightly raised by communism, namely, to establish among men relations that are human."[71] I agree with Merleau-Ponty's contention that human relationality is the central and defining question of communism. This imbues my own position with a certain irreducible humanism.

Camatte, although a theorist of catastrophe and despair, nonetheless remains a communist. Being communist is, for Camatte, the only position in which any future hope can be rooted. Also, being communist means insisting on the community that abolishes alienation. Communism is largely defined by its opposition to capitalist alienation. As Camatte puts it himself: "In communism, humanity dominates its production and reproduction as well as its history; there will be becoming and becoming other, but no longer alienation."[72] This is one of the ways in which the communist theory of community can bypass or postpone the politics of the state and the law and can focus instead on what is today often called "communization." Beyond analysis, then, a communist would seek to organize or experiment with forms of life and modes of thought that work against the logic of capitalist alienation, and according to Camatte's communism, new formations of being-together *may be* the only hope for praxis.

When I think about alienation and despair in our present-day capitalist societies, I worry about the prospects for new forms of being-together, of coming to identify one's self as inextricably linked to other persons. On the

---

71. Maurice Merleau-Ponty, *Humanism and Terror: An Essay on the Communist Problem*, trans. John O'Neill (Boston: Beacon, 1969), xv.

72. Camatte, *Capital and Community*, 254.

one hand, I think that new formations of being-together may be more diffi-cult than ever before, given that the privatization of social life has perhaps outpaced the privatization of the economy. Yet on the other hand—and for the same reasons of privatization—communist forms of being-together may be more important than ever. Consider the general social scene: we are learning more and more how to be together while remaining total-ly apart. This being-together-apart is technologically mediated through screens. And this fragmentary scaffolding of the human community—this form of separated sociality—is coming to mean community as such. Resist-ing this community of separated sociality could become a politics, but what would that look like? To return to Levinas's idea, one wants to be face-to-face with their beloved children, parents, friends, and lovers, and the sepa-rated sociality is always only accepted as a temporary stopgap that should hopefully give way to proper forms of togetherness. What role might love play in a politics of sociality? Is love only possible in community, or is com-munity only possible with love? Is love without community a false form (that is to say, a spectacle) of love, and community without love a false form of community? These questions will be taken up more fully later.

Camatte does recognize a severe difficulty: "Capital's community can-not be replaced immediately by a human community."[73] While this diffi-culty may appear obvious, it is a warning to any who might seek to create communism right now, as in autonomous zones or prefigurative projects. The difficulty should also be kept in mind by those who are partial to recent trends in communization that would hope for some direct replace-ment of the capitalist lifeworld with communist practices. I find Camatte's warning against immediacy convincing and would encourage us to be sus-picious of anything that claims to be a clear communist path. I wish this were not the case, but temporary interruptions of or solutions to capitalist forms of life are neither real interruptions nor real solutions. On the ideo-logical terrain, we need not only a new idea of community but, first of all, a new idea of value. Yet according to Camatte: "Capitalism had a personal way of negating value; that of becoming its presupposition."[74] I argue that love relations contain valuations that do not obey the presuppositions of capital.

How can we identify and assert the importance of noncapitalist val-ues, that is, values beyond exchange value? Selma James, Mariarosa Dalla Costa, and Silvia Federici have helped with this going back to the 1970s,

---

73. Ibid., 264.
74. Ibid., 298.

showing us how so much of what human communities need and value the most cannot be valued with money, by capital.[75] This was the enduring message from the movement known as Wages for Housework. The point was not to ask governments or wealthy private citizens to pay women wages for housework, but rather to expose the obscured importance of reproductive labor, to show how women's work has provided a constant global and historical stream of labor and capital and, most importantly, to demonstrate that women's work cannot be appropriately valued by capital. Capital cannot value real community because the *Gemeinwesen* is not governed by money, is not formed for the accumulation of capital, and eludes any exchange value. Like the unpaid housework, childcare, and eldercare done by so many women, community is also necessary for a healthy society of human beings. As well, love given in exchange for money is not *actually* love, just as paying for friendship is not friendship and cannot be if it comes with a bill of sale. Some of these points appear as easy common sense. Even those without a single cell of communist sensibility seem to understand that things like love and friendship retain a value that is not, and cannot be, a capitalist exchange value.

Camatte argues that community is, in its most meaningful realization, not only *not capitalist* but also very clearly communist. Camatte quotes Marx at length in text after text writing about the *Gemeinwesen* as the realization of a distinctly human and healthfully communal form of life. He also draws from the *Economic and Philosophic Manuscripts of 1844*, saying that if we assume the basic humanity of others, and if you assume a human relationship to others and the world, "then you can exchange love only for love, trust for trust, etc."[76] Then Camatte sums up as follows: "Communism is the true human community where the mediation is man himself. The human being is the real *Gemeinwesen* of man."[77] One of the problems within Camatte's theory, which I intend to overcome, is the unsubstantiated yet repeatedly posited differentiation between *real* and *unreal* community. The assertion that there is a true, authentic *Gemeinwesen*, which stands incompatibly opposed to the disfigured and destroyed capitalist *Gemeinwesen*, requires substantiation or should be abandoned. One should anticipate the obvious question: "How can you say that my

---

75. See Selma James, *Sex, Race, and Class* (Oakland: PM Press, 2012); Mariarosa Dalla Costa and Selma James, *The Power of Women and the Subversion of Community* (Bristol, UK: Falling Wall, 1972); and Silvia Federici, *Revolution at Point Zero* (Oakland: PM Press, 2012).

76. As quoted in Camatte, *Capital and Community*, 305.

77. Ibid.

community is *unreal* or *inauthentic*?" And to that question we cannot answer with a base assertion as Camatte does. I think Camatte is right about the irreconcilable logics of capital and community, but I also think that an unsubstantiated discourse on authenticity is neither helpful nor necessary.

What is absolutely indispensable in Camatte's analysis is his total rejection of the notion that Marx's work—and capital itself—is distinctly (or even especially) economic. "The critique of capital ought to be, therefore, a critique of the racket in all its forms, of capital as social organism; capital becomes the real life of the individual and his mode of being with others."[78] This means that, when we speak of value and when we speak of exchange relations, we are speaking about the social organism, about the form of human society. We are never speaking only about how commodities are produced, labor is divided, and markets function. Capitalism is about the structure of our being-in-the-world with others, and we have to understand its existential implications in determining the purposes of our lives. So when we ask fundamental questions about capital and community, we are asking about various ways of being-in-the-world. Camatte's Marxism is very clear about this fact, and even if we do not accept his claims about *real* and *unreal* community, we must keep in mind capital's uses and abuses of the human being.

Politically, Camatte recognizes the absolute necessity for some "revolutionary explosion" capable of forming new communist forms of life, and yet he simultaneously asserts that "due to the weakness of the world revolutionary movement, we have to exclude an immediate becoming of communism."[79] On the question of how to strengthen the chances for a communist revolution, Camatte is variously silent, unpersuasive, and even dissuasive. Between his short and fleeting invocations for revolutionary activity, Camatte is more often cynical and negative, as in other writings such as *This World We Must Leave and Other Essays*.[80] Nonetheless, Camatte's basic analysis in *Capital and Community* establishes for us a preliminary way to differentiate rival logics of relationality, different modalities of being-together. Leaving aside other considerations in Camatte's complex and multifarious writing, we can take his basic analysis—in conjunction with our assessments of Weil, Levinas, and Blanchot—as establishing for the present study a rudimentary theory of the communism of love. Yet

---

78. Ibid., 373.
79. Ibid., 395–96.
80. Jacques Camatte, *This World We Must Leave and Other Essays*, ed. Alex Trotter (Brooklyn: Autonomedia, 1995). See also *The Selected Works of Jacques Camatte* (New York: Prism Key, 2011).

none of this helps us to think clearly enough about the singular concept of love or about the implications of a practice of love for the health of the social organism. As we draw chapter 1 to its close and look toward chapter 2, just around the corner, we take up love with a bit more focus.

Srećko Horvat's 2016 book, *The Radicality of Love*, attempts to move beyond thinking about love as a human relation toward a more political formulation. We will take a closer and much more critical look at Horvat's problematic work in chapter 7 of this book, but several of his thoughts will help here to make the segue we need. Horvat thinks about love and capitalism, and about the radical and political logic of love, and yet he tends to think and write about love in a distinctly romantic or erotic sense, which is to say in more individualistic and less social or public contexts. (We will of course need to distinguish between different kinds of love, such as romantic, sexual, parental, familial, humanistic, and so on.) But for Horvat, the capitalist organization and management of love is a problem.

Within the milieu of romantic love, dating, and searching for a life partner, Horvat observes a pattern of outsourcing love relations to private, for-profit match-making corporations. For Horvat, this represents the direct intrusion of the "capitalist model into the most intimate sphere: into the sphere of dating."[81] Remarkably, this particular commodification of love relations is a booming global business, which is successfully marketizing longing and loneliness rather than being rejected as an obvious corruption of love. Horvat observes that this is not only an issue of capital and commodification, but also of technology. Problems in social affairs are increasingly addressed with technological fixes or with the assistance of applications, which makes them "appear" as technical difficulties rather than interpersonal or social ones. According to Horvat, any critical theory of human relationality today must keep the technological question clearly in mind. Horvat's analysis hones in on developments of technology that create situations in which "you do not even need the other anymore, you can satisfy your every desire without it."[82] He claims that "very few sociologists or philosophers today tackle the problem of technology" and that "people who work on technology are not interested in feelings and emotions."[83]

However, those claims are not accurate. We should not overdetermine the technological dimension of our problem, for these technologies are—properly speaking—just the latest instruments of capital. Moreover,

---

81. Srećko Horvat, *Advancing Conversations: Sre ko Horvat: Subversion! Interviews with Alfie Brown* (Winchester: Zero Books, 2017), 38.

82. Ibid., 43.

83. Ibid., 44.

from the ethics of robotics to artificial intelligence, major philosophers and sociologists have indeed focused on technology in human relations, but this goes back in sociology and philosophy to long before Neil Postman and Martin Heidegger. At a more recent conference in 2014 at the New School for Social Research titled "Digital Labor," many hundreds of major scholars across every discipline of the social sciences and humanities (prominently from sociology and philosophy) gathered to discuss a large and growing field of research focused on technology and human relations. Suffice it to say that I do not agree with Horvat that the people working on technology are not interested in feelings and emotions. To the contrary, the entire marketization and integration of new technologies is developed within a careful and stunningly sophisticated attention to feelings and emotions.

In chapter 2, I show that problems of human relationality—and specifically those forms we identify as "love relations"—predate not only contemporary technology but also capitalism itself. Capitalism and capitalist technology exacerbate problems of human relationality that go back to antiquity. While I take Plato's *Symposium* as my central focus in chapter 2, I do not intend to cut off that inquiry from distinctly contemporary problems. Horvat characterizes the main argument of Plato's *Symposium* as suggesting a "soul-mates" theory in which "one part is trying to find the other complementary part and as long as it doesn't find this missing part it will never be complete."[84] He then says we need a totally opposite vision, where the other is not a missing part of us but rather a totally different and autonomous being, not *of us* or *from us*. Horvat here repeats a common misreading of Plato's *Symposium*, since the soul-mate theory of the halves is *not* the theory of Plato or Socrates. It is imputed to Aristophanes in Plato's *Symposium* and is rejected rather promptly in the text. *Symposium* presents love in many different ways, several of them still subversive. From chapter 2 to the end of this book, we will not analyze love by technologizing it or shrinking it down to its interpersonal and romantic articulations.

While I agree with Horvat that love is a political concept, we must do better to resist conflations of love and desire, for although they interact, each can be practiced without the other. For now, let me only note that love can keep people together in the absence of desire and that love is not capable of reliably producing desire where there is none. Unlike love, desire is not itself a practice. Desire may govern human activity, however,

---

84. Ibid., 46.

as it refers to affective or libidinal longings, desires for particular feelings, experiences, or acquisitions. Love, in contrast, is a power and practice. Love is a power and practice of human relationality that always implicates others and necessarily negates the privatization of feeling and experience as the properties of individual persons.

Guillaume Paoli says that "everything is subject to commerce: every desire, every aspiration, and every impulse."[85] Paoli is right. Everything one desires has long been subject to commodification or will be subject to commodification. Desire can be commodified, and if enough people express the same desire to constitute viable grounds for commerce, the commodity will come. This is partly why those working on technology are never indifferent to human feelings and emotions. But love is not desire, and I want to think through the differences. For example, why does love (unlike desire) cease to be love when it becomes a commodity? Love cannot be a commodity without ceasing to be love; at the moment of commodification it is no longer love. Love shares this in common with friendship, but not with desire. Love only deserves its name as long as it exists outside of or against the logic of capitalist exchange, whereas desire is not obliterated in or by capitalist exchange relations.

Paoli sums up well how capital tries to capture the whole of human relations:

> All relations involving at least two individuals can be seen in terms of service, can be based on a contractual relationship, can be negotiated with one another as equals and thus can have a price. From that point on, there is no limit to the extension of this model. In the past it would never have occurred to anyone that all aspects of human existence could be turned into markets in which each person is in competition with everyone else to create consistent demand. But as soon as a sufficient number of "actors" understand their relations as being determined by this unavoidable model, all others effectively are as well.[86]

Paoli's overarching argument is that capitalism needs us to remain motivated as active agents of consumption and has therefore found ways to motivate human life and activity through commercial, contractual, and market forces. For this reason, victims or opponents of capital, who have

---

85. Guillaume Paoli, *Demotivational Training*, trans. Vincent Stone (Berkeley: Cruel Hospice, 2013), 6.
86. Ibid., 30.

had their lives disfigured or destroyed by "market colonization," should look to forms of "demotivation" as a subversive politics.[87] We should be either demotivated, following Paoli, or, as I will argue instead, *antagonistically motivated*.

What if relations involving two or more individuals could be differently motivated, governed by a logic opposite and antithetical to that of capital? If love, unlike desire, is abolished by its commodity form, then has love become obsolete to human relations? Theories of a totalitarian capitalist colonization of life may suggest demotivation as the only or most sensible response, whereas I recommend instead rival motivations for a relationality incommensurate with capitalist exchange relations. The logic of capitalist relationality (which is taken up with dedicated focus in chapter 3) is not merely a set of principles, a *logos* to theorize, for it actually organizes real relations of life, from childhood education to work to phases of retirement, slowing down, and death. The logic of capital organizes what we see as valuable in life, which partly explains why otherwise reasonable people place their lives in the unhappy service of work that they despise, often for fifty years or more, day in and day out.

Our basic theorization, however, seeks to retrieve and develop a rival logic in love. Despite the fact that "love" is a dangerous and sullied word replete with ideological triggers, it appears here—and is increasingly shown throughout this book—as an irreducibly communist power. This can only be true, of course, if what we mean by "communism" is also well defined. We have already established that what we mean by communism is no political state in history, no form of government; it refers instead to forms of life, forms of being-in-the-world with others. We have, for example, considered the *Gemeinwesen* as the beating heart of the communist idea (a thesis that we will further explore in chapter 3's reading of Marx's *Grundrisse*).

You may bristle at the joining together of the usually disparate languages of love and communism; some will surely react against the faintest suggestion of love as a communist power. I should therefore warn you that long before the philosophical lexicons of capitalism and communism, indeed long before those words even existed for any discourse, love was already understood as an unruly practice, as a subversive power, as a thing that—as a god on earth—could organize or reorganize one's entire life, establishing the basis for the constitution of the human being and its community.

---

87. Ibid., 7–10.

CHAPTER 2

Plato's *Symposium* and the Many Powers of Love

"[Love] is a vagrant with tough, parched skin. He is always barefoot and homeless, sleeping under a roof of sky or in the doorways of strangers. Sometimes you can hear him snoring in ditches by the side of the road."

—Diotima and Socrates, *Symposium*

"Eskimos have 120 different expressions for snow, because it's life-threatening for them. In Germany we have only one word for love; Greeks have 20."

—Alexander Kluge, *BOMB Magazine*

Plato's *Symposium* is an unpredictable text, a misfit among Plato's works. It is not a conventional Socratic dialogue where Socrates goes on a conversational journey about some specific subject with various interlocutors who compel detours or compromises yet never fully derail Socrates from his course. Instead, *Symposium* is a series of speeches made in praise of love, and when Socrates finally offers his own speech, he gives credit for its content to an old woman, Diotima, a philosopher and priestess from around 440 BCE. Socrates tells us that Diotima taught him what he now teaches about love. Diotima is, like Plato himself, thus simultaneously absent and present in the dialogue. And Socrates is neither his own nor Plato's mouthpiece here. We cannot say that Plato's *Symposium* presents Socrates's theory of love or even Plato's. Much of the text presents the speeches of others, all of which Plato clearly wanted us to think about. One could easily imagine a text on love that took the form of most other Socratic dialogues, where eager friends and colleagues gather to engage Socrates on the central question, throwing different positions into the dialogue for consideration, refutation, and context. One could just as easily imagine a dialogue that is more cohesive and singular in its ultimate development of a philosophical perspective. Instead, *Symposium* begins and ends as a complex of rival visions. The only cohesive view we are left with is that love is a tumultuous power that, despite its passionate upheavals, is called upon to be praised instead of condemned. Love appears here as *unlike* the upheavals that statesmen denounce—love is often tumultuous, but it is not a riot or a revolution.

While all of the text's speech-givers contribute some understanding and reflection on the question of love, Socrates is extremely harsh in criticizing them. Yet in a peculiar twist, Socrates is not the last word on the subject. The conclusion of Socrates's speech is in fact a kind of dead end, which perhaps Plato knew was *not* and *could not* be the end, as Diotima, with Socrates in full agreement, ties love to the human desire for immortality, and also to heterosexual procreation. But the text begins with the homosexuality of Apollodorus, and just as it is to this day, when love traverses sexuality its "politicalness" can be seen immediately. This is true at any point in history. But in *Symposium*, love appears, even to the ordering mind of Socrates, as not simply beautiful and perfect. Love appears not as a perfect completion, but as something in the middle in want of something else, as an active aspiration for the not-yet.

To set the stage, Socrates and his friend Aristodemus are walking together to join a gathering of friends over dinner at Agathon's house. Aristodemus was accompanying Socrates as a guest, but Socrates kept falling behind, lost in thought, and despite their walking together, Socrates ended up trailing on his own. They were together and apart in the walking, and throughout the text Socrates never appears too eager to join the symposium at Agathon's. It is almost as in the opening pages of *The Republic*, where he is compelled by the force of his interlocutors to join the conversation. Soon enough, it is proposed that all those gathering at Agathon's should give "the finest speech he can in praise of Love."[1] It is agreed that love is too often neglected, and Socrates says, "I myself could never refuse, since the art of love is the only subject I've ever claimed to understand."[2] This interesting proclamation of confidence from the start is a bit unusual for Socrates, but perhaps it explains the ferocity with which Socrates ultimately presents his (and Diotima's) view in a strangely nondialogical form.

2.1 Too Many Aphrodites

"For it is Love, far more than family, connections, or wealth, which must guide any of us who wish to live a good life."[3] Following this declaration, Phaedrus hopes to answer the question of *how* love can be such a guide to the good life. Our present project is to some extent well-aligned with Phaedrus's basic premise. Love would be some other way of arranging a life. I am not sure that love is a guide like a compass for a person on a

---

1. Plato, *Symposium*, trans. Avi Sharon (Newburyport, MA: Focus Philosophical Library, 1998), 22 [177d].
2. Ibid., [177e].
3. Ibid., 23 [178d].

journey. To say that love is a practice and power is not the same as to say that it is an instrument or a tool utilized to help us get from here to there. But, human sexuality is the real star of the opening scenes. In our present time, we have seen that same-gender or transgender sexuality reveals the subversive power of a maligned Aphrodite. Pausanias—a figure also known from Plato's *Protagoras* as having studied under the tutelage of Prodicus the sophist—could not speak of love without sexuality.

Pausanias distinguishes between two Aphrodites, the elder Ouranian and the younger Pandemian. Ouranian Aphrodite is the heavenly or higher love, whereas Pandemian Aphrodite refers to the common love of the people. In fact, the word "Pandemian" means "of the people," and, according to Pausanias, it is not only common but vulgar, a low form.[4] According to Pausanias, the common Pandemian love is properly understood as a wild and unruly lust, "which oversees and guides the baser, more common sort of men. Such men desire women as much as boys, prefer the body to the mind and often choose the dumbest mates they can find since they are interested only in the physical act and could not care less whether it were done honorably or ill."[5] It is both basic and necessary to characterize Pausanias's own homosexuality as that of an elitist misogynist who favors men for their intellects, unlike the lowly desires of the many. We could devote this whole book to unpacking the historical, patriarchal, and misogynistic content of Pausanias's speech, but there is perhaps something more interesting in his characterization of the common love of everyday people as vulgar.

The assumption that a man seeking higher forms of love would avoid the allure of a female body and be attracted instead to the mind of a young man, a boy apprentice, reflects the position of males in antiquity as the ones afforded the space, time, and resources (or the freedom) to live a life of the mind and to be raised from childhood to cultivate their intellect. Thus, the higher love is more an intellectual relationality than a libidinal-sexual and bodily one. Here Pausanias's homosexuality is more precisely defined as not centering on sex as much as on philosophy. As Pausanias puts it: "However, the Love that accompanies Heavenly Aphrodite has no trace of the female in him: he is thoroughly male. Hence this Love instills in us a fondness for boys. Moreover, Ouranian or Heavenly Aphrodite is older and therefore more mature, having no part in juvenile recklessness."[6] This means that as a person matures, he moves on a

---

4. Ibid., 26 [180e, 181a].
5. Ibid., 27 [181b].
6. Ibid., [181c].

path toward the abolition of the feminine. To say that the highest love leaves "no trace of the female" is first of all to recognize the female in the male (an important point to be sure), but second of all to condemn the female in the male as an immature phase tending toward recklessness. Pausanias's homosexuality is thus rooted in a hatred of the female, a fundamental misogyny. At the same time, however, because the basest form of love is the common Pandemian one, Pausanias claims that the many are feminine, including and especially the males in Greek society. Most men are too feminine, which Pausanias identifies as a problem to be solved through a maturation toward homosexuality. This means, among other things, the eventual abolition of the feminine.

Pausanias recommends a law against pedophilia, prohibiting relations with the youngest boys, yet he does so not out of concern for the child. He is more worried about the investment of the older lover being wasted on "so uncertain a goal. For one can never tell whether a boy will develop properly or not, physically and mentally."[7] He goes on to say that such a law will be superfluous to the best of men who would not, whether it were legal or otherwise, pursue relations with the youngest boys, and so the law would mainly regulate "the vulgar sort of lovers."[8]

To the normative morality of twenty-first-century readers, this open discourse about the inferiority of the feminine and the love of young boys is immediately unacceptable. We cannot (and should not) defend Pausanias's argument on those scores. His major insight, however, derives from this discussion of the legal prohibition of pedophilic relations. While we agree with the prohibition against pedophilia—and, I would hope, for nobler reasons than Pausanias gives—we should observe that the law is always worried about *how* "love" gets expressed.[9] The concern of the law about appropriate love relations is not a worry that died in antiquity. Today, politics and law continue to concern themselves with men loving men, women loving women, transgender love, and polyamorous activity. Of course, interfaith and interracial love have long had their legal problems too. Pausanias, having agreed with the prohibition against pedophilia, singles out one of the subversive powers of homosexual love. He observes that despots and tyrants always worry about love and that "tyrants here in Athens learned the truth of this by hard experience when Aristogeiton's love for the boy Harmodius and young

---

7. Ibid., [181e].

8. Ibid.

9. I place the word "love" here in quotation marks because, although Pausanias claims to be speaking of love, I do not recognize the sexual desire for children as love.

Harmodius' affection for Aristogeiton grew so strong that together they caused the downfall of the regime."[10] We thus turn our attention to a love that toppled a regime.

Here, Pausanias is referring to the story about the end of Hippias's regime in 514 BCE, which is recounted in Thucydides's *History of the Peloponnesian War*. Hippias of Athens was an infamous tyrant who ruled from roughly 527 BCE to 510 BCE, when he was forced during an invasion to flee Athens. Hippias's brother Hipparchus was murdered by Harmodius and Aristogeiton in 514 BCE, and for this, Harmodius and Aristogeiton were executed by Hippias. According to the story, the killing of his brother by the homosexual lovers (Aristogeiton and Harmodius) is the event that compelled Hippias to tyranny, the murder of many of his own citizens, and the imposition of brutal taxes. Hippias's infamous cruelty turned his own citizens into revolutionaries against him. It is no doubt a stretch for Pausanias to characterize the end of Hippias's regime as being caused by Aristogeiton's love of Harmodius. However, Pausanias means to show that love encourages people to form new loyalties and friendships, "the sorts of things which Love has the greatest likelihood of fostering," and this proliferation of feeling for others, leading to new lines of alliance and common cause, can be very bad news for tyrants.[11]

If we step back from the example of Hippias, we can see how the point holds true within the context of war. Fostering feelings of friendship—let alone love—with enemies is tantamount to ending the war, to making it impossible. War works best when heads of state are obeyed, variously loved or feared, and when the enemies are reliably hated. Historically cultivated and racialized hatreds have long been integral to war-making. It is no accident that the protest slogan "Make Love, Not War" was always also intended as a dissent against state power. Heads of state, whether or not we call them tyrants, always prefer to cultivate and foster loyalty to and friendship with the state and its governors, for they need to be able to turn their citizens against others who would purportedly harm us, whether or not those "others" are called barbarians, Jews, Arabs, Muslims, or gays and lesbians. Within this context, love and friendship, especially for and with those who are meant to be enemies, weakens or breaks political power; it directly challenges the regime.

Now, Pausanias also sees Pandemian love as vulgar because, according to him, it is attached to superficial and perishable things like the

---

10. Plato, *Symposium*, 28 [182c].
11. Ibid.

appearance of the youthful body and our visceral attraction to it. This love is only a base pleasure because, as youthful beauty fades with age, the love would fade too. This is why the higher Ouranian love is preferred by Pausanias, because it attaches itself to an intellect that gets better with age.[12] So for Pausanias, the ideal attachment is not bodily, nor is it based on wealth, which Pausanias identifies as a shameful motivation.[13] Despite other problems, in these specific regards our basic theorization resonates with Pausanias's claim that love is neither fixated on physical beauty nor governed by an interest in monetary gain. Moreover, the theory of love as a communist power especially appreciates any understanding of love that sees it as a threat to tyrannical regimes, even if Pausanias overdetermines its power in the case of Hippias's downfall.

However, Pausanias makes some dire mistakes. Worse, some of his mistakes are still made today and thus cannot be treated as merely ancient errors. We cannot accept that the intellect is male, and we cannot accept that homosexuality is about abolishing the female. And we cannot accept that what Pausanias calls Pandemian love is even love at all. What he is in fact describing is a superficial attachment to a passing passion. We cannot give such a superficial attraction the name "love," and we must resist a bifurcation of love as either vulgar or heavenly. The main reason we cannot accept Pausanias's Pandemian love as any kind of love at all is because *we do not reduce love to sexual relations, lust, or to the private desires of individual persons. The sexual life of individuals, our feelings of lust, and the satisfaction of our private desires may well be a feature of love relations, but in and of themselves, they constitute no form of love.* We must not mistake what may be attributes of love for love itself.

Yet, Pausanias's understanding of and insistence on the subversive power of love is not to be thrown out but built upon. What if everyday people could practice a love that is not vulgar? If that is the case—and I shall argue that it is—then what we are after is not the end of Pandemian love but rather a different kind of Pandemian love, a love that is common, subversive, and praiseworthy.

Eryximachus's speech shifts our attention to the health of the lover. He points out that an unhealthy person cannot love well, whereas a healthy person is capable of loving. He also praises love for its power to bring hostile elements together.[14] Eryximachus's main interest is in love's power to unify oppositional and hostile elements and to heal sickness. According to

---

12. Ibid., 29 [183e].
13. Ibid., 31 [185a].
14. Ibid., 33 [186e].

Eryximachus: "You might even say that his power is omnipresent. But it is actually when Love is directed, with restraint and justice, simply toward the good in itself that it truly has the most power of all and is the source of our greatest happiness. For it is then that it enables the bonds of human fellowship and harmony with the gods above."[15] Here again, love appears as a power with political implications, a power that needs the guidance of "restraint and justice," for otherwise it may not tend toward good things like happiness and human fellowship.

It would be easy to anticipate Socrates's objection to any theory of love that sees love as sometimes good and sometimes bad (not only in Eryximachus's speech but also in Pausanias's). The Socrates of *The Republic* or *Crito*, for example, understands that good things are always worth doing and denies that they are properly defined if doing them causes ill. I cannot say with confidence what exactly Plato wanted us to take from Eryximachus's speech, but one of its key insights stands out as instructive: when Eryximachus speaks of love as a power that "enables the bonds of human fellowship" to flourish and grow, we are speaking—long before any communist theory of the *Gemeinwesen*—of a communizing power. Even if we cannot call this idea "communist" as it appears in the context of Eryximachus, the causal relation of love to human fellowship was already and irreducibly a part of the philosophical discussion in ancient Greece. And, indeed, it is a theme carried on throughout the whole of Plato's *Symposium*.

Aristophanes's speech takes the theory of love to a very different destination. He begins by stating that he will take a different approach, proclaiming "that mankind still hasn't learned the power of Love, not in the least."[16] His speech is the source of the famous fable of halved humans in search of their other half to make them whole. In this tale, Zeus cuts every human in two, and when "our original nature had thus been cut in two, each half immediately began to long for its complementary half."[17] This story, often incorrectly attributed to Socrates and Plato (see the discussion of Horvat's mistake in chapter 1 above, for example), is found in Aristophanes's speech and presents what we may refer to as the "completion theory of love." According to the completion theory of love, the other, the beloved, makes us whole. We cannot be whole without completion by the other. We will show why it is necessary to reject this version of the completion theory and to recommend another one instead.

---

15. Ibid., 35 [188d].
16. Ibid., 36 [189d].
17. Ibid., 37 [191a].

Aristophanes argues: "It is Love that draws together the severed halves of our original state as we desperately try to make one out of two, to heal the human condition."[18] Aristophanes retains the healing power of love previously discussed by Eryximachus, though he specifies that what is being healed by love is not an unwell person, but rather the human condition. Notice also that, after Zeus's halving, we begin with a broken starting position: we start off in life with a severed being, incomplete, and sick. To fix the problem of being, we need to find our other half. We desire to find the half that will complete us, and we live in search of that person until we do. If we do not, then we live a life of incomplete being. According to this theory, love is essentially an ontological problem. While Aristophanes's theory cannot be followed or maintained, we retain his ontological focus.

A different completion theory of love could be the one we outlined in chapter 1, one focused on repairing a fragmented and privatized social body through a resurgent *Gemeinwesen*. Camatte was thinking about health and the human condition too, albeit without any reassurances of restoring well-being through personal or sexual relationships. Aristophanes's tale, although ancient, is perfectly suited to the present neoliberal practice of match-making and the privatization of love relations. Aristophanes's theory is *not* a social theory of love in that it imagines the achievement of a human wholeness within the parameters of a private love relation between two individuals. Assuming that each person is indeed the appropriate half for the other person, love would work just as well regardless of broader social, political, or economic crises. You could have a fully realized love in an apocalyptic world on fire. It would be romantic, perhaps, to imagine two lovers kissing as they're engulfed in the flames of wildfires, or to envision a happy couple standing in a warzone decimated by poverty and neglect, surrounded by misery and death but nonetheless happy with their love. I want to challenge this idea at its roots. Aristophanes's completion theory of love inadvertently prefigures what has become the prevalent capitalist conception of human happiness and health as the private properties of individual persons who have sought and acquired them.

Aristophanes approaches human sexuality differently than Pausanias, although he also affirms the superiority of homosexual love:

All of those men who were split off from the combined male-female

---

18. Ibid., 38 [191d].

gender (the type we call androgynous) spend their lives chasing after women. Most of them happen to be adulterers and so are the women who come from this group. However, women who were severed from the all-female type have no interest in men. Their desires are directed only toward other women and it's from this antique hybrid that lesbians have come. Finally, all those cut from the all-male group are drawn always to other men. Once severed from another man, they naturally fall in love with men, and, as I see it, they are the finest sort we know.[19]

Both gay and lesbian love are here presented as superior to heterosexual love. One of the distinguishing features of Aristophanes's account, compared to that of Pausanias, is that Aristophanes recognizes homosexual love as not only superior in a philosophical or intellectual sense, but also as *natural*. Pausanias appears to present homosexuality as the choice of enlightened men, and, of course, he scarcely appreciates lesbian love as belonging to any similar category. With Aristophanes, however, people are born heterosexual or homosexual, depending on the gender of the one they were split off from, and the heterosexuals have the baser tendencies toward bodily pleasure-seeking, dishonesty, and infidelity. We may presume that Aristophanes prefers the homosexual love of men to that of women because Aristophanes shares Pausanias's misogynistic view of the superior male intellect.

The important story of the historical inversion of these ancient valuations of human sexuality is not the subject of our present study. But suffice it to say here that there is a long history of heterosexual dominance and normalization entrenched in the theological, religious, and patriarchal powers that have governed social and political affairs in and after the transition to the Common Era. In humanity's passage to the Common Era, much of the world eventually saw an inversion of Greek valuations of sexuality, and not only an inversion but an effective vilification and criminalization of homosexual love as deviant, religiously transgressive, and morally unacceptable. Despite present criticisms of these theories of love, there are ongoing and pressing political abuses of this hidden and inverted history, some of which continue to demand our attention—perhaps the most obvious of all is the idiotic notion that homosexual love is a distinctly contemporary issue. Homosexual love long predates the discourses that condemn it.

---

19. Ibid., 38 [191e].

For Aristophanes, a life of piety and good faith is the prerequisite for the reward of love. This means we have to "become Love's friends," and only then will we be rewarded by the gods who will "help us find and love those youngsters who were truly meant for us, our own matching halves—a very rare achievement these days."[20] Youth is a recurring theme in *Symposium*, though we should wonder why youth is so valorized if the highest form of Ouranian love takes its primary interest in the intellect, and not in our sexual attraction to bodies. Aristophanes is obviously not referring to the Pandemian love of common people if what he's talking about is, as cited above, "a very rare achievement these days." But Aristophanes also presents love as a kind of individualist pursuit. A man or a woman must know how to praise love first in their individual life, to know what love is, and then must be obedient to the gods and search for their missing half. The goal of this journey is the completion of the self. Love is positioned in the theory of the matching halves as an outcome of obedient good behavior that makes one whole.

We quickly see that many different images of Aphrodite are painted in *Symposium*, yet too much of the discussion centers on the private concerns of individual persons. No one who has read Plato's Socratic texts can accuse either Plato or Socrates of forgetting the social. To read any of Plato's major works in political philosophy—from *The Republic*, *Crito*, *Apology*, and *Laws* to *Meno* and *Gorgias*, among others—is to consider the health of the social body, of the body politic, its legal order and justice. In Plato's political thought, the structure and harmony of the constitutive organs of political society are paramount concerns. A good political society aims at "making the weaker, the stronger and those in the middle—whether you wish to view them as such in terms of prudence, or, if you wish, in terms of strength, or multitude, money or anything else whatsoever of the sort—sing the same chant together."[21] Now, while it is true that we have not yet arrived at Socrates's speech, love has so far been cut off from this broader social concern. Plato's *Symposium* is not, therefore, immediately recognizable as a political text. And yet, we find a pregnant tension: love is clearly a great power, among the greatest powers on earth, and all politics is concerned with power. Let us be the midwives, then, helping to bring out the political content of this power.

Note that the entire setting of the symposium is infused with sexual innuendo and flirtation, as Phaedrus points out toward the end of

---

20. Ibid., 40 [193b].
21. Plato, *The Republic of Plato: Second Edition*, trans. Allan Bloom (New York: Basic Books, 1991), 110 [432a].

Aristophanes's speech.[22] The background flirtations and sexual connections of the interlocutors are further disclosed in Alcibiades's speech, but we must ask: Why this setting at all? That the discussion of love is to be continually pursued within the context of interpersonal sexual attractions can only necessitate a relative depoliticization of the philosophy of love. In *Symposium*, we are largely (although not entirely, as we shall soon see) pushed to think of love as a mainly asocial affair between two persons. And if you look at dominant thinking about love after Plato, you will find a long history of thinking of love as exactly such a private affair, a fact that can be traced back to this text of Plato's. Although the privatization of love has been challenged by many philosophers since, it still survives and thrives in the most common idealizations of romantic love. This is one of the more unfortunate legacies of *Symposium*.

Things do take a turn, though, when Agathon insists on adding a defining characteristic to the nature of love, claiming that "violence is everywhere incompatible with Love."[23] This expands on Pausanias's discussion of Hippias and my earlier comments on the opposition of love to war. Love must be located outside of (and perhaps even against) war because it is incompatible with violence, and there is no war without violence. I am not convinced by Agathon's assertion and will show the occasional but important compatibility of love with certain forms of violence in the complicating analyses to come. For now, however, let us acknowledge that so much depends on what we call "violence." If, for example, we established that poverty and racism are *forms* of violence, would Agathon have to say that love opposes them? Agathon is at least open to appreciating the social and political dimensions of love. For example, he says: "Love diminishes our insularity and replenishes our collegiality."[24] This is to say that Agathon praises a notion of love that works against social privatization and encourages at least some forms of human solidarity.

Agathon's speech is followed by applause, and Socrates only makes his way into the conversation toward its conclusion. At this point we discover Socrates's total dissatisfaction with all of the foregoing speeches. Although Socrates is often associated with the theories of love in *Symposium*, and most egregiously with Aristophanes's completion theory of love, he in fact rejects all of these theories and is hardly ever as fierce and brazenly critical as he is in response to them:

---

22. Plato, *Symposium*, 41 [194d].
23. Ibid., 43 [196c].
24. Ibid., 45 [197d].

The method which all of you have been using is quite different: you gather together the largest and most outlandish attributes you can find, whether they're true or false and whether they belong to the subject or not. That's why all of you have spent so much time and effort ascribing so many preposterous qualities to Love: that he looks like this, that he gives us that. You're only doing this to make him seem as beautiful and perfect as possible. You're obviously not trying to convince those of us who already know the truth, but simply hoping to dazzle the ignorant.... I won't make a fool of myself by imitating your example.[25]

Needless to say, Socrates is unimpressed. But how does he turn the conversation in opposite directions, and does he move beyond the failures of his colleagues in ways we can develop for a contemporary theory of love?

2.2 From Socrates to Spartacus: Love in War and Revolt

Socrates begins his intervention in conversation with Agathon. Socrates observes first of all that when you love and desire a thing, it is because you do not yet have it in your possession. He takes care to establish this as a basic principle with Agathon, saying: "We must be certain about this, Agathon. Is it just probable or entirely necessary that all desires are desires for things which are absent or lacking? I feel quite certain that this must be so."[26] Agathon agrees, and Socrates goes on to take certain examples, such as that a strong person would not desire to be strong and a tall person could not desire to be tall. Socrates points out that when a wealthy person says they desire to be wealthy or a healthy person says they desire to be healthy, what they really mean is that they want to go on being wealthy or healthy in the future, out of a concern to keep possessing tomorrow what they already have today. Even here, desire depends on the absence of its object. A future possibility of becoming sick or poor is the basis for the healthy and the wealthy to desire future health and wealth. Without the possibility of an absent or lost object or possession, desire becomes nonsense. We desire either *what* we do not possess or *that* we will continue to keep our possessions in the future.

---

25. Ibid., 46 [198e–199b].
26. Ibid., 47 [200a].

Socrates's opening declarations are already problematic. First of all, keep in mind our discussion in chapter 1 warning us against the conflation of desire and love. We have already established, albeit in a preliminary way, that love and desire are not identical. So we have to proceed with caution, watching to see if the difference between the two is in fact lost on Socrates. More importantly, we do not want to ground a theory of love in thinking about what we have, about our properties and possessions. In every chapter of this book, we will, in fact, argue against this assumption. We will show, following Erich Fromm and others, why love is more concerned with being than having. But it is not a detour to see that this is how Socrates begins thinking about love, for an understanding of the history of the private property conception of love is necessary to the present study. It is worth noting as well that grounding discussion about desire and love in having and possession long predates capitalism.

Socrates's speech is, as mentioned above, a recounting of his conversation with Diotima, "a priestess from Mantinea."[27] Essentially, the theory of love that Socrates presents is Diotima's theory, which Socrates claims to find fully convincing. And in the theory of Diotima, we may find a fruitful starting point for a more interesting and critical theory of love than one centered on property and possession. There is another and more promising premise here that states that love is neither beautiful nor good.[28] Socrates represents this as Diotima's argument, and because Diotima and Socrates are saying the same thing, I will present what follows as their view.

We have different starting positions to consider. According to the opening premise, accepted by both Agathon and Socrates, desire would be greatest where want and need are most severe—that is to say, those who have the most to desire have the greatest desire. Socially, this starting position would turn our attention to the "have-nots," to the people or class without much, yet with much to desire. When we look at the wealthy and strong and beautiful and happy, we would therefore find very little desire beyond the desire to continue having the same good fortune tomorrow. This is what we may call a "status quo desire." Status quo desire can be contrasted to the first desire Socrates identifies, which we may call a "desire for something else." Status quo desire is the desire of the healthy, wealthy, and powerful, whereas a desire for something else is the desire of the sick, poor, and exploited. But again, is what is true of desire also true of love?

---

27. Ibid., 49 [201d].
28. Ibid., 50 [201e].

Articulating a connection between love and human need is a more expansive formulation than the privatizing premise regarding possessions. Diotima and Socrates articulate the point with moving clarity: "Love has not fallen far from the tree. His Mother's son, he is ever wanting and, although some may find this hard to believe, he is not the least bit delicate or handsome. On the contrary, he is a vagrant with tough, parched skin. He is always barefoot and homeless, sleeping under a roof of sky or in the doorways of strangers. Sometimes you can hear him snoring in ditches by the side of the road. In all this he takes after his poor mother and is always in need."[29] Love is ever wanting, much like the halved being in pursuit of its other. But Diotima and Socrates are not reiterating Aristophanes's story about incomplete halves. Whereas beauty—albeit an intellectual and not physical beauty—is the centerpiece for Aristophanes, ugliness is the heart of love for Diotima and Socrates. The ugly should not here be confused with the vulgar of Pausanias's speech. Here the ugly is the homeless, downtrodden, barefoot, impoverished, and beaten being, an unloved person trampled underfoot, full of failure, and hidden from view. He or she is *not* to be envied like the beautiful and well-off. He or she is nothing but need, want, and dispossession. And yet it is this being of such a lamentable condition who is given the name "Love." Here love and desire are interwoven and inextricable.

This being is an open field of desire, but the desire is not at all a status quo desire. No, this is the picture of a desire for something else at its ground zero. Diotima and Socrates continue through to the end of the text with a certain conflation of desire and love. Let us say now that they are *at least* right about desire. Diotima and Socrates say that even if Love (the vagrant son above) has some good days, Love deteriorates into sadness each night, and because Love cannot be omniscient, *Love is not a god*.[30] Diotima and Socrates say that "gods and those few men whom we consider to be truly wise never feel any love or desire for wisdom since they already possess it."[31] What is remarkable in this account is that for the first time in *Symposium*, love is categorically a thing of this world—it is human, not divine—and it is to be found in the most imperfect and ugly humanity.

But human love does not mean relative love. Inquiring about the universality of love, Socrates ask Diotima: "And this desire for happiness,

---

29. Ibid., 53 [203d].

30. I capitalize "Love" in these few instances only where, following Diotima and Socrates, we are talking about the proper name of the mother's son as in the passage quoted just above.

31. Plato, *Symposium*, 53 [203e–204a].

this love, do you think it's universal, does everyone want to have good things and to have them forever?"[32] Diotima agrees to this universality, and they move on to explore why not everyone could be called a lover. But I want to observe the new content smuggled into this question. Notice that the desire for happiness is here specified as love. So Socrates is not only thinking of love and desire as parts of a unitary whole, often treating love and desire synonymously, but he is now qualifying the specific desire for happiness as love. Desire for happiness is a loftier desire than, say, a fleeting sexual desire satisfied by masturbation. This is a qualification that matters because happiness is a vast subject unto itself, and not every desire—once satisfied—results in it. So we could say, following Socrates and Diotima, that love desires happiness, and this connects with the previous discussion about want because the want of happiness naturally emanates from the unhappy. Does this mean that love is the desire of the unhappy? To some extent, this may well be the case, and it is consistent with Diotima and Socrates's picture of the homeless vagrant snoring in ditches.

Diotima correctly addresses the tendency to single out sexual love as the only or primary form of love whenever, in fact, what is actually being discussed more properly refers "to the whole range of passionate activities associated with love."[33] She argues that we impoverish the term when we use it only to describe one of its forms. Diotima is right to highlight the reductionist practice of thinking of love in its sexual form alone. Previous speeches did well to show how, in many instances, the passionate activity of sexual intercourse is based less on love than on fleeting attractions and gratifications. Diotima and Socrates would have to say that some passionate activity, including if not especially sexual activity, may be a practice of things other than love. This can be seen in many examples, including in the principled distinction between the instant gratification of bodily desires, on the one hand, and human happiness, on the other. But I want to be clear that we are not criticizing sexual activity that is not a practice of love. There are many activities that are not practices of love that are nonetheless worth doing for their own reasons. With sexual activity beyond procreation, there is also intimacy, experimentation, and pleasure. There is a whole field of sexual pleasure that, on the grounds of human feeling alone, has every justification it needs. We cannot moralize about sexual pleasure in any categorical way without exercising a perverse morality, a

---

32. Ibid., 54 [205a].
33. Ibid., 55 [205c].

morality perverted by some ideological or theological disposition, which is usually easy to discern. While we advance no arguments against sexual activity without love, we nonetheless recognize other forms of love that are nonsexual, which would include social or political love, kinship and friendship, paternal and familial love, and the affective bases for human solidarity. Shifting onto that path in the early stages of a theory of love sets us in the direction of driving against the privatization of love in the interpersonal relationality of two or three individuals.

But Diotima and Socrates ultimately drive down the wrong path, go off the proverbial rails, and ultimately fall off a fatal cliff. They take their catastrophic turn at the moment when Diotima asserts that the true aim of love is giving birth and parenting, understood as a desire for immortality.[34] While one could simply defend that ancient love cannot be held to contemporary standards, I would point out that ancient love has set many of the standards that we now venture to transgress. On this question, Diotima is unequivocal: "For the love and care which all parents show toward their offspring is just an expression of this all-consuming desire for immortality."[35]

In a brief departure from the present analysis, allow me to outline a personal and anecdotal articulation of a rival vision: I am, at the time of this writing, the father of two young children. They are separated by seven years, and the oldest is moving from elementary to middle school. I am daily involved in my children's lives, although my teaching and research take me away from them at various points every day—except during the weekend, when I defend the old convention of doing no teaching and research until Monday. My love for my children is a deep and abiding practice of my everyday life. I do not claim to be a perfect father, and one day my children will surely share with me the vast catalog of my errors. But I love my children to their bones. What does this mean? It does not mean that I seek to live forever through them. I have no idea who they will become. Giving birth to them with my partner was not the act of love that mattered most. Many children are born yet live unloved. The act of love is the one that is practiced in the process of their becoming who they will be. Consider, then, a rival proposition: *the parent's love is practiced by way of participation in the child becoming what she ought to be.* This proposition is rival to the one articulated by Diotima about the parental desire for immortality.

---

34. Ibid., 56–57 [206b–207a].
35. Ibid., 59 [208b].

Our rival proposition was already introduced in chapter 1 in the discussion of Levinas. When I say that I want to participate in my children becoming what they ought to be, *I do not* mean that I have some specific idea of who or what they ought to be. I mean, rather, that *precisely because I love them*, I do not want to preserve them as fixed objects of love, and I do not want to use any parental force to press them into a path of becoming against their wills. Yet they do need guidance. My children's wills to become are in an early formative stage. If they are asked who they should become, one may say the Flash and the other may say a FIFA soccer player in the World Cup. These wills to becoming are very likely to change and have probably already changed several times by the time your eyes are passing over these words. Regardless of the specific wills of my children, I would like to participate in their becoming what they are not yet, following their mutual self-understandings about what they feel they could and should be. This is a nonteleological notion of becoming in the sense that some single destination cannot be specified by anyone, neither by me nor by my children. And I do not need my children to make me immortal in the way that James Mill and Jeremy Bentham had hoped John Stuart Mill would do for them and utilitarianism. Here, and following Diotima and Socrates, we transition from sexual love to the parental love of the child. Yet in *Symposium*, neither one of these is recognizably social or political. They are forms of love that arrange the private affairs of individuals and in some sense can be practiced fully in the privacy of the home, cut off from the social and political life of a town, city, or community.

Diotima and Socrates continue to press their critical points about the imperfect and the ugly, arguing that love of a beautiful partner is not as durable as love of an ugly partner because, as mentioned earlier, youthful and bodily beauty can fade whereas a beautiful mind can last and grow for a lifetime of companionship. They work out their speech toward its disappointing conclusion, to its veritable dead end. Socrates finishes: "I am convinced that there is no better ally than Love for those who want life immortal."[36] The philosophy of love articulated by Diotima and Socrates ultimately posits a desire for one's self in an infinite perpetuity as the height of love. In their discussion of parental love, the beloved—in that case the child—is mainly instrumental to the purposes of one's desire for immortality. We have seen that Socrates is not always the patient interlocutor or gentle midwife of philosophy, especially not after having to

---

36. Ibid., 63 [212b].

sit through too many speeches he despised. And yet, in the case of *Symposium*, the friends he criticizes with so much ferocity often have the better ideas. The authorship of Plato complicates our final analysis because, obviously, Plato wanted us to have all of these speeches, not only that of Diotima and Socrates. There are certain incompatibilities between the speeches, and there is much to criticize and reject, but the contribution of Diotima and Socrates is not the main theory. Indeed, the bulk of the text already precedes it, and Alcibiades enters after all of the others are finished for a final flourish.

Alcibiades was known as a wealthy and handsome military genius. He was also an athlete, decorated with prizes in chariot races at the Olympics. He became a politician and, as a military commander, was sent to lead the conquest of Sicily. After Socrates had finished his speech and as the rousing applause for it had died down, Alcibiades was heard coming in through the hallway in a drunken display. He was accompanied by a posse of doting admirers. By this point in his life, he had risen to fame. He was encouraged by the others to join the symposium, especially by Agathon who wanted the handsome young latecomer to join them on *his* couch. Socrates soon lets on that Alcibiades is in love with him, or at least passionately attracted to him and fiercely jealous of any sexual attention that Socrates might receive from other men, saying: "Ever since we fell in together, I haven't been free to look at or speak to another soul, and if I do he burns with jealousy.... I'm afraid he'll explode again tonight. Please, Agathon, try to settle things between us, and if he gets violent, you'll have to protect me."[37] Does Alcibiades really love Socrates? What is the relationship of jealousy to love? Socrates worries about Alcibiades getting violent. Recall that it was Agathon who earlier declared that "violence is everywhere incompatible with Love."[38]

But Alcibiades denies Socrates's characterization: "I certainly hope you didn't believe a word he just said about me, did you? Why it's just the reverse. He's the one who gives me a beating whenever I praise anyone other than him, god or man."[39] So each man claims that the other is unreasonably infatuated with him, that he is the object of the other's violent jealousy. And this is the prelude to Alcibiades's strange concluding speech.

Unkindly, Alcibiades begins his speech by comparing Socrates to statues of Silenoi, usually depicted as unattractive Satyrs, predatory men with

---

37. Ibid., 65 [231d].
38. Ibid., 43 [196c].
39. Ibid., 66 [214d].

huge erections who were famously rapacious.[40] Unlike Silenoi and Satyrs, however, Socrates charms his prey with words instead of music. Alcibiades confesses to having been the prey of Socrates and, because of their intimacy, claims to have also glimpsed Socrates's true nature, a nature not visible in his public persona. Alcibiades claims that Socrates does not share the values of the broader society and "couldn't give a damn whether a boy is beautiful or rich or famous or any of the things that most people care about. I tell you he has contempt for all of that, and he thinks that we ourselves are totally worthless."[41] But behind his public persona, Alcibiades claims that Socrates is "radiant and beautiful."[42] Alcibiades, the young and handsome, presents himself as smitten with the unkempt Socrates at the start of their relationship, and tells how he eventually came to think that Socrates had fallen in love with him. According to Alcibiades, Socrates "deceives us all by making us think he is in love with us, when suddenly you realize that you're the one in love with him."[43] Socrates listened patiently, likely more amused than during any of the previous speeches, given Alcibiades's humor and affection in speaking about him and their "love" directly out in the open.

Socrates interrupts the speech toward its end saying that Alcibiades has exaggerated Socrates's beauty and love, and insists that the true story is quite different. But Alcibiades persists and tells of how, in a reversal of the usual position of Silenoi and Satyrs, it was he the young and handsome man who ended up in sexual pursuit of Socrates. They'd spent a night together, where Alcibiades had become like a predator yet was surprisingly rebuffed by Socrates: "But in spite of my efforts, this insolent man turned me down, scorned my beauty.... You've got to believe me. I swear by the gods and goddesses together: my night with Socrates was as chaste as if I'd spent it with my own father or brother!"[44] But we want to know what this tale has to do with love and how or why it belongs to the famous ancient text on love. It has to do with sexual desire, yet there is little by way of any clear connection to a philosophy of love. So far, it gives us only a tabloid-like glimpse at the confounding agency of the lovers, each with regard to the other. One thinks he is in control, only to discover he is under the control of the other, and the reality is too tangled to unravel.

---

40. Ibid., 67 [215b]; see also translator's footnote 1.
41. Ibid., 69 [216e].
42. Ibid., 69 [217a].
43. Ibid., 74 [222b].
44. Ibid., 71 [219d].

But then, in a peculiar twist, the theme of war makes a surprising return. Alcibiades tells of his service in the military alongside Socrates when Athens invaded Potidaea in Northern Greece in 432 BCE. This invasion marked the beginning of the Peloponnesian War. Alcibiades recounts Socrates's remarkable bravery and calm in battle, and his "inhuman ability to resist the cold."[45] In fact, Socrates impressed Alcibiades all around, as he did not complain about the food or about the toil of marching over difficult terrain, and he made no ado about his ability to bear the physicality of the invasion far better than his much younger comrades. Most importantly, Alcibiades recounts: "You should keep in mind his conduct during the heat and press of battle. For though I was the one who was decorated for bravery during that campaign it was Socrates, alone of the whole battalion, who intervened to save my life. You see, I'd been wounded in a skirmish when Socrates found me and refused to leave me behind, pulling me from certain death and rescuing my shield as well."[46]

Here is an example that may well demonstrate Socrates's love of Alcibiades more than any sexual affection. What did Socrates do? His friend and comrade had fallen to die in battle, and Socrates did everything he could to save him from death. Even if Socrates had failed to save Alcibiades, the effort could be seen as a practice of love. Love in war is a love that matters because it is a practice of human solidarity at the critical moment, at the moment when that solidarity may be decisive for the human being. Love in war is a love at war with death. Love in war, especially if it transgresses boundaries between friend and foe, can be a power to end war. Above all, one must not love an enemy that one is charged to kill. This lesson, perhaps more than any other in *Symposium*, hews most closely to my theoretical and political arguments.

However, Plato's *Symposium* remains a major problem in the history of the philosophy of love. First of all, the multifarious philosophy of these speeches only touches love lightly as it passes by. More substantively, *Symposium* takes up the question of love from problematic starting positions that lead variously to dangerous and unhelpful destinations. The speech-givers do not agree on many things, but too much agreement coalesces around the idea of love as a logic of sexual relationality. There is also insufficient differentiation between love and desire; far too frequently, the terms are used synonymously. Then, with Diotima and Socrates, love would have its highest articulation in the sexual and procreative

---

45. Ibid., 72 [220b].
46. Ibid., 73 [220e].

mode of wanting to live forever, in the desire for immortality. And finally, aside from precious few reflections on war and subversion, love is not described as a social or political concept. These are some of the limitations of *Symposium* that we will surpass. Although these errors and limitations come out of a short, ancient text, they continue to shape contemporary understandings of love, which is on the whole still regarded as a subject of romantic life and sexual desire, of self-interest and self-completion, and as mostly alien to political inquiry.

Our arguments, grounded in the preliminary inquiry of the first chapter, assert contrary directions to those explored in *Symposium*. The sexual relationality of two individual persons may or may not embody and reflect a love relation in miniature. But love is not the private property of a little duet, and it exceeds that relation. To view love as the relation of two is the common reductionist romanticization of erotic love that still needs challenging today. Also, love and desire are not the same thing. Many objects of our desire, such as money, a particular commodity like a phone, or a sexual experience, may be desires without connection to love. All of us have such desires. More precisely, love can motivate actions that are not particularly desirable but that promote the well-being of the other. Much of parental love functions in this way, as does the love of one comrade rescuing another on the battlefield. Finally, procreation and a desire for immortality through procreation are cut off from anything we will call love. This is not to say that procreation must happen outside of love, but, rather, that *love does not need procreation*. Indeed, the desire for immortality through raising a child who would bear one's family name is among the very worst of all motivations for bringing new life into this world. Beyond reductionist romanticization and the privatizing permutations of erotic relationality (that is, "I am yours, you are mine"), *love is a social concept and power*. Furthermore, if love is the great power that philosophy proclaims it to be, then politics, which is fundamentally concerned with power relations in the human world, has got to take up the question of love.

Long after Plato and Socrates, but still before the life and times of Jesus Christ, in the decades of 109 BCE to 71 BCE, lived another great historical figure who led an infamous slave revolt, a great ancient uprising against empire. I am of course referring to Spartacus, who just so happened to be a great hero of Karl Marx's.[47] Spartacus led the slave rebellion of the Third Servile War, or the Gladiator War, from 73 BCE until his death in 71. In concluding the present chapter, I want to further—but only very

---

47. See the "Confessions of Marx" in Kamenka, *The Portable Marx*, 53.

briefly—explore the extent to which love participates in war and revolt. The issue will be taken up more extensively and in more contemporary contexts in chapters 7 and 8.

Most of the major accounts of political history have embodied and reflected the patriarchal masculinity of their heroic protagonists, the leading men in stories of war, conquest, and rebellion. We always hear the names of the men, but their lovers—and especially when those lovers are women—are not only the casualties of history but of its telling. When we think of the slave revolt of Spartacus we think of a brave and rebellious fugitive turned commander, rising up in arms with fighting comrades like Crixus, facing off against other male foes like Crassus and Glaber, and even against the lanistae who purchased and kept them. But a recent study by Aldo Schiavone, one of the world's leading scholars of Roman history and law, has finally helped a mysterious woman appear. Schiavone reconstructs the story of Spartacus by way of a rigorous analysis of the incomplete fragments from Appian and Florus, Livy, Plutarch and Sallust, and other sources of ancient documentary detritus. The story told by Schiavone, which appears in a short book published by Harvard University Press titled *Spartacus*, is the best we have yet.[48]

It turns out that Spartacus had a woman by his side for much of his capture, enslavement, escape, and revolt during the Third Servile War. This woman, whose name we do not know, may well have been with Spartacus at every step of his journey. We know very little about her beyond that she was there, but Schiavone thinks her presence was important. This woman, the beloved of Spartacus, "was a priestess, dedicated to making prophecies."[49] In the fragmentary sources documenting her presence, she seems to represent a mysterious and mystical power. Indeed, her presence and power were understood as subversive by the Roman ruling class: "Plutarch talks of her as being possessed by trances ("ton Dionyson orghiasmois")—situations in which female sexuality, completely transgressing the rules of everyday life, became a direct sign of the divinity, and the path to communion with it. It was all very familiar to the Roman ruling circles: around a century earlier they had issued a harsh senatorial decree to put a stop to the spread of these practices in the lower layers of society, well aware of their potentially subversive effects on the social order."[50] People in positions of power have a long history of worrying about

---

48. Aldo Schiavone, *Spartacus*, trans. Jeremy Carden (Cambridge, MA: Harvard University Press, 2013).

49. Ibid., 27.

50. Ibid., 28.

women's subversive powers and about sexuality. Some of this has been touched on in our discussion of *Symposium*. The concern over sexuality goes back at the very least to Pausanias's retelling of the story of Hippias and the fall of his regime in 514 BCE. I cannot speculate about the form of transgressive female sexuality that Schiavone mentions, but we are talking about what seemed like a mystical allure, a power within human sexuality that was seen as treasonous for its ability to attract the desires of everyday people who could be driven to question the power of the state. The image of the woman by Spartacus's side shows that passion is close to subversion.

Schiavone attests that this woman likely accompanied Spartacus in the revolt. Prisoners were often traded along with their loved ones, "and in our case the woman might quite easily have been captured together with Spartacus, having shared his life as a fugitive and guerrilla fighter."[51] So the subversive power of his lover may well have been a significant power at play in the plans of Spartacus to escape and then to fight against the Roman system. According to Schiavone, Spartacus could not accept a life of fighting as a gladiator in an arena, against his will and for the pleasure of his captors. But why not, especially since so many others *had* accepted that fate, and for so many generations? Schiavone answers: "The gods—his Dionysius, who spoke through his woman—had foreseen other things for him."[52] How to make this concrete? Human relationality is always a critical part of the context of human action. This means that in order to understand the historical contexts of human action, we must understand how actors related to the others around them: Who did they love? Who loved them? How did that love mobilize their life activity? Answering those questions is not always easy to do, but if we can do it even a little bit with figures as distant as Socrates and Spartacus, then we can do it with others who have lived much closer to us in time. Indeed, this will be a major theme of the next chapter.

At the time of his escape, Spartacus and his small company of insurrectionist slaves overpowered the guards and ran off into the cover of darkness, the first space and moment of liberation. Schiavone is confident that Spartacus's beloved would have gone with him into that emancipatory night, for "if she had remained she would have been tortured and killed as an accomplice. And it is quite possible that she was not the only woman."[53] It is important to emphasize the fact that the revolt did not simply

---

51. Ibid., 29.
52. Ibid., 33.
53. Ibid., 34.

comprise of the insurgent acts of brave men, therefore, but was also made by courageous women and accompanied by a kind of insurgent love, a love that could not be contained in a *ludus*.

Spartacus was part of a larger vision of rebellion. As Schiavone has it, Spartacus was sending a "political signal" to "the heart of the empire" rejecting "the corrupting power of wealth and acquisitive greed. And this in the face of a society that was making money and opulence the measure of the world."[54] Spartacus moved *against* the empire and its heart made of money, and for that very reason he became an iconic figure of revolt against brutal exploitation maintained by and for people of power. Spartacus shows a power other than the power of money, an insurgent power from below, from inside prison cells. That the revolt was full of violence makes it appear far removed from Agathon's pacifistic notion of love. Yet is it possible to say, at least to some extent, that this revolt, this slave uprising, this war waged by fugitive gladiators against state power was itself a practice of love? Such a conclusion perhaps seems like the stretch of a generous imagination. But at least this is beyond question: There was an active sense of possibility and dignity beyond a life of brutal captivity. There was also a company, full of companionship, kinship, intimacy, and human solidarity, a company—a collectivity—of men and women, some (if not many) of them in love. There is no speculation in saying that revolt desires a new becoming, not only personal but also always implicating social, political, and economic dimensions. From where does it grow? What are its roots? To what extent does the violence of revolt betray love? Alternatively, we could ask to what extent revolt needs love and depends on it.

Those who are mobilized or empowered by relations of love and human solidarity sometimes become figures of history. But what of the nameless men and women who surrounded them? And what of the corrupting power of wealth and greed within a society ruled by money, like the protocapitalist ancient world in which Spartacus became a transformative force of history? What I am appealing to in these questions is too elusive to touch in our ancient examples, but it is fundamentally a question about the role of love in the life of insurgents. How do revolutionary figures interact with love as a practice and a power, even if not as a concrete concept of political theory?

Let us move now to the terrain of such questions.

---

54. Ibid., 60.

CHAPTER 3

The Love of Communists

"Love is communism within capitalism; misers give
their all and this makes them blissful."

–Ulrich Beck and Elisabeth Beck-Gernsheim, *The Normal Chaos of Love*

"In place of the individual and egoistic family, a great universal
family of workers will develop, in which all the workers, men
and women, will above all be comrades. This is what relations
between men and women in the communist society will be like.
These new relations will ensure for humanity all the joys of a
love unknown in the commercial society of capitalism."

–Alexandra Kollontai, *Selected Writings of Alexandra Kollontai*

Money abuses and disfigures human relations. Marx understood this with the greatest profundity:

> Money thereby directly and simultaneously becomes the *real community* [*Gemeinwesen*], since it is the general substance of survival for all, and at the same time the social product of all. But as we have seen, in money the community [*Gemeinwesen*] is at the same time a mere abstraction, a mere external, accidental thing for the individual, and at the same time merely a means for his satisfaction as an isolated individual. The community of antiquity presupposes a quite different relation to, and on the part of, the individual. The development of money in its third role therefore smashes this community.[1]

Money transforms social relations by way of organizing community against itself. Marx maintained that "the *real community*" was nothing other than the community that humans live and experience. As a materialist, Marx was not interested in comparing and contrasting an ideal-typical concept of community with the community of our lived experience. But the community of our lived experience is not *the only possible* form of community, and throughout history, community has taken various forms. In capitalist societies, where everyday life is governed by money, the human community is organized in accordance with that reality. What humans may need to subsist and survive is not a given security. It is instead monetized and available consistent with one's ability to pay. Accordingly, we structure

---

1. Karl Marx, *Grundrisse: Foundations of the Critique of Political Economy (Rough Draft)*, trans. Martin Nicolaus (New York: Penguin Books, 1993), 225–26.

our education, our adult lives, our weekdays, weekends, and recreation, around a centerpiece of capital, around the business of tending to money, to its acquisition and exchange. This is not hypothetical; it is actual. But it is not the only possible arrangement.

Driven by what we identify as the reality and accept as the necessity, we reproduce in our daily lives a social organization that reproduces the capitalist community and its logic. Marx sees a problem with this community in that it comprises a collectivity of individuals in pursuit of the satisfaction of their own private needs, and is in fact a community of isolation. The other human person is confronted as a competitor, a measurable commodity, an employer, and the other—*just like you*—cannot live for the overall health of the social body because each individual understands that the social body is composed of organs looking after their own health and well-being. When Marx considers the alternative "community of antiquity," he is not making a romantic plea for a return to some past era. Rather, he is pointing out a different arrangement, a different logic of relationality, that was abolished by the development of money as the sovereign power in the capitalist form of life.

Marx was not a communitarian, and I am not making a communitarian argument. I am not transfixed by the concept of community. I am not wanting—*not in the least*—to centralize a theory of community. What I am interested in are possible and desirable forms of life, human health and well-being, and social and political movements capable of addressing and ultimately transforming conditions of life that make us sick, that deplete our compassion and diminish human solidarity. I am opposed to a form of life that pits us against one another as if we are all runners in a rigged race in which too few runners ever win. I am interested in thinking about logics of life capable of contesting and subverting a logic of life governed by money, where even the most ordinary daily activities (such as watching a movie or listening to music) are ruled by capital. Marx understood with more dedicated focus and understanding than anyone else the irremediable problems of the capitalist rule of life.

In this chapter I explore how some of the major communists have thought about and practiced love. I undertake this exploration by considering both philosophical and biographical discourses on the love of communists. The love of communists is not impervious to the disfigurations of life in a capitalist society. The love of communists—or communist love—is enacted and realized (just like the love of anyone else) within the limits of the existing reality. The love of communists has been the hopeful refuge of communists like Marx, Rosa Luxemburg, and so many others. Love is in fact a refuge for anyone, *regardless of whether or not they are communist.* But because the communist consciously opposes the logic of capital, love provides him or her with a direct experience of noncapitalist relationality, which can be understood as such. While I ultimately argue that all love is necessarily communist in fundamental ways, this chapter looks at what love has meant to and for communists confronting the demands of life in a capitalist society and what love has meant in the imaginaries of a post-capitalist future.

First, we work through Marx's theories of community and alienation as they are elaborated in *Grundrisse*, because in that work they are far more sharply developed and clarified than in the earlier works, and with a more sustained focus than in the works that came after. I aim to show that Marx understood with remarkable prescience the isolating and disfiguring tendencies of a life governed by money and organized by capital. I explore this in *Grundrisse* in order to set the stage for thinking about the shape that love takes in such a disfigured society—that is, what love means in communities of alienation. How does love function in a society of individualist separation, dependency, and alienation from the human community? Next, in the remaining sections of this chapter we consider the love of communist women, and specifically love from the point of view of socialist-feminist theory. Thus, we shall turn from Karl Marx to Jenny Marx, Rosa Luxemburg, and Alexandra Kollontai.

3.1 Capitalist Disfiguration:
Grundrisse and the Community of Alienation

Marx wrote about alienation in the important section focused on "Estranged Labor" in his *Economic and Philosophic Manuscripts of 1844,* one of his earliest works, written when he was twenty-six years old. He remained focused on various forms of alienation from that young age until his death. The same could be said about the concept of community, which was always linked to his study of capital and to his understanding of the communism that preceded capitalist society. But Marx was no communitarian, and he meant nothing by "community" that would have been acceptable to North American social theorists and analytical philosophers who speak of "communitarianism." For Marx, a central and enduring (indeed, lifelong) interest in alienation and community led him to explain transformations in human relationality using the social sciences, just as evolution was being explained in the natural sciences. In 1857 and

1858, Marx produced the massive work of *Grundrisse*, in which he carried forward his earlier theories from the *Manuscripts of 1844*, *The German Ideology*, and *The Communist Manifesto*, moving his thinking in the direction of the final masterpiece that would ultimately (and posthumously) emerge as the volumes that comprise *Capital*.

The massive and sprawling notebooks that make up Marx's *Grundrisse* can be summarily described, despite their complexity and depth, as an inquiry into the ways that capitalist exchange relations damage and disfigure human society and well-being. Not only was Marx *not* a communitarian, but the very concept of "community" was always suspicious to him, as it appears more often as an abstract concept than a material actuality that we experience or study. Marx was inclined, from as early as *The German Ideology* (1845–1846), to point out the deceptions of the "illusory community."[2] Nonetheless, he thought it was both possible and necessary to speak of a damaged and disfigured human community without defending any ideal concept of community. The way to do this, for Marx, was to specify the *Gemeinwesen* that counteracts the separation and alienation within social life that leads to privatization, isolation, and human misery. Being alone is not the issue. A person can be healthy and happy all by herself so long as her isolation is temporary and not forced against inclinations for meaningful social relations. Having the latter, most people will healthfully seek out periods of solitude useful and necessary for attending to matters best addressed alone.

Marx singles out a defining feature of capitalist society, a belief in "the constant necessity for exchange, and in exchange value as the all-sided mediation."[3] On the premise of this basic belief in exchange and exchange value rests the idea that the pursuit of private self-interest will ultimately serve the interests of all. To get what I want, I must give you what you want, and this will lead to everyone getting what they want and need within a system of exchange relations. Thus, as in Adam Smith's often-abused idea of the "invisible hand," we arrive at the welfare of everyone through the adding up of private self-interest. According to Marx, however, the basic logic of exchange, which grounds the organization of capitalist society, should not be mistaken for a primordial human nature. Exchange is only the nature of this or that society, but a different society may have a different nature. Marx points out that "private interest is itself already a socially determined interest, which can be achieved only within

2. For Marx's discussion of the illusory community, see Marx, *The German Ideology*, 191–93.
3. Marx, *Grundrisse*, 156.

the conditions laid down by society … hence it is bound to the reproduction of these conditions and means."[4]

When we speak of human nature, what we generally mean is that whatever we see human beings doing most of the time in most of the places must be their human nature.[5] This is why people who focus on wars and their carnage tend to think that human nature is violent, since war is always somewhere happening or somewhere on the horizon; whereas other people who focus on the fact that most of humanity is not fighting, killing, or dying in wars—*even during wartime*—tend to think that human nature is peaceably inclined. If you look around for a lifetime and study human history, you will find that there are certain things humans seem to do time and again, and you may therefore conclude that their so doing is decided by an immutable human nature. But that is an analytical error. Whatever human beings are doing at *any given time* must be within their nature to do, or else they would not be doing it. But humans are also capable of doing other things than the things we observe them doing at any given time, which suggests that human nature also includes other and possible behaviors that are not characteristic. Human nature is not immutable: whenever humans start doing something *new*, we have to change our understanding of their nature. For example, it is not in the nature of human beings to fly, until we find ways to do it. We must therefore conclude that the only thing human nature is truly incapable of doing is that which human beings cannot—under any circumstances—do.

Arguments about politics from human nature are almost always flawed by their selective isolation of some one part of human behavior that is chosen to show whatever one wants to show about human nature. To expound on the example above: My students often declare that because humans are always somewhere at war, then it must be human nature to fight wars. When I point out to them that in every war there are always fewer people fighting the war than not, this challenges not only their ideas about human nature but also their ideas about possibility. States usually fight wars with the often-involuntary help of a small subset of their own populations, and we should never mistake states for the whole of humanity. Likewise, living in a capitalist world, human nature appears to be capitalist. So we have to imagine that if we lived in a

---

4. Ibid.

5. Here, I say "generally" (not always) because other dimensions of human nature have been studied and demonstrated by cognitive science, neuropsychology, and linguistics, largely at the level of proclivities that appear as distinguishing features of the human being.

noncapitalist world, human nature would appear differently. Capitalist societies necessitate and acculturate certain ways of being-in-the-world, but other ways of being could be necessitated and acculturated in a society that is not ruled by exchange relations.

According to Marx, a society that is oriented around private self-interest generates an orientation of general indifference to others. We tend to look on other people—at least insofar as they are not our children, parents, or siblings—as factors more or less helpful or harmful to our private interests. This calculated indifference shapes our sociality and reduces the social bond to a peculiar kind of instrumentality. This is the necessary trajectory of subjecting human life to capitalist exchange relations. The social bond is mainly held together by money relations. Marx puts it as follows: "The individual carries his social power, as well as his bond with society, in his pocket."[6] Capital makes money into a social power, and our relationships with others are mediated by money. Capital does not foreclose the possibility of different and nonmonetary human relationality, which is why we can still speak of real experiences of friendship and camaraderie. We are not talking about a totality, but rather, a tendency. Love and friendship still happen in this world, and we could say that they actively resist capitalist totality; inasmuch as they exist, we can touch other powers than the relative power of the money in our pockets.

In the chapter on money in *Grundrisse*, Marx sharply diagnosed problems in the social bond between individuals as stemming from capital, noting:

> [I]t is clear to the economists that the existence of money presupposes the objectification [*Versachlichung*] of the social bond; in so far, that is, as money appears in the form of *collateral* which one individual must leave with another in order to obtain a commodity from him. Here the economists themselves say that people place in a thing (money) the faith which they do not place in each other. But why do they have faith in a thing? Obviously only because that thing is an *objectified relation* between persons; because it is objectified exchange value, and exchange value is nothing more than a mutual relation between people's productive activities.[7]

In my view, there is no better summation of the basic problem of capitalist

6. Marx, *Grundrisse*, 157.
7. Ibid., 160.

exchange relations than Marx's explanation here. Capitalist economists are aware of the power of money as a social bond, and this is crucial to capitalist economics because it entrenches human society in a web of dependency on capital. Marx is talking about the displacement of faith in the human person by faith in money. While we may not take someone's word for it when they promise to return a borrowed car, we *will* "take their word for it" if they leave a deposit or some other collateral. In this way, the person's word is *valued* less than his or her money. There is a debasement in this valuation—namely, a devaluation of faith in other people. Why does the deposit of money make our faith stronger? Why does faith in others require the deposit? We could perhaps answer that people are prone to lying, deception, and self-interest. If they know they can borrow the car and simply drive off with it, then they would be likely to take it and lose nothing. In contrast, if they promise to return the car and can reclaim a sizable deposit upon the car's receipt, then the cost of driving off with the car could be too high. This is called "a security." That means that faith in the other without a deposit is an "insecurity." Thus, faith in money both leads to and paradoxically ameliorates social insecurity.

All of this is only sensible because it follows the foundational belief system of existing society: *faith in money*. And yet, if I lend a book to a trusted friend, I will not ask for a deposit. If I lend my car to a family member, I do not ask for a contract. The reasons for this are too obvious to state. But this demarcates a limit of capital's totalitarian tendencies. Capital organizes society and our social life at a very foundational level, having established the rules according to which faith in a friend or a loved one becomes exceptional. We would not lend our cars or books to just anyone unless we did not care to see them again. Here we see that the rule is that of capital, but we also see that friendship and love are exceptions to the rules of capital.

Marx further explains the basic idea as follows: "*Comparison* in place of real community and generality."[8] We each ask the other, what do you have, and how does it compare to what I can give you in exchange for it? Whether we are talking about labor, commodities, services, or favors, a quantification of comparative exchange values takes the place of other valuations. Personal relationships that are not governed by exchange values and money are minimal, mostly relegated to your closest circle of family and friends. However, what is true about those few people in whom you have faith is also potentially true about others considered too

---

8. Ibid., 161.

strange to trust without a collateral security or deposit. Each of the others in whom you do not place your faith are at the same time familiar to other people who *do* trust them without demanding a deposit. Moreover, many of your trusted friends were strangers at some point. Therefore, we cannot conclude that faith in other people is against human nature. It is not against human nature, but rather against the nature of a society ruled by exchange relations. Marx explains this by speaking about the value of the human person and the valuation of money as the *objectified relation*. The deposit of money is a demonstration of the other's goodwill, as if capital were indicative of goodwill. It is no accident or surprise that the impoverished and homeless are often viewed with the greatest suspicion. Marx helps us to understand that the impoverished and homeless are not the original cause of the suspicion against them; rather, this suspicion (or lack of faith) derives from the basic structure of a society that distrusts the absence of money.

Marx focuses on how social relations are developed in a system of exchange, extending the destructive force of capital into the more familiar sphere of personal relations. He claims: "In the money relation, in the developed system of exchange ... the ties of personal dependence, of distinctions of blood, education, etc. are in fact exploded, ripped up (at least, personal ties all appear as *personal* relations); and individuals *seem* independent (this is an independence which is at bottom merely an illusion, and it is more correctly called indifference)."[9] It would thus be a mistake to treat all family relationships and friendships as a refuge from capital. The fact is that many marriages, families, and friendships are undone by financial insecurity. Humans do and must continue to interact and to form associations. But Marx means to warn us about how many of our apparently warmer personal relations may also be illusory.

Consider the connections of employees working together in an office or two individuals working together on a project. We may even include sustained interaction in cyberspace, for example a friendship or membership sustained by a social networking application or a long-term email correspondence. In these cases, one often comes to know the other and to develop rapport through daily interactions. Within the daily interactions—perhaps regular lunch or coffee meetings—one learns something about the other's private life. They talk about their unhappiness, share their victories, their good news and bad. From all appearances, this looks like friendship. If we were to invoke the problematic notion of authenticity, we

9. Ibid., 163.

might specify sincere interest, sincere concern, honest and mutual affection. But how do we distinguish between what Marx calls "personal ties" and "*personal* relations"? This is the key: What happens when one or the other leaves the job, breaks from the project, or ceases to stay in the social network or keep up the correspondence? We have all had the experience of losing the basis of a former relationality. Now you are disconnected. A personal tie is not a connection regularized by a project or external obligation. If you have a personal tie, the connection to the other remains even when you are no longer working with them on a project, seeing them on a daily basis, or engaging in some normalized correspondence. But how many of our "ties" prove to be *merely* "relations"?

Marx observes that capitalist exchange relations promote a form of relationality that functions like a stand-in for the personal ties that it has ripped up and exploded. I think he is all the more right nearly two hundred years on, when we simply expect the departed employee to fall out of touch because, after all, they will have a new life and new projects. What may have seemed like a tie was in the end just a project-relationality. When we lose our circumstantial reason for daily interaction, the connection is broken. This is simply to say that human relationality is a circumstantial contingency. Perhaps this has always been true. This is not some unique property of capitalist society. But we nonetheless long for transcircumstantial connections, connections that can survive leaving the workplace. While the phenomenon is easily explicable, I have been sad and surprised to learn that I could so easily fall entirely out of touch with colleagues I considered real friends as soon as they left the university to live and work elsewhere. One has to wonder about a friendship that cannot bear such movement. Marx wants us to see this otherwise invisible degradation of human relationality in the system of exchange. Personal ties that may have seemed deep enough to hold people together are often ripped up and exploded by a simple movement of the friend's body from one building to another.

Marx does not neglect the other illusion—that of individual independence—which he claims is more accurately called indifference. The indifference that subordinates human connection to projects and work is often lauded as independence. The friend or dear colleague leaves the office or the project, and you just keep on going. Perhaps you get a promotion. Maybe it happens that you can maintain and survive the semiregular dissolution of human connections, and more than surviving, you even find yourself thriving. In a capitalist system of exchange, this appears as independence. But such independence is an illusion. The human being does not exist, and cannot exist for long, alone. We are only alive to read and think together because others than ourselves took care of us until we were able to "take care of ourselves." No one is "independent" for very long until becoming an adult, but, even then, the system of exchange is a system of dependence and interdependence. Even if you distinguish yourself, it is a distinction made visible by the others around you. Marx points out that we too often mistake our indifference toward other human beings as independence. He is right that caring too much about others (the opposite of indifference) is often not advisable in a capitalist system of exchange, which is competitive: you cannot simply ignore your competition. Indifference does not mean that you ignore other people. Indifference is the absence of real care for the other person.

This privatization of care is found also in the productive apparatus in which a whole association of people works to make a product that belongs to *none of them*. The basic premise of John Locke's labor concept of property from his *Two Treatises of Government* is smashed to pieces by capital.[10] Working to make the thing does not make the thing into your property, not even in part. Labor does not establish ownership. Your labor, in the system of exchange, belongs to the one who purchases it with a wage, and whatever comes from that labor belongs to that employer. The employer exists in a competitive framework of his or her own, and while he or she pays mind to the worker, the employer is indifferent to the worker in the sense discussed above. Marx explains how, even though communality is the prerequisite for any kind of production, the products of labor are distinctly noncommunal.[11] It is no wonder that, according to Marx, capitalist "independence" is more connected to alienation than to freedom. Marx shows us how readily we make such mistakes, as capital would have us declare alienation as liberation.

What is the role of money in a system of exchange? Often, when my students read Marx, they wonder about the relationship between capital and money and whether or not Marx means to abolish money in all its forms. Marx defines money as "an individuated, tangible object."[12] He claims that money has had a servile role, as simply a marker for circulation and exchange, but that it quickly became "lord and god of the world of commodities."[13] This is to say that money was invented to serve

---

10. See "Chapter V: Of Property" in John Locke, *Two Treatises of Government*, ed. Peter Laslett (Cambridge: Cambridge University Press, 1988).

11. Marx, *Grundrisse*, 171–72.

12. Ibid., 221.

13. Ibid.

exchange, but it eventually came to rule the world. Marx decisively states that money is "not only *an* object, but is *the* object of greed."[14] He claims that greed in the capitalist world tends to fixate on commodities, and even on commodified human beings (as in the context of slavery and certain permutations of sexual objectification). But because all things are coveted and acquired *through money*, money becomes the object of greed par excellence. Marx observes that this "mania for possessions," as he calls it, is possible without money, but money becomes the possession that rules all possessions.[15] Since money can always be utilized to possess new possessions, money becomes the object of the mania. This mania, according to Marx, is directly and ruthlessly destructive to human community everywhere: "Monetary greed, or mania for wealth, necessarily brings with it the decline and fall of the ancient communities [*Gemeinwesen*]. Hence it is the antithesis to them. It is itself the community [*Gemeinwesen*], and can tolerate none other standing above it. But this presupposes the full development of exchange values, hence a corresponding organization of society.... A particular individual may even today come into money by chance, and the possession of this money can undermine him just as it undermined the communities of antiquity."[16]

When a community becomes maniacally fixated on money, it becomes sick, as Plato said in *The Republic* long before Marx. A community can be destroyed by monetary greed, just as an individual person can be. When community becomes an instrument of monetary greed, it cannot abide the social purposes of a healthy human community. What does Marx mean by the decline, fall, and undermining of the community or individual? He means that the desire for money is *not* bound by any particular desire for one commodity or another. One can be desirous of more money even without a desire for a thing, and since a system of exchange makes such a desire perfectly rational, the desire for money (monetary greed) becomes the rationality of the community. Marx claims that money overtakes the community "since it is the general substance of survival for all, and at the same time the social product of all."[17] This is what Marx means when he writes that money, in its development from the eighteenth to the nineteenth century, "smashes community."[18] There is the *Gemeinwesen* for human well-being, for the development of talents and possibilities, but

---

14. Ibid., 222.
15. Ibid.
16. Ibid., 223.
17. Ibid., 226.
18. Ibid.

then there is the *Gemeinwesen* of money, in which the whole association is governed by capital. The latter destroys the former in a dialectical and irreducibly antagonistic confrontation.

The particular form of life and being that a human person takes *within a particular society* is sociologically (and this includes politically and economically) produced and is not the form necessitated by an immutable nature. This basic insight of Marx has for a long time been fundamental to sociology. The basic principle is that the person is an expression of a complex system of interrelations. Outside of any social setting, a person would be a human being alone with her nature, yet within a social setting—as everyone is—she is *not* simply a human nature. Marx puts it this way: "To be a slave, to be a citizen, are social characteristics, relations between human beings A and B. Human being A, as such, is not a slave. He is a slave in and through society."[19] Slavery is an economic, political, and social relation, and not a human nature. But insisting that slavery was natural was for a long time its central defense. Yet slaves can become not-slaves, and free people can be enslaved. Slavery is something that is done, and it can be undone without undoing the humanity that is only organized into one specific relation or another. That is, the undoing (or abolishing) of slavery calls for a different relationality and not for a different human nature. It is the specific relationality that matters to both the slave and the master. All of this is to say that the kind of *Gemeinwesen* we make matters. The capitalist *Gemeinwesen* of exchange value necessarily creates forms of relationality that first and foremost serve money and capital, which is precisely why it needs to be abolished.

Marx specifies that "as a slave, the worker has *exchange value*, a *value*; as a free wage-worker he has *no value*; it is rather his power of disposing of his labour, effected by exchange with him, which has value. It is not he who stands towards the capitalist as exchange value, but the capitalist towards him. His *valuelessness* and *devaluation* is the presupposition of capital and the precondition of *free* labour in general."[20] The slave's entire being is a pure commodity, whereas most of the being of the wage-worker is irrelevant since the only thing of value is his labor. One way we can know that this valuation and commodification are capitalist is that neither slaves nor wage-workers are valued according to their own point of view, according to their own sense of what they—or their labor—are worth. Slaves and wage-workers may demand whatever they like. Today, one

---

19. Ibid., 265.
20. Ibid., 288–89.

may post any old collector's item for any price on eBay. But the question of the value (or devaluation) of the thing is not determined by that demand. The capitalist only assesses the value of the thing from the perspective of capital. That is, the value of the slave or the worker's labor or the collector's item is not determined by the slave or the worker or the collector, but by how much someone else is willing and able to pay. The slave and the worker are not free to establish their own value in a capitalist society; if that were the case, they would never have existed as such. A similar and very important point can be made about democracy today. Most of the people (the *demos*) of the world are poor, a fact that undermines any serious claims about growing global democracy. If there were growing global democracy, would the world's *demos* demand their own impoverishment? We can learn a lot about any society by asking ourselves whose interests are best served by the existing state of affairs.

Marx observes a further degradation of the human person and community by capital. Each capitalist looks at his own workers only as workers, but views the rest of the working class "as *consumer* and *participant in exchange*, as money-spender, and not as worker."[21] This is an important feature of the reduction of the human being to an instrument of capital. The reductionist perspective of capital that establishes the value (in a devaluation) of workers exceeds at the same time the narrow boundaries of each capitalist's business and makes the capitalist look upon other workers in a differently devalued way, only inasmuch as they may buy his products or participate in profitable exchange by other means. This is why the establishment of value according to capitalist exchange relations ends up erecting a *Gemeinwesen* of association that is ruthless, reductionist, calculating, competitive, cruel, and exploitative.

One may wonder how we can think about love in such a reality as that described and analyzed by Marx. But the importance of love is bolstered in such a reality because love is a tendency contrary to that of the system of exchange. Love, as we shall see throughout this study, can only be understood as antithetical to the calculating reductions of money mania. Not only are there other ways of valuing one another and of valuing ourselves, not only have there been other modes of relationality, but direct experiences with the antithetical power of love remain possible and actual.

While the humanist dimensions of Marx's work could be said to have been obscured in (or dismissed from) his writings from the 1850s, 1860s, and 1870s (at least more than they were in those from the 1840s),

---

21. Ibid., 420.

Grundrisse can only be understood as a sustained inquiry into the ways that capital and money disfigure and destroy healthy human community. Marx's overarching concern in *Grundrisse* is to understand the necessary devaluation, dehumanization, and alienation of the human being in capitalist society. The humanism of *Grundrisse* is scarcely obscure, and any reading that misses the central importance of this is a misreading. Those who categorically reject the basic premises of Marxist-humanism do not do so only by selectively reading the *Economic and Philosophic Manuscripts of 1844* but also by failing to read *Grundrisse* well or even at all.

Marx's analysis is not only descriptive and theoretical but also based on practical activity. Indeed, the activity—the collective action—of the healthy *Gemeinwesen* is central to Marx's concept of communism: "The *commune* thus appears as a *coming-together* [*Vereinigung*], not as a *being-together* [*Verein*]; as a unification made up of independent subjects, landed proprietors, and not as a unity. The commune therefore does not in fact exist as a *state* or a *political body*, as in classical antiquity, because it does not exist as a *city*."[22] In this passage, Marx is not talking about the commune of communism that emerges in opposition to the capitalist reality. Instead, he is talking about an illusory commune. He is isolating the sense of the commons or commonwealth, for example, of a small neighborhood, a group of employers, a group of workers, or some other group of groups. Such a "commune" is not a *being-together* because its members may be practically cut off and apart from each other. Marx specifies a *coming-together* instead of a *being-together* in order to capture the difference between willful *acts* of human association and the creation of a new form of being-in-the-world. The *coming-together* creates an apparent commune, but it is an association that can be destroyed from within by the *coming-apart* of its competitive and highly individualistic being. Marx distinguishes the commune, the heart of the communist idea, from the *state*, *political body*, or *city*. The *state*, *political body*, or *city* appears as a unification, but its real being is one of class division, internal hostility, racial hatred, and so on. Such a *coming-together* is not a *being-together*. The commune of Marx's idea would have to be more than a cardholder membership (such as legal citizenship or nationality). It would have to be a new kind of *coming-together* of some part of humanity for itself, establishing a *being-together* for the health of its heterogeneous membership as a whole.

For Marx, the commune is a natural outgrowth of our social instincts,

---

22. Ibid., 483.

of the sense of ourselves as a *species-being*, as part of a larger organism. Communism is only made to appear impractical from the vantage point of the historical movements that destroyed it. In fact, Marx claims that "human beings become individuals only through the process of history.... Exchange itself is a chief means of this individuation [*Vereinzelung*].... Soon the matter [has] turned in such a way that as an individual he relates himself only to himself."[23] Processes of individuation that remove us from the *being-together* of the commune motivate a *coming-together* of noncommunist associations, such as the *coming-together* of corporations or cities. As Marx says here unequivocally, exchange is the main mechanism of capitalist individuation. Embedded within a world of exchange relations, each individual trades what he has for what he wants, without any regard for the other extending beyond that narrow calculation. Although some will continue to resist that narrowing, a long history of exchange relations has militated against such resistance, and Marx concludes that the individual has overwhelmingly come to value one relation above all, his relation to himself. As Marx puts it, in "bourgeois society ... the thing which *stands opposite* him has now become the *true community* [*Gemeinwesen*], which he tries to make a meal of, and which makes a meal of him."[24]

This last line reveals the remarkable depth of Marx's analysis. That we become alienated from the human community is among Marx's earliest important insights, which he had already written about with impressive profundity by the age of twenty-six. We see others as a means to our own edification and private gain, and we try to find ways to situate ourselves— in the office, the department, the congregation, the neighborhood, the conference—by which we can be the gainers. We try to place ourselves into a relationship with the community in such a way that the community becomes a means of satisfying our own private interest. But all the while, we are being killed by that effort. Most people live in poverty and quite reasonably worry about their present and future security. Moreover, loneliness is not an abstract private condition but a growing global epidemic that creates *real* sadness, misery, and death (the psychosocial toll of loneliness has been well researched empirically, and the subject will be taken up in a sustained way in chapters 4 and 6). Isolation is a real problem, and it is harder to solve real problems alone. We think we are looking out for ourselves by way of an individuation from community, but we do not properly appreciate the catastrophes of an individuated form of life.

---

23. Ibid., 496.
24. Ibid.

Hannah Arendt ends *The Origins of Totalitarianism* with a serious reflection on isolation and terror. Arendt distinguished solitude from loneliness in the following way: "In solitude, in other words, I am 'by myself,'
together with my self, and therefore two-in-one, whereas in loneliness I
am actually one, deserted by all others."[25] Arendt understands isolation
as a particular form of loneliness, but these are to be distinguished from
solitude. Solitude is something we seek out, as when we create the space
and time necessary to think and be by ourselves, and solitude can be opted in and out of voluntarily. In contrast, loneliness and isolation are the
outcomes of desertion. We have been deserted, and in thinking only about
care of ourselves, we have deserted others as well. Arendt is not talking
about being deserted for a weekend, but rather about desertion as a general condition. And here is the problem from her point of view: "What
prepares men for totalitarian domination in the non-totalitarian world is
the fact that loneliness, once a borderline experience usually suffered in
certain marginal social conditions like old age, has become an everyday
experience of the evergrowing masses of our century."[26] Politics preys on
isolation and fear, and terror comes from the acceleration and exacerba-
tion of fear. It is easy to be afraid alone. It is easier to be *unafraid* with
others. When one is all alone and afraid, one turns on the lights or calls
for a friend; when alone and afraid, the young child climbs into her mother's bed and arms. Isolation is a social problem, and Arendt saw it as integral to twentieth-century totalitarianism. Marx understood isolation in
a different context in the nineteenth century, that of bourgeois society.
In our present twenty-first century, we are seeing some of isolation's new
mutations and maladies in things like *hikikomori* and *karoshi* and the violent outbursts of "lone gunmen," among other things.

Hikikomori refers to the phenomenon of a growing subset of the Japanese population who remove themselves from school and work, shut
themselves up into little self-made worlds within rooms of their homes,
and reduce their interactions with people to mainly computerized contact. *Karoshi*, also a Japanese term, refers to death by overworking. The
term is invoked to describe a general increase of work-related sudden
deaths, often caused by heart attacks, strokes, stress, suicides, and mal-
nutrition. Both of these phenomena are widespread not only in Japan but
also throughout other regions of Asia and have various permutations all
around the world. Wherever highly technological intensely competitive

---

25. Hannah Arendt, *The Origins of Totalitarianism* (New York: Harcourt Brace Jo-
vanovich, 1968), 476.
26. Ibid., 478.

capitalist societies impose an accelerating pace of life and work on an increasingly anxious and insecure people with uncertain futures, isolation and death may appear as the only ways out. *Hikikomori* and *karoshi* may be recent afflictions of alienation, but inasmuch as they center on the existential tolls of work, they have their roots in earlier political economy.

Marx was among the first and remains among the very best to make a close and critical analysis of widespread human alienation as a structural problem rooted in the exchange relations of political economy. *Grundrisse* contains a thoroughgoing analysis of the anticommunist, commune-dissolving tendencies of capitalist exchange relations: "Exchange begins not between the individuals within a community, but rather at the point where the communities end—at their boundary, at the point of contact between different communities. . . . The system of production founded on private exchange is, to begin with, the historic dissolution of this naturally arisen communism."[27] This text appears just before the text of *Grundrisse* breaks off and ends in an uncompleted sentence. The first part of the first sentence establishes that exchange is foreign to the community. Exchange does not begin within the community, but at the point where the community ends. For Marx, it was not natural within the human community to give someone some water to drink or food to eat only in exchange for some other thing. Within the community, one individual asks another if he or she knows how to get to the center of town, and the other one answers if she can. She does not hold the answer hostage in exchange for something else. When one is dying of thirst, the other does not withhold water for a "good deal." Where such practices did emerge was at the boundary of the community. Within my own family, and within many other families and friendships, we know that exchange is alien. It would be cruel to hold my young son's dinner hostage in exchange for work. I would rather not introduce such exchange relations to my family and parenting. Indeed, there is nothing for which I would hold water or food hostage from my sons. This is not an extraordinary moral sensibility. It is just the common sense of a communist sensibility that naturally arises in a loving family.

When Marx says that the system of private exchange opposes "naturally arisen communism," we can finally grasp his meaning in full.[28] In any decent family, you will find the basic caretaking of the very young and most vulnerable members. This communism is a natural necessity, without

---

27. Marx, *Grundrisse*, 882.
28. Ibid.

which no baby could survive. We do not give our babies what they need only in exchange for something they can give to us because the logic of exchange is impractical and inappropriate there; it is even unnatural. But not only there. The same basic sensibility governs the healthy relationships of adults and friends. When two adult lovers start to measure their contributions in a competitive accounting of who does what for what reward, resentment is the inevitable outcome. You may worry about how to guard against a disparity of contributions. Better than a tally of exchanges would be a natural communism that motivates each to do what they can and must do to keep the little commune of the family healthy and well. Of course, that would not always happen. But it also *does* happen already, even in a world ruled by exchange relations.

Finally, it is worth pointing out that accepting capitalist exchange relations as the basic mechanism through which to address unfairness would not guard us against a disparity of contributions. We live in capitalist societies that have not solved the fundamental problems that people worry about when thinking about communism. "What about crime?" "What about inequality?" "What about incentive?" "What about fairness?" "What about individuality?" All questions that can and must be asked about the present world order! And a world governed by the logic of capital, by a life of exchange relations, has created problems much greater than the ones that exchange originally sought to address at the boundaries of community. The destruction and replacement of our healthiest forms of relationality with a system of exchange relations has been fatally damaging to human life and to the planet's ecology, and that system of exchange must be resisted and ultimately abolished, if not by some form of communism, then by love—or by the communism of love. What is love without communism?

3.2 Jenny, Rosa, and the Significance of Revolutionary Affection

Jenny Marx

Gender is an artifact inasmuch as it is made. And today gender is in many ways undergoing processes of being unmade, deconstructed, or radically reconstructed. We can and do accept this premise, yet at the same time we must also recognize important historical differences between revolutionary men and revolutionary women. The transposition of patriarchy and sexism from dominant culture into early revolutionary cultures was automatic because the critique of patriarchy and sexism had yet to be developed—much less made hegemonic—in radical milieus. The revolutionary movements of anarchists and communists have long challenged and rethought gender, and specifically the political agency of women; there is ample evidence to support the claim.[29] Nonetheless, we also know that the major syllabi on world revolutionary figures, much like the major syllabi in the history of philosophy, have been dominated by men, and mainly Western European men. This is not simply a problem to blame on the composers of syllabi: women have in fact been locked out of meetings, overburdened with care-work, blockaded from education and politics, even rampantly throughout radical associations. But revolutionary women have gotten their voices into the conversations and onto the stage, and when they got their bodies and brains onto editorial boards and political struggles, they never merely echoed the activities of their male comrades. Revolutionary women did not and do not duplicate the focus and feeling of revolutionary men; rather, they expand and challenge it in important ways, many of which bear directly on the subjects of our study.

Within Marxist circles, there has been an effort to properly appreciate how much Frederick Engels was responsible for Marx's body of work. For example, in a conversation between Mary Gabriel and Bertell Ollman on C-SPAN's *After Words* on October 6, 2011, the two highlighted the oft-neglected importance of Engels. Ollman appreciates that in Gabriel's book, *Love and Capital: Karl and Jenny Marx and the Birth of a Revolution*, "you make clear that it's really Engels who brought Marx to a good deal of what he came to present as his economic theories of capitalism."[30] This is of course true and has by now been rather well documented. But Gabriel also discusses in the same conversation with Ollman that Jenny Marx was Marx's "intellectual equal."[31]

Gabriel's remarkable book offers a rare and sustained focus on Jenny Marx and the immediate Marx family, with special attention to the relationship between Jenny and Karl and their harrowing lives. *Love and Capital* is not simply a biography of Karl Marx but an important installment of the intellectual and political history of the Marxes. Jenny Marx is portrayed as a loving and devoted partner and mother, and as a revolutionary and thinker in her own right. But, even here, Jenny is depicted as much

---

29. Most any of Sheila Rowbotham's books substantiate this claim. See, especially, her classic study, *Women, Resistance and Revolution: A History of Women and Revolution in the Modern World* (London: Verso, 2014).

30. "*After Words* with Mary Gabriel," C-SPAN2, *BookTV*, October 6, 2011, https://www.c-span.org/video/?301873-1/after-words-mary-gabriel.

31. Ibid.

farther away from Karl than Engels is. Engels appears as a theoretical and economistic genius equal to Karl, as one who should receive as much credit as Marx, if not more in some cases, for the development of Marx's work. Jenny, in contrast, appears as an intellectually astute and politically revolutionary homemaker who created the supportive space within which Marx (and often Engels) could carry out their work. Here I want to challenge this general view of Jenny Marx, suggesting that her role in the development of Marxist philosophy was of even greater importance, and I will show this with the help of Gabriel's own study. The question is not whether Gabriel describes Jenny's life and activity accurately. The question is how we interpret and understand the significance of that life activity. I argue that Jenny was in fact much more substantively involved in the development of the revolutionary *writing* of communist philosophy than is typically appreciated, even among those who aim to appreciate her more fully. To sharpen the point: if Engels is raised to the status of an author, so too should Jenny. But who cares about authorship? What difference does it make? And why argue anything about this in a book about love?

The fact is that philosophy does not come only from the heads of philosophers but also from their experiences and their conditions of life. This even belongs to the fundamental premise of Marx's own materialism. No philosophy is written solely by those who hold the pens or type the words, but philosophy is written by the conditions and experiences of the life in which the thinking is articulated.[32] But I will not make "writing" into an easy metaphor in order to recognize the authorship of Jenny Marx. She herself wrote much and importantly about the world around her, and her point of view—her distinct rootedness in the world—was written and communicated in a well-documented and dialectical relationship with Marx from the time he was seventeen years old until his death. The communist philosophy of Marx, which would become known as Marxism, was in fact produced from a *love relation*, and not out of an *exchange relation*, meaning precisely—and in no way metaphorically—that the living love of the Marxes generated, to a large extent, the Marxist philosophies of communism and revolution. The ghost that haunts the works of Karl Marx is a ghostwriter named Jenny Marx. In short, Jenny and Karl developed *their* thinking through their living relationality, and they did so from the beginning to the bitter end. This particular claim is not Gabriel's, yet it is supported in her work.

---

32. I have argued this point more fully in *Specters of Revolt* (London: Repeater, 2016).

Upon meeting Jenny, Marx wrote a letter to his father stating that "a new world has come into existence for me, that of love."[33] Gabriel notes that this new love immediately drove Marx to writing as his "first inclina-tion."[34] This early writing was poetry: Marx's very first books were actually books of poetry titled *The Book of Love* (he wrote two volumes under that title), which he delivered to Jenny on Christmas in 1836, the same year that Jenny agreed to marry him. Marx the revolutionary thinker and radical scholar began, then, with voluminous writings on love. Although his subjects of study would soon change, the inclination to write from love remained a constant for Marx.

Jenny imagined herself in the role of helping Karl get his thoughts down onto paper and "carefully preserved for other people," but she also had her own appetite for reading serious scholarly books, as she put it, "no fairy-tales and no poetry, I can't bear it."[35] This is to say that Jenny wanted to participate in Karl's thinking and writing, although she viewed herself in a mainly supportive role (in much the same way as Gabriel characterizes her). Like so many radical women then and now, Jenny always had to be much more than an intellectual buried in books in a library. What is the status of an accomplice who stares down every struggle at your side? On their honeymoon, Karl brought along Hegel, Rousseau, Machiavelli, and Chateaubriand. Marx would only emerge as a major figure of history within the context of this marriage, and only with Jenny's active involvement. Gabriel attests that "their marriage would be a mutual cultivation of flame. Her love enabled him."[36] I do not want to romanticize or valorize marriage as an institution, neither this particular marriage nor any other one. Rather, I aim to extract a substantive sense of the ways that a love relation participates in and generates new thinking. I am here interested in where the text comes from, what is before a text, what enables its existence as such, and not merely what comprises it.

The problem is that when we sit down to read and write about someone else's thinking, we begin with a completed or given text. What enables it is often invisible. When we find a text that says something profound or new, we wonder where it came from. We can ask a series of questions: How did you come to think that way? What led you to those conclusions? When did you have that insight or epiphany? The real answers to all such

---

33. Mary Gabriel, *Love and Capital: Karl and Jenny Marx and the Birth of a Revolution* (New York: Back Bay Books, 2011), 25.

34. Ibid.

35. Ibid., 33.

36. Ibid., 46.

questions are given in the form of stories: "Well, let's see ... When I was at X, I was wondering about Y. Then, all around us, Z was happening. At the same time, I was reading R and wondering about how to consider the question of Q." The author may tell the story of the text, and only then do we understand that factors X, Y, Z, R, and Q, among other variables, participated in the thinking *of and within* the text itself. They are inextricable from its being.

From the beginning of their relationship, Marx "regarded Jenny as an intellectual equal, and that was no mere token sentiment: Marx was ruthless when it came to things of the mind, and he would not have relied on Jenny's judgment if he did not think she was in fact brilliant."[37] Jenny's judgment, thus, was inside Marx's writing. At the very least Jenny is variously before, behind, and within the texts of Karl Marx. The point here is not, as I have said, to credit Jenny for the writings of Marx and Engels but to understand the relationality of the Marx family as indispensable to the development of what is today called Marxism. And, crucial to our inquiry, the relationality of the Marx family was not that of exchange relations. While many features of their history could show this, just consider, for example, that Jenny did not marry Marx for money and that the two lived in various forms of dilapidation their entire lives together (and their life together was just about the length of their entire lives). The things they did for one another (*and not everything was kindness*) were done in accordance with logics other than exchange. It is true that they daily confronted the problem of poverty and tried to secure advances and payments for Marx's published writing. More often than not, however, Marx was not paid for this writing. Jenny never was. Indeed, neither the writing nor the relationship was governed by money. This perhaps seems not so remarkable. After all, many people past and present could say the same thing about their own familial relations. It is not, however, unremarkable, since family economics (that is, *oikonomia*) have also caused the dissolution of countless familial relations.

When Engels lived for a time with the Marxes, Jenny reported that their "little colony lived together harmoniously and sympathetically ... sharing their meager resources. The success of one, she said, was the success of all."[38] Recalling our discussion of *Grundrisse*, it is not hard to see the concept of the commune in this report. The *coming-together* of the miniature commune of the Marx family could not have rested on capitalist

---

37. Ibid., 53.
38. Ibid., 82.

exchange relations precisely because the latter were decisively damaging to the overall health of the family. Again, this experience of an alter-relational *coming-together* is probably not alien to most of us (at least I hope not). My sincere hope is that you have experienced some similar form of being-with-others, even if not with your biological family. Some people experience a nonmonetary form of human relationality more readily with friends, comrades, or even with colleagues who share common concerns. What is different in the Marx family is that when most people experience real friendship and love they are not busy making arguments about the capitalist disfiguration of the *Gemeinwesen*. Marx was nearly transfixed by that problem in his research, and he left us with a library devoted to considering it.

At times the closeness of the productive side of Marx's writing was literally and physically embodied through Jenny: "Their handwriting intertwined on the page as he scribbled his thoughts on paper and she followed in an elegant, feminine hand, patiently copying out and making legible her husband's blistering indictment of the bourgeoisie and his belief that revolution was right, inevitable, and imminent."[39] Gabriel's account ultimately makes it very difficult to see Engels's influence on the intellectual and material production of Marx's work as any more important than Jenny's.

But Jenny was not the secretary that Gabriel says she was during this period of intertwining handwriting in 1848. Jenny had every reason to reject Karl's commitments and thinking, for that commitment and thinking mired the whole family (including the children) in a life of total insecurity, political persecution, and financial catastrophe. If she—or *if they*—would have broken with the revolutionary work and taken a different path, there would have been more chance at a life of peace, stability, and at least some modicum of financial security. But reviewing all of Jenny's letters, her unfinished autobiography, and other accounts, Gabriel concludes that "Jenny *was* fully committed to Marx's work and truly did recognize and understand the needs of the rare genius she had chosen as a husband.... [S]he saw his life's work as her own."[40]

That last line could be read in several ways, and Gabriel's intention is to convey the unwavering commitment, loyalty, and love of Jenny to Karl. I'd like to juxtapose that reading, however, to a different reading that I propose here. I do not disagree with Gabriel's position; I only think that it

---

39. Ibid., 116–17.
40. Ibid., 190.

stops too short. At this juncture, it would appear that Jenny is more than a faithful and trusted accomplice: she is an indispensable aid to the fruition of Karl's genius. Gabriel has substantiated that point well, but I think that in both *literal* (that is, historical, experiential, and developmental) and *figurative* (that is, creating and guarding the space and time needed for Marx's theoretical and political work) terms, *Jenny precedes Marx and his work, creates the conditions for its existence, and shapes its form and content as a body of work.* This reading, unlike Gabriel's, places Jenny clearly beyond the limit of the secretary or faithful wife. This reading puts Jenny into a position more commonly defended for Engels. But Jenny's role is even deeper than that of Engels, who after all is still positioned in relation *to* Marx. Jenny's relation *with* Marx is largely (not entirely) responsible for Marx's work. That is to say, whereas Marx's work depends on Engels's work (and vice versa), *Marx's work is Jenny's work* (and vice versa) from its earliest conception.

I should stress again that we are not talking about the relative crediting of individuals, but about love relationality and what it does—*how it works*. This discourse in no way implies or attempts any erasure of Karl Marx. Rather, we may understand a deindividuating and deprivatizing concept of agency capable of explaining how a complex of human relations actively shapes the positionality and thinking of each person. In its least controversial formulation this initiative appears, at bottom, as a basic sociological insight.

The love relation had its flaws. Jenny wanted Karl's fidelity to monogamy, and that was betrayed in an affair between Marx and one of their most important adopted family members, Lenchen, a woman who lived with the Marxes for years as a kind of housekeeper for the family. Little is known about how much Jenny learned of this betrayal, but we do know that it would have been extremely painful for her. The marriage was not open or polygamous, nor was it replete with common betrayals; it was otherwise a union of remarkable intimacy, fidelity, and solidarity. And Jenny and Karl's love and solidarity were often tested, particularly surrounding the deaths of their children, to which they had become horrifically accustomed in the 1850s.

But it is important to appreciate the failures and imperfections in the little commune of the Marx family. It is important not only because the betrayal was real, but also because we cannot be seduced by any notion of some perfected love relation of romance and family. Any family that appears to us as perfect only appears so in a superficial way. If you look closely enough into any family or love relationship, you would likely find not only many problems but also secrets and failures. No one else could hurt Jenny as Karl could. Psychology has long conveyed that the traumas of family life are unlike any others in terms of influence and severity. But a perfect commune is also an ideological fiction of political theory, and neither Engels nor Marx thought that communist revolution would create an infallible utopia. It is perhaps a small consolation to say that failure is everywhere, both inside the family and beyond it in society. But it is a critical political insight. Often, the capitalist response to communists is to assert that this or that imaginable problem—some hypothetical crime, murder, incident of greed, catastrophe of laziness, or failure—will not be solved by communism, and thus they arrive at their predetermined conclusion that the communists have nothing to offer. What they forget is that they are asking about problems that already exist in the capitalist reality, problems also unsolved by the system they defend. The same problems of crime, murder, greed, laziness, and failure plague the capitalist world of the present; capitalism does not "solve" the problems its defenders pretend to worry about. If one has to wholly reject every position that cannot perfectly answer every imaginable problem, then one could take no position at all. Despite the infidelity and other failures, Jenny and Karl endured by way of a well-practiced but imperfect love.

The indispensable and enduring importance of Jenny and Karl's love to Marx's work is beautifully captured by Gabriel:

> To be able to work (which is to say, to be able to live), Marx needed the anchor that Jenny and the children provided. He ordered his thoughts only in the midst of their disorder. Throughout his life, theirs was the society he craved. This man, who from age seventeen committed himself to the work of humankind, apparently could not rise to the task in the absence of the women who made up his small household. He longed particularly for Jenny. She was not only his friend and lover, but had been his most trusted intellectual sounding board since their honeymoon thirteen years earlier. Neither his heart nor his head functioned without her.[41]

Every line of this passage demands attention. Marx's work was not done for money. His work did not have a high exchange value, and thus it was a work that never functioned as a sensible "job" in the world of capital. Despite this, his work was his life. This means that his work defined his

---

41. Ibid., 254–55.

life's purpose, justified his existence, and, perhaps most importantly, was his main durable commitment and connection to the world beyond his household. Marx's work could only be undertaken and developed within the very concrete context of his life with Jenny. Moreover, he found in the happiest moments of that little commune with Jenny the forms of relationality and qualities of life that he wanted to see extended everywhere, enlarged and enjoyed throughout the social body. That their familial society was the society that he craved means that he theorized a communization from the limited, known commune. As Gabriel documents here and throughout *Love and Capital*, Marx could only work well—could only live well—within the context of his home life. And it was, once again, not only Jenny's presence and effort in maintaining the household but also her intellect that made her such an integral part of his life's work and purpose.

I would like now to present the particular content of this extrapolation as the inevitable hypothesis: *If Marx only did that which had capitalist exchange value (that is, for money), he would have lived a very different life of lesser meaning and minimal historical significance.* Yet perhaps this is true of everyone in any society. One need not make one's work into one's life as Marx did, nor does one need to work and live within the context of a beloved family of husband, wife, and children. The specific details pertaining to Marx's life can be scrubbed from the speculation without negating it. If a woman works at the local animal shelter and regularly pays out of her pocket for expenses attending to fostering cats, the question of how much money she makes from this activity is inappropriate to the situation. The person volunteers her time and money for a reason other than profit, and even if it is a comparatively small thing like fostering cats, tending to a community garden, feeding and clothing the homeless, or helping friends build a website or edit a text, it may be enough—both qualitatively and quantitatively—to create meaning in a lifetime of sustained activity. This "work," if we would call it that, holds a value that we can speak of and measure. But it is not an exchange value, and the value of the thing (that is, the commitment or the activity) is in no way diminished by that fact. We know that Marx understood this well, and he learned it in his daily life.

Jenny died shortly before Karl, at the age of sixty-seven, and so she did not live to see Marx's work fully realized or taken up in the ways that they had both hoped to witness. Yet she remained committed to their shared vision on her deathbed. At her funeral, Engels eulogized that the "contribution made by this woman, with such a sharp and critical intelligence, with such political tact, a character of such energy and passion, with such dedication to her comrades in struggle—her contribution to the movement over almost forty years has not become public knowledge; it is not inscribed in the annals of the contemporary press."[42] While Engels sought to convey that she had not been appreciated appropriately, this appreciation has still not come to pass. In her own life, Jenny was too often seen as a being in the orbit of the great genius Marx, even by so many who knew and appreciated her. But I do not think she orbited him. With Jenny, we are not talking about an acknowledgment in a book, a dedication, or some other stated gratitude, all of which are inadequate to the task of truly appreciating her intellectual contributions to—and the causal forces of her love on—the form and content of Marxism. When we speak of Marx's work, we must think and speak not only of Karl. As for Karl, he did not attend Jenny's funeral; he was ill and weak and discouraged from leaving his home and venturing into the cold. But he was also in a new lifeless condition without his Jenny. Engels declared that Karl Marx had also died on the day of Jenny's death.[43]

Following this, it is not far-fetched to say that Jenny was perhaps the most unrecognized coauthor of Marx's work. But the same creative agency can be found in many if not all of the love relations of creative figures of history, both within and beyond the family unit, including of course within the relations of same-gender family units, of the unmarried, or of the imprisoned. The point is not to romanticize the particular example of the Marx family but to recognize the role that the love relation plays in the development of both thinking and being-in-the-world, and in the becoming of individual persons. However, we also must confront the problem of a long history of women like Jenny who have only been seen in "supporting roles" or not seen at all.

While I have not done the substantive work here of properly appreciating Jenny's role in the writing of Marx's philosophy, I do hope that I have made the case for such an appreciation. Within the context of this book, which is not dedicated to the study of Jenny Marx, I intend to establish that the relative obscurity of women in radical history is more often a kind of erasure. This is not only an erasure made by patriarchal and sexist exclusion, but also by the capitalist individualizing of thought as private property, which is called today "intellectual property." I do not think that Marx would have ultimately wanted his work to be his private property, despite bouts of vanity and protective ownership, as could be seen, for

---

42. Ibid., 490.
43. Ibid., 491.

example, in the brutally corrective form and content of *Critique of the Gotha Programme* (1875). Some of Marx's infamous rebuttals and righteous self-defenses were considered a necessary part of defending and insisting on a vision that Marx and Engels knew could be turned in unintended and dangerous directions if their positions were not clarified and defended.[44] Marx was suspicious of hijackers and manipulators who might instrumentalize and abuse his work. But it has to be said that the participation of revolutionary women was necessary in the development of revolutionary theory in primary ways, and Jenny Marx is only one of many such women. Other revolutionary women were integral to theorizing new forms of life in very different ways. But in Jenny's case, love appears as a substance of history directly and concretely related to the generation of the most important social and political theory of the nineteenth century.

Silvia Federici has shown how capitalism extracted more from women than it could ever possibly pay for. Capital has done this by refusing to appreciate the value of women's work, even though the history of capitalism has both depended on and expected a free supply of "women's work" in perpetuity.[45] Capitalist societies have only recognized the care-work, housework, and reproductive labor done throughout global human history by way of depending on them. But by denying all such forms of labor any exchange value, capital refuses to value (by its own mode of valuation) what human beings value the most. And capital is incapable of any such valuation. Consider the long history of women bearing and rearing children, and tending to the most vulnerable members of every society—the very young and the elderly—without any form of payment or capitalist valuation. That history reveals that affective care-work, taking care of those who need care the most, has remained a kind of *necessary communism* within capitalist societies, much as in the household of the Marx family. Here, we could speak of the communism of care, which I shall regard as a feature of the communism of love.

For these and other reasons, when thinking about love as a communist power, it is essential to consult communist women. To that end, I now consider Rosa Luxemburg's *feeling for suffering* and, finally, Alexandra Kollontai's notion of a *communist Eros*.

---

44. See Engels's letter to Weydemeyer of April 12, 1853, for evidence of Marx's and Engels's concern over such dangerous directions as cited in Gabriel, *Love and Capital*, 236.

45. See Silvia Federici, *Caliban and the Witch* (Brooklyn: Autonomedia, 2004); and Federici, *Revolution at Point Zero* (Oakland: PM Press, 2012).

Rosa Luxemburg

In a moving scene in the film by Margarethe von Trotta titled *Rosa Luxemburg*, where Barbara Sukowa (who more recently played the role of Hannah Arendt) portrays Luxemburg, Luxemburg reflects on how she has enough courage and strength to bear most anything, including prison and death, for herself, but not when she sees and feels the suffering of others. With footage of belabored and abused oxen pulling a wagon in the snow, Luxemburg recounts having "seen a terrible thing":

> A few days ago a wagon laden with sacks arrived. The load was so heavy the oxen could not pull it through the gate. The driver, a brutal fellow, began to beat them so hard that one of them bled. During the unloading, the animals stood there so silent and exhausted, and the one that bled had a look on his black muzzle like an unhappy child. I stood before him and he looked at me. The tears flowed down my cheeks as if they were his tears. One could not feel more pain for the dearest brother as I in my helplessness watched his silent suffering. Oh my poor ox. My poor dear brother. Both of us stand here so mute and are one in suffering, in powerlessness, and yearning.... Such is life and we must face it.[46]

Luxemburg's letters are full of similar expressions of acute feeling for the most vulnerable animals in our world, which therefore includes non-human animals such as cats and even dung beetles. Indeed, the scene above was based on an actual letter we will look at more closely below. Within the realm of humanity, Luxemburg thought much about women and children too, as she understood and appreciated their relative vulnerability in a world run by men (we should recall that in Zurich she was one of very few women with a doctorate in *Staatswissenschaft*).

So striking is Luxemburg's affection for oxen, beetles, and cats that one wonders whether her affection was an outgrowth of her communism or her communism an outgrowth of her affection. Of course, it is possible that neither is the outgrowth of the other, since as we know, such feeling for animals is not universal among communists, and most animal lovers are not revolutionaries. Scientism, and specifically the purported objectivity of the social sciences, is meant to guard against the biases of affection. For Marx, historical materialism could eventually purge its moral or emotional content: one could condemn the existing conditions of the world

---

46. *Rosa Luxemburg* (film), directed by Margarethe von Trotta, Germany, 1986.

perfectly well on a materialist account of human misery alone. Such a materialist basis gave stronger footing to Marx's thought, especially given the opposite tendencies of religious belief based in feeling and faith. The communists, as has been held since Marx himself, could and should avoid the trappings of utopian sentimentality. Yet Luxemburg refused to abandon affection, which often appears in her writing as a revolutionary affection. One of the most beautiful and recurring themes in Luxemburg's writings is her expression of love and solidarity for suffering nonhuman animals, as when she writes about the miseries of buffaloes, which she understood as victims of human warfare. This emphatic and empathetic feeling for other beings was inextricably linked to Luxemburg's revolutionary commitments.

Notice, for example, that Luxemburg speaks of the oxen as comrades, calling the bleeding one "dear brother." She interprets her own tears as an expression of the animal's pain, and she declares a unity between human and nonhuman suffering, powerlessness, and yearning. To Luxemburg, the oppressed share a lot in life with abused and beaten animals, and this likeness is more than a comparison, for it results from *relations of power* that organize the world. Many will not like thinking about human beings in community with bugs, cats, dogs, or cows because they will see such a unification as a degradation of their humanity. In the long history of Western philosophy, including in Marx (see the opening of *The German Ideology*), there is a generally reliable insistence on isolating what is unique about the human being at the level of *species-being* or production.[47] But seeing one's self in the oxen or cat is only considered degrading if we look on nonhuman animals from the perspective of a self-assured superiority. If we could appreciate their unique intelligences, and even their unique superiorities, then perhaps we would not view every likeness as a debasement. Furthermore, the reason we do not like to be "treated like animals" is because the human treatment of animals is notoriously exploitative and murderous.

This is not an argument for veganism or animal rights, although it certainly lends itself to those causes. But here, in the context of this book, my aim is to consider how a broadening sphere of affection, *broad enough to encompass deep feeling for others unlike us*, is a shared basic principle of both the communist idea and of love. In other words, a broadening sphere of affection is not the sole private property of liberal cosmopolitans and non-Marxian humanists. It is also deeply embedded in the internationalism of socialist philosophy, an internationalism that was fully understood

---

47. See, for example, Marx, *The German Ideology*, 164.

and defended by Luxemburg (something that could be seen especially in her antiwar politics).

But what of her feeling for the bleeding ox? Luxemburg identifies in the nonhuman animal certain key features: (a) personality, (b) preferences, and (c) capacity to suffer. In her letters, Luxemburg wrote often and warmly about her beloved cat, Mimi. No cat could be more fortunate than to live with this communist revolutionary. But we should also acknowledge that Luxemburg was perhaps equally fortunate to have had such a companion as Mimi. Many times, Luxemburg preferred Mimi to her comrades, sought refuge in Mimi's company, and credited her for the best attributes of her demeanor and thinking.

Regarding (a) *personality*, it is obvious to anyone who has spent time with a cat or a dog that individual animals of the same species do not have the same personalities. Of course, it is possible to catalog the general traits of breeds and species, yet despite generalities each individual develops, possesses, and expresses a personality. Personality is the substance of the person, necessary for personhood (here, I mean personhood conceptually and not necessarily legally). When we remember the deceased, be it a cat or a human, we recall the ways that the personality was in the world—the mannerisms, behaviors, movements, and traits that distinguished him or her from others. I can recall finding one of my beloved cats after he died under my bed. As I picked up his lifeless body, my first thought was, "This is not my cat. Where is my cat?" Some may prefer to speak of the soul as the substance that animates the body, as Franco Berardi in his *The Soul at Work*,[48] but it is also the active personality of the being that embodies and expresses the particular life form's being-in-the-world.

Regarding (b) *preferences*, nonhuman animals do not like everything equally, and some things they decisively dislike, whether getting shots, being petted, being held, or eating particular foods. They also prefer things, such as being scratched right behind the ear, hiding in one hole in the ground as opposed to another, and so on. And they have ways of *communicating* these preferences too. That nonhuman animals of the same species (much like humans) express a manifold of diverse preferences is noncontroversial. The ability to express real preferences is a necessary prerequisite for any expectation of appropriate regard and care. To do right by you—as my son, as my student, as my lover, as my cat—it will help to know what you like, what works best for you, and the communicability

---

48. Franco "Bifo" Berardi, *The Soul at Work: From Alienation to Autonomy* (Los Angeles: Semiotext(e), 2009)

of your preferences opens up a space in which I can develop my consideration of you and henceforth avoid being inconsiderate. We can be considerate of others radically unlike us, whether we are talking about the consideration of women by men, of transgender people, of gays and lesbians, of people with disabilities, of nonhuman animals by humans, and of all such considerations involving the preferences of individual persons. Consideration of personality and preferences tends toward a form of human relationality that is *better* than one ruled by exchange value.

Finally, regarding (c) the *capacity to suffer,* anyone who has seen slaughterhouse footage, witnessed a young child chasing after an animal against that animal's preferences, comforted a sick or wounded animal in pain, or weighed the pain of a pet against its continued existence knows without question that nonhuman animals can suffer. Human suffering need not be pitted against the suffering of nonhuman animals, as if to say that it is either their suffering or ours. We might consider how our feeling for the helpless and abused animal—wherever such feeling is present— should or could shape our feeling about abused humanity that is unlike us in different ways than the animal. Or, we might interrogate why different feelings attend to the miseries of different beings, even within the boundaries of our own species. And indeed, we may see the absence of feeling for nonhuman animals as an obstacle (if not a fixed limit) to the capacity of individual persons to feel love and solidarity for beings other than themselves.

What is certain is that Luxemburg saw all these features in the oxen, in her cat Mimi, and also in the impoverished workers of the world. Luxemburg was not an animal rights activist. She was a communist revolutionary with a generous sphere of affection capable of encompassing the pain and suffering of every being she encountered. But what is the importance of recognizing these affections to our study? The depth and breadth of feeling for other beings is a major factor in the healthy relationality of human beings. Deep and abiding affection for others is not only a defining feature of what we call love—whether familial, erotic, or friendly—but also a defining feature of communism in the sense of the *Gemeinwesen* we have discussed, not only with Marx but also with Weil and Levinas, as demonstrated in the first chapter.

Luxemburg often wrote about her cat Mimi as her most faithful comrade. She regularly signed her letters with kisses from her and from "M," her beloved Mimi. Luxemburg shared her life with Mimi from roughly 1904 until about 1917, for approximately fourteen years, until shortly before her death. It is even possible that Luxemburg lived with Mimi before

1904 or that Mimi outlived Luxemburg, for all we have to go by is when she started to mention the cat in her letters and when she stopped.

Luxemburg observed that, after returning home from her frequent long trips away from Mimi, the cat was visibly happy to have her and her doting attentions back.[49] Mimi would keep Luxemburg company on lonely days at home and would roll over "teasingly on the carpet, saying *prau* ['meow']."[50] As happens whenever one gets to know the personality of the other, Luxemburg developed the ability to "read" Mimi's behavior as asking to be tickled or fed, as being hungry or tired or grumpy or playful or affectionate. But Luxemburg also credited Mimi for reminding her of basic principles for clear thinking and commitment. She refers to

> the basic rule I've made for my life: To be kind and good is the main thing! Plainly and simply, to be good—that resolves and unites everything and is better than all cleverness and insistence on "being right." But who is here to remind me of that since Mimi is not here? At home so many times she knew how to lead me onto the right road with her long, silent look, so that I always had to smother her with kisses ... and say to her: You're right, being kind and good is the main thing. So if you sometimes notice from my talk or my silence that I am contrary or grim, just remind me of that truthful saying of Mimi's.[51]

Plainly, Luxemburg anthropomorphizes Mimi in this passage, since a cat does not have sayings made up of words in human languages. One gets the sense (here and elsewhere) that Luxemburg talked regularly to her cat as a way of thinking things through. Anthropomorphism involves attributing human traits, emotions, or intentions to nonhuman animals. As a tendency among humans it is widely documented in fables and children's tales that depict animals with human traits in most cultures back to antiquity. Science cautions us against wrongly imputing human emotions to animals, such as attributing to an animal that it must miss its mother or is watching you in moral judgment of your actions. At its worst, anthropomorphism is in fact a way of *only* valuing the animal insofar as it can be made to *seem like you*. Thus, it is not really the other being that we appreciate, but the ways in which we can project our own being onto it.

---

49. Rosa Luxemburg, *The Letters of Rosa Luxemburg*, ed. Georg Adler, Peter Hudis, and Annelies Laschitza, trans. George Shriver (London: Verso Books, 2013), 314.
50. Ibid., 320.
51. Ibid., 378.

Philosophically, however, there is a more hopeful side to the anthropomorphic tendency. Anthropomorphism also shows an ability to perceive a proximity between beings who do not even share a basic phenotypical structure. One could say that this proximity is more imaginary than actual in anthropomorphism, but I suggest that—*at the affective level of feeling for the other*—this proximity is not *merely* imaginary. Often, the problem of cruelty to others is a problem of insufficient imagination.[52] Human societies are to some extent governed by human imaginaries, and cruelty can be mitigated by an ability to imagine other people and our own proximity to them. Indeed, our actual relationships in the world, whether between two lovers or among foreigners at a border or between Luxemburg and Mimi, are *relationships constituted by a peculiar way of seeing the other*. My sister and I, to take a simple example, shared the same father yet hold him in our memories very differently, a product of variously generous imaginings, distinct experiences, and selective remembering. One could ask who is right and who is wrong, but doing so misses a deeper insight: each one of us is right inasmuch as our memory is based in a real relationality, an actual relationship with a father rooted in a real history comprised of experiences and events.

But let us not abandon the discourse on Mimi, which may still appear as an unusual digression. Luxemburg cared deeply and worried much about Mimi throughout her life. Luxemburg once wrote to Mathilde Jacob, her comrade and secretary, that she detected Jacob's growing indifference to the cat. Luxemburg appealed to Jacob on Mimi's behalf: "I feel hurt by that. Believe me, she surely feels it. She will become apathetic, sluggish, and inactive. Do be kind to her, as before!"[53] Luxemburg's deep, abiding, open, and unashamed love of Mimi is consistently expressed. Such an affection as this is not easy to find in the writings of revolutionary men, which for a long time faithfully reflected the masculinities expected of working-class and revolutionary men in the nineteenth and early twentieth centuries. Within that context, there is something distinctly "feminine" about a revolutionary expressing such feelings for a cat, which even today may be regarded as emasculating by those in the mainstream. I do not say that any of this is *essentially* or *biologically* true, only *sociologically* true within given historical and cultural contexts. For this reason, questions of affect, feeling, and love have either been neglected or marginal in male-dominated political philosophy. For the same reason, we still have

---

52. See Elaine Scarry, "The Difficulty of Imagining Other People," in Martha C. Nussbaum's *For Love of Country?*, ed. Joshua Cohen (Boston: Beacon, 2002), 98–110.

53. Luxemburg, *Letters of Rosa Luxemburg*, 434.

much to retrieve from the distinctive contributions of women who were not held hostage to the straitjacket masculinity embedded in politics and its study in the social sciences. The contributions of Jenny Marx and Rosa Luxemburg were also very different from each other. Women should not be counted on for the same thing, but for different things.

Consider the worldview of a woman who conveys the following perspective: "I know that for every person, for every creature, one's own life is the only single possession one really has, and with every little fly that one carelessly swats and crushes, the entire world comes to an end, in the refracting eye of the little fly it is the same as if the end of the world had destroyed all life."[54] Luxemburg's anthropomorphism did not diminish but rather enlarged her perspective. She did not insist on seeing the fly as herself, but on trying to see the world from the fly's point of view. In this, she may or may not have attributed the correct content to the perspective of cows, oxen, cats, flies, and beetles, but that is not important. What is important is the effort to see the world from the other being's perspective, especially for those on the losing end of power. This perspective is connected with Luxemburg's notion of love, which she claimed "brings out the noblest and most beautiful qualities in each person, because it raises up the most ordinary and insignificant detail and sets it around with diamonds."[55] It is with love that the little things appear to us in their most sympathetic light. An effort to see the world from the other's point of view, with genuine affection (and attention, as Weil said) through love, is an instinct against cruelty. And so much of the cruelty that concerned Luxemburg (as well as Weil) includes capitalist exploitation and capitalism itself.

Connecting this constellation of thoughts on flies and cats and oxen to capitalism is not some fanciful flight if one takes a close look at Luxemburg's writing. The above-referenced scene from the von Trotta film is an adaptation of an actual letter written to Sophie Liebknecht by Luxemburg in 1917. In the original letter, Luxemburg is much clearer about the connection between the suffering animals (who were, in fact, water buffaloes) and the capitalist world. First, she observes that the animals themselves came from Romania as "spoils of war."[56] She then describes much the same scene as depicted in von Trotta's film, with the heavy wagon load, the brutal fellow whipping the animals, the bleeding buffalo, and

---

54. Ibid., 449.
55. Ibid.
56. Ibid., 457.

the same tears of the buffalo running down Luxemburg's face.[57] But here is the part that von Trotta left out: A kind attendant nearby witnessed the whipping and asked the cruel soldier leading the wagon if "he had no pity for the animals?"[58] Luxemburg recalls that the soldier answered: "'No one has pity for us humans,' ... and started in again beating them harder than ever."[59] She described the animal as "like an abused child" and the animal's face as having "the expression of a child that has been punished and doesn't know why or what for, doesn't know how to get away from this torment and raw violence.... No one can flinch more painfully on behalf of a beloved brother than I flinched in my helplessness over this mute suffering. How far away, how irretrievably lost were the beautiful, free, tender-green fields of Romania!"[60]

Clearly, as the soldier's response asserts, there is a fluid relation between cruelty in the worlds of both human and nonhuman animals. And in the relation to the abused child, Luxemburg expresses a kind of maternal feeling, a motherly love and solidarity, not for one's own child but for a being of an entirely "other" kind. How can we not long for a world of such affection according to which every being is seen as an individual, with a personality with preferences and a capacity to suffer, which we should take care to look after?

Yet a sincere concern for the vulnerable can go wrong. Here Luxemburg considers a "dubious favor" she once paid to a dung beetle:

Last spring, I was coming home from a walk in the fields, along my silent, empty street, when I noticed a little dark spot on the pavement. I bent down and saw a silent tragedy: a big dung beetle lay on its back, helplessly defending itself with its legs, while a large group of tiny ants swarmed around on top of it and ate it alive! It made my flesh crawl! I took out my handkerchief and began to chase away the brutal little beasts. But, they were so insolent and stubborn that I had to fight a long struggle against them. When I finally freed the poor victim, and placed it faraway on the grass, I saw that two of its legs had already been eaten away.... I walked away with the agonizing feeling that in the long run I had done it a very dubious favor.[61]

57. Ibid.
58. Ibid.
59. Ibid.
60. Ibid.
61. Rosa Luxemburg, *The Rosa Luxemburg Reader*, ed. Peter Hudis and Kevin B. Anderson (New York: Monthly Review Press, 2004), 391.

We may marvel once again at Luxemburg's striking affection for this tiny creature, although not for the even tinier hungry ants. But we have read her consideration of the fly, so perhaps what inclined her toward the beetle and against the ants was the position of each. The tragedy was the beetle's present helplessness and desperate struggle for life. That is why Luxemburg takes the beetle's side. But she acknowledges also that such affection could be unhelpful. Here it would have perhaps been better and more natural to allow the ants their meal. The beetle's struggle, it turns out, did not come to an end as it was left to scurry off without two of its legs. Thus, Luxemburg's effort to end the beetle's struggle may have inadvertently elongated it.

Still, her affection for the beetle, the buffalo, the fly, and the cat is an affection for the vulnerable, for those susceptible to or presently suffering abuse and death, and her affection for the trampled upon and abused is clearly carried over into her politics. I am still not sure whether her affection shapes her politics or vice versa, but we can see the importance of the connection most in Luxemburg's writings on women. To restate a critical proviso, *we* do not liken the woman to a nonhuman animal. But women have been treated as nonhuman or not-fully-human animals in a long history ruled by men in power, and within societies where to be treated like an animal means to be mistreated. Perhaps men and women would embrace their animality more consciously if nonhuman animals were not so brutalized and disposable within human societies.

Luxemburg discussed why the capitalist state did not want working women to vote. "It rightly fears they will threaten the traditional institutions of class rule, for instance militarism (of which no thinking proletarian woman can help being a deadly enemy), monarchy, the systematic robbery of duties and taxes on groceries, etc."[62] Women are positioned in society such that politicizing their preferences, taking seriously what they want or suffer, and appreciating their personhood fully and equally with men encroaches on the patriarchal power men seek to defend. It is not hard to see that the interest of the abused and bleeding buffalo is not the same as the interest of those who look upon that animal as a machine. One principle of the dialectical thinking of Marxism is to look to those positioned on the losing end of the existing state of affairs and to take their side against the established power. As a principle of class struggle, this predisposes us to taking sides with the abused, beaten, locked out, and excluded.

---

62. Ibid., 240.

Luxemburg understood well that work is predominantly imagined and defined as the work that men do. Luxemburg grasped that much of the work of women is not even recognized as work at all. The only work considered by capital as productive is that "which creates capitalist profit. From this point of view, the music-hall dancer whose legs sweep profit in her employer's pocket is a productive worker, whereas all the toil of the proletarian women and mothers in the four walls of their homes is considered unproductive. This sounds brutal and insane, but corresponds exactly to the brutality and insanity of our present capitalist economy."[63] But here is where the point of view of the other is instructive. We must look at work from the woman's point of view (which is not to say that all women will view it the same way). Many mothers know that their unpaid work is not only difficult and unending, but no less important than the man's work on a factory floor. And the daily work of the impoverished mother is all the more difficult because of immediate and pressing wants of her children and because every form of assistance with her children and life is a commodity available only to those with the ability to pay. This point of view may be that of the proletarian woman or mother, but if we do not retrieve and consult it, it is likely to be left out of the analysis—as it has been for so much of history.

At the same time, we have to be careful not to treat the perspective of some working-class women as that of every woman. Not all women are communists. Luxemburg understood the division of perspectives among women along conventional lines of a Marxian class analysis. She put it this way: "For the property-owning bourgeois woman, her house is the world. *For the proletarian woman, the whole world is her house*, the world with its sorrow and joy, with its cold cruelty and its raw size."[64] As beautiful as this articulation may be, we know that not even all proletarian women share this hopeful perspective full of internationalist feeling and solidarity. But I think that what is most important in this passage is its least poetic content. Notice that what Luxemburg juxtaposes to the privatized worldview of capital is a worldview that takes up the *sorrow, joy, cruelty*, and *size* of life. This is a worldview comprising feeling for others than one's self. Wherever that feeling is greater, we find a broader sphere of affection, and I claim that the *Gemeinwesen* Marx sought after depends on the breadth and depth of such affection. Marx could not and would not put it that way. That is one of the many reasons we need Luxemburg.

---

63. Ibid., 241.
64. Ibid., 243.

Luxemburg's life and politics were full of revolutionary affection. She never underestimated the political power of human emotion. She wrote to Leo Jogiches in 1899, "I want to affect people like a clap of thunder, to inflame their minds not by speechifying but with the breadth of my vision, the strength of my conviction, and the power of my expression."[65] The simple insight here is that for social and political movements and transformations, people have got to be moved. Reasonable arguments alone will never win the day. Marx agreed with Luxemburg on this on materialist grounds. For him, transformative movements would come from the disaffections of the exploited class of workers; while he focused on the material conditions that bring the workers to the point of revolution, their disaffection was also important. Marx felt that the disaffection would be an inevitable and inexorable result of the material conditions of life in the capitalist world, so he somewhat took for granted that the requisite affections would appear in the ideological field of the superstructure when material conditions compelled them to emerge. Luxemburg did not disagree, but she saw how, in the political parties of the left, people could be—and indeed had to be—moved by emotional appeals (not merely by reason). She highlighted this especially with regard to socialists taking one position or another during the First World War. No position was guaranteed among the proletariat, and logical argument often failed. To oppose the war seemed logical and reasonable to Luxemburg, and she articulated those arguments sharply in the final chapter of *The Accumulation of Capital* on "Militarism as a Province of Accumulation."[66] But she saw that such argumentation did not always win. Opposition to the war had first and foremost to be rooted in a visceral disaffection, a powerful feeling.

At this juncture, we have a fairly good but still underdeveloped idea of Luxemburg's communism as an expression of affection for the beaten, vulnerable, and abused. What is missing is an understanding of any connection to a concept or theory of love. To preliminarily consider the place of love in Luxemburg's life and politics, I consult her letters to Leo Jogiches in *Comrade and Lover*.[67]

Jogiches was an influential revolutionary active in the Russian, German, and Polish socialist movements of his day, and he was in a romantic relationship with Luxemburg from the early 1890s until about 1907.

---

65. Ibid., 382.
66. See Rosa Luxemburg, *The Accumulation of Capital*, trans. Agnes Schwarzschild (New York: Routledge, 2003).
67. Rosa Luxemburg, *Comrade and Lover: Rosa Luxemburg's Letters to Leo Jogiches*, ed. and trans. Elżbieta Ettinger (Cambridge, MA: MIT Press, 1981).

Reading *Comrade and Lover* is a bit like prying into the most intimate and private life of a figure who would have likely preferred to keep much of this trapped in shoeboxes or deposited in a future library archive opened only posthumously. But for our present purposes, there is one critical conclusion we can draw from this book: Luxemburg's letters to Jogiches are full of warmth, anger, disappointment, frustration, and tension. In her life, *love was not a calming force.* Love was nothing short of a tumultuous upheaval. As Elżbieta Ettinger put it: "Their happy times were bliss. Their battles were bloody. They parted, loving each other, defeated."[68]

But I do not want to tell you about Luxemburg and Jogiches's love life. If you would like to pursue that story, you will have to do it elsewhere. I would like to say something instead about Luxemburg's ideas on love and then connect them to her communism. As a teenage schoolgirl, Luxemburg wrote: "My ideal is a social system that allows one to love everybody with a clear conscience. Striving after it, defending it, I may perhaps even learn to hate."[69] This interesting early formulation notably resonates with our whole inquiry up to this point. More importantly, the centrality of love here would soon drive Luxemburg to adopt communism as the theory that demands a social system based on the love of everybody. Communism as a system based on love, as a system of love, was for Luxemburg an early notion that would determine her future course and commitments.

Luxemburg often demanded that Jogiches should write more about himself.[70] She was regularly frustrated by his communicating with her mainly at the level of any other comrade, as any other fellow revolutionary. Of course, she was a comrade to Jogiches, but Luxemburg held that being a comrade was not the same as being a lover. With a comrade, one shares issues of common concern, develops a critique, and joins a cause to fight for together. With a lover, everything else before and beyond the political is also relevant and of great interest. While everything else may be irrelevant to a comrade, it is necessary for lovers. Without the "everything else" there is a cold distance. Politics alone is inadequate. Love demands more than work and politics for Luxemburg, for it aims to gather everything else besides work and politics into a shared life. Luxemburg writes to Jogiches:

> You don't seem to see that all your letters are systematically and colossally distasteful; they boil down to one long, drawn-out stuffy

---

68. Ibid., xiii.
69. Ibid., 1–2.
70. Ibid., 69.

mentorship like "the letters of a schoolmaster to his favorite pupil." ... by now the whole thing has become a *disease*, an addiction! ... No matter what I'm writing about, my articles, my visits, my newspaper subscriptions, dresses, family relations, anything I care about and share with you—none of it escapes your advice and directions. I swear to god this is getting to be boring! Even more so because it is one-sided. You never give me your work to criticize, not that I would care to instruct you ... and, even if I did, you wouldn't listen anyhow.[71]

We will not psychoanalyze Luxemburg; we are incapable of doing so and, even if we were not, it is irrelevant to this project. Yet Luxemburg's expectations for love are both clear and frustrated here. Luxemburg expects a certain equality in the love relation, by which I mean that one should not assert oneself as a master over the other. While Jogiches was by no means a slave master, it is easy to see that a master-slave relation is not a love relation, and Luxemburg did not want her lover to treat her like a schoolchild under his tutelage. While this imbalance of power and authority may be appropriate in a classroom or a doctor's office, it was maddening to Luxemburg in love. Also, as Jogiches's lover, Luxemburg wanted to speak of all the things she cared about. Much of what she lists are nonpolitical topics, meant more for a love relation than for a meeting of comrades. She wanted not only to be advised but to be listened to and thought of. She expressed this frequently in her letters. Finally, Luxemburg expresses frustration in what she calls a "one-sided" relation: Jogiches constantly offered criticism, advice, and direction while requesting and accepting none of that from her. One of the dynamics that Luxemburg's love seeks out, we might say, is a reciprocity of interest and attention. Luxemburg expects from love a certain equality, attention, affection, and mutuality. These expectations, each one of recurring importance in the relationship between Luxemburg and Jogiches, are generalizable for the present discussion.

By 1900 it was becoming clear that Luxemburg and Jogiches may not be able to make the happy life together they had been trying to build. She reflected on a recent visit to Jogiches in Zurich and wrote that she felt invisible to him, only distinguished from other women by the fact that she wrote articles. She noted that men treat some women with adoration. While Luxemburg was not the kind of woman she observed in

---

71. Ibid., 88.

Berlin—women who seemed to her like they expected to be worshipped—she did want to be sought after for company, conversation, and, above all, what she called a "common spiritual life."[72] Luxemburg writes to Jogiches that it is "impossible to build a *common* spiritual life if we continue to live as we do. An agreement between us is possible only if you get rid of your mistrust and if you believe that I'm capable of understanding you and that I do care about your inner life."[73] Inner life refers here to Jogiches's anxieties, his nonpolitical desires, personal hopes, familial concerns—in short, the content of his private life. Luxemburg felt both that Jogiches did not attend to her inner life and that he did not want to share his. She does not think that anything like the little commune of a loving family is possible without sharing real concerns for the other's inner life.

There was also a sense that politics could destroy the love relation. As Luxemburg wrote in one letter: "My success and the public recognition I am getting are likely to *poison our relationship* because of your pride and suspicion."[74] Luxemburg long worried that the competitive power relations of politics could ruin the love relation between her and Jogiches. How could he bear it if she had more recognition than him? Competition, central not only to politics but irreducibly so to capitalism, is quite damaging to human relationality. Outside of business and politics, one wants comrades, lovers, and friends to win, and one may even see in the triumph of loved ones and dear friends one's own triumph. It is difficult if not impossible to be with another, *for their well-being*, if you perceive their thriving as a threat. In that context, for example, you may secretly hope for the failure of the other so as to maintain your superior position.

One conclusion is clear from Luxemburg's relationship with Jogiches: effort is not enough. You cannot generate love solely by trying. It was not for lack of trying that this relationship failed, but rather for lack of real interest, affection, and mutuality.

By now, readers may wonder if these features of a private love affair can tell us anything about power, politics, and society. I think that they can and do. Most men and women, regardless of their politics, want a love relation like that longed for by Luxemburg. The desire for such a love is by no means a distinctly "communist" or "revolutionary" desire. So why not characterize Luxemburg's love as just like any near-universal aspiration of any human person? Alternatively, why not find in her humanistic instincts and affections a basic liberalism or cosmopolitan feeling? The answer is

72. Ibid., 98.
73. Ibid.
74. Ibid., 27.

that, for Luxemburg, everything in life was connected to questions of capital and revolution, something that is not true of liberals, conservatives, cosmopolitans, and humanists of other kinds. Like most people then and now, Luxemburg sought in love a real and reliable refuge from a world of hostile competition and individualist assertion, from a world plagued by regular deficits of real concern for other beings. But unlike most others, Luxemburg comprehended these as the defining features of the capitalist world. A different logic would be necessary for the establishment of the hopeful little commune of Luxemburg and Jogiches, yet that different logic failed to materialize a real relation, as sometimes happens. This is why we have to understand that love is not merely a theory but also always a practice that must be realized in activity (this practical activity is the sustained focus of chapter 4).

The distinction that makes the difference in the present study is that we are talking here—with Jenny Marx and Rosa Luxemburg—about the power and importance of love in a life of struggle for a *different world*. We are talking about the love of women in search of a different world. We are talking about love as a refuge from persecution, poverty, war, and death. Yes, we are talking about the love of communist women because we are considering a communist theory of love. And we are learning that we do not need to theorize from scratch. Indeed, another communist woman, Alexandra Kollontai—a woman with the courage and intellect to treat the intimate spaces of human affection as the vital terrain of emancipation— wrote an early and formative communist theory of love.

3.3 Kollontai's Communist Theory of Love

Alexandra Kollontai lived from 1872 to 1952, and, although she was not trained as a political theorist or philosopher, she developed many important theories during the revolutionary period in Russia. While Kollontai occupied various official positions in the Soviet Union, her greatest gift was a treasure trove of writings on the development of communist morality for the construction of new modes of being-in-the-world, for a new family organization, and for new social and political relations. Kollontai wrote a lot about love and human relations, and she did so with sustained focus on the difference between capitalist and communist relationality. She closely considered gender inequality and the unique ways in which women were exploited (for example, the expectation that women should raise children alone). For Kollontai, there could be no real revolution without a total transformation in our thinking about sex, sexuality, marriage, and the family. For example, Kollontai understood the existing structures of marriage and family as emerging from a capitalist history of converting loved ones into private property. She therefore argued that we must not bring such understandings of women and family forward into a new society.

In her "Theses on Communist Morality in the Sphere of Marital Relations," Kollontai says:

> The fact that with the consolidation of the capitalist system of production, the marital/family union develops from a production unit into a legal arrangement concerned only with consumption, leads inevitably to the weakening of marital/family ties. In the era of private property and the bourgeois-capitalist economic system, marriage and the family are grounded in (a) material and financial considerations, (b) economic dependence of the female sex on the breadwinner— the husband—rather than the social collective, and (c) the need to care for the rising generation. Capitalism maintains a system of individual economies; the family has a role to play in performing economic tasks and functions within the national capitalist economy.[75]

Kollontai observes how capitalist societies turn family units into little bunkers of consumption. Marriage and family become economic units within which parents and children attempt to get what they need according to the rules of the economy. Thus, monetary considerations govern the familial unit, converting togetherness into a modality of positional economic advantage. Kollontai identifies three features of the capitalist relationality of marriage and family life. The first function is to survive financially. The second function is to maintain the economic dependence of women on men. While women's economic dependence on men has evolved and diminished significantly *within capitalism*, Kollontai specifies a privatization of responsibility such that the well-being of women and children is cut off from any broader social responsibility. This aspect has not changed much, as families continue to regard their own immediate members as wholly their responsibility, *and not as the responsibility of nonmembers*. This privatization of concern is connected with Kollontai's third observation about the privatization of child-rearing and childcare.

Thus, capitalist relationality configures each family as an island unto

---

75. Alexandra Kollontai, *Selected Writings of Alexandra Kollontai*, trans. Alix Holt (New York: W. W. Norton, 1980), 225.

itself. The marital/family unit fares well or not, and if it is wracked by economic insecurity, that is no one's business beyond the familial boundary. This shrinks our sense of responsibility and social solidarity, keeping each little island cut off from the larger social body and reality, but it also reduces the power of each island to the resources at its sole disposal. These tendencies of individuation, privatization, and economic instrumentality are, as we have seen, characteristic tendencies of capital. Kollontai understands communist relationality as directly and necessarily antithetical to such tendencies.

Kollontai makes moral arguments about marital/family relations, distinguishing between "bourgeois morality" and "communist morality."[76] She specifies that the key distinction centers on gender: bourgeois morality promulgates different codes of behavior for men than for women, such that men can lead the most depraved lives so long as they maintain an appearance of respectability. A totally different set of rules and expectations applies to women. Kollontai's 1921 feminism belonged to the field of communist morality. This is crucial because we are not accustomed to thinking of feminist and communist arguments as necessarily imbricated; it is easy and common to claim feminism and not communism, and there is also a long history of communists who have not been feminists. But this is not how things appear to Kollontai. Inasmuch as communism is fundamentally about the transformation of social relations and of relations of power, relationships between the sexes must be treated as fundamental questions of communist morality. Kollontai saw communism as including what we would call feminist thinking on sex and gender, but, perhaps more interestingly, she also contended that the feminist movement would generate communism. How could one wish for a total transformation of capitalist sexual relations without communism?

Kollontai argued against the island notion of the family as follows: "In view of the need to encourage the development and growth of feelings of solidarity and to strengthen the bonds of the work collective, it should above all be established that the isolation of the 'couple' as a special unit does not answer the interests of communism. Communist morality requires the education of the working class in comradeship and the fusion of the hearts and minds of the separate members of this collective."[77] Thus, the romantic relationality that forms a couple should not effectively cut the couple off from the broader social body. Rather, coupling should serve

---

76. Ibid., 229.
77. Ibid., 230.

as a kind of connective tissue that moves us to feelings of solidarity with others outside of the biological family unit. A couple, as such, is evidence that we can feel a great or even greater connection to a former stranger from another family, from another place in the world, a person we may have happened to meet at some point in our adult life. Communism would not, therefore, oppose the couple or even the basic marital/family unit, but would seek to turn its affection against privatization. We often see in the family or the couple a love that can shrink our feeling for others, but it could instead grow our feeling for others, which is for Kollontai both a power of love and a principle of communism.

Whereas with other writers, we had to connect a theory of love to questions of capitalism or connect communist theory to questions about love, Kollontai consistently and clearly connects these for us. When she writes about communist social relations, she writes about love. Kollontai insists: "Love is only one aspect of life, and must not be allowed to over-shadow the other facets of the relationships between individual and collective."[78] She attacks what she regards as bourgeois morality, according to which the couple is so perfectly complementary and complete that they no longer need a connection to any others outside of their union. Kollontai seeks to abolish this still-prevalent idea of the perfect couple that needs nothing outside of itself. The couple and its love may be celebrated and commended, but it is only healthy within the context of "the development of many and varied bonds of love and friendship among people."[79] Kollontai criticizes the notion that everything of each person's inner life should be given only to the other beloved person who comprises the couple. A human being is capable of a multiplicity of love relations, yet bourgeois concepts of ownership (i.e., private property) tend to promote the dangerous notion that love of everyone is promiscuity or betrayal. In this way, capitalism promotes what I call a "shrinking love."

What I mean by "shrinking love" is twofold. Firstly, in a shrinking love, a person's feelings of love are to be gathered up and shrunk down into an exclusive gift to the beloved. In this sense of shrinking love, a love that enlarges and spills over the boundaries of the couple would be viewed as unrefined, unwieldy, dangerous, and possibly immoral. In this itera-tion, shrinking means a forcible restraint on the experience and expression of love. Secondly, I regard "shrinking love" as the love that shrinks us. We ourselves become small private properties of someone else, with

---

78. Ibid.
79. Ibid., 231.

miniaturized spheres of affection. Here shrinking love fits each one of us into autonomous units cut off from the world, little islands of humanity. In this second iteration, shrinking loves make us smaller. As a whole, then, shrinking love both shrinks love, domesticating it and stripping it of its social dimensions, and shrinks us down to the little commodities of some present or future family/marital unit, complete with private purposes and concerns.

Though Kollontai does not use the term, she describes what I am calling shrinking love as a mortal enemy of communist morality and revolutionary movement. Communist love is not only expansive (instead of shrinking), but, according to Kollontai, it grows "the whole gamut of joyful love-experience that enriches life and makes for greater happiness."[80]

Because the whole gamut of love experience includes intellectual components of life and other forms of companionship and gratification, it can never be reduced to sexual activity. Yet one of the most common tendencies of shrinking love is to shrink love down to sexual activity. Consider, for example, the double standard implied by cheating or by a betrayal of monogamous relationality. Rarely is a person considered to be cheating when that person speaks more with a close friend than with the person's own partner. Yet it often happens that a companion outside the romantic unit gets more of your being and time, more of your attention, both quantitatively and qualitatively. Why should betrayal be limited to the sexual act and not the "emotional infidelity" through which one shares their darkest desires and brightest hopes? The reason derives from the fact that sexual activity is taken to be the apex of intimacy, so all of the conversation and companionship that precedes or surrounds it is not quite the forbidden intimacy. Kollontai is not suggesting, however, that the solution to sexual possessiveness is to become more possessive about other aspects of the beloved's life.

Kollontai addresses this directly, criticizing that present-day "lovers with all their respect for freedom are not satisfied by the knowledge of the physical faithfulness alone of the person they love.... We demand the right to know every secret of this person's being. The modern lover would forgive physical unfaithfulness sooner than 'spiritual' unfaithfulness. He sees any emotion experienced outside the boundaries of the 'free' relationship as the loss of his own personal treasure."[81] So the point of view that mistakes physical sexual activity for love is factually wrong not only

---

80. Ibid.
81. Ibid., 243.

because sexual activity can be unloving and scarcely intimate at all. But, more importantly, in raising sexual activity to the apex of human intimacy, there is also an egregious shrinking of love to only one of countless other (and in many cases more meaningful) acts of love. Kollontai argues that we should strive to unleash and expand love rather than aim for its total ownership and domestication. She contends that the morality of capitalist society "has carefully cultivated the idea that one partner should completely 'possess' the other."[82] This idea has triumphed and has expanded nothing but the reign of shrinking love.

Kollontai proposes an alternative: "A jealous and proprietary attitude to the person loved must be replaced by a comradely understanding of the other and an acceptance of his or her freedom. Jealousy is a destructive force of which communist morality cannot approve.... The individual has the opportunity to develop intellectually and emotionally as never before.... [N]ew forms of relationships are maturing and the concept of love is extended and expanded."[83] One way to interpret this would be to read Kollontai as opposing monogamy, which may indeed be one possible experiment. But that is not her recommendation. While Kollontai is not opposed to "open relationships" as such, her argument is more for an "open love," a love compatible with monogamy so long as each partner understands, appreciates, and encourages that the other may have other passions and commitments (indeed, other loves) that expand beyond the purview of the marital/family/couple unit. These other loves would not cancel out or shrink the love of the couple, but rather would be practiced as expansive connections with other people and projects.

Aside from the fact that Kollontai speaks consistently and directly about love, she is actually quite close to Marx in *Grundrisse*. Like Marx, and also like Luxemburg in "The Dissolution of Primitive Communism," Kollontai claims that communist forms of life are destroyed by capitalist forms of life.[84] She says: "Under capitalism the ethic of competition, the triumphant principles of individualism and exclusive private property, grew and destroyed whatever remained of the idea of the community, which was to some extent common to all types of tribal life."[85] Generation after generation born and raised in a world governed by capital is

---

82. Ibid., 242.
83. Ibid., 231.
84. See Rosa Luxemburg's "The Dissolution of Primitive Communism: From the Ancient Germans and the Incas to India, Russia, and Southern Africa," in Hudis and Anderson, *Rosa Luxemburg Reader*, 71–110.
85. Kollontai, *Selected Writings*, 238.

educated to learn the trappings of human solidarity and affection for other people. When you live in a world so thoroughly competitive, individualistic, and pathologically private, you must learn how to be ruthless and
self-centered, how to turn your own relationships into tools for surviving
and winning. You know that if you don't look out for your own private
interests, few others, if any, will. Some outcomes of inconsiderate inattention are catastrophic in real life.

Yet, for Kollontai, there is another important catastrophe beyond the
questions of morality and immediate need, one that has to do with the
sadness of the human person: "We are people living in the world of property relationships, a world of sharp class contradictions and of an individualistic morality. We still live and think under the heavy hand of an
unavoidable loneliness of spirit.... People have perhaps never in any age
felt spiritual loneliness as deeply and persistently as at the present time.
People have probably never become so depressed and fallen so fully under
the numbing influence of this loneliness."[86] We could think about these
lines for the next hundred pages, so I shall use some restraint and make
only three related points here. Firstly, our capitalist societies have created
the loneliest ways of being together. A century later, with our social-medi-
ated relations, we are *literally* together alone. Our problem today is that
we falsely believe that any form of togetherness counteracts loneliness,
which is not even true in many marriages and families. Secondly, Kollontai writes of the problem of loneliness as a spiritual one. In those passages where Marx wrote about spirituality in *The Economic and Philosophic
Manuscripts of 1844*, spirituality was for him a matter of alienation, being
cut off from others, from one's self. A theory of love helps us extend and
deepen the analysis of alienation. Finally, and perhaps most sadly, from
more contemporary perspectives of social psychology, critical theory, and
cognitive science (all of which we shall consult in the next two chapters),
Kollontai appears to be right about the basic condition, which has not im-
proved and in some ways has gotten worse.

Kollontai connects the problem of loneliness not only to capitalism
but to love. "We are unable to follow the simplest rule of love—that another person should be treated with great consideration."[87] This isolation
of love's simplest rule is not, of course, to specify it as the only rule of
love. Great consideration of another person is simply impossible when
and where one considers only one's self. Love demands not some passing

---

86. Ibid., 240.
87. Ibid., 241.

consideration, not a small or fleeting consideration, but rather consideration with depth and duration, which recalls our discussions of Luxemburg, Weil, and Levinas. Loving consideration means that we have to work to know who the other is, what they would like, what they desire, and how to help them avoid or bear suffering if at all possible. But that great consideration is the simplest rule of love also means that there is no love without it. For Kollontai, this consideration belongs to communist morality and promotes communist forms of life.

We should appreciate here a bit more of the feminist content of Kollontai's communism. She argues in "Sexual Relations and the Class Struggle" that women are placed into a kind of captivity in the marital/family/couple units of capitalist society, and that the implementation of property rights appears to go only to the husband over the wife, and not in the other direction.[88] Kollontai advances an analysis of women and capitalism similar to that of Luxemburg. Kollontai observes: "Capitalism has placed a crushing burden on women's shoulders: it has made her a wage-worker without having reduced her cares as housekeeper or mother."[89] Importantly, Kollontai's feminist-communism makes the confrontation with sexist bourgeois morality into a necessity of women's liberation. It is not lost on Kollontai that if men were to accept the notion of a more expansive (rather than shrinking) love, it is unlikely they would advocate an equal expansion for the love of their wives because doing so would loosen their grip over women as property. Unlike the theories of many communists, Kollontai's communist theory of love is also always feminist. For Kollontai, any theory of communism as a form of life (which is always superior to the bankrupt notion of communism as a form of government) *must be feminist if it is to be communist in any meaningful sense.* Following Kollontai, we must ruthlessly criticize and ultimately reject any antifeminist communism as well as any anticommunist feminism, since both are contradictions in terms.

Part of what capitalists fear most in communism is its feminism. Kollontai adds the following:

> Even in capitalist society the needs of the workers were to some extent met by the provision of playgrounds, kindergartens, play groups, etc.... But bourgeois society was afraid of going too far towards meeting the interests of the working class, lest this contribute to the

---

88. Ibid., 248.
89. Ibid., 252.

break-up of the family. For the capitalists are well aware that the old type of family, where the woman is a slave and where the husband is responsible for the well-being of his wife and children, constitutes the best weapon in the struggle to stifle the desire of the working class for freedom and to weaken the revolutionary spirit of the working man and working woman.... The father and mother are ready to agree to any terms when their children are hungry.[90]

Thus, keeping women in the captivity of domestic life and keeping the family unit functioning as an autonomous economy that sinks or floats on its own, not only operates on the basis of a shrinking love, but also shrinks the aspirations of the unit to its most immediate needs and economic concerns. People can scarcely think about radical social or political transformation when everyday concerns about the security of their basic existence colonize their consciousness. Provisions granted within capitalist society are partly meant to preserve the basic situation of privatized family life while preventing conditions from getting so miserable as to make revolution worth the risk.

The economic position of the whole family, but particularly of women, makes both communism and feminism necessary, a point Kollontai argues in "Prostitution and Ways of Fighting It." We should keep in mind that it was not capital all by itself that incentivized prostitution. That is only one part of the story, according to which many girls are "forced into the streets by poverty, homelessness, unemployment and other social circumstances which derive from the existence of capitalism and private property."[91] Women's economic dependence on men is best informed by a feminist understanding of women's historical lack of opportunity. When the opportunity structure effectively blockades women from managing their own financial security, women are driven to seek such security by other means. The production of women-as-sex-objects is a form of sexual commodification. Within the market of sexual exchange relations, capitalism alone is insufficient to answer why most of the "consumers" are men and most of the "commodified humanity" are young girls and women. At the same time, however, we cannot simply reproduce Kollontai's 1921 view on prostitution today. Many contemporary sex workers and feminists challenge and reject the stigma of sex work, insisting that other jobs considered "more respectable" under capitalism are not necessarily better—or

---

90. Ibid., 257.
91. Ibid., 262.

even fundamentally different—and also that some of the women who do sex work are not forced into it.[92] Nonetheless, any good analysis of sex work will focus on its gendered dimensions, hence the necessity of feminism to the political economy of prostitution.

While we have been reviewing Kollontai's communist theory of love, we have yet to touch on her most important essay on the subject. In "Make Way for Winged Eros: A Letter to Working Youth," we can fully and finally elucidate Kollontai's theory of love and move to concluding critical reflections on the theory and its problems. In "Winged Eros," Kollontai takes up love as a sociopsychological factor. She observes that the joys and pains of loving require time and strength, by which she specified "social and psychological energy."[93] Kollontai views love as dependent on "energy," so when our daily lives are spent wholly investing our social and psychological energy into other projects, jobs, or responsibilities, there simply may not be enough "energy" left over for love. People who are physically and emotionally exhausted do not have the energy for love. Love is not a background setting that stays healthy and in place without any investment of energy. One of the best ways to suffocate love is to exhaust the human person through work or other obligations. Not only energy but also time is necessary. Here we have to wonder about the contemporary technologies of love that, in exchange for a fee, promise expert match-making by processing online profiles and survey data. This algorithmic approach to "finding love" has been appealing primarily because of its promise to save time and energy. But at some point, for example when the matches actually work, time and energy will inevitably have to be committed to the growth and tending of the love. Time and energy (both social and psychological) are the oxygen of love, without which it cannot breathe. We might say that the suffocation of love from inadequate time and energy is yet another form of its shrinking.

Here, too, Kollontai continues to make the case for a more expansive love against a shrinking love, even forecasting central issues in present-day sexuality politics. "Love is not in the least a 'private' matter concerning only the two loving persons: love possesses a uniting element which is valuable to the collective. This is clear from the fact that at all stages of historical development society has established norms defining when and

---

92. See, for example, Leopoldina Fortunati, *The Arcane of Reproduction: Housework, Prostitution, Labor and Capital*, trans. Hilary Creek (New York: Autonomedia, 1995); and Molly Smith and Juno Mac, *Revolting Prostitutes: The Fight for Sex Workers' Rights* (London: Verso, 2018).

93. Kollontai, *Selected Writings*, 277.

under what conditions love is 'legal' (i.e. corresponds to the interests of the given social collective), and when and under what conditions love is sinful and criminal (i.e. contradicts the tasks of the given society)."[94] The extent to which Kollontai grasped the future of sexuality politics in the early 1920s is astounding. Evidence that love is never a private affair can be found in governmental and legal concerns over who loves who and in what ways. Most notably, the global history of same-gender love relations, recent sodomy laws, and the criminalization of despised sexuality provides mountains of evidence corroborating Kollontai's claim. When one starts to think of love as sin and crime, love's political side becomes visible. States and laws must deal with criminals, so if certain expressions or practices of love become criminalized, then those love practices become political and legal problems.[95]

Kollontai provides historical notes reviewing how "humanity has sought to regulate not only sexual relations but love itself," pointing out, for example, that there is even a history of kinship communities within which falling in love with blood relations was the highest love.[96] So when the collective's sense of what love can do changes, the laws and norms are invariably changed too.[97] This is one of the ways that love and its forms influence history. Legal and political histories also shape, contain, and variously imprison love. Kollontai is specifically interested in how the history of capitalism transitioned the family from a wealth-sharing unit to a unit structured around the accumulation and safeguarding of its capital. A certain economic logic functioned in the wealth-sharing unit too, but one could say that the miniature economy of the family was subordinate to the family's existence as a little commune, as with the Marx family. Thus, sharing, caring, and solidarity primarily governed the family's collective needs and secondarily governed its finances. The shift to the accumulation and guardianship of capital essentially modified the family into a competitive modality in which it defends its wealth not just from the state but from other families. So for Kollontai, what fundamentally changes is the basic *orientation* of the family.

Regarding the orientation of the family, Kollontai constantly emphasizes comradeship throughout all her writings. The word "comrade" and

94. Ibid., 279.

95. We should note the language of sin here, which belongs to the history of religious concern over love and its forms.

96. Kollontai, *Selected Writings*, 279.

97. Kollontai uses the term "collective" to mean the social body, polity, or political association/community.

the concept of "comradeship" is consistent and prominent. While Jodi Dean has recently gone to Kollontai's work to develop a theory of the comrade, I see the concept of the comrade as just one possible expression of a more expansive love.[98] This can be seen throughout Kollontai's writings on love, the family, sexuality, and communist human relationality. The basic theme is everywhere the same: *We must acculturate and practice expanding and deepening forms of human solidarity*. When we look on the other as a comrade—whenever it makes sense to do so (after all, not all enemies are imaginary)—the name "comrade" indicates a decision to view the other as part of *our* collective. The comrade is, by definition, not a rival or a competitor against whom our interests are set. According to Kollontai, the capitalist ideal is "the married couple, working together to improve their welfare and to increase the wealth of their particular family unit, divorced as it was from society."[99] The others outside of the family were to be of little concern, which is to say that they are not regarded as comrades. Communism turns "comrade" into one way of loving beyond the family.

Like Luxemburg, Kollontai appreciates the importance of affection: "Solidarity is not only an awareness of common interests; it depends also on the intellectual and emotional ties linking the members of the collective. For a social system to be built on solidarity and co-operation it is essential that people should be capable of love and warm emotions."[100] Thus, the awareness of common interests and a shared theoretical position must be supplemented with real emotional connections. A comradely greeting can be a formality like any other. What matters are real feelings, love, and warm emotions. To say that the other is a comrade because of a common worldview means nothing if one secretly wants to beat that comrade in a competitive game of life. Consider a banal example of the problem. One time before a lecture I gave at a conference of Marxists, I greeted the packed room full of (mostly) strangers as "comrades." I meant it, and, while it was a sincere gesture, the nominal greeting was not accompanied with real love or warm emotions for the people in that room. I would have wished no one there any ill, and I took great pleasure in conversation with the activists and academics I spoke with, but none of that amounts to a substantive or sustained relationship that affords any one of us a reliable solidarity we may draw on. And this says nothing about the

---

98. See Jodi Dean, "Four Theses on the Comrade," *E-Flux Journal*, no. 86 (November 2017), https://www.e-flux.com/journal/86/160585/four-theses-on-the-comrade.

99. Kollontai, *Selected Writings*, 284.

100. Ibid., 285.

peculiar competitive—and sometimes hostile—interactions among radical intellectuals of a common milieu. "Stop! You are comrades!" someone may say. But perhaps they are not really comrades.

For Kollontai, one of the most important attributes of love is that while states and laws and capital may seek to hold it captive, to shrink it down to serve their purposes, love cannot be held at bay indefinitely. Kollontai observes how "love could not be contained within the limits set down by bourgeois ideologists.... Love constantly escaped from the narrow framework of legal marriage relations set for it."[101] Kollontai is not advocating or celebrating adultery, but she offers an interesting analysis of it. She argues that bourgeois capitalist morality condemns the "infidelity" or "cheating" called adultery but has no interest in exploring the sources of the dissatisfactions that motivate it. If adultery is a problem, then it will not do to simply condemn its immorality. What is necessary—especially for any critical theory—is to identify the root causes of the dissatisfaction.

Part of the problem is that we are living and working without sufficient time and energy necessary for healthy love, and we are expected (especially and historically women and gays and lesbians) to accept unacceptable captivities of love, where real feelings are held hostage to commitments we'd rather not make. It is crucial to stress that this point, much like adultery, is not fundamentally about sexual activity. Kollontai is consistent. It is not only the case that so many of our material needs are not satisfied, but that so many of our psychological and emotional needs are not satisfied either. Because people are often mobilized by their real needs, they are eventually driven to breach the boundaries of capitalist morality. If we want to increase fidelity and trust within love relations, then we have to create the conditions (material, psychological, and social) under which love can flourish.

From this point, there are essentially two opposing directions Kollontai charts for love:

> Love has become a psychological and social factor. Under the impact of economic and social forces, the biological instinct for reproduction has been transformed in two diametrically opposed directions. On the one hand the healthy sexual instinct has been turned by monstrous social and economic relations, particularly those of capitalism, into unhealthy carnality.... On the other hand ... a web of emotional and

---

101. Ibid., 284.

intellectual experiences has come to surround the physical attraction of the sexes.... Love is intricately woven from friendship, passion, maternal tenderness, infatuation, mutual compatibility, sympathy, admiration, familiarity and many other shades of emotion.[102]

Here Kollontai juxtaposes the first possibility (that of a wingless Eros) to a preferable second path (that of a winged Eros). With winged Eros, love takes flight from its shrinking captivity and breaks with the reductionist view of sexual intercourse as its highest expression. With winged Eros, "physical attraction and emotional warmth are fused. The existence of love-friendship where the element of physical attraction is absent, of love for one's work or for a cause, and of love for the collective, testify to the extent to which love has become 'spiritualised' and separated from its biological base."[103] Love in the phase of winged Eros is a renewed and unwieldy force that can only be shrunk down to narrow economic and biological expressions by means of its destruction. As can be seen in love-friendship and other forms of love, the ultimately irrepressible tendency of love is to *enlarge* and *deepen* the *Gemeinwesen* of a healthy community. This tendency is fundamentally and irreducibly communist.

Kollontai finally proposes a new morality for human relationality according to her theory of love. This morality of relationality consists of three principles. The first is that of equality, which in practice would tend toward the abolition of gender inequality, the inequality of the sexes. The second principle involves a total rejection of any tendency to convert another person into someone else's private property, insisting "that one does not own the heart and soul of the other."[104] Third and finally, Kollontai posits "comradely sensitivity" as a moral principle where we would cultivate "the ability to listen and understand the inner workings of the loved person (bourgeois culture demanded this only from the woman)."[105] If we can restructure love relations along these lines, "men and women will strive to express their love not only in kisses and embraces but in joint creativity and activity."[106]

Kollontai's communist theory of love is persuasive and useful in several ways. Even those who are not anticapitalists may be drawn to her critique of what we have been calling a shrinking love and to her preference

---

102. Ibid., 286.
103. Ibid.
104. Ibid., 291.
105. Ibid.
106. Ibid.

for the expanding love of winged Eros. Even those who have no interest in a structural transformation of political economy might like to think of love as a soothing balm against the harsh realities of everyday life and work. For those of us who genuinely worry about our ability to survive capitalism before it destroys us—not only ecologically and economically, but also psychologically—Kollontai offers a moral and political theory that can be practiced within our own spheres of human activity to address at least some of those concerns. In short, Kollontai's communist theory of love suggests that love tends toward communist forms of life, and communist forms of life tend toward love. Kollontai's communism is a philosophy of struggle against inequality, for mutual respect of the complex needs of people, and toward real comradely sensitivity. Kollontai's communist theory of love is calibrated for the acculturation of a social relation of warmth, solidarity, and meaningful human connections. In short, Kollontai's theory makes love central to the restoration and flourishing of the *Gemeinwesen* at the heart of Marx's communism.

I shall offer only two disagreements with Kollontai here.

First, in the 1920s Kollontai's hope was anchored to a period of radical experimentation in the organization of social life, and much of her very specific hope, connected as it was to the Russian Revolution, has been dashed not only in the world at large but also in the particular context and history of the Soviet Union. Today, we are facing many of the same problems so astutely diagnosed by Kollontai almost one hundred years ago; it is for precisely that reason that I claim the enduring relevance of her theory of love. The problem is that, whereas love appeared to Kollontai poised to burst asunder its long captivity to bourgeois morality, love has since—in many of the same ways discussed above—been fairly well beaten into submission. It is worth pointing out that social, legal, and political developments on gay and lesbian love relations, and now hopefully with transgender relationality, do constitute real evidence that love does not obey the rules of its criminalization. Sometimes it changes those rules. There are many cases in the annals of queer sexuality that prove that sometimes love wins out against the vilification of its forms. However, our most hopeful global uprisings and social movements are rarely about love and its dilapidated state.

Love would almost appear as a corpse in waiting, a corpse stored in the next room unburied, as the Marx family lived with the body of their deceased daughter Franzisca when they could not afford a coffin.[107] What

---

107. Gabriel, *Love and Capital*, 222.

I mean by this perhaps-too-morbid analogy is that we have lived with a dead love set down beside us, attending to what we regard as our more pressing and immediate concerns. Love is often an aspiration, a hope, but not a living activity that one can practice *right now*. Other matters take precedence. In this way, the first problem with Kollontai's theory is not really with the theory per se. Rather, the century since she developed it has given us worsening problems of privatization, growing inequality, and a more and more pervasive loneliness of spirit. Sad to say, but our first disagreement must be with the hopeful disposition toward winged Eros. In the decades following World War II, the Marxist critical theorists from Germany and France would do much to articulate the negation of Kollontai's hope. I do not want to abandon that hope, but it is not appropriate to the present era.

My second disagreement is the more significant one. Kollontai fixed her hope to the Soviet Union, and she thought that her theory of love could be administered through national policy. My disagreement here is with Kollontai's faith in the compatibility of her theory with purportedly communist government. Kollontai did not need to wait for decades of disillusionment to conclude that her theory of love would be murdered by the state instead of practiced by it. Already in the nineteenth century, those debates had defined the thinking of so many revolutionaries, and Lenin was surrounded not only by critics from the right but by those from the left, and not only by anarchist critics but by Left communists whom he accused in 1920 of having an "infantile disorder."[108]

But beyond the well-known actuality of communist critics of statism, it is strange that Kollontai could have considered government of any kind as capable of abolishing shrinking love and helping to usher in the reign of the more expansive love of winged Eros. One may retort that this is only easy to say now, in the twenty-first century, for hindsight has made clearer what the anarchists and communists of the nineteenth and twentieth centuries got right (and wrong). But that retort doesn't work. Can you imagine any implementation of Kollontai's theory by a political state? Kollontai was thinking about love and capitalism, about bourgeois and communist morality, about gender and relationality, and her thinking was hardly suitable for a top-down implementation of domestic policy. Love cannot be administered like taxation.

Clear as this may seem, Kollontai was a member of Lenin's government,

---

108. See V. L. Lenin, "'Left-Wing' Communism: An Infantile Disorder," in *Collected Works*, vol. 31 (Moscow: Progress Publishers, 1964), 17–118.

and she believed in it. Her political career began immediately following the 1917 revolution. Kollontai was People's Commissar for Social Welfare, and she founded the Women's Department in 1919. In this latter role in particular, Kollontai felt that she could implement at least some of her ideas about improving the conditions of women's lives, and she even took up some of the specific causes articulated in her theory of love. For example, the Women's Department sought to aid in educating women about the communist theory of marital/family relations, and it is noteworthy that she worked out her arguments on these subjects *while* directing the department. By 1930, the Women's Department was closed. As we know, Kollontai's feminist ideas scarcely made their way from the Soviet state into Russian society. This was not for lack of trying; rather, I think it was just an inevitable expression of the limitations of trying to transform society through state departments.

Kollontai's political career was rather short-lived, and she was herself aware of its limitations. She eventually participated in the formation of a left-wing faction, the Workers' Opposition, which was seen by Lenin as a threat to his power. In government, Kollontai's influence was minimized and minimal. Perhaps this is the bias of a writer, but I think her writings were her major contribution to politics, history, and the world. Yet she did not totally abandon Soviet politics. She served in various roles as ambassador and diplomat of the Soviet Union in Norway, Mexico, and Sweden. She stayed involved in professional politics well into the 1940s, and so it is unlikely that she ever totally disconnected her hopes from the official politics of the Soviet Union. Her political career was not catastrophic for her theory, but it was totally discordant with it. What Kollontai talks about in her communist theory of love is simply *not the business* of bureaucratic state power. By this point in our study it is clear that when we speak of the communism of love—*of communism itself*—we are talking about forms of life, not about forms of government. However one characterizes the early days of the Soviet Union, it is outlandish to imagine it having anything to do with winged Eros taking flight. Such a project must take place from below, from within a revolutionary relationality, motivated and mobilized by the indignant affections that communist women have so aptly written about and lived. Communism and love can grow larger from our little communes of human life, experience, and thought, and if they ever do reach the bureaucratic offices of government, they will be greeted as hostile forces. As they should be.

Kollontai's communism as a practice of love is and must be a communism from below (like *all* communism worthy of the name). But this conclusion leaves us to ask about the means by which a winged Eros could possibly take flight (if indeed it can take flight), since it cannot be imposed by government or policy. We turn now to explore this and other related questions through more recent research, focusing on practices of love theorized from the 1950s on up to present-day considerations in critical theory and psychoanalysis.

CHAPTER 4

Love as Praxis:
Critical Theory and Psychoanalysis

"The child's creativity—indeed, the human faculty of imagination
in general—presupposes a 'capacity to be alone,' which itself can
arise only out of a basic confidence in the care of a loved one."

–Axel Honneth, *The Struggle for Recognition*

"It takes powerful constellations and circumstances to pervert and stifle
this innate striving for sanity; and indeed, throughout the greater part
of known history, the use of man by man has produced such perversion.
To believe that this perversion is inherent in man is like throwing seeds
in the soil of the desert and claiming they were not meant to grow."

–Erich Fromm, *The Sane Society*

4.1 Insanity: *Après Moi, le Déluge*

In my view, one of the most brilliantly written and penetratingly insightful books of the twentieth century is Erich Fromm's 1955 *The Sane Society*. Although we can identify problems in the work and can recognize many of the limitations of language and knowledge in the 1950s, Fromm's book continues to offer a complex and nuanced study of psychology and life in capitalist society. The central message of *The Sane Society* is that capitalism tends toward a peculiar yet diagnosable insanity that we can and must guard against by understanding it psychoanalytically and then must counteract through a restorative socialism of health and well-being.[1] The insanity of capitalism is that it variously promotes and requires forms of alienation that give rise to isolation, loneliness, anxiety, and unhappiness, yet we have come to defend it, reproduce it, and tout its great victories. Severely alienated persons are both psychologically and sociologically deprived to the point that they become incapable of love. This thesis appears in a different way in Fromm's later and much shorter *The Art of Loving*. With these works, and with the help of present-day critical theory, psychological research, and psychoanalytic theory, we may be able to understand how love and capitalism not only structure our being-in-the-world and the human community but also affect human health in concrete psychosocial terms.

Fromm is first of all concerned with the pathology of normalcy, which refers to deeply entrenched presuppositions and beliefs that support the

---

1. Within the context of our discussion of Fromm, I use the term "insanity" because he does and not because it is the most appropriate term. In what follows, the problems with declaring peoples and society "sane" or "insane" will be made clearer.

basic morality of the existing capitalist society. Within this pathology we find the belief that everything that we see is more or less reasonable and right, and that those who oppose, question, or confront the existing reality—those who break with the pathology of normalcy—are wrong and misguided. As was characteristic of the critical theory of Fromm's generation, this pathology of normalcy is based on instrumental reason, according to which any reasonable understanding of the society is presupposed to include the idea that that society is perfectly reasonable. In this way, our own discourse on the society is the property and product of the society itself. Stated in a different way, every social and political regime depends on a hegemonic belief in its own reason and rationality. As a result, whatever happens or is done there will appear rational and right.

One of the common articulations of instrumental reason says that the form of life we now have is simply an embodiment of human nature, and therefore the existing society must be natural. This gloss on the naturalness of everything that is already established smuggles in an endorsement of the existing society from the start. Fromm points out, however, that what we call "'human nature' is but one of many manifestations—and often a pathological one—and the function of such mistaken definition usually has been to defend a particular type of society as being the necessary outcome of man's mental constitution."[2] This notion of functional understanding, that is, a way of thinking promulgated because it justifies the social system, is an example of instrumental reason. Central to Fromm's thinking is that, from a clinical and psychoanalytic perspective, we can speak not only about sick persons but also about sick societies, and we can do this precisely at the point where we can identify pathologies at the societal level.

Many of the basic observations of Fromm's psychoanalysis are wholly consistent with and corroborate Marx's work and Marxist philosophy. Marx predates Freud, but Fromm used Freud's innovations to revise and extend Marxist theory into the late twentieth century. For example, Fromm observes that the human person needs to unite with other human persons in order to be healthy and well. This tendency toward the *Gemeinwesen* is a basic communist notion, as we have seen, but Fromm goes further: "This need is behind all phenomena which constitute the whole gamut of intimate human relations, of all passions which are called love in the broadest sense of the word."[3] Thus, the communist tendencies of the human

---

2. Erich Fromm, *The Sane Society* (New York: Henry Holt and Company, 1955), 13.
3. Ibid., 30.

person *precede* and *motivate* efforts to establish intimate human relations. This raises the question of whether or not it is precisely the communistic propensity of humanity that tends toward loving.

Suffice it to say for now that, according to Fromm, the question of love enters early as a concrete scientific term. In an early definition, Fromm writes: "There is only one passion which satisfies man's need to unite himself with the world, and to acquire at the same time a sense of integrity and individuality, and this is *love*. *Love is union* with somebody, or something, outside oneself, *under the condition of retaining the separateness and integrity of one's own self*."[4] I do not want to describe love as a passion, and, frankly, Fromm himself does not keep to this designation. But the core idea of this definition is worth explication, and it reflects a position also taken up by Axel Honneth, as we shall soon see. The core idea is that love is a union with someone or something outside of oneself that in no way diminishes one's own individuality or sense of self. The notion that displaced attention from one's own self to another shrinks oneself is false; in fact, the individual person actually grows only in unity with others. Already in *The Sane Society*, Fromm is writing about love as an action, which turns out to be one of his most defining contributions to the theory of love.[5]

Fromm speaks of love as a productive action in that it generates feeling that is inclusive and expansive, not only with a beloved object or person but also with other things and people, including oneself. This would be a healthy orientation; however, many people practice disfigured and unhealthy relations that are wrongly mistaken for genuine love. Fromm points out that self-love is the opposite of selfishness, for selfishness "is actually a greedy concern with oneself which springs from and compensates for the lack of genuine love for oneself.... If I love, I care—that is, I am actively concerned with the other person's growth and happiness."[6] In this sense, love is understood as productive because it is an activity that generates real things such as care and concern for other people.

One of the difficulties in Fromm, especially when comparing his work with more contemporary critical and psychoanalytic theory, is that he seems to view society and politics as a terrain of psychosocial battle on which love must fight against the various tendencies of capitalist alienation. Love, if properly understood and practiced, could potentially win. Fromm wrote about love precisely because he thought it was the most

---

4. Ibid., 31, italics in original.
5. Ibid., 32.
6. Ibid., 32–33.

hopeful dis-alienating power at our disposal. But his view was oversimply dialectical to the point of being dichotomous. One either understands and practices love properly, as a form of resistance against capitalist alienation, or abandons love for the disfigured form it takes in existing society. More recent theorists have come to see a less dichotomous opposition, and the status of love in current society is generally seen as muddier and, worse, as a more intractable problem than it appeared to Fromm in the 1950s.

Fromm defends primary narcissism as "the normal physiological and mental development of the child," meaning that young children cannot be expected to tend to anything beyond their most immediate individual wants.[7] They are hungry, they are tired, they are bored, they are mad, they want this or that thing, and frustrated desires mean unhappiness for the child. This is, for Fromm, the emotional and physiological disposition appropriate to the youngest and most vulnerable lives. This primary narcissism is not to be condemned or challenged but understood and appreciated as a necessary phase of the development of the child's preferences, pleasures, and self-understanding.

However, as the child grows, Fromm sees healthy development as moving away from narcissism, through love, and if a growing child—and later, an adult—remains in a state of narcissism, then that person develops pathologies that are unhealthy from both a psychic and a social point of view. For such a narcissistic adult, "there is only one reality, that of his own thought process, feelings and needs."[8] The narcissistic person has not learned to appreciate and care for the fact that other persons have their own frustrated desires that can be understood and attended to apart from one's own desires. But the major and overarching points that Fromm wants to make in his research are that "failure to relate oneself to the world is insanity" and that "relatedness is the condition for any kind of sane living."[9] To speak of generalized social insanity today almost sounds old-fashioned. Or perhaps it sounds hyperbolic. We live in a world where words like "insanity" should be and have been largely replaced by proper terms naming specific diagnoses or pathologies. "Insanity" carries within it the ultimate insult for the human person who understands his or her species by way of its cognitive powers and rational faculties. To be insane would be to have a deficit in the most defining dimension of the human being as *Homo sapiens*.

---

7. Ibid., 35.
8. Ibid., 35–36.
9. Ibid., 36.

Let us look at the etymological and conceptual roots of sanity and insanity. The word "sanity" goes back to the early fifteenth century and essentially means "healthy condition." One could see here the connection to "sanitary," which draws on the same roots, the Latin *sanitatem* or *sanitas*. To be sanitary in the familiar sense of keeping oneself clean and well-kempt is one of the pathways to healthy living. Only later on, closer to the seventeenth century, did sanity start to mean "soundness of mind." Although it may be better to return to the broader concept of healthy condition, there is no doubt that Fromm the psychoanalyst was working with the notion of health in terms of "soundness of mind." Insanity, dating from roughly the 1580s, indicated the impairment of mental functioning and therefore also indicates an unhealthy condition of life. Of course, it is still necessary to speak of health and sickness. But it is better to confront what is insane in the world such as it is and to avoid calling people sane or insane. Fromm was concerned about an insane society, which he thought already existed to some extent. What is especially useful in Fromm's work is the analysis of sanity and insanity in political theory. For example, when Fromm calls nationalism a form of insanity, he is making a critical point in the wake of the Nazi regime and the Second World War. He held that the idolatrous worship of one's own country, "which excludes the love for others … which is not part of one's love for humanity is not love."[10] Fromm was right to worry about how certain ideas like nationalism, patriotism, and racism can take hold of clear thinking and derail it. But this presupposes the existence of an alternative clear thinking, something we can never take for granted.

One of the major advances of Fromm over Freud was in the research on love. Prior to Fromm, psychoanalysis followed Freud's theory of love as an expression of sexual desire, which is essentially egotistical and antisocial.[11] Fromm notes: "For Freud, love was basically a sexual phenomenon."[12] Fromm rightly rejects Freud's narrow conception of love and insists instead on defining it as a social power of healthy human connection. Also unlike Freud, Fromm worries about the fate and state of love particularly in capitalist society. On this latter point, however, Fromm is guilty of a different kind of reduction. He defines capitalism as a Western economic system increasingly dominant and global since the seventeenth and eighteenth centuries. Capitalism, Fromm maintains, arranges economy in

---

10. Ibid., 59.
11. Ibid., 75.
12. Erich Fromm, *The Art of Loving* (New York: Harper Perennial Modern Classics, 2006), 83.

a particular way. He is correct that we can speak of an economy ruled by the logic of capital (that is to say, designed to accumulate the private ownership of capital). But capitalism was never merely an economic system. Capitalism determines far too much at social, legal, political, ecological, psychological, and cultural levels to be regarded as merely economic. Capitalism is a complex social system within which the economy is one of many moving parts. This is not to accuse Fromm of a narrowly economistic Marxism. He is also widely interested in the psychosocial and political effects of the capitalist economy, not only "economic problems."

It has been a long time since anyone should have been allowed to get away with treating capitalism as if it were only an economic system. The critical theorists taught us so well about the social, psychological, cultural, and technological features of capitalism. Today, capitalism has to be understood in its systemic complexity, as an encompassing lifeworld governed by the logic and power of capital, governed by the dictatorial rule of life by money. Fromm observes that the "capitalistic principle that each one seeks his own profit and thus contributes to the happiness of all becomes the guiding principle of human behavior."[13] Once the capitalist principle configures human behavior, however, that behavior subsists and continues even against economic countertrends, crises, and other changes of direction. Here we will challenge Fromm's treatment of capitalism as fundamentally economic, and later we will challenge his idea of socialism, which is dangerously narrow in other ways.

However, one of the things that is underappreciated in Fromm's work is the extent to which he read and discussed the ideas of anarchists. He viewed anarchism and Marxism as different forms of socialism, all of which—despite important differences—"emphasized the necessity for abolishing exploitation and transforming the workingman into an independent, free and respected human being."[14] Fromm's humanism starts to come through in his discussions of socialism and its various forms. Socialism, for Fromm, is always ultimately about the restoration of health—that is to say, of sanity—through anticapitalist practice and political movements. But capitalist society is structured to produce the kind of people that suit it. This means, for Fromm, the intergenerational production of people with a social character defined by obedience, consumption, and predictable gullibility. This type of person will go along with the most insane social relations, will view generalized insanity as perfectly sane,

---

13. Fromm, *Sane Society*, 86.
14. Ibid., 100.

and will identify a sick state of affairs as healthy and good. All of this is acculturated in capitalist society and becomes cemented as a psychological disposition.

From here, Fromm focuses his attention on alienation, which can be battled with acts of love. Fromm restates without modification the basic insights of Marx's chapter on alienation and estranged labor from *Economic and Philosophic Manuscripts of 1844*. While Fromm accepts Marx's basic theory of alienation, he connects alienation to the subversion of psychological well-being. When you worship another person whom you call the beloved, your disposition is more appropriate to idolatry than love.[15] If you worship the beloved, or if you seek to become their private property (or make them into yours), alienation may return and come to characterize your relationship with the other. We have seen this point in other contexts, particularly in our discussions of Luxemburg and Kollontai. If being with the other does not meaningfully connect the two of you to each other with attention and mutuality, or to others beyond the home, family, job, or apartment, then this form of togetherness may do nothing to counteract alienation. Sometimes, such relations are called love, but one can see in their privatizing and isolating tendencies that they are not the love praised by any good theory of love. Here is further evidence of Fromm's advance beyond Freud, the latter of whom saw no problem with isolating and privatizing love.

According to Fromm, alienation is no minor problem: "Alienation as we find it in modern society is almost total; it pervades the relationship of man to his work, to the things he consumes, to the state, to his fellow man, and to himself."[16] While technological advances since the 1950s have evolved well beyond Fromm's imagination, current research shows that they have done little to reverse alienation. We can see dangerous new developments of alienation from the twentieth into the twenty-first century in the writings of Bernard Stiegler, Franco Berardi, John Cacioppo, and Julia Kristeva, all of whom we take up in forthcoming sections. Using technology, people have tried to create surrogates for lost human connections, none of which have overcome growing isolation, partially because they accept and presuppose our already-existing and ongoing separation in the world. Our technological "fixes" do not actually connect human beings but instead only facilitate cognitive intersections on a map that is not itself a relationship. That despair and loneliness are not resolved by

---

15. Ibid., 123.
16. Ibid., 124.

contemporary technological relationality is a point very well documented below, and the sad fact is that Fromm was right to worry about catastrophic alienation. Some permutations of alienation are today being expressed in violent acts of murder, mass shootings, and generalized anxiety that threatens to ruin countless lives.

Alienation tends toward atomization, the production of discrete, atom-like individuals who are more and more estranged from one another. This breaking up of a fundamental social substance—the connective tissue of actual sociality—cannot be healed by technology, but only through love. Sociality has been reduced to a facade comprised of self-interested exchange relations.

> The employer uses the ones whom he employs; the salesman uses his customers. Everybody is to everybody else a commodity, always to be treated with a certain friendliness, because even if he is not of use now, he may be later. There is not much love or hate to be found in human relations of our day. There is, rather, a superficial friendliness, and a more than superficial fairness, but behind that surface is distance and indifference. There is also a good deal of subtle distrust.... Modern society consists of "atoms" (if we use the Greek equivalent of "individual"), little particles estranged from each other but held together by selfish interests and by the necessity to make use of each other.[17]

Fromm's description, no less true today, is also a picture of the total opposite of what I call "communism." The key component of Fromm's description is that behind the superficial friendliness of social relations lurks distance, indifference, distrust, and utilitarian calculation. Even apart from the question of communism, we must at least condemn this situation as unpropitious to love.

The communist reversal would be something like this: No human person is seen as a commodity. To look on a person and, worse, to treat a person as a commodity would be taken as the greatest offense. Superficial friendliness would still be practiced, but it would be consciously regarded as nicety, a sociable demeanor, and would not be mistaken for real friendship. Instead, friendship would comprise deep, active, and meaningful concern for the friend, without calculations of cost. If that friend would join you, and you her, in a common struggle or cause, you would become

---

17. Ibid., 139–40.

comrades. Real friendship would be seen not in niceties but in meaningful acts of solidarity and practices of care, or in an everyday consideration for other people that is given and received as genuine. We would try to calculate only the use of things, and not the use of people, and we would share a vital sense of what is worthy of our love and hatred. There is plenty of distance and indifference in the world, as there would probably have to be no matter the form of life and society. However, we could understand this reality *as such*, and never mistake distance for intimacy and indifference for care. Society would be understood as an effort that does not always succeed but that nonetheless attempts to counteract human estrangement and to move beyond (leaving behind) the interests that capitalism both generates and feeds on.

This imagined reality is not a bad idea of communism, and notice that it is not a fundamentally economic idea, although it would certainly necessitate radically different economic relations. Such a communism, in practice, would push against the capitalist orientation of existing society. Communism would demand a multiplicity of pushes that would probably not effectively reverse things very quickly but would make clear the desire for a total reversal.

This pushing back is perhaps what Fromm calls "socialism." But Fromm's concept of socialism is wanting, to say the least. In his essay "Humanist Socialism," Fromm argued for a political program through the SP-SDF (Socialist Party–Social Democratic Foundation), and he enumerated a political program involving foreign policy, economic aid, social security, and many other mainly economic policy measures.[18] Fromm insists that socialism must be radical and that capitalism is hostile to humanism, but his program and politics tended to favor professional political-economic analysis coupled with party and policy recommendations. He generally avoided serious consideration of social movements (aside from a somewhat fleeting appreciation for spontaneity), creative acts of subversion, and art; he appeared totally uninterested in revolution. In this way, Fromm's old friend Herbert Marcuse kept his finger better on the pulse of a contentious politics from below, keeping closer ties to radical social movements and new creative forms of rebellion.

That said, I am not sure that anyone—Marcuse included—had a better understanding of capitalist insanity than Fromm. The commodification of the human person in capitalist society is an idea going back to Marx,

---

18. See Fromm's essay "Humanist Socialism" in his *On Disobedience: Why Freedom Means Saying "NO" to Power* (New York: HarperCollins, 2010), 67–91.

but not until Fromm did we get a real analysis of how commodification functions at the level of human psychology, particularly with regard to self-understanding and identity.

> If things could speak, a typewriter would answer the question "Who are you?" by saying "I am a typewriter," and an automobile, by saying "I am an automobile," or more specifically by saying "I am a Ford," or "a Buick," or "a Cadillac." If you ask a man "Who are you?," he answers "I am a manufacturer," "I am a clerk," "I am a doctor"— or "I am a married man," "I am the father of two kids," and his answer has pretty much the same meaning as that of the speaking *thing* would have.... *Things* have no self and men who have become things can have no self.[19]

When people come to identify themselves by saying *what* they are and *what* they do, they lose sight of the often important difference between *what* one is and *who* one is. It is true that some small number of human beings feel so perfectly embodied by being a doctor or a musician or a professor that there is scarcely any reduction or misnomer in saying that they are a doctor, musician, or professor. However, most people in capitalist societies end up doing something every day for most of their lives that *does not* embody and reflect their aspirational or actual being-in-the-world. We all know that many service-sector workers would sooner say they are musicians than waiters, but such an identity may be rejected by those who only want to know what one is paid to do. Moreover, while we may accept some identifications not tied to paid employment, like "father of two kids," such an identification raises the question of whether the father was anything at all prior to the first child's birth. Did his own becoming commence on the child's birthdate? Who is he when the children are old enough to have no need for his fathering?

I would probably answer the question by saying that I am an author and a philosopher, although being the father of two children is deeply meaningful to me. I am mostly paid to teach, although I would likely consider "teacher" a secondary identification. In contrast, I am scarcely paid anything at all for my writing. Either I am a terrible writer or capitalism has no way to "value" radical theory. By now you will have made up your mind on the question of whether I write well, but since I am the one speaking, I will go with the latter explanation (especially since the radical

---

19. Fromm, *Sane Society*, 142–43.

theorists you like better than me are also scarcely paid for *their* writing). But it is easy to see that I would not like my sons to answer the question by saying: "I am Richard Gilman-Opalsky's son." "No," I would tell them, "even though you *are* my son, who you are is not determined that way." Fromm prefers an identity claim that resists commodification best, one that says, "I am not a thing."

One reason we must resist being things, against the capitalist tendency to see us as such, is that we seek relations beyond exchange relations. For Fromm, this is why and where love matters most. But thinking is also a casualty. The alienated and commodified person can scarcely think, certainly not critically, deeply, or against the grain. Fromm argues that the alienated man "takes his reality for granted; he wants to eat it, consume it, touch it, manipulate it. He does not even ask what is behind it, why things are as they are, and where they are going. You cannot eat the meaning, you cannot consume the sense, and as far as the future is concerned—*après nous le déluge!*"[20] The brazen selfishness of the demeanor made by capital is, predictably, perfectly suited to capitalist society. Things are as they are, so we may as well accept them, and we can navigate our happiness through consumption. *Après nous, le déluge*: After us, let the flood come and wash away everything else on earth; let chaos reign after we pass, for only we ourselves and our present moment are of concern.

The cruel inconsideration of "après nous, le déluge" was actually not cruel enough to capture the shrinking regard of capitalism. So Marx tweaked the phrase to "après moi, le deluge," which better captures the shrinking of "we" (for the "we" was at least a collective concern) to "me" (the individual alone): "*Après moi le déluge!* is the watchword of every capitalist and of every capitalist nation. Capital therefore takes no account of the health and the length of life of the worker, unless society forces it to do so. Its answer to the outcry about the physical and mental degradation, the premature death, the torture of over-work, is this: Should that pain trouble us, since it increases our pleasure (profit)?"[21] This position, which rests on the logic of capital, is a form of the insanity that we have been discussing. We can see this best today with regard to the ecological crisis. To heed what geologists and ecologists are telling us with the reply "après moi, le déluge" is nothing short of ecological insanity, yet it is an insanity that still reigns. What does love look like in an era of *après moi, le déluge*? There, love appears as an antagonist countercurrent to the existing order.

---

20. Ibid., 171–72.
21. Karl Marx, *Capital: A Critique of Political Economy, Vol. 1*, trans. Ben Fowkes (New York: Penguin Books, 1990), 381.

Indeed, that is what love needs to be, but how can we make this into a concrete theory and praxis? Is it possible to materialize love as a real antagonistic power (which would also make love into a protagonist, though not in the ways of Plato's *Symposium*)?

Another problem with accepting and reproducing the insanity of the society of *après moi, le déluge* is that "the concepts of health and illness are the products of those men who formulate them—hence of the culture in which these men live. Alienated psychiatrists will define mental health in terms of the alienated personality," and thus they will consider as normal and healthy whatever they observe as the normalcy of the alienated person.[22] We might declare the same condition sick, but that is only if we take a critical view of what has been normalized, which we—following Fromm—may deem pathological. How can we know which picture of health and sickness to accept or to challenge? It is not enough to say, as Fromm says, "The alienated person ... cannot be healthy."[23] We cannot count on people to recognize their alienation, and many of the most alienated and selfish people will insist on their sociability and deep concern for others. We cannot tell someone they are insane and expect them to agree.

We should now more properly appreciate the fact that Fromm—more than most of the Marxists of his generation—paid close attention to anarchists. In *The Sane Society*, Fromm writes about Proudhon, Kropotkin, Tolstoy, Landauer, and Bakunin, as well as about Marx, Luxemburg, and others. Fromm asserts the defining contention of classical critical theory in describing these and other radicals of the nineteenth century as follows: "By criticizing their own society they transcended it."[24] We begin to move beyond the existing reality by subjecting it to ruthless criticism. My own work belongs to the field of critical theory and I accept its basic premise to a point, although I also maintain that the limitations of critical theory are greater than its possibilities. This is because our societies absorb and allow our fiercest criticism of them in order to demonstrate their openness; in this way, our criticism is used to substantiate the virtue of the systems it criticizes.

But Fromm takes important lessons from the anarchists, and he both reads and defends Marx as an antistatist toward the end of *The Sane Society*. Fromm reads Marx as only differing from the anarchists in the journey they would take to arrive at the abolition of the state, and here I fully

---

22. Fromm, *Sane Society*, 192.
23. Ibid., 204.
24. Ibid., 233.

concur with Fromm's reading.[25] Marxist-humanism, the position Fromm claims, is not a top-down politics, a fact that is ultimately quite difficult to reconcile with his disinterest in social movements and revolution and with his alignment with the SP-SDF. I suspect that Fromm supported the socialist push against *après moi, le déluge* and for a sane society but felt that the organized politics of a socialist party would be the most promising way to do that in his own day. While I do not agree with this, many today do, a fact that can be seen throughout North America and Western Europe in renewed efforts to transpose a democratic socialist politics into capitalist elections and even into capitalist political parties.

At the end of his book, Fromm paints the most ominous illustration of the major impasse of modern capitalist society:

> In the nineteenth century the problem was that *God is dead*; in the twentieth century the problem is that *man is dead*. In the nineteenth century inhumanity meant cruelty; in the twentieth century it meant schizoid self-alienation. The danger of the past was that men became slaves. The danger of the future is that men may become robots. True enough, robots do not rebel. But given man's nature, robots cannot live and remain sane, they become "Golems," they will destroy their world and themselves because they cannot stand any longer the boredom of a meaningless life.[26]

So, what is the major impasse of the twenty-first century? Maybe it is still too soon to say. If Fromm is right about the sequence from Nietzsche to the middle of the twentieth century, then perhaps today the impasse is that *society is dead*. After all, the slaves could gather for revolts and escape plans, and robots can associate and work together on a program. But slaves and robots could not predict the present violence of new abreactions to boredom, developments such as *hikikomori*, *karoshi*, terrorism, mass murder, and the breaking-point dysfunctionality of human anxiety. The ecological crisis may be less of a crisis than the actual end of the world. Fromm had some faith in the powers of psychology and psychoanalysis to keep us in touch with a humanity that could resist robotification in the twentieth century. Today, however, psychology and psychoanalysis seem—at their best—to help us understand what is happening. More often, they are practices of adjustment and conformity. That psychology and psychoanalysis

---

25. Ibid., 257–58.
26. Ibid., 360.

are mainly adaptive and palliative leads to the new possibility that there may be no more "roads to sanity," to use Fromm's term.[27]

What if the roads to sanity are only traveled when the dead ends of consumption, pathology, and alienation bring us to the point of material destruction? This possibility would map onto the current ecological crisis. Even with all of the evidence in the world, ecological catastrophe remains an abstraction to most anyone who can continue to reproduce their daily lives tomorrow in the same way as yesterday. You may say, "Here are the facts," but in the face of those facts, if the water and lights turn on and people are expected to go to work and shop, they will keep up the old patterns as long as they can. For the sake of life on earth, ecologists hope this is not true, but reason alone does not motivate action. This brings us to a crisis theory according to which only catastrophe drives us down a different road, but we will not—or cannot—go down that road until the current path is obstructed by the certainty of death. This is the dark cloud that hangs over the present ecological insanity and other pathologies of the twenty-first century.

Before moving on to some of the relevant twenty-first-century interventions by Axel Honneth and John Cacioppo, let us consider Fromm's own follow-up, his short 1956 study, *The Art of Loving*. Our exploration of the more extensive 1955 *The Sane Society* lays the groundwork for an engagement with this one. *The Art of Loving* is Fromm's focused effort to single out love as a practice necessary to the restoration of sanity within and against the capitalist world. Here we shall consider whether the act and art of loving gives us an active, hopeful praxis in a world in which God, human health, conventional politics, and psychological roads to sanity have been variously blockaded, murdered, or forsaken in our sick societies. I claim that there are some ideas worth taking from Fromm here, if only in the way that one loots abandoned buildings after the flood. Perhaps that is where we are now in psychological (and maybe ecological) terms—after the flood.

Fromm challenges conventional discourses on love, noting: "Most people see the problem of love primarily as that of *being loved*, rather than that of *loving*, of one's capacity to love. Hence the problem to them is how to be loved, how to be lovable."[28] Fromm's goal is to overturn this proprietary understanding of love. We must stop looking on love as something to acquire and possess, to hold and have like a private property. People

---

27. Ibid., 270.
28. Fromm, *Art of Loving*, 1.

have become accustomed to thinking about everything that they want in terms of exchange and acquisition. But for Fromm, love is an action, not an exchange relation.

Fromm claims that separateness is "the source of all anxiety."[29] This overgeneralization is demonstrably false. We know from current research—and I suspect that much the same was true in the 1950s—that people are able to feel the worst depths of the most debilitating forms of anxiety while in close relationships with others (some such research will be consulted in this chapter). However, Fromm's overly general view of human anxiety does not negate his insight into the importance of being-with-others as a way to contextualize, mitigate, and combat anxiety. Another person, a friend acting out of genuine love and concern for you, can help you to confront your anxieties, even if not in all cases. This qualification is important because I shall argue that love is one power among others, that love is not omnipotent, and that it cannot address many of our most pressing problems, no matter how well it is defined and practiced. Love cannot cure all anxiety; love cannot save a sick partner from dying from cancer. Sometimes, the very practice of love generates anxiety and other troubling disruptions.

Contrary to this view of mine, Fromm asserts a sweeping, life-giving power: "The desire for interpersonal fusion is the most powerful striving in man. It is the most fundamental passion, it is the force which keeps the human race together, the clan, the family, society. The failure to achieve it means insanity or destruction—self-destruction or destruction of others. Without love, humanity could not exist for a day."[30] We have to get off the bus here. Yes, we are social beings who are deprived and made sick by isolation from others, by a lack of human solidarity and relationality (alienation from *species-being*). But this striving desire for interpersonal fusion that Fromm speaks of is often absent or weak in families, clans, and societies that *do keep together*, that even survive and reproduce in perpetuity. Sick societies do not go quickly to their deaths, and their sickness often becomes a functional insanity. Human beings often go on living without love, and while we can agree that the absence of love is a serious problem, there is no reason to think that we will embrace loving as a means to make ourselves healthy. Some even paradoxically turn away from love: the possibility of loving *causes* their anxiety because they have become accustomed to living without love. This could be likened

---

29. Ibid., 8.
30. Ibid., 17.

to people stressed out on vacations because they no longer know how to relax, because the break from work induces anxiety. We must break with Fromm on all sweeping generalizations about the power of love.

But we must *not* break with Fromm in his theorization of love as an action. "Love is an activity, not a passive affect; it is a 'standing in,' not a 'falling for.' In the most general way, the active character of love can be described by stating that love is primarily *giving*, not receiving."[31] So then, love is not something that happens to you but something you do, and when you stop actively loving, love stops too. Love demands action and activation, and a human who is capable of love is not always in the process of loving.

The notion of *giving* is central to breaking the logic of *exchange*. Many times, people give to others in the hopes that they will get something in exchange for the giving, even if that return is not requested or required. People often announce their charitable giving because they want to get something (even if just some recognition of their good morality) in exchange for their giving. Such giving is not maligned by Fromm. If one gives a generous gift to a noble cause and wants to be known for doing so, the recipient may be more than happy to let it be known and would be no less well-off for the public nature of the gift (unless the giver was a bad association). But giving is only an active form of love whenever there is no expectation for something else in exchange.

From this point of view, we can see that in relationships there is often an *appearance* of love in everything that the one partner does for the other partner. Yet if the giver feels crossed for not getting an equal exchange in return, then the love of the giver becomes suspect. Nobody should monitor or measure this from the outside. And nobody can. There are times when a person does not track the giving and getting and gives actively out of a genuine love, refusing to keep tabs on gifts given or received. In the example of young children, a loving parent gives while knowing full well that expecting an equal exchange from the child would be inappropriate to the relationship. I do not tell my young sons that they can only eat if they clean their rooms; I prepare and give them food no matter what they do or do not do.

Fromm takes the opportunity in *The Art of Loving* to develop his theory of love further, going beyond his formulations in *The Sane Society*. He specifies four basic features that are present and observable in all forms of love: (1) care, (2) responsibility, (3) respect, and (4) knowledge.

---

31. Ibid., 21.

Wherever there is love there is care, by which Fromm means *"the active concern for the life and the growth of that which we love."*[32] And, wherever there is love there must also be responsibility, by which Fromm means a voluntary—not compulsory—sense of duty, to be ready to respond to the needs of another because one feels that such responsiveness is part of one's responsibility. Wherever there is love, there is also respect, by which Fromm means that we strive to see the other as the other is now and as the other wants to become, to look closely at the other person and want to see them become what they want to be or ought to be. This is perhaps a peculiar notion of respect; we tend to think of respect as the feeling (accompanied with some awe) that one has for a person who is already accomplished. But Fromm's concept of respect can be applied at the earliest stages of becoming, well before the other person's journey leads to accomplishments. That is to say, I can respect my young children by looking at who they are, at how they are different from each other and from me, and I should want to support their becoming. That would be a form of respect that my children should not have to "earn." Finally, there is no love without knowledge, by which Fromm means understanding coupled with and even motivated by concern, so that it is never enough to understand a problem without real concern for its consequences. With immigration, for example, insufficient love means bad knowledge, which can be seen wherever we find efforts to stop or manage immigration without equal or greater efforts at understanding the real motivations of migrants, without real concern for their well-being.

Fromm's work here helps us to develop a theory of love that still holds today. If Fromm's theory of love were well read and actively pursued in life, it would likely improve things in various ways for real people in the world. So I recommend reading Fromm to anyone interested in the subject of love.

But Fromm's theory of love is also insufficiently variegated and far too categorical in normative terms. The core of his argument is something like this: love is good, capitalism is bad, all of which becomes perfectly clear from a humanist perspective informed by psychoanalysis. However, humanism, psychoanalysis, and socialism are not enough to clarify these points, and practices of love do not only unify people—they can also divide. Politics, and especially projects aiming for the radical transformation of the world, still depend on certain hatreds and benefit from a concept of the enemy. Love is a real power, yes, but maybe it is a minor power

---

32. Ibid., 25.

in the grand scheme of things, and racist violence deserves our hatred and contempt, even if that *hatred comes from love* (such a notion as this is alien to Fromm). For a concept of the enemy, we do not need to resort to vilification in the way that governments, white supremacists, and anti-communists are so well-practiced in doing. No, the fact is that there are real enemies in this world, and they are not only people but logics. We will have fully explored and argued these points by the end of this book.

In order to move toward a practice or politics of love, Fromm maintains self-love as a prerequisite. That you cannot love another until you love yourself has become a familiar cliché. However, it is more important to Fromm that we understand that self-love and selfishness are incommensurate and opposite. Fromm claims: *"It is true that selfish persons are incapable of loving others, but they are not capable of loving themselves either."*[33] A person could be very selfish indeed while in no way adequately caring for themselves, being completely unresponsive to their own real needs or relatively devoid of self-knowledge. It is likely for this reason that Fromm maintains his faith in psychoanalysis. While he sharply disagrees with Freud on the question of love, he follows Freud's commitment "to the process of psychoanalytic therapy, the ever deepening experience of oneself."[34] But what is most difficult to imagine is the therapeutic movement occurring at a social level. The therapeutic movement at a social level is, for me, something like a revolt, an idea I have developed elsewhere following Julia Kristeva's psychoanalytic theory of revolt.[35] But Fromm does not see revolt in this way. For Fromm, it would seem that we can only intervene at the social level by way of socialist-humanist politics or a popular text, perhaps he hoped by way of one of his books.

To Fromm's great credit, he never abandons his sustained critique of capitalism as antithetical to love. It is perhaps for that reason that the present study could be taken as a contemporary and critical reworking of Fromm's basic theory. Capitalism is the dedicated subject of the third part of *The Art of Loving*, which is titled "Love and Its Disintegration in Contemporary Western Society." There, Fromm discusses how capitalism shapes human values, shifting us toward *things* and *having* as opposed to *people* and *being*. Capitalism strives for a society full of people wanting

---

33. Ibid., 56.

34. Ibid., 73.

35. For a dedicated book-length study of the social, cognitive, emotional, and healthy dimensions of riot, revolt, and other social upheaval, see Richard Gilman-Opalsky, *Specters of Revolt: On the Intellect of Insurrection and Philosophy from Below* (London: Repeater Books, 2016).

things, less concerned with being than with having, and it has largely achieved this acculturation. "Modern man is alienated from himself, from his fellow men, and from nature. He has been transformed into a commodity, experiences his life forces as an investment which must bring him the maximum profit obtainable under existing market conditions."[36] In this, Fromm is foreshadowing what would be more fully developed in his major work, *To Have or to Be?*, from the 1970s.[37]

This leads us to the important concept of "pseudo-love," which enables Fromm to discuss forms of human feeling and desire that are commonly mistaken for love. For example, he discusses "idolatrous love" and "sentimental love," among other misnomers.[38] And he addresses the "frequent error" of thinking that love means the total absence of conflict.[39] When two people honestly communicate about real problems or issues between them, in their lives and relationship or in the world, this conversation could lead to severe disagreement, hurt feelings, real conflict. This is the way that Fromm includes conflict in his theory of love as a practice. When he thinks about conflict in or from love, he thinks mainly about interpersonal conflicts that emerge from difficult but important, healthy conversations. Here again, we see the importance of psychoanalysis to Fromm's theory, for it enables him to identify healthy conflict at microsocial and micropolitical levels.

At this point in our analysis certain lines of divergence must be clarified. I break with Fromm in two important ways: First, love is not a great omnipotence that can save and heal us from capitalist disfiguration. I agree with Fromm that love is necessarily anticapitalist. Fromm is right when he says, "The *principle* underlying capitalistic society and the *principle* of love are incompatible."[40] Love is an oppositional organization of life and human relations that provides a relative—and often fleeting—refuge from capitalism. Love as a lived practice provides real experience with a rival (and I would say communist) logic of life. But life itself does not depend on love, and our acts of love cannot overpower the much larger and ubiquitous capitalist reality. Inasmuch as Fromm makes love appear omnipotent, he is wrong, and I will show it. Second, psychoanalysis is not emancipatory in the ways Fromm had hoped. Fromm's general disregard for social upheaval, revolts, and riots—and even for the possibility of

---

36. Fromm, *Art of Loving*, 79–80.
37. See Erich Fromm, *To Have or To Be?* (London: Bloomsbury, 2013).
38. Fromm, *Art of Loving*, 92–93.
39. Ibid., 95.
40. Ibid., 121.

revolution and its insurrectionary nodal points—does not go away in his post-1968 writings. Rather, he retains a consistent interest in the disobedient person in the form of a critic or actor who may or may not align with a political party or social movement. In fact, Fromm's work reliably makes social analysis with an individualist appeal. That is, he astutely analyzes social, economic, cultural, political, and psychological problems, yet calls on us to adopt a better interpersonal comportment in our individual lives. The problems that Fromm diagnoses so well are too pervasive throughout the social body to be adequately addressed by way of analysis and individual action.

These departures do not mean that Fromm is wrong but rather (1) that he overdetermines and generalizes from categorical thinking and (2) that his theory of practice (that is, praxis) is held hostage to the clinical orientations of psychoanalysis. The former leads to *descriptive* problems, while the latter leads to *prescriptive* ones.

I want to help Fromm's theory overcome its descriptive and prescriptive limitations, and I also want to bring his theory to bear on a twenty-first-century reality. Fromm always understood the importance of connecting his work to the political, even if he could not quite manage to move from clinical thinking to political thinking. But we do want to build on his critique of capitalist society, which remains helpful. In Fromm's work, the critique of capitalism is grounded in ethical argument, which is common to Marxist-humanism. "'I give you as much as you give me,' in material goods as well as in love, is the prevalent ethical maxim in capitalist society."[41] The so-called ethical maxim of capitalist society is shown to be immoral from the point of view of Fromm's humanism, so his argument *for love* ends up as a moral as well as a political imperative.

In the end, Fromm recognizes the precarious and marginalized position of love in a capitalist society, and his rather considerable optimism (especially for a critical theorist of his generation) is eventually kept in check.

> Even if one recognizes the principle of capitalism as being incompatible with the principle of love, one must admit that "capitalism" is in itself a complex and constantly changing structure which still permits of a good deal of non-conformity and of personal latitude.... People capable of love, under the present system, are necessarily the exceptions; love is by necessity a marginal phenomenon in present-day

41. Ibid., 119.

Western society.... Those who are seriously concerned with love as the only rational answer to the problem of human existence must, then, arrive at the conclusion that important and radical changes in our social structure are necessary, if love is to become a social and not a highly individualistic, marginal phenomenon.[42]

This conclusion to Fromm's famous study is fascinating and clearly anticipates certain problems. People could try harder to betray the expectations and values of capitalist society. It is not that capitalism fully restricts the individual person's freedom to think critically about the normative orientations of their society. Perhaps critical theory, with the help of psychoanalysis, could help people take advantage of their freedom, but Fromm worries that we have lost the instinct and appetite for radical criticism. To really move love out of the margins and to remake society as a loving body—*to bring real sociality back from the dead*—we would need a structural transformation. Marxists have usually meant by radical structural change something like revolution. But not Fromm. For him, *movement* is ultimately analytical and critical: "To analyze the nature of love is to discover its general absence today and to criticize the social conditions which are responsible for this absence."[43]

It is striking to behold how much Fromm got right in the 1950s that remains useful if not necessary to a deep understanding the world today. Fromm's body of work is a treasure trove of Freudian-Marxist analysis of life in the Western world (Western Europe and the United States) in the twentieth century, a century that Marx did not live to see. But we are nonetheless left with diagnostic and practical questions that require us to surpass Fromm's theories. It is not only technology that has changed things since Fromm. We now know that human beings can live indefinitely into the future in a state of severe, intergenerational, and damaging sickness. The insanity that Fromm diagnosed was not a terminal condition, or at least it has not yet been. There is not only growing alienation and anxiety, but catastrophic global poverty, increasing inequality, and ecological crises on the near horizon; so when I say "not yet terminal," I mean inasmuch as we have managed the relative avoidance of present and looming insecurities.

Despite his focus on action, I can find no politics or praxis in Fromm that can help us today. Fromm's major contribution was diagnostic,

---

42. Ibid., 121–22.
43. Ibid., 123.

a still-useful diagnosis that moves us beyond the limitations of earlier Marxisms that were less attentive to human feeling and psychology. But Fromm's theory of love cannot, without critical assistance, help us to understand the therapeutic movements of May–June 1968, uprisings against bureaucratic capitalism throughout Eastern and Western Europe in the 1970s and 1980s, the Zapatista rebellion of the 1990s, the anti-globalization movements at the turn to the twenty-first century, revolts in France and London, the Arab Spring, Occupy Wall Street, Black Lives Matter, new protest movements in Hong Kong, and many other recent and ongoing upheavals. We need a theory of love capable of speaking to such phenomena as these, where real people rise up to address their own unhappiness.

Does contemporary critical theory do better to move beyond the outstripped socialism of the Cold War era and the clinical-analytical orientation of psychoanalytic thinking? To help assess the present position of critical theory on these questions, I turn to Axel Honneth. In particular, I look at Honneth's theory of recognition and defense of sociality against capitalist tendencies of total individuation, which are well articulated in *The I in We* (2014). There, he explores the psychoanalytic and social dimensions of individuation, self-realization, group identity, recognition, and self-confidence. However, it is only in *The Idea of Socialism* (2017) that Honneth's theory of recognition clearly appears as the core content of his twenty-first-century socialist theory. There he situates socialism as a transformative politics liberated from the context of industrial capitalism and the economic conditions of the nineteenth century. Socialism, according to Honneth, must be about new forms of life, new practices of intersubjectivity and relationality from within the family to the broader community of citizens. Thus, Honneth claims that socialism is and must be understood as a philosophy and politics focused on becoming social in the fullest sense of the term. That is, socialism is *becoming-social* in an increasingly alienated and asocial world. Unfortunately, making the connection between Honneth's thinking and the theory of love will take some effort because love has not been central to critical theory since Fromm.

But Honneth is at least thinking about love as an important if marginal issue related to his theories of recognition and socialism: "In my view, during the last two centuries, new needs have constantly been asserted by invoking the normative meaning of 'love'—the well-being of the child, the wife's need for autonomy, and so on. These needs have gradually led to a deepening of reciprocal care and affection; the same dynamic can be observed in the relations of recognition obtaining in modern law, where legal proceedings pertaining to previously neglected life-situations have brought about an unambiguous increase in legal equality."[44] Here Honneth recognizes social, political, and legal progress as partly a result of arguments or demands about love. For example, we have seen more attention to the needs of young children and greater gender equality, and many such advances have been codified in laws about equality as well as in cultural attitudes. Honneth recognizes these advances as real improvements in the lives of real people, and attributes their realization to two hundred years of argumentation about what the love of others should demand in practice. Indeed, there is more light and optimism in Honneth's critical theory (and in the critical theory of other contemporaries such as Jürgen Habermas and Nancy Fraser) when we jump fifty years forward from Fromm.[45] We have to remember, of course, that the first critical theorists were thinking and writing in the midst and wake of the ominous terrors of totalitarianism.

But this does not mean that contemporary critical theory has become uncritical of existing society. According to Honneth, "the processes of instrumentalization, standardization and fictionalization have turned the individualism of self-realization, which has been gradually developing over the last half-century, into an emotionally barren system of demands within which individuals today seem more likely to suffer than to prosper."[46] So though there have been positive shifts in normative valuations pertaining to gender and racial equality, and legal advances that reflect those norms, people are still suffering the new maladies of a differently "insane" society. Honneth speaks about new forms of "social suffering" that are actually only several decades old, which are "without precedent in the history of capitalist societies. They are much less accessible to empirical observation because they exist in the sphere of psychological illness, and thus there are only clinical indicators available to detect them."[47] The bad news is that while the problems are largely invisible, the methods available for their detection and treatment are incapable of working well at the social

---

44. Axel Honneth, *The I in We: Studies in the Theory of Recognition*, trans. Joseph Ganahl (Cambridge: Polity, 2014), 89.

45. This is especially true as regards Habermas's optimism for the European Union. See, for example, Jürgen Habermas, *The Postnational Constellation: Political Essays*, trans. Max Pensky (Cambridge, MA: MIT Press, 2001). There, Habermas's cosmopolitan faith rivals even Kant's, and his hope for what the EU may become is both staggering and unconvincing.

46. Honneth, *I in We*, 164.

47. Ibid., 165.

level. This was one of the problems identified in Fromm's work, but can Honneth better address the problem by proposing a politics we can take seriously?

Following the research of Alain Ehrenberg's influential book, *The Weariness of the Self: Diagnosing the History of Depression in the Contemporary Age* (2010), Honneth tells us that a "growing number of therapeutic findings, along with the unprecedented trend towards the use of pharmaceutical anti-depressants, indicate that depression-related illnesses are displacing neurosis.... The permanent compulsion to draw on one's own inner life to find the material needed for authentic self-realization demands from subjects a constant form of introspection that at some point has to come up empty."[48] The central problem, Honneth argues, is that we have come to think that the "I" is separate from and often opposed to the "we," and that this juxtaposition of "I" to "we" makes each one of us into our own sole responsibility. The pressure we place on ourselves is so great that we cannot bear it. The pressure on the "I" causes terrible anxiety and pathology, coupled with exhaustion, despair, and widespread depression. Honneth argues that we need to work through and ultimately abolish dichotomous thinking about the "I" and the "we," and work collectively to find the "I" in the "we." If we could overcome this false dichotomy and realize that human individuality is produced by and within a social collectivity, then this would dissolve oppositional juxtapositions between each of us and the rest of us. For Honneth, the "I" is not really possible—*or psychologically bearable*—without the "we."

We immediately return to the predicament of *après moi, le deluge*. But today, the pathology of *après moi, le deluge* may be reaching its breaking point. Such a narrowly self-interested disposition was perhaps functional within the context of hyperindividualistic competition where one would be hobbled and disadvantaged by any communist regard for other people. Tending to the concerns of others could slow you down or hold you back and keep you from winning. But today we are seeing some of the new maladies of the isolation of the "I" from the "we." The disposition of *après moi, le deluge* has shifted so much of the burden of each life onto each individual, and the individuals—already as young adults—are buckling under the pressure. This is evidenced in Ehrenberg's and Honneth's research, and is also taken up in other ways by Julia Kristeva, Bernard Stiegler, and Franco Berardi, among others. If it could be said that capitalism previously drove us to the functional insanity of *après moi, le deluge*, as Fromm

---

48. Ibid., 165–66.

contended, then perhaps today we should say that *après moi, le deluge* has finally become dysfunctional.

Honneth discusses that "with the romantic idea of love a utopian vanishing point emerged that allowed members of society increasingly subject to economic pressures to preserve the vision of an emotional transcendence of day-to-day instrumentalism."[49] Thus, anxious and depressed people who feel helpless and broken, people who are struggling economically, often feel that the only escape from the world can be found in romantic love. But romantic love is no real solution to any social or political problem, and in fact this formulation makes love less a practice against the ills of the world than a way to flee the world, to escape it. For many people, there is a real hope that the ills of life can be overcome in the private spaces of romantic love, where we live after work or school, or on the weekends. Honneth calls this a form of "romantic individualism" that becomes an ideology.[50] It is a problematic ideology for many reasons, not the least of which is that the love relationship or family is subjected to the same economic pressures as the individual. If romantic individualism becomes a part of our worldview, then we come to think wrongly of our homes and love relationships as autonomous from the pressures of capitalist society. In this sense, Fromm's hope for love may have gone in an opposite direction. Instead of love appearing as a counterpower to what he regarded as capitalist insanity, romantic individualist love is subsumed fully into, and rendered compatible with, capitalist society. In romantic love, the couple can and often does say *après moi, le deluge.*

This is where Honneth is most illuminating. He claims that the ideology of opposing love to the world of capitalist exchange relations "was probably always a typical product of bourgeois illusion."[51] Not only does the escapist idea of romantic love never really provide an escape for those suffering socially, economically, and psychologically, but the loving couple also becomes "ever more dependent on consumption."[52] Utopian thinking about romantic love relations is thus a part of bourgeois ideology and ends up endorsing a different set of exchange relations—that is, romantic love relations that are themselves organized and ruled by the capitalist logic they want to escape or break.

It was in the 1980s and 1990s, according to Honneth, that the bourgeois idea of love relations as an alternative or escape came under the

---

49. Ibid., 170.
50. Ibid., 179.
51. Ibid., 186.
52. Ibid.

greatest pressure. In those decades, more families required both partners to go to work, and new demands for flexibility and overwork seized the time that was previously leftover for home life. Also, there was greater mobility in labor, and not only more movement from one job to the next but also movable time, work expected at home, on phones, and ultimately anywhere that a cell phone is charged in hand. There has been a growing expectation over the last thirty years for more "emotional engagement at work," making it "more and more difficult to bring into the private domain that creative virtuosity that is necessary to maintain 'pure' relationships founded on inclination alone."[53] In the light of these developments, the separate and rival space of romantic love has been all the more exposed as the bourgeois illusion that it always was.

In perhaps the most important passage from *The I in We*, Honneth claims that

> the new "spirit" of capitalism, which transfers the entrepreneurial idea of calculative action to subjects' self-relations, penetrates into the capillaries of intimate relationships, so that the model of utility-oriented calculation begins to predominate.... [W]hat rather seems to be emerging as a new model of behaviour is the tendency to calculate the long-term chances of such love relationships according to their compatibility with the future mobility demands of a career path that can only be planned in the short term. If so, this would mean that what now dominates the innermost core of love would be something that has long had a place in consumer practices, but has never overwhelmed the power of feelings: economic rationality. Until now, this was something partners took into account together to make their precarious relationships last, but now they are becoming a tool they apply to evaluate one another as partners.[54]

Honneth's insights here indicate something like a capitalist colonization of love, and that things have gone in the opposite direction from what Fromm would have hoped for in the 1950s. Even if Honneth is not entirely correct—*and I do not think he is*—the problem cannot be easily overcome. To confront the problem of love subordinated to an economic rationality, we have to define love in such a way as to offend the bourgeois ideal of romance. This means that—in the same way that Berardi refused to

---

53. Ibid., 187.
54. Ibid., 188.

surrender the notion of the soul to theology—we cannot allow bourgeois romanticism to claim love.[55] Berardi did not abandon the concept of the soul; he reclaimed it. The same must be done with love.

But Honneth is not entirely correct. The breadth and depth of human feeling has not been fully colonized by an economic rationality, and I do not think that love relations have been totally reconfigured by consumption and capitalist exchange values. The utopianism of romantic individualism has to be abandoned, but there is still evidence in the family, in love, between the mother and the father and the child, between brothers and sisters, and between friends, of an alter-relationality that is not ruled by economic rationality. Saying that Honneth is not wholly correct only means that he (and we) should avoid overdetermining the negativity of his critical insights. Wherever love relations are not colonized and determined by the privatizing logic of capital, what love *shows us, what it reveals in practice*, is a logic of life that we can and must expand. Even if *après moi, le deluge* is only rolled back to the formulation *après nous, le deluge*, we have to appreciate the retrieval of a "we" from the "I." There is still enough experience of love in this world to show us a rival model of being-in-the-world.

Honneth observes that "there is something coincidental about the cooperation between Critical Theory and psychoanalysis, envisaged by Horkheimer and brought about by Fromm. At the time there was a broad current of attempts to integrate Marxism and psychoanalysis, with the main purpose of supplementing the social-theoretical core of historical materialism with a psychological theory that could explain the absence of revolutionary uprising."[56] This only appears as coincidental today because the fusion of Marxism and psychoanalysis has departed from its original motivations over the question of revolution. I would say that for Fromm, shortly after Horkheimer, critical theory had already begun to run away from the question of revolution. Fromm wanted to explain obedience, he wanted to explain conformity to dangerous ideas and practices, but psychoanalysis was not for him a pathway to the revitalization of revolutionary sensibilities. Revolution was more dissuasive to Fromm and Horkheimer than, say, to Marcuse. But Marcuse remained strangely invested in "Soviet communism," whereas Fromm was much more sympathetic to Raya Dunayevskaya's characterization of the Soviet Union as

---

55. See Franco "Bifo" Berardi, *The Soul and Work: From Alienation to Autonomy*, trans. Francesca Cadel and Giuseppina Mecchia (Los Angeles: Semiotext(e), 2009).

56. Honneth, *I in We*, 193–94.

bureaucratic state capitalism.[57] But unlike most of the critical theorists, Dunayevskaya's disaffection over developments in Russia did not lead her away from revolution (she was among the most unwavering revolutionists of the Marxists of her generation).

However one wants to read this philosophical and political history, the fact is that, like Fromm, Honneth is ultimately not interested in revolution. For Honneth, the present purposes of psychoanalysis should be to understand identification and recognition. In other words, Honneth is interested in how each person develops her sense of self, her individual identity—in both sociological and psychological terms—and in how well she is recognized by others. Psychoanalysis can help us to substantiate the necessary defense of sociality and group identity and, at the same time, to cultivate and keep the "I" fully and properly recognized within the "we." Psychoanalysis can therefore help us destroy the false and fatal opposition of each person to everyone else.

Honneth argues against the historical tendency to vilify groups as regressive spaces of conformity (i.e., group thinking) where human individuality goes to die. He laments that even "psychoanalysis is dominated by a negative image of the group," a fact that is likely connected to the clinical tendency to attend to the isolated individual and her personal history alone.[58] But according to Honneth, the development of the human individual's personality and being-in-the-world only takes place within social groups. That the formation of the "I" is dialectically developed in a web of intersubjective relations is key, for example, to the development of a young child's personality, to the child's relationship to himself or herself. The approval, encouragement, and affirmation of those around young children are essential to their becoming.

Key to these processes of becoming are respect and recognition. "Children develop initial, germinating forms of self-respect by experiencing themselves at play as an interaction partner whose judgment is regarded as valuable or reliable. Of course, what also plays a role in this process is the experience of being increasingly respected by other members of the family as a subject whose beliefs are no longer wholly irrelevant

---

57. For documentation and discussion of Marcuse's analysis of the Soviet Union, and the relation of that position to criticisms made by Fromm and Dunayevskaya, I recommend two books: Herbert Marcuse, *Soviet Marxism: A Critical Analysis* (New York: Columbia University Press, 1958); and Kevin B. Anderson and Russell Rockwell, eds., *The Dunayevskaya-Marcuse-Fromm Correspondence, 1954–1978: Dialogues on Hegel, Marx, and Critical Theory* (Lanham, MD: Lexington Books, 2012).

58. Honneth, *I in We*, 202.

for common decision-making."[59] For these reasons, it is necessary to say that the "I" forms within a "we," and any pretension about the opposition of individual and collective is demonstrably false. The child's individual identity grows only in the context of some "we," some of which can cause an unhealthy development of the "I," especially where there is nonrecognition, misrecognition, or various other forms of neglect and abuse.

Individuals from childhood to death "have a very normal and even natural need to be recognized as members in social groups in which they can receive constant affirmation of their needs, judgment and various skills in direct interaction with others.... In order to maintain and perhaps even strengthen their self-confidence, subjects need to receive constant reliable affection, which for the most part they encounter in relationships of friendship and love."[60] That human sociality is not only normal but natural is a recurring theme for us, but if being-with-others is necessitated by human nature, and if friendship and love are the most common modes of healthy interaction and affection, then Honneth is locating love and friendship on the stage of universal aspiration. Can we say that love is a universal human aspiration? Love and friendship may well be as close as we get to identifying universal human aspirations. And if these aspirations are also irreducibly antagonistic to capitalism, what would that say about human nature and capital? Yes, human beings live and love within capitalist societies, but perhaps love and friendship are tendencies *against capital*, tendencies that mitigate the worst elements of life in our societies. If love is a near-universal human aspiration, and it is also irreducibly communist, then can we not speak of the universality of the communism of love?

Honneth can raise this question but cannot answer it. He insists that discrete experiences with love are never enough to generate a lifetime of self-confidence. What matters far more than a single experience is an *ongoing* experience of love, friendship, respect, and recognition. When those things go away or pause for too long, it does not matter that one once had a friend or once experienced love. After a while without respect or recognition, starved of love, a person's self-confidence erodes, and he or she longs ever more pressingly for affirmation and human solidarity. We are, in this sense, very vulnerable beings. "As a response to this vulnerability, the desire for concrete approval and affirmation grows. In the need to directly experience the esteem of one's peers lies *one*, if not *the*, central

---

59. Ibid., 205.
60. Ibid., 206.

motive behind group formation today."[61] Thus, according to Honneth, we form groups (the "we") not only to make ourselves but to take care of ourselves (the "I"), and so we must criticize and reject *all* valuations within capitalist society that valorize the heroic and wholly "free" individual who stands alone with bravery, fights alone, and wins. This is indeed the image of heroism central to capitalist mythology, yet it is fatally unhealthy to human beings in both psychological and social terms. According to Honneth, the catastrophic unsustainability of this "I" has become increasingly clear.

Honneth knows that he is at the same time challenging tendencies in critical theory, not only those that were prevalent in Fromm but also those in Adorno and Horkheimer, all of whom worried about (in the context of Nazi Germany) how groups could follow fatal and murderous pathologies of obedience. The concept of the group-as-herd traveled well from Nietzsche to critical theory in German philosophy, and seemed confirmed in the wake of World War II as producing sameness and predictable behavior. The worry was about the preparatory manipulation of groups not only for fascism, but also for capitalist consumption. While critical theory has tended to focus on the dark side of groups, Honneth insists that "even after maturity, we are dependent on forms of social recognition imbued with direct encouragement and affirmation."[62] We can remain concerned about things like conformity, obedience, standardization of taste, loss of individuality, and the other things that occupied the minds of early critical theorists, but such problems are not intrinsic to sociality. As Honneth argues, groups can do many things, some good and some bad, and groups of people do many essential things for individual people throughout each and every lifetime.

Consider the powerful example Honneth provides in the last chapter of *The I in We*, where he takes up a discussion about the human need for consolation after the death of a loved one. He notes the tendency to accept strange behaviors such as talking to tombstones or maintaining the bedroom of a deceased family member, and he considers participation and acceptance of such seemingly odd rituals as part of our sociality. Even those who do not believe in God or the human soul may speak to a tombstone or a deceased loved one. This is allowed within a supportive sociality because what we want from others is respect and recognition of the difficult effort needed to grapple with and survive the most trying events of a human life. Allowing space for shared rituals and collective

---

61. Ibid., 207.
62. Ibid., 214.

mourning—withholding judgment for otherwise irrational behavior—is, according to Honneth, just one of many ways we relate to other people in order to bear the world as individual persons. The group is necessary not only in the formative and developmental stages from birth to adulthood, but also in crises at the end of a human life.

When Honneth writes about these matters, it is not always clear that he does so as a socialist. Indeed, Honneth's own Marxism often appears irrelevant to his overarching arguments, and it can be easily avoided by readers who would rather take Honneth's insights without their Marxist content or grounding. Honneth has written scores of essays and delivered countless lectures in which a discussion about capitalism and Marxism would indeed seem quite superfluous. That Honneth's work is connected to and consistent with his Marxism was made most clear in his 2017 book, *The Idea of Socialism: Towards a Renewal*. Here the necessary, natural, and healthy sociality discussed in *The I in We* appears as the basic substance and commitment of socialism.

Honneth explains that in the second half of the eighteenth century, "the polemical expression 'socialistae' (a neologism derived from the Latin 'socialis') referred to a tendency in the works of Grotius and Pufendorf, who were accused of claiming that the legal order of society should be founded on the human need for 'sociality' rather than divine revelation."[63] So when Honneth retrieves the earlier idea from the century before Marx, he finds that socialism is basically the concept of society grounded in and committed to the "we." The prefigurative notion of socialism centers on the healthy development of human association, of a primary and foundational mode of being-together. The early socialist thinkers used the concepts of association, cooperation, and community to say what they meant, what they wanted, and their basic formulation—it turns out—is much like what Honneth calls for in *The I in We*. In *The Idea of Socialism*, however, he more explicitly claims that the basic socialist principle is that "the self-fulfillment of each must depend on the self-fulfillment of the other."[64] Honneth also sums up the challenge of capitalism to our healthy sociality: "Because market participants encounter each other as subjects interested in their own private advantage, they are incapable of feeling sympathy for each other and offering each other the support required by social relationships of fraternity or solidarity."[65]

---

63. Axel Honneth, *The Idea of Socialism: Towards a Renewal*, trans. Joseph Ganahl (Cambridge: Polity, 2017), 6.

64. Ibid., 13.

65. Ibid., 16–17.

This way of thinking about socialism is not simply a reflection of Honneth's theory of recognition. It is intended as a real and practical path to a renewal of socialism in the world. The problem dating from Karl Marx to the present, according to Honneth, is that socialism has been too rigidly tied to the Industrial Revolution, too tied to the idea of the revolutionary proletariat. That way of thinking about socialism has held a good idea hostage in ways that may ultimately kill it. For Honneth, the time has come to confront the fact that Marxian class analysis, the notion of a revolutionary subject position, and modes of production that determine most everything are ideas that fail to capture the realities of the twenty-first century. Imagine if, when thinking of socialism and capitalism, one thought mainly of muscular male workers in factories, of workers on labor strikes, or about the imagery of Charlie Chaplin's *Modern Times*. If this is the image of socialism, then socialists are hopelessly out of touch. Too many socialists think about such a socialism from the past. A socialism for the industrial-male proletariat should not have survived the twentieth century, let alone made it into the twenty-first century. Honneth points out that our capitalist societies are scarcely anything like the Manchester capitalism of the nineteenth century. In a way somewhat similar to Alain Badiou's discussion of communism in *The Communist Hypothesis* (2010), Honneth urges us to think of socialism as a form of historical experimentalism, of people playing with new forms of relationality, new forms of life.

To keep the idea of socialism alive and relevant to the present century, Honneth contends that we need to liberate socialism from its conceptual anchoring to the economic reality of the industrial era. We need to free the idea of socialism from the political imagination encompassing the late eighteenth century to the late nineteenth century. Honneth declares the reasons the early socialists were so fixated on a narrow economistic view (although I am not convinced that they were) to be a mystery, observing that "the founders of the socialist movement located the cause of what they called 'private egotism' solely in the behavioral constraints of the market economy. They therefore believed they must direct all their political efforts toward overcoming this economic order."[66] But what if we were to think about socialism as a project equally concerned with the social order, with *how* we relate to one another?

If we had a more sociological and less economistic idea of socialism, we would have been better equipped to carry the idea of socialism forward into the postindustrial (or post-Fordist) political imagination. Honneth is

---

66. Ibid., 76.

right to remind us of the *status*—both ideological and actual—of socialism in the world of politics today. The idea of socialism, notwithstanding the recent burst of interest in democratic socialism in several locations, largely appears outflanked by the privatizing dominance of neoliberal capital, despite the fact that human loneliness and anxiety—as well as economic measures like inequality—are everywhere on the rise. That being said, Honneth pays surprisingly scarce attention to the fate of the idea of socialism in the ideological disputes of the Cold War, where the word and concept "socialism" was wielded far more effectively by capitalists and anticommunists than by socialist theorists or revolutionaries. I would argue that the cumulative effect of state capitalist regimes calling themselves "socialist," and in turn being called "socialist" by their enemies, throughout the whole of the short twentieth century (1914–1991) had a significant destructive effect on the socialist idea.

How is any of this connected to love? In a rare and striking moment, Honneth makes an important yet undeveloped point about love and socialism: "Even though they obviously based their whole concept of social freedom in the economic sphere on the model of love, early socialists made no effort to apply this concept to the project of emancipating women from the constraints of marriage and the family. This, however, would have been the right path, for all relationships of love and affection since the beginning of modernity can be understood as relations founded on the normative idea that those involved mutually supplement and enable each other to realize themselves."[67] Quite obviously, Honneth is unaware of the life and work of Alexandra Kollontai, or he is—like so many others—insufficiently attentive to it. Worse, Honneth mistakenly lays the blame of the lack of attention to women, marriage, and the family at the feet of the socialists, who, even going back to Marx himself, were actually ahead of the curve on such matters.

But let us not lose the point for the problems. The most important aspect of this formulation is that Honneth describes the socialist idea as modeled on love, and he draws comparisons between love relations and the kinds of relations idealized by socialists. Also, as he does several times throughout this book, Honneth aligns his own theory of recognition, of self-realization of each one within the group, with *both* love and socialism. The central aim of all three—Honneth's theory, socialism, and love—is to construct a world of mutually supplementary relations, to construct a world of healthy spaces for human cooperation, recognition, and

---

67. Ibid., 84.

flourishing, and not of hostile competition and insecurity. For example, Honneth states: "For the sphere of love, marriage, and the family, the realization of social freedom means realizing new forms of relationships in which the mutual care promised by these relationships is only possible if the members involved can freely articulate their actual needs and interests with the aid of others."[68] This passage, meant to characterize the sphere of love, is at the same time a perfect characterization of the central argument in *The I in We*, and of the socialist idea.

While one must be at least a little suspicious when an author makes all of the good ideas appear to support his own theory so consistently and without much trouble, I would like to follow Honneth's general direction. Yes, we must renew thinking about socialism as a form of life and not mainly as an economic theory. The communism of love requires us to see more clearly all of the para-economic aspects of capitalism. Honneth thinks that socialism must aim, above all, at making contemporary societies more social. This would *include* economic transformation without specifying economy as the single most defining feature. "Only if all members of society can satisfy the needs they share with all others—physical and emotional intimacy, economic independence and political self-determination—by relying on the sympathy and support of their partners in interaction will our society have become social in the full sense of the term."[69] This would be the highest goal of socialism, of Honneth's theory of recognition and realization, and perhaps of love as well. If we can move toward such a society as this, however difficult and slow that process might be, we could create better conditions of life for a growing number of us as we struggle against the tendencies of the societies diagnosed by Fromm and Honneth. For both Fromm and Honneth, this is what socialism is for—creating a healthy sociality that can defend itself against capitalist disfiguration and destruction.

Aside from my relatively minor criticisms of Fromm and Honneth, I agree with the general analysis and recommendations of critical theory on the subjects of love and capitalism. By now we have a good picture of the basic problems, aspirations, and directions. But we have also arrived at a terrible impasse: we are moving in the real world in a direction exactly opposite to the ones proposed by Fromm and Honneth. Recent research provides terrifying evidence of looming catastrophe in the psychic and social life of capitalist societies today (in addition to the problems

---

68. Ibid., 89.
69. Ibid., 107–8.

of ecology). Let us take some time to consider the present danger and whether or not there is a hope we can reach from despair.

4.2 Danger and Hope of Despair

The systems of the human being—the biological, neurological, physical, and psychological systems—always need social connection to other humans for maintaining health. We have been discussing this through the major relevant philosophies from Plato to Marx to Honneth.

John Cacioppo's research substantiates—*in the field of cognitive neuro-science*—the now-familiar claim that human health and well-being depend on healthy and sustained social connections. While the word "capitalism" appears only once in the entirety of Cacioppo's book *Loneliness: Human Nature and the Need for Social Connection*, and not in any sharply critical terms, the author confirms that monetary pathology, the logic of wealth acquisition, and poverty exacerbate problems of isolation and loneliness. He even holds that an opposite orientation is absolutely necessary. While we may call that opposing orientation "communism," Cacioppo does not. He ends up by recommending that each individual do his or her part to make the world a little bit less lonely, an unsatisfying and unserious solution to the problem he so expertly diagnoses.

Here we should observe as an aside the remarkable fact that so many liberals who are so quick to disqualify communist or socialist analyses and recommendations as "impractical" and "unserious" typically prefer their own benign mix of (a) *keep doing what we're doing* while (b) *being as nice or good as possible*. This familiar combination is more or less Cacioppo's final word, and because of its unimaginative hopelessness, we know from the start that we have no use for his recommendations on what to do. Despite this, his research in cognitive neuroscience substantiates some of our basic claims by looking closely at the current psychosocial state of the human condition.

Cacioppo reviews survey data that shows people prefer love, intimacy, and social connection over wealth, fame, or physical health when they are asked to consider what makes for a happy life. This is at least what people claim to want, so "it is all the more troubling that, at any given time, roughly twenty percent of individuals—that would be sixty million people in the U.S. alone—feel sufficiently isolated for it to be a major source of unhappiness in their lives.... Our research in the past decade or so demonstrates that the culprit behind these dire statistics is not usually being literally alone, but the subjective *experience* known as lone-liness."[70] Cacioppo affirms here that loneliness is something often experienced when surrounded by other people. The problem is the feeling of loneliness. Most people will have experienced it in a room full of people at some point in their lives. Loneliness is widespread, and, according to Cacioppo, it is a large and growing source of unhappiness. If loneliness can be experienced *while being with others*, then it must be the *relation to others* and not the *presence of others* that matters.

But Cacioppo does not want us simply to wage war against loneliness. As with many forms of pain, loneliness has a purpose. Cacioppo puts this in biological and existential terms, pointing out that the purpose of physical pain is to alert us of physical danger. If my young son did not feel pain when touching a stove, then he might keep his hand on the stovetop, which would result in injury. The pain that he feels causes him to withdraw his hand and therefore protects him from danger. Cacioppo says that loneliness has a similar purpose because the experience of loneliness has historically driven us to find others to be with. When my son feels lonely, he asks for a friend. If we had no pain of loneliness, we might remain isolated in a world where social bonds are necessary for a healthy life. At certain points in human history, the danger of isolation meant death. A young child left alone is left for dead in most cases because the child relies on the care of others. As Honneth argued, to become a confident and healthy person who realizes who you want to be requires love, support, and encouragement from others who recognize and respect you. Thus, loneliness, much like physical pain, can push us toward safety and well-being. This alone should put us off any misguided project like the abolition of loneliness. Not only can loneliness not be abolished, its abolition would also be bad for us.

The problem in our societies is therefore something else. Loneliness becomes a problem when it is felt as a more-or-less-constant pain that does *not* help us avoid danger or push us to safety. Loneliness is a problem when it makes it hard or impossible for us to live as we might like to live. Not all pain can be defended. Some pain is too much, and in the case of loneliness in our present world, we are talking about a pain that has become destructive, that is wrecking more than it is protecting. Cacioppo refers to studies he and his colleagues have conducted that show that loneliness is causally related to the progression of Alzheimer's and

---

70. John T. Cacioppo and William Patrick, *Loneliness: Human Nature and the Need for Social Connection* (New York: W. W. Norton, 2008), 5.

that it alters DNA affecting the immune system; it also accelerates degenerative health problems of both the young and old.[71] Loneliness causes real measurable problems, and is only misunderstood if it is treated solely as a nonphysiological, or "merely psychological," problem. Cacioppo reminds us that, "at least among young adults, those who feel lonely actually spend no more time alone than do those who feel more connected."[72] Loneliness is caused by insufficient human connection, a state of being that shortens life, accelerates illnesses, and creates sadness.

This research helps us to understand why social media and metatopical human connection through screens and computers cannot cure loneliness. Loneliness may drive a person to seek technologically mediated connections, but if the resulting experience is the *mere* presence of others, loneliness will persist. Without the *kinds* of relationships we long for and need (recall Honneth's guidelines), one can be popular online and lonely in the world. The experience of loneliness can, in certain cases, be exacerbated by online connections that lead to cruelty, bullying, shaming, competition, and jealousy. This does not mean that technology is always harmful to social connection, only that if Cacioppo is right to separate loneliness from being alone, the solution to loneliness cannot be *not being alone*. Being alone may or may not factor into loneliness. In short, "you can have all the 'right' friends in terms of social prestige, in-group cachet, or business connections, or a spouse who is rich, brilliant, and fabulous looking, but if there is no deep, emotional resonance—specifically for you—then none of these relationships will satisfy the hunger for connection or ease the pain of feeling isolated."[73] A person with fewer friends, living in poverty and without a partner, may feel less lonely than a person with opposite fortunes.

Cacioppo addresses the fact that "proponents of technology tell us that computer-mediated social encounters will fill the void left by the decline of community in the real world."[74] Such faith in a technological fix is demonstrably false. Cacioppo explains that many of these technologies are "single-stranded interactions," lacking the multiple textures, dimensions, and richness of embodied human interaction, the latter of which goes much further than screen-interfaced connections in satisfying what people crave from human connections.[75]

---

71. Ibid., 12.
72. Ibid., 13.
73. Ibid., 77.
74. Ibid., 259.
75. Ibid.

Consider the diverse field of experiences (the many "strands" or "textures") that are often absent in computer-mediated sociality: bodily gestures, organic mimicry, improvisation, real-time humor, accidents, subliminal cues, and different energetic feelings in different rooms full of different people. All of this goes beyond the minimal, less fully textured, and often simulated connections readily available through social technologies. While this is not intended to degrade or dismiss all online connections, we should appreciate how they differ from face-to-face and in-person relationality. According to Cacioppo (whose argument here is much like that of Levinas), in-person relationality is empirically, psychologically, and experientially *fuller* than single-stranded interactions. In-person relationality entails more of the experience of the other than that found in single-stranded interactions, which put us in touch with one or a few aspects of the other, usually in only one or two of many possible ways. Thus, although social technologies like email and social media *do help* us address deficits in human connection, Cacioppo says that such technology does not fill the void of real community in the world.

In order to drill down on what exactly it is, then, that makes us experience the pain of loneliness, Cacioppo consults psychological research on people's sense of self. When people are asked to say who they are, their answers tend to fall into one of three categories. Respondents may answer by explaining a *personal or intimate self*, which would consist in self-descriptions like height, weight, and taste in art or food. Some respondents will answer by describing a *social or relational self*, which would consist in saying that they are so-and-so's sister, mother, or spouse, something that names them by way of a relation to another person than themselves. Still others may answer by describing a *collective self*, which would include naming their national or ethnic identity, their identity as a Republican or a Democrat, a Jew or a Muslim, and so on.[76]

Rather than rating these categories comparatively, Cacioppo speaks of them as comprising three dimensions of the self and social connection. "For the self, the essential dimensions are personal, relational, and collective, onto which we can map the three corresponding categories of social connection: intimate connectedness, relational connectedness, and collective connectedness."[77] A person with robust descriptions of real and active connections at all three levels would have a strong sense of self and would therefore be less susceptible (although not immune) to loneliness. For

---

76. Ibid., 78–79.
77. Ibid., 80.

example, a person with well-defined musical tastes who is proud to be the husband or mother of so-and-so, and who identifies with several active social groups, whether religious or political or cultural, is a person with a clear sense of self and social connection. This is not to say that an individual with amorphous tastes in food and music, no close family or friends, and no strong group identity is a person with no self. But such a person may be more susceptible to loneliness.

Cacioppo is especially interested in the physiological impact of loneliness, which is part of his commitment to showing the bodily and biological significance of psychology. Thus, it is important for him to show how loneliness causes bad health. Summing up the data from his research, Cacioppo discusses five ways that loneliness causes harm. First, those suffering loneliness are more likely to pursue unhealthy behaviors, such as poor eating habits or drug use. Second, there is greater exposure to stressors and major life events. Loneliness exacerbates feelings of stress and frustration at work, and makes it harder to deal with major life events such as the death of a loved one. Third, people experiencing loneliness have a diminished sense of potency (that is, the sense that one can do what one wants to do) in the face of stress or even minor hardships. For the less lonely adult, a little stress can serve to motivate, whereas for the very lonely, even small stressors can be demotivating and demobilizing. Fourth, Cacioppo points out that a person who is not suffering loneliness is likely to have a more developed and prepared nervous system. Cacioppo and his colleagues "found loneliness to be associated with higher traces of the stress hormone epinephrine in the morning urine of older adults. Other studies have shown that the allostatic load of feeling lonely also affects the body's immune and cardiovascular function."[78] A long review of physiological data ranging from DNA transcriptions to blood pressure show that loneliness exacerbates and accelerates illness of the human body. Finally, Cacioppo looks at rest and recuperation, as people experiencing severe loneliness recover more slowly from a wide range of afflictions, and social alienation is causally related to fatigue, even during the daytime, as well as poor sleep at night.

The findings demonstrate why we must take human loneliness seriously as a central and growing global problem. Meanwhile, social and political science continues to treat notions like loneliness—and, even more so, love—as too soft, too amorphous, immaterial, and emotional, to be of any clear significance to the study of society and politics. Despite notable

---

78. Ibid., 105.

exceptions to this generalization, the sciences dedicated to the study of society and politics remain indefinitely hobbled by chronic inattention to key questions of human relationality.

One of the more powerful conclusions Cacioppo establishes in his focus on the physiological impact of loneliness is the phenomenon of "cause at a distance," seen in a web of empirically measured effects showing loneliness as causally related to many problems throughout contemporary society.[79] Cacioppo highlights one example of cause at a distance as follows: "Our physiology is tuned to others in ways we barely consider, but the depth and pervasiveness of the linkages suggest why frustration of the desire to connect can throw us into a tailspin."[80] Sustained deprivations of healthy human sociality not only make us ill as individuals, but make others ill as well, as if loneliness were a kind of contagion.

Loneliness can also be a punishment. When we want to punish a young child, we may remove her from play with her friends, put her in a "time out," send her to her room, refuse a dessert after dinner, or deny some other reward. When we are really angry with a friend or a family member, we may withhold ourselves from them, stop talking to them, stop calling them, or stop returning their calls. Cacioppo observes: "For social behavior, the warmth of connection is the carrot; the pain of feeling isolated, also known as loneliness, is the stick."[81]

Unfortunately, Cacioppo fails to notice the most glaring and catastrophic example of the phenomenon he describes: mass incarceration. Mass incarceration, a problem very well diagnosed not only by Michel Foucault many decades ago but more recently by Angela Y. Davis and Michelle Alexander, furnishes the most vivid example of Cacioppo's point with regard to social behavior and punishment.[82] Those deemed criminals are separated from their families and cut off from others in prison cells everywhere. In the example of mass incarceration, notice the measured doses of "common time" where prisoners are allowed to congregate and socialize. This sociality is doled out in specific units of time as part of the prison's basic understanding of the maintenance of prisoners' health. Some common time with others may be permitted in order

---

79. Ibid., 114.
80. Ibid., 118.
81. Ibid., 120.
82. See Michel Foucault, *Discipline and Punishment: The Birth of the Prison* (New York: Random House and Vintage Books, 1977); Angela Y. Davis, *Are Prisons Obsolete?* (New York: Seven Stories, 2003); and Michelle Alexander, *The New Jim Crow: Mass Incarceration in the Age of Colorblindness* (New York: New Press, 2012).

to keep prisoners well enough and alive, but not so much as to ease the punishment, a punishment that can largely be summed up as *isolation from the social*.

Biologically and psychologically, sociality is necessary for humanity, thus the deprivation of sociality is dehumanizing. Indeed, the heart of Cacioppo's argument is that we are "an obligatorily gregarious species. The attempt to function in denial of our need for others, whether that need is great or small in any given individual, violates our design specifications.... Social connection is a fundamental part of the human operating (and organizing) system itself."[83] This would mean that, as we were wondering above, the human instinct for deep, meaningful, and sustained relationships with other people is a universal fact of the human being. If we agree with Cacioppo, this indeed makes love into one force or activity of a universal human aspiration, helping us to answer the question raised by Honneth about love's universality.

For Cacioppo, love is only one dimension of sociality, and it is not a topic of sustained attention in his research. He is more concerned with immediate crises than with a theory of love. Loneliness can interfere with every aspect of a human life, can affect the well-being of households and workplaces, and can spread like an "emotional contagion."[84] This provides us with a different dimension to explore beyond Honneth's concerns about capitalist tendencies toward detachment of individuals from groups. Honneth's concerns over such individuation are variously social, political, and economic, whereas Cacioppo's are mostly social and psychological; better would be a synthetic understanding that is always social, political, economic, and psychological at the same time. Consider that Cacioppo's discussion of the spreading of loneliness like an emotional contagion is social in a mimetic sense; it is entirely disconnected from anything like Honneth's political concerns as a socialist and a critical theorist. Cacioppo is relatively silent on political-economic questions of capitalism and capitalist culture, whereas Honneth is not terribly interested in the biological and physiological dimensions of loneliness. Both Honneth and Cacioppo are right, but each approach is inadequate on its own.

One thing is certain: Cacioppo is diagnosing a problem for which his recommended solutions are mismatched and unsatisfactory. He tells us that, in 1985, when researchers asked American subjects how many confidants they had, they most commonly said three, whereas in 2004 the most

---

83. Cacioppo, *Loneliness*, 127.
84. Ibid., 165–66.

common response was none. Twenty-five percent of Americans in a 2001 study reported that they had no one to talk to. The World Health Organization and Harvard University also found in 2004 that eating disorders, binge drinking, childhood depression, and attention deficit disorder had shot up, while UNICEF has been showing that wealthy nations (such as the United States and UK in particular) had very poor measures of child welfare, a terrible infant mortality record, and high levels of exposure to violence, bullying, and insecure family relations.[85] Cacioppo makes only fleeting connections to Honneth's main concerns and to ours, observing that "independence is the rallying point for our culture" and that "a rising tide can indeed lift a variety of boats, but in a culture of social isolates, atomized by social and economic upheaval and separated by vast inequalities, it can also cause millions to drown."[86] Cacioppo does not think or write about capitalism; he accepts it as a foregone conclusion or as an intractable context to simply presuppose. He does not think of capitalism as generating the problems he diagnoses, and this marks his sharpest break with the psychoanalytic theories of Fromm. However, some of Cacioppo's fleeting remarks clarify that he is aware that the problems he has identified are exacerbated by capitalism.

Cacioppo observes, for example, that in "many parts of the world, older societies are rushing to embrace the American commodity culture and the casual disregard for social bonds that gave rise to the exurb's anomie."[87] And, in the one line where he mentions capitalism in *Loneliness*: "In China a society built on Confucian regard for the collective has been suddenly thrust into the aggressive individualism of capitalism."[88] In these lines, Cacioppo is specifically identifying American-style capitalism as reconfiguring global culture toward the individuation Honneth condemns. For Cacioppo, socialism (or, for that matter, a resurgent Confucianism) is not the appropriate response to this problem. But he does call for better relationality. Cacioppo presses his readers as follows: "A landscape built for disconnection simply makes it even more urgent to work consciously and deliberately to build stronger human bonds at every opportunity, in every day-to-day exchange."[89] I agree, and while we might name this urgent work "communism," Cacioppo would find no value in such an identification. To the contrary, I argue that calling this urgent

---

85. Data cited in Cacioppo, *Loneliness*, 247–48.
86. Ibid., 248 and 264, respectively.
87. Ibid., 254.
88. Ibid., 255.
89. Ibid.

work "communism" and targeting capitalism as one of the root causes of the loneliness that Cacioppo condemns is far more than a semantic or political point.

For example, if our urgent work is called communism, then we *must* think about the problem of loneliness as always also a political problem demanding some form of collective action. Also, with communism, we cannot relieve ourselves of the burden of considering the relationship of all problems to capitalism. We ultimately need far more than clinical and individualistic interventions. I am in favor of a micropolitics of love, but we must not forget that when Félix Guattari wrote about micropolitics and microrevolutions, he was always concerned with their potential to link up and create transformative (that is to say, *really revolutionary*) movements.[90] This is, indeed, how Guattari wanted to reconceive communism, as a movement of particulars, of the subversive creativities of a multiplicity of insurgent actors. That is quite far from Cacioppo's purportedly apolitical cognitive science. The point is that naming the counterposition "communist" enables and encourages us to make a move that Cacioppo cannot make—namely, to identify capitalism as causally related to the problems we are discussing.

While addressing loneliness through the communism of love moves beyond Cacioppo's conclusions, it does not contradict them. This is a case of surpassing, not opposing. Cacioppo writes:

> Money appears to have a positive impact on people's motivation, but a negative impact on their behavior toward others. There are data to suggest that merely having money on the periphery of consciousness is sufficient to skew us away from prosocial behavior. The psychologist Kathleen Vohs and her colleagues did a series of nine experiments that primed certain participants with thoughts of money.... In all nine tests, those who were given the subtle suggestions of money were not only less likely to ask for help, but also less likely to help others. When a lab assistant staged an accident by dropping a box of pencils, those primed with thoughts of money picked up fewer.[91]

In a society ruled by money, we always have money *at least* on the periphery of our consciousness, we are all primed with thoughts of money, and the suggestions are far from subtle. Cacioppo and Vohs should have noted

---

90. See Félix Guattari's essays "The Proliferation of Margins" and "Why Italy?" both in *Autonomia: Post-Political Politics* (Los Angeles: Semiotext(e), 2007).

91. Cacioppo, *Loneliness*, 264–65.

that this "priming" is the basic consciousness of life in a capitalist society. We live in societies where money determines what we have, how we live, which opportunities are foreclosed or open to us, where economic power is political power and vice versa. It is therefore no wonder that loneliness grows in such a society. Our society is capitalist, and Cacioppo could and should have brought that basic insight forward from Fromm into his twenty-first-century research.

But, alas, Cacioppo does not follow his own conclusions to their ends. "Of course vast economic, political, and cultural forces are also at play, but ultimately, human beings shape their environment through individual, iterative behaviors. As a free agent within such a system, each of us has a certain degree of power, through our individual actions, to continuously adjust the social environment toward something slightly better or something slightly worse."[92] Certainly, Cacioppo will never stand accused of impractical utopianism. Unfortunately, this twist renders Cacioppo's recommendations (though not his findings) useless for political theory.

Cacioppo would have us sidestep the vast economic, political, and cultural forces he reviews in favor of doing what we can as individual "free agents" (whatever that means), to slightly adjust our social environment more or less favorably. But even if we followed this advice, which individuals are the ones who can do this, and how? We should have to count out all of those who are severely lonely from any such slight adjusting, since Cacioppo has already argued that the mobilization of the loneliest among us (for far lesser and more minor activities) becomes difficult. He did not describe the total freedom of those debilitated by loneliness, but rather demonstrated that their agency was frustrated and undermined by loneliness, shrinking their central human powers. So then, is Cacioppo's recommendation only really practical for the least lonely persons, for those who see relief in the results of their efforts to improve their social environment? Where is the place for collective action of any kind, for a subset of humanity to confront and overturn the massive growing global crisis of loneliness?

There is no such place or idea in Cacioppo's research. But if we could understand our small, minor power to adjust the social environment—to try to change it—as part of a politics, then we could perhaps find a formulation for praxis. We could possibly return to Fromm and Honneth for help with that project, but, for reasons that will become clear below, that will not be enough either. One conclusion we may draw at this juncture

---

92. Ibid., 266.

is this: loneliness is the emotional contagion of our times, which spreads disaffection through our mimetic sociality, as a disastrous epiphenomenon of capitalist causes.

Julia Kristeva, a psychoanalyst committed to critical social theory, deals with love and despair in a different way. She claims that the main purpose of psychoanalysis is love. "For what is psychoanalysis if not an infinite quest for rebirths through the experience of love, which is begun again only to be displaced, renewed, and, if not abreacted, at least collected and set up at the heart of the analysand's ulterior life as an auspicious condition for his personal renewal, his non-death?"[93] Problems in human relationality pertaining to love are the kinds of problems that drive individuals to seek psychoanalysis. Love is the business of psychoanalysis.

I suppose this follows from the above discussion. If one has more or less optimal relations as per Fromm, Honneth, or Cacioppo, the motivation for psychoanalysis would be low. Ideally, Kristeva suggests, the analysand could leave psychoanalysis with a well-calibrated preparation for love in her life, which when disturbed or broken, would drive the analysand back to the analyst. Here too, we find the idea that the individuated therapy relationship of analyst to analysand can maintain or revivify healthy love relations. Kristeva's clinical orientation homes in on the interpersonal context of love as a miniature social relation. But we have seen that the problems of love (and loneliness) are large-scale social problems. The question of how to address problems of human sadness at a social level remains. It is worth asking at this juncture whether or not theorizing love at the social level is an insurmountable limitation of psychoanalysis. I am inclined to say yes, that the problems of love and loneliness are ultimately—*however well illuminated by psychoanalysis*—demarcations of the limit point at which psychoanalysis fails.

We can acknowledge that the analyst may be uniquely situated to have her finger on the pulse of the most pressing social problems. What the analyst sees walking through the doors are social problems concentrated variously into the bodies of analysands. "What are analysands complaining of, dwellers in giant cities who have lost their bearings? Can we isolate *The* contemporary sickness, the one that colors the end of the twentieth century and slips it into the third millennium? ... What analysands are henceforth suffering from is *the abolition of psychic space*."[94] For Kristeva, psychic space means both the space and time necessary for

---

93. Julia Kristeva, *Tales of Love*, trans. Leon S. Roudiez (New York: Columbia University Press, 1987), 1.

94. Ibid., 373.

inquiry, reflection, creative and critical thought, and the processing of information sufficient for its conversion into human understanding. The psychoanalyst primarily sees people who need to carve out and dedicate some space and time for this psychic activity in a world designed to seize and use up all of their attentions. The abolition of psychic space impedes self-understanding and makes loving—*which demands substantial psychic space*—all the more difficult. Psychic space is something like the oxygen of love. People with no space and time to think, reflect, wonder, and explore are incapacitated for loving.

In *Tales of Love*, Kristeva gives sustained attention to the figure of Narcissus and the problem of narcissism. She does not think that the primary narcissism of childhood withers away in adulthood. People do not have the sufficient psychic space to regard and attend to other people. "The one in love with his fleeting reflection is in fact someone deprived of his own proper space."[95] What can be done about this abolition of space? Kristeva favors a psychoanalysis that encourages radical breaks with—or breakdowns of—the existing psychological state. It is not true that the analyst only wants to alleviate pain, for the analyst also wants to help people move into "unstable, open, undecidable spaces."[96] While it may sound odd that a psychoanalyst would encourage the unstable or undecidable, Kristeva sees such psychic space as the place of imagination and possibility. By going into such open and dangerous territory the analyst hopes to guide the analysand into the psychic space necessary to think in open, new ways about the psychological crisis.

Kristeva thinks that we have become like extraterrestrials suffering in our search of love. She calls us extraterrestrials (or "ET's") to capture the alien and alienating nature of life in contemporary capitalist society. We do not fit comfortably into this world we have made, into this world we reproduce through our predictable daily behaviors. Rather, we are like extraterrestrials who are visiting our own world for a time, and what we really want to know is how to love in a place like this. For that, we will need imagination: "I speak in favor of imagination as antidote for the crisis. Not in favor of 'power to the imagination,' which is the rallying cry of perverts longing for the law. But in favor of saturating powers and counterpowers with imaginary constructions—phantasmatic, daring, violent, critical, demanding, shy.... Let them speak, the ET's shall live. Imagination succeeds where the narcissist becomes hollowed out and the paranoid fails."[97] We

95. Ibid., 376.
96. Ibid., 380.
97. Ibid., 381.

do not want to empower anything that anyone might imagine, because human beings are capable of imagining the most horrific things. Such an invitation is just calling out for punishment or repression by the law. The point is to liberate and encourage everything *within* the imagination to be explored, to be spoken out loud. This counteracts the repression of a life of alienation and would be, for Kristeva, a healthy exercise. Kristeva believes that we will have to become more imaginative at precisely those junctures where our narcissism and paranoia leave us most miserable. Without imagination, we are likely to accept our own misery as an incontrovertible fact. It is not necessary to realize everything imaginable, but without imagination, the existing reality is all there is.

According to Kristeva, alienation, loneliness, narcissism, privation of our sociality deepens the longing for love, since love appears (and feels) like the only road to a different destination. "An uneasy child, all scratched up, somewhat disgusting, without a precise body or image, having lost his specificity, an alien in a world of desire and power, he longs only to reinvent love. The ET's are more and more numerous. We are all ET's."[98] Kristeva's account of ET's, unlike Cacioppo's account of loneliness, is meant to report on the existential condition of life in contemporary capitalist societies. The abolition of psychic space, brutal competition, hyperindividuation, and loneliness have made us all into extraterrestrials who cannot but hope for some form of love—some revived practice and experience of human relationality that may be capable of making us feel better. I would say that the psychoanalytic and psychological view running from Fromm to Honneth to Cacioppo to Kristeva situates love as a kind of medicine for a sick society, for a society undermined by various forms of privatization.

In a different deployment, Dominic Pettman claims we should think of love as a technology—instead of a medicine—that repairs our broken sociality. In his book, *Love and Other Technologies*, Pettman claims that the three words "love," "technology," and "community" "in fact designate the same thing, or at least the same movement—specifically, a movement toward the other."[99] So far we have thought of love as a movement toward the other but not as a technology. We have also discussed how technology can be a separating and individuating movement *away* from the other. It is not at all clear that technology facilitates being-together more than being-apart. Pettman's counterintuitive proposal is meant to help us rethink

98. Ibid., 382–83.

99. Dominic Pettman, *Love and Other Technologies: Retrofitting Eros for the Information Age* (New York: Fordham University Press, 2006), xiii.

love and how it works in the information age. While I find some insights in Pettman's work, I think we have to resist imagining love as if it were a technology. To map love over present technological sociality is to make it follow a logic other than its own.

It makes sense to think of love as an effort to extend one's self toward the other, as a movement toward other people, and as an expression of our will to connect and communicate. Inasmuch as technology is an expression of that same will, Pettman may be right to see love as a technology.[100] The problem is that Pettman chronically overlooks the extent to which the history of technological development has tended to create greater distance between people.

For example, in the capitalist workplace (a major terrain of technological innovation), it is often understood that the worker's proximity to his or her work and to other workers is a danger; thus, the question of technology is how to continue the work at the greatest distance. The historical development of cotton gins, for example, slowly yet increasingly distanced the subject (worker) from the object (cotton). Closeness is not always a benefit! The worker exhausted from separating cotton fibers from seeds by hand would long for a way to do this labor at a distance afforded by machines. That same technology that makes the worker's life easier is also celebrated by the capitalist who wants more cotton in less time, and who wants to justify cutting the costs of human labor. The move from hands on fibers to hands on cranks or levers still maintains a relatively close proximity. But it would get farther soon. Efficiency and speed—as the real central logics of technology—created more distance still, eventually giving rise to the "future" cotton gin where the whole process can be controlled remotely through a screen. This is not necessarily bad news. Indeed, it may be good for most everyone involved in cotton production. But it may not create any more "leisure time" for workers and is most certainly not ruled by a logic or a movement of being-together. The central logics of love, unlike technology, could never be efficiency and speed.

Likewise, email, text messaging, and social media are considered technologies of human connection only to the most superficial analysis. These are, to go back to Cacioppo, single-stranded interactions, meaning that they put each one in touch with some minor strand of the other's being-in-the-world. These technologies of "togetherness" also often serve to separate and create greater distance. A person often emails a colleague sitting right next to them precisely to avoid the multistranded connectivity

---

100. Ibid., 17.

of an embodied conversation of gesture and open improvisation. Most people today have some experience with text messaging and email as a shorthand that is *preferred* precisely because they minimize connection to other people, because they provide distance. Pettman is aware of these criticisms, but he passes over them too easily.

Pettman is working within the milieus of critical theory and late-twentieth-century Marxisms, and he by no means endorses the uncritical technophilia of capitalist innovation. He is concerned with many of the problems we have been discussing in this book. But Pettman worries more about belief in a bad notion of "authentic love" that leads to our pining away for an ideal love that never was. If we do not rethink love for the information age, then we may not have any future love, since those who want idealized love cannot expect to find it on any near horizon. Pettman criticizes the old-fashioned and erroneous idea that things like online dating services and apps that arrange people according to algorithms are qualitatively worse than meeting people in real life. He notes that people look down on those who use new technologies for love in the place of old-fashioned methods, saying that "the joke is on those who find humor in such behavior and who stubbornly labor under the delusion that their own relationships IRL (in real life) are anything other than a complex social algorithm."[101]

But can we equivocate the complex social algorithm with the algorithms used on dating apps? Must we really accept either some old misguided romantic theory of authentic love or the theory of love as a technology? I would prefer to reject both. If what brought me and my partner together was a complex social algorithm, then it would have been an algorithm that guaranteed nothing for either of us. Whether brought together in real life or online, keeping together is another story. It is not the coming-together but the being-together that matters, regardless of how one "finds love." As for being-together, it is quite clear that there are differences between IRL relationality and single-stranded or screen-mediated relationality. Such differences can make a big difference. For example, perhaps one only wants to text message or email a father or mother who is abusive IRL. The distance that technology affords may be preferable or even necessary to maintain any relationship at all. But it would be unacceptable (and to some extent impossible) for me to parent my young children through a screen, and that is not because I am romanticizing IRL interactions as being more authentic. The bodily and embodied presence

---

101. Ibid., 190.

of regular and sustained attention, including the whole ensemble of performative interactions (such as humor, play, teaching by doing, eating, sharing, physical affection, and the like) is qualitatively different—even if it is not always ideal—and Pettman knows this.

To be fair, Pettman calls for a profound rethinking of technology, and his theory of love is not a simple capitulation or assimilation to the current status of technology. Pettman means to speak of technology only "in the spirit of *techne* and *poiesis*, as a mode of revealing or 'bringing forth.'"[102] The problem is that Pettman seeks to establish some notion of an "authentic" or "better" technology than the capitalist one that has prevailed up to this point. Two of our biggest mistakes, says Pettman, "occurred when we decided to place humans at the center of the universe, and then the self at the center of humanity."[103] With such priorities as those, what other form could our technology have taken than that of ecological abuse, self-interest, and a culture of grown-up narcissism? What we need, he argues, is a different technology, and the one that brings us together best is love.

I oppose thinking of love as a technology not only because existing technology is capitalist and rests on the two mistakes Pettman rightly observes, but also because such a formulation leads us to think of solutions in terms of technological development. The motivations for human community and being-in-the-world are not retooled at the level of technology but at the levels of ethical and moral commitment and social and political movement, and they are mobilized by real experiences, desires, and disaffections. I imagine that Pettman would call ethics a technology, just as he calls stubbornness and ideology (including communism, patriotism, racism, and religion) technologies too.[104] In Pettman's etymological and conceptual frame, most anything can be called a technology.

Thinking of love as a technology in the context of the present study would be to concede that technology may also be a universal aspiration, but it would have to be a benevolent technology that moves us toward each other. The fact is, however, that our increasingly technologized lives are coincident with (and causally related to) higher degrees of isolation, loneliness, anxiety, and other disaffections that we may not be able to survive. In the end, I reply to the metaphorical appeal of Pettman's counterintuitive discourse with something simple yet important: *Let's take fatal affairs more seriously! What we gain from thinking about and treating love as a technology is a more benevolent view of technology and a more*

---

102. Ibid., 198.
103. Ibid., 204.
104. Ibid., 205.

instrumental view of love, whereas what we need is an understanding of love as a practice and power of life and death.

That course is far better abided in the work of one of Pettman's favorite thinkers, Bernard Stiegler. Stiegler is concerned with what he calls "spiritual misery," where the word "spirit" refers to psychic and collective processes (cerebral and social) that move us beyond "I" to "we." Spirit is not, for Stiegler, some kind of metaphysical or invisible substance, but is the human connectivity that moves people beyond their bodies into a sense of being-together.[105] Societies composed of disaffected individuals are thus societies of spiritual misery. This destruction of human spirit is essentially the result of a profound fragmentation of the "we," which for Stiegler is both (1) a result of capitalism and (2) a source of hopelessness. All of this is by now well-traveled terrain, but Stiegler notes that in the psychological sphere, spiritual misery leads to "the outright *liquidation of the super-ego* as a system of prohibitions."[106] A general breakdown of prohibitions gives rise to less-predictable behavior, some of which is violent and reveals to us the real danger of living in a world of disaffected individuals.

Our societies want to exert control over us, but Stiegler claims they cannot do so indefinitely. "Contrary to what Peter Sloterdijk seems to believe, I do not think that humanity can be domesticated. I believe, on the contrary, that human beings ceaselessly oscillate between the *desire for taming* and the *temptation of fury*.... Control societies, in other words, are not sustainable."[107] Thus, we have not only to worry about despair and loneliness but also about the reactions that come from them. People may want to live calm, ordered, and settled lives full of security and personal safety, but they also want to release energy, are attracted to breaking rules (especially when the rules appear to harm them), and eventually let out what has been bottled up. These are real and present tendencies, and societies would do well to beware the effects—sometimes terrorist and murderous—of human despair and spiritual misery.

Sounding a bit like Fromm and Honneth, Stiegler says that "being-together can be bound and maintained only through *philia*, that is, through an affective relation of esteem, respect, friendship, familiarity," which is intended to signal "*love* in all its diverse forms."[108] But when such

---

105. Bernard Stiegler, *Uncontrollable Societies of Disaffected Individuals: Disbelief and Discredit, Volume 2*, trans. Daniel Ross (Cambridge: Polity, 2013), 2–3.

106. Ibid., 5.

107. Ibid., 10–11.

108. Ibid., 18.

being-together is broken up in our societies, we will not only get sadness and loneliness; we will also see riots, school shootings, vandalism, murder, and suicide. Lost confidence, a lost sense of self, generates mental health situations fit not only for clinicians like Kristeva, but also for mayors and police forces.

But politicians, police, military, and law are not capable of addressing the problem. These are not fundamentally problems of management or containment; rather, they are problems of human misery. Thinking about rebellious young people who made recent uprisings in France, Stiegler says that these youth "have lost confidence in themselves, no longer believe in the authority of their parents, and are confronted with the *structural cynicism of the society* in which they live.... [T]his is a generation *psychiatrically* confronted with a situation of *extreme danger*."[109] We simply cannot pretend that human disaffection and spiritual misery will always take the same form as in the past. New opioid epidemics, killing sprees, and psychological conditions emerge alongside old disaffections. Yet we tend to think of these problems as societies of control. This means that, for example, the growing number of mass shootings in the United States has become a debate between Republicans and Democrats that mainly centers on questions of control. First, there is gun control. Then you have questions about controlling doors at schools, controlling emergency procedures, being in control of the situation, with some saying that more guns means more control and others saying that fewer guns and more healthcare is the pathway to getting the problem under control.

Both sides seem incapable of confronting—or unwilling to confront—the fact that things may be "uncontrollable" precisely because they are really beyond our control. Societies of control resist thinking about the category of the "uncontrollable," so they try to control everything—terrorism, drug abuse, and borders—and they often fail to notice that their efforts are met with measurable increases of the behaviors they aim to diminish. Stiegler confesses his fear. He is worried about his children and their future, and he knows that the problems we face are beyond the control of the apparatuses of established power today, if they ever were under control at all. The only thing Stiegler can think to do is to return in the end to the subject of love: "Our epoch does not love itself. And a world that does not love itself is a world that does not believe in the world: we can believe only in what we love. This is what makes the atmosphere of this world so heavy, stifling, and anguished. The world of the hyper-market, which is

---

109. Ibid., 44.

the effective reality of the hyper-industrial epoch, is, as an assemblage of cash registers and barcode readers, a world in which loving must become synonymous with buying, which is in fact a world without love."[110]

The problem identified by Stiegler's analysis is actually much worse than what we have previously discussed: while we must try to reestablish and revive love in the world, this requires first that we can believe in something and that the world itself can give us cause for such belief, for faith in a future horizon. It seems trite at best to suggest that communism is something to believe in, especially in the world such as it is. Instead of restorative movements of human health and well-being toward community and love relations that can shield us from the brutal individualism of our societies, we are experiencing the opposite.

Whereas Cacioppo spoke of growing loneliness, Stiegler writes about *hikikomori* and *otaku* in Japan. As mentioned above, *hikikomori* refers to the hundreds of thousands who have cut themselves off from the world outside, living in isolated spaces and only interacting with other people through screens. *Otaku* is a different phenomenon in which people opt to live in a world of video games and comic books with other *otaku* who share their disaffections and lack of faith in the *actual world*.[111] None of the worlds they love is the actual world outside.

Otaku and *hikikomori* are unpredictable disturbances. They are mutations in our sociality that only make sense after the fact. They will not be—and have not been—the only mutations. *Otaku* and *hikikomori* are disturbances that cause real problems for schools, families, and labor markets, as well as for the afflicted individuals who have opted out of living in the world. How could they be expected to choose the world as it really is after having found miniature worlds to live in that seem to them far less threatening? Our capitalist societies are worlds of precarity, terror, and real danger, much of which we cannot predict and, more importantly, cannot control. *Otaku* and *hikikomori* have given up on the ulterior world to some extent, but that means they have no resolve to change it. Perhaps they know or feel *that they cannot change a thing*.

It is critical to point out that the uncontrollable society is not *only* a terrible thing, for uncontrollable activity may sometimes be insurrectionary, and the insurrection may be the indispensable, productive, and transformative development that we need. Broken control can come in the form of a revolt or an uprising, which says something perhaps even

---

110. Ibid., 82–83.
111. Ibid., 88–89.

hopeful about intolerable realties in societies of control. Such breaks could also open new psychic space in which imagination can be set loose and new understandings can emerge. Uncontrollable societies may or may not do good things, and societies of control may do worse in terms of what they normalize, reproduce, and preserve.

According to Stiegler, in his book *What Makes Life Worth Living*: "Attention is the psychic faculty that allows us to concentrate on an object, that is, to give ourselves over to an object, but it is also the social faculty that allows us to take care of this object—or of another, or of the representative of another, or of the object of the other: attention is also the name of that civility that is grounded in *philia*, that is, socialized libidinal energy."[112] Stiegler's focus on attention here recalls what Simone Weil has said about attention as the highest form of human generosity (see chapter 1). A central problem of contemporary life is that the human faculty most necessary for care—*attention*—is fragmented, divided, and unreliable, so our ability to care for each other is broken down.

Stiegler identifies attention as a civility grounded in love—*philia*—which follows from his previous claim that we do not love our world. But attention in Stiegler's discussion, unlike in Weil's, is not a matter of generosity or the lack thereof. We no longer know how to pay attention. For Stiegler, "the destruction of attention implies the destruction of both the *psychic apparatus* and the *social apparatus* (formed through collective individuation), insofar as the latter constitutes a system of care, given that to pay attention is also to take care."[113] The degradation of our common ability to pay attention is, for Stiegler, an outcome of capitalism. Our consumerist societies and commodity cultures have figured out how to "capture and harness attention" for the purposes of making human psychology serve capital.[114]

The relationship between attention and care was taken up in the July–August 2018 issue of the *Atlantic*, where Erika Christakis focuses on the divided attention of parents who have normalized a semiconstant interaction with screens. In "The Dangers of Distracted Parenting" Christakis points out that parents' usual worry is how much time their children spend looking at tablets and smartphones, when in fact, the parents' screen time is the greater danger. "Child development is relational," and a new danger "arises when the emotionally resonant adult-child cueing

112. Bernard Stiegler, *What Makes Life Worth Living: On Pharmacology*, trans. Daniel Ross (Cambridge: Polity, 2013), 81.

113. Ibid., 82.

114. Ibid., 88.

system so essential to early learning is interrupted—by a text, for example, or a quick check-in on Instagram."[115] What is deceiving about this situation is that parents now spend more time with their children, in their presence and around them, than at any previous point in history. So we may inaccurately think that the greater physical presence makes up for interrupted attention. But the opposite is true: "This is the worst possible model of parenting—we are always present physically, thereby blocking kids' autonomy, yet only fitfully present emotionally."[116]

This provides yet another reason we must reject Pettman's characterization of love as a technology, despite Pettman's own qualifications. Technology often has an interrupting, distancing, and fragmenting impact on human relationality, and it does not reliably increase our attention to or interaction with others. Stiegler and Christakis reveal that technologies that move us away from each other also distance us from critical forms of care. And I share Stiegler's concern for his children in a concern for my own. I agree that human attentions have been effectively seized and cut up by predatory interests hiding out in the open behind the screens we so fully attend to. It is too easy to say that we need to learn how to love when we do not have the emotional resources, psychological space, and social environment conducive to learn such an attentive practice. When we look at the world from the perspective of love, we can see that we are in trouble. We may want to practice love as Fromm, Honneth, Kristeva, and others would have us do, and we may want to use love as an antithetical force against the growing loneliness that Cacioppo diagnosed so well. But it may well be that all we can practice of the communism of love is its radical critique of the existing state of affairs.

While I think Stiegler is right to consider the psychological and social limits of capitalist individuation—the points where we found mutations like *hikikomori* and *otaku*—I also think that some expressions of disaffection are practical manifestations of the human aspiration for love. In response to Black revolt in Ferguson, Missouri, after the police shooting of Michael Brown in 2014, both liberals and conservatives on US television often said that the insurrectionists must not love their community because they were in the streets looting and destroying it. But we should consider the revolt as a love asserted against the racist violence of police, capital, and law. It is precisely because one both loves and wants to love one's self and community that one may join the uprising.

---

115. Erika Christakis, "The Dangers of Distracted Parenting," *Atlantic* 322, no. 1 (July/August 2018): 12.

116. Ibid.

Black revolt, for example, gives a loud voice to neglected disaffections, and it visibly demonstrates indignation, the latter of which is impossible without love. Indignation, inasmuch as it is centered on the privation of dignity, is the modality of an explosive demand for the worth and concern of the self and community in the face of their denial. As it was with the Mexican Zapatistas in the 1990s, communities that long live in oblivion may one day refuse the inaudibility and invisibility imposed on them. Indignation is a demand for a dignity that is self-consciously deserved. It is impossible to express the disaffection of indignation without a basis of self-love.

This is why, as discussed in Blanchot's consideration of the community of lovers of May 1968 (chapter 1), love sometimes takes the form of revolt. This is also why it was so important to consider the question of love from the perspective of women (chapter 3). Love does not appear as one and the same thing in every place and time (as we saw in chapter 2). Let us now consider its specific form and content in current contexts of patriarchal marginalization, racialization, and the latest phase of resurgent white supremacy.

CHAPTER 5

Love and White Supremacist Capitalist Patriarchy

"Love can't flourish in a society based upon money and meaningless work: it requires complete economic as well as personal freedom, leisure time and the opportunity to engage in intensely absorbing, emotionally satisfying activities which, when shared with those you respect, lead to deep friendship."

–Valerie Solanas, *SCUM Manifesto*

"Bourgeois values define the family situation in America, give it certain goals. Oppressed and poor people who try to reach these goals fail because of the very conditions that the bourgeoisie has established. There is the dilemma. We need a family, because every man and woman deserves the kind of spiritual support and unity a family provides. Black people try to reach the goals set by the dominant culture and fail without knowing why."

–Huey P. Newton, *Revolutionary Suicide*

5.1 Unlike Loves: Racialization and Consumption

The concept of "love" has long been the centerpiece of bell hooks's feminism, a feminism that is always simultaneously critical of capitalism and racism.[1] The focus on love in hooks's feminism culminated in a quartet of books, published from 2000 to 2004, devoted to the study of love as a social and political power: *All about Love: New Visions* (2000), *Salvation: Black People and Love* (2001), *Communion: The Female Search for Love* (2002), and *The Will to Change: Men, Masculinity, and Love* (2004).

hooks has consistently argued that self-love—including a loving concern for one's own life possibilities—is an essential prerequisite for a love of the other that could motivate politics. Self-love is differentiated by racism and classism because impoverished people of color are inculcated by capitalist culture from childhood to confront their "lesser valuation." In a white supremacist society, which can be seen wherever the most dominant icons of beauty and success are white people, Black people and other people of color have to find pathways to self-love without constant and pervasive reassurances of their value in society. People of color often must work hard for self-love, and community spaces may help to build and reinforce a sense of worth that does not otherwise pervade the racist and classist reality. Adding to the dimensions of race and class, hooks focuses also on the imperialism of mainstream feminisms that tie the grievances of women's struggles to the concerns of Western white women. Countering all of this, hooks calls for a "decolonized feminist perspective" that "would first and foremost examine how sexist practices in relation to

---

1. I retain bell hooks's own convention of writing her name in lowercase.

women's bodies globally are linked.... When issues are addressed in this manner Western imperialism is not reinscribed and feminism cannot be appropriated by transnational capitalism as yet another luxury product from the West."[2] Therefore, when hooks looks at love, she always does so from the perspective of a feminist theory that is consistently conscious of race, class, and gender.

An anarchist sensibility runs clearly through hooks's work. This anarchism—which hooks does not herself claim—is expressed in two consistent ways. First, her arguments on race, class, and gender never rest on an inversion of the oppressed/oppressor relation, since she always names domination as the fourth major concern. Domination, from a feminist perspective, is typically viewed as patriarchal, but hooks adds capitalism as an intersecting and necessarily hierarchical tendency. A principled critique of domination and hierarchy is one of the distinguishing features of anarchism, from at least the second half of the nineteenth century through to the middle of the twentieth (following Bakunin and others who worried about the hierarchical tendencies of authoritarian socialists and revolutionary statists). Second, hooks never trusts governmental solutions to the problems she diagnoses, and she points instead to bottom-up forms of activist and community politics. Her diagnostic and antistatist positions situate her within the milieu of an anarchist orientation, even though she seems uninterested in anarchism. Yet her critique of domination, which is at least substantively anarchist, is inextricably linked to her basic theory of love. In *Feminism Is for Everybody*, hooks writes: "Whenever domination is present love is lacking."[3] This simple generalization contains a basic logic that hooks develops more fully throughout her work. The critique of domination enables hooks to condemn not only capitalism, but also sexism, patriarchy, racism, and imperialism.

hooks observes a problem with loving in accordance with exchange relations, for love cannot genuinely be given to another in exchange for something else. But in patriarchal society, "women being the gender in touch with caring emotions would give men love, and in return men, being in touch with power and aggression, would provide and protect."[4] A conscious trading of love and care for security and protection is a measurable exchange, one which fails to recognize that both sides need all of these things. She applies her critique of domination to patriarchy:

2. bell hooks, *Feminism Is for Everybody: Passionate Politics* (Cambridge, MA: South End, 2000), 46–47.

3. Ibid., 77.

4. Ibid., 101.

"Love can never take root in a relationship based on domination and coercion.... [T]here can be no love when there is domination."[5] Domination, for hooks, indicates a "power over" relation, where the dominant power keeps an oppressed subject or group in a state of subordination, repression, abuse, exploitation, inequality, or exclusion. Domination can be seen in the ways that class power, racism, heterosexism, imperial power, and patriarchy keep—and have historically kept—women, sexual minorities, the poor, and people of color in place, against the interests and wills of those subjects. This raises the question of how people practice love under domination.

When hooks argues that domination is incommensurate with love, she means that whatever looks like love in a context of domination where an overpowering figure claims to love a subordinate subject will eventually reveal itself as not the real thing. The presence of such domination in interpersonal relationships always indicates, for hooks, a deficit of love. She argues that "love is rooted in recognition and acceptance, that love combines acknowledgement, care, responsibility, commitment, and knowledge" and that ultimately love is a power that opposes domination.[6] It sometimes seems that hooks is closer to speaking about the anarchism of love than the communism of love. If there is patriarchy and sexism and racism at the starting position, love growing from there will inevitably challenge, oppose, and shrink the forms of domination where the love was not-yet. In this way, love appears in hooks's basic theorization as something like an antidote or medicine, but not a *pharmakon* of which there could be too much. The notion of love as *pharmakon*, as both remedy (in the right proportions) and poison (in the wrong proportions) is worthy of further attention, although hooks holds a more dichotomous—and I will argue an insufficiently nuanced—view of love as a power that can do no wrong. In hooks's analysis, wherever love does seem to do wrong, it is probably not love at all. I will challenge that position, yet retain and build on hooks's interest in a variegated analysis imbued with feminist considerations of race, class, and gender.

People often receive their primary education about how to love or how to survive without being loved in the family. For hooks, the home is an essential location of love or its absence. "When we evoke a sense of home as a place where we can renew ourselves, where we can know love and the sweet communion of shared spirit, I think it's important for us

---

5. Ibid., 103.
6. Ibid., 104.

to remember that this location of well-being cannot exist in a context of sexist domination, in a setting where children are the objects of parental domination and abuse."[7] Clearly, hooks does not romanticize the home as a haven for all people, as she is well attuned to the fact that the family home is often not the space that it should be. We like to think of the family home as a safe space, even as a refuge from the outside world, when it is often a domain of cruelty and injury, full of violent forms of patriarchy, sexual and emotional abuse, and terrible fear. Love cannot be learned or experienced well within such a home. Not until one flees the dangerous space of the home can one assemble a new family of choice capable of providing the loving relationality denied in and by one's earlier family.

In conversation with Cornel West, hooks focuses on Black family life and Black community and culture, mainly in the United States. West and hooks contend that Black family and community in the United States differ from familial and community spaces that have not been consistently shaped by histories of racism, white supremacy, classism, exclusion, and abuse. Histories of dehumanization make for different orientations to the world. West observes that "the very notion that Black people are human beings is a new notion in Western Civilization and is still not widely accepted in practice.... [I]t is very difficult for Black men and women to remain attuned to each other's humanity, so when bell talks about Black women's agency and some of the problems Black men have when asked to acknowledge Black women's humanity, it must be remembered that this refusal to acknowledge each other's humanity is a reflection of the way we are seen and treated in the larger society."[8] West was not offering this up as an excuse for Black male sexism, but rather as a way of understanding the origin of certain attitudes. West connects the problem of sexism within the Black community to a long history of racism. It stands to reason that living on the losing end of a racist past and present affects one's understanding of one's self and of the world. And it is also true—as can be seen throughout the present book—that many radical theorists in the Marxian milieu or its orbit have been less committed to this analysis. When one reads critical theory from Fromm to Honneth, for example, the impact of racialization on relationality appears as basically insignificant.

In hooks's first book-length study of love, *All about Love: New Visions*, the family continues to be the primary location for learning relationality. She writes: "Love and abuse cannot coexist. Abuse and neglect are, by

---

7. bell hooks and Cornel West, *Breaking Bread: Insurgent Black Intellectual Life* (Boston: South End, 1991), 18.

8. Ibid., 12.

definition, the opposite of nurturance and care. Often we hear of a man who beats his children and wife and then goes to the corner bar and passionately proclaims how much he loves them."[9] Proclamations of love for a victim made by an abuser generate confusion. It's not that the abuser is lying. The abuser may well be telling the truth as well as he knows it. Passionate proclamations of love can be honestly believed by an abuser in moments of repentance, and every child or adult partner wants to believe that she is really loved. The reassurance that one is loved can be difficult to resist because love is considered palliative to abuse. Some abusers are, to be sure, consciously lying. They may want to keep what they have, so they sing a desperate, apologetic song of love until the abuse can be forgiven as a rare transgression. Abusers who honestly repent for the harm they have done, and who plead their case of love, may genuinely not know what love is, may never have thought about it, or may never have experienced it firsthand. The problem here is that love and its surrogates may be indistinguishable.

hooks also underscores the lies of capitalism. As she puts it: "Advertising is one of the cultural mediums that has most sanctioned lying. Keeping people in a constant state of lack, in perpetual desire, strengthens the marketplace economy. Lovelessness is a boon to consumerism. And lies strengthen the world of predatory advertising."[10] We are always being lied to in our capitalist societies where all *things* are sold to us. Even things that are not in fact things (like love and time and attention) are made into things for sale, which is to say: they are commodified. Sophisticated methods of selling home in on and produce particular feelings of lack, or of desire for something that one does not have but can acquire with money. From this capitalist point of view, lovelessness appears as an ideal condition. Deprived of love and its experiences, people are full of longing, a longing seized by capital. Thus, with hooks, we arrive at a different way of saying, indeed of showing, that capital is dissuasive of love. Previously, we have looked at the logics of love and capital, about the ways that capital disfigures and subverts love relations and the human community through the rule of exchange relations. However, with hooks, we see that capital profits from deficits of love, from human dissatisfactions that predatory consumerism can seize on. Here the now-classical idea of first-generation critical theory gets a better theorization through hooks's Black radical feminism—better because hooks's theory of love never glosses over the

9. bell hooks, *All about Love: New Visions* (New York: Harper Perennial, 2000), 6.
10. Ibid., 47.

racial and gendered components of the question, which we discuss more fully below. She recommends a moral commitment to practicing a "love ethic."[11] And here again, hooks returns to her unwittingly anarchist rejection of domination: "Domination cannot exist in any social situation where a love ethic prevails."[12]

To define what exactly hooks means by "love ethic" we should return to love as attention, acknowledgment, care, respect, understanding, well-being, and opposition to domination. A love ethic tells us that it is best to attend to other people by listening to them and acknowledging the seriousness of their concerns and problems. A love ethic recommends trying to understand where the unfamiliar feelings of other people may come from by way of real attention to the other, listening with respect, and resisting any solution to the crisis that calls for their domination or yours. This can be applied in particular cases. For example, if my son comes home from sixth grade, talks back to me angrily and slams the door in my face, hooks's love ethic would recommend a practical response. I can begin by taking seriously the sources of his disaffection and trying to understand them. But the instinct to domination is always close by. I am bigger than he is (at least for now), and, at twelve years old, he is to some extent under my power. I can shout at him and punish him, and in the years to come I can kick him out of the house. But I love him deeply, so I should try something else.

I should try to talk to him, but it may not work. I should try genuine attention. But as any parent knows, problems are not always solved that way. The child may not want to speak with a parent, and even the most caring efforts can be shut down (perhaps even as an attempt to exercise power by the relatively powerless child). Is hooks saying that the parent who shouts down, hits, or evicts the child cannot possibly love that child? Or are we talking instead about a lapse or deficit or breakdown of love made possible by a failure of understanding? These are difficult questions, but one thing is certain: love may recommend certain actions, yet it will not solve every problem. What good is a love ethic that cannot solve our problems? I would suggest, along with hooks, that the whole deliberation is ultimately helpful, as are the actions it recommends, and they are better in practice than some of the known alternatives, even if the results are not immediate. Perhaps, then, a love ethic can be a good guide for human action even if it cannot guarantee any outcomes. Love should not

---

11. Ibid., 87.
12. Ibid., 98.

be a results-oriented practice in any case, for it is a relation and an ethic, something that exceeds a specific moment or effort. This is to say that love can organize and guide a life, but it cannot be tested like a spot remover bought in a grocery store. I agree with and defend hooks's recommended orientation toward love as an ethic and a practice, a position she has extended from Fromm's work in important ways, and I will save my criticisms for later.

Also like Fromm (and like Cacioppo and Stiegler), hooks attends to alienation and loneliness in contemporary capitalist society. She claims that the sadness and despair of alienation is "the outcome of life in a culture where things matter more than people."[13] Narcissism grows from this alienation and the capitalist valuation of things, and narcissism is hostile to love. Instead of love, hooks argues, we see the rampant growth of greed, which is not the self-love that it is often mistaken to be. But unlike Fromm, Stiegler, and Cacioppo, hooks resists generalizations beyond stratifications of race and class. She writes about how the culture of greed and consumption differently affects the poor, who often resort to crime "to satisfy the same material longings as the rich."[14] Because class maps over race in white supremacist societies, communities of color living in consumerist societies governed by money may be incentivized to crime by a system that devalues them—not only in work but with regard to education, food access, heated or air-conditioned housing, safe public parks, and so forth. Self-interest and greed function differently in different communities based on relative socioeconomic positionality and the available opportunity structures. We must therefore be careful when we speak about alienation, anxiety, and depression to avoid generalizations that level out real differences of race, class, and gender. Critical theory never struggled enough to do this, and even prominent contemporary social theorists such as Berardi, Stiegler, and Honneth, who write book after book diagnosing the social reality, pay fleeting attention to stratifications of race and gender, and sometimes even scarce attention to class.

This may sound odd to any reader familiar with hooks, since she is not the least bit afraid to make general observations and, indeed, is often read as making too many. hooks's writing is never short on platitudes about her subject matter, or on conclusions that sum everything up without leftover troubles. Nonetheless, hooks reliably returns to qualifications about how the problems she studies are impacted by imperialist white

---

13. Ibid., 105.
14. Ibid., 109.

supremacist capitalist patriarchy. It is necessary in any case to critically assess some of the major conclusions of hooks's theory of love.

hooks argues that love has to be extricated from the culture of consumption that wants to make it into a fast gratification for sale in the capitalist marketplace. She points out that "love is rarely an emotional space where needs are instantly gratified."[15] We have to learn to think about love as something outside of "the culture of exchange."[16] The culture of exchange, according to hooks, acculturates greed, and in her theorization, greed appears as perhaps the largest obstacle to living in accordance with a love ethic. Greed is a human feeling and tendency, and it cannot be abolished, but it should not be allowed to govern human affairs. hooks worries about the connection to poverty here, observing that "we ignore the starving masses in *this* society, the thirty-eight million poor people whose lives are testimony to our nation's failure to share resources in a charitable and equitable manner."[17] This is one of the cases where hooks identifies a form of greed that has effectively derailed our societies from acting in accordance with a love ethic. The love ethic would always make attending to the well-being of others less of a *peripheral* and *ineffectual*— and more of a *central* and *determinant*—commitment in both politics and everyday life.

Ultimately, hooks argues for a communalism in the face of the failures of communism. Her idea is a kind of anarchist communism influenced by the best aspects of what she has seen and experienced in Black communities in the United States. In other words, hooks thinks of solutions to problems carried out in the networked kindnesses of neighbors, family, and close community. She knows that there is a communist tendency in all of this, but refuses to embrace the communist idea. She argues instead: "While communism has suffered political defeat globally, the politics of communalism continue to matter."[18] Although hooks was never committed to any kind of communism, she has always been a fierce and unrelenting critic of capitalism. We know what she means by the global political defeat of communism. She is referring to the end of the Cold War and the failures of the so-called "communist" projects of the twentieth century. But hooks's communalism is egregiously inadequate.

Communalism, as hooks defines it, must be distinguished from communitarianism. For hooks, communalism is a much more rhizomatic and

---

15. Ibid., 114.
16. Ibid., 115.
17. Ibid., 120.
18. Ibid., 125.

anarchistic way of developing the healthy *Gemeinwesen* of small groups. hooks's communalism is something like a highly localized coming-together for mutual aid, solidarity, care, and healing. Communalism of this kind sounds better than the narrow essentialism of communitarian philosophies that resist any sense of social responsibility that exceeds the boundaries of the community on the grounds that an appeal to universal values such as dignity and autonomy are dangerous or impossible.[19] The problem with hooks's communalism, however, is that it views big political-economic, social, and structural issues through a "think globally, act locally" lens. Such an approach to politics is abysmally inappropriate to problems like ecological crisis, and even to problems of special concern to hooks such as imperialism and white supremacy. Although I share hooks's rejection of state-administered solutions to these same problems, we need to make the miniature *Gemeinwesen* of families and neighborhoods into a coordinated movement of movements, which I would call communism. Today, we have to think communism through some such movement of movements from below, and not through the hackneyed image of the failed and collapsed bureaucracies of the previous century.

While hooks is not a communist, she does indicate that moving beyond the smallest units of the human community would be necessary eventually: "Capitalism and patriarchy together, as structures of domination, have worked overtime to undermine and destroy this larger unit of extended kin. Replacing the family community with a more privatized small autocratic unit helped increase alienation and made abuses of power more possible.... The failure of the patriarchal nuclear family has been utterly documented. Exposed as dysfunctional more often than not, as a place of emotional chaos, neglect, and abuse, only those in denial continue to insist that this is the best environment for raising children."[20] Here hooks appears to be to carrying forward Kollontai's basic thinking about the family. So hooks's communalism is not suggesting hyperindividualistic and privatized communities, but rather a growing and encircling family of extended kin that draws more humanity into the fold.

hooks argues that extended family networks are essential to the health and well-being of children, who can otherwise be victimized in the privacy of small autocratic family units. Because of abuse in the smallest

---

19. For good discussions of communitarianism see Michael Walzer, *Thick and Thin: Moral Argument at Home and Abroad* (Notre Dame: University of Notre Dame Press, 1994); and Janna Thompson, *Justice and World Order: A Philosophical Inquiry* (London: Routledge, 1992). ·

20. hooks, *All about Love*, 130–31.

spheres of family life, "friendship is the place in which a great majority of us have our first glimpse of redemptive love and caring community."[21] Many people flee the dangers of family for the refuge of friendship. Whether in the family or elsewhere, the search for love is clear evidence of an irrepressibly human search for community. I read hooks as arguing for something like little anarcho-communist islands that, although surrounded by hostile opposition, nonetheless provide enough caring community to protect us from the most dangerous abuses of home, family, work, domestic violence, and so on.

And we have to follow the love ethic toward the expansion of these little islands, toward the inclusion of strangers. According to hooks, there is a certain madness in not moving in that direction: "We cannot embrace the stranger with love for we fear the stranger. We believe the stranger is a messenger of death who wants our life. This irrational fear is an expression of madness if we think of madness as meaning we are out of touch with reality. Even though we are more likely to be hurt by someone we know than a stranger, our fear is directed toward the unknown and the unfamiliar."[22] This is connected to hooks's concerns about racism and imperialism. If we can understand that most of the dangers we face come from those closest to and most like us, then the rationality of racism and imperialism may be weakened. Racism and imperialism depend on and are mobilized by vilifying strangers. Fundamentally, hooks is not telling us that we have nothing to fear, but instead that we tend to be afraid of the wrong things. White supremacists are dangerous largely because they are full of fear and hatred. Following hooks, they are nonetheless much more likely to be hurt, abused, unwanted, neglected, and unloved by the white people in their closest vicinity than by the Black people they profess to hate.

hooks specifically takes up the question of love in US Black community and politics in *Salvation: Black People and Love*.[23] Here hooks tells a tale of a Black radical politics that pushed Black community away from the love ethic and toward the idealized Black, male, patriarchal militants and freedom fighters in the liberation struggles of the second half of the twentieth century. While hooks supported—then and now—Black liberation struggles, she lamented and regrets the ascendancy of a certain Black masculinity that, she claims, diminished love to a mere romantic

---

21. Ibid., 134.
22. Ibid., 193.
23. bell hooks, *Salvation: Black People and Love* (New York: Harper Perennial, 2001).

substance deemed both effeminate and emasculating. (This view has been taken up and challenged by Tommy J. Curry, whose more recent critical intervention is discussed below.) hooks argues that love, stripped of anything but its most inoffensive romantic identity, became extraneous to the struggle of Black radical politics, but it should not have been: "Love is profoundly political."[24] hooks is interested in the ways that love functions in white supremacist society. She points out that love was even a matter of survival when "enslaved black people worked to create a subculture where bonds of affection could be forged and sustained."[25]

Love must do different things in the context of white supremacist domination. hooks argues that Black families cannot do the same kind of loving as white families. Black families must construct and cultivate homes as spaces of refuge from a racist world, a world in which Black children are daily subjected to discrimination, exclusion, police profiling, and suspicion. Black children need reinforcements for self-love, acceptance, and confidence that the world at large does not offer, and thus they may need different lessons from loving parents about their health and well-being in a society of mass incarceration and racism. Consider, for example, that while I try to teach my own children about abuses of power and police brutality, I am less worried about their being the targets of police violence than Black mothers and fathers are accustomed to being about their children. My particular love for my sons, one could say, does not need to take the form of *that* active concern. Many white parents may reassure their children of their safety, saying "the police will be there," whereas Black parents may say the same thing as a warning.

hooks prefers to speak of white supremacy instead of racism. White supremacy names non-Black people as agents of racism and anchors the discussion of racism against false distractions and derailments about "reverse racism." But also, hooks wants Black people to consider how white supremacist thinking has been internalized in their own lack of confidence, self-doubt, and deficits of self-love. As she puts it: "As a strategy of colonization, encouraging enslaved blacks to embrace and uphold white supremacist aesthetics was a masterstroke. Teaching black folks to hate dark skin was one way to ensure that whether white oppressors were present or not, the values of white supremacy would still rule the day."[26] Negative images of Black people in the news and an early understanding of the lopsided likelihood that Black boys will spend time in prison and be

---

24. Ibid., 16.
25. Ibid., 20.
26. Ibid., 59.

surrounded by drugs, gangs, and the like are parts of a culture of white supremacy in which racialized and devalued selves are formed within Black communities in America.

It is worth emphasizing again that critical theory and Marxist philosophy have not done very well with sustained attention to these problems. Certainly, some radical thinkers such as Nancy Fraser, C. L. R. James, Raya Dunayevskaya, Robin D. G. Kelley, and Angela Y. Davis did (and do) maintain a focus on race and gender, in addition to class. But for the most part, white supremacy appears in critical and Marxian theory as epiphenomenal to capitalism. While I am not necessarily opposed to the epiphenomenal view and retain a central focus on capitalism and its crises, I am convinced that critical and Marxian theory needs a more sustained focus on white supremacy. And this focus definitely impacts the present study of love. Take, for example, hooks's insight that people without race or class privilege have always experienced "love in those places where material plenty was lacking. Love is especially available to us because it is a non-market value."[27] True, Fromm also insisted on love as a nonmarket value, and he did so decades before hooks, but in his theory racial stratification is near-totally insignificant. hooks helps us see that the marketization of love is perhaps more dangerous for those who are fully integrated into capitalist exchange relations. Those who do not have the capital to get in, who have scarce access to commodities, and who have been locked out of commercial activity can only seek and experience love in noncommercial ways and places.

The problem, which can be traced back to slavery and segregation, is that white supremacy expects Black people to accept their own subordination. You can very reliably spot white supremacy wherever white people minimize and dismiss Black disaffection. Indeed, the acceptance of unacceptable forms of domination and subordination is the basic expectation of "white supremacist capitalist patriarchy."[28] Whereas most Marxists and critical theorists concentrate on capitalism, hooks defines the enemy as "white supremacist capitalist patriarchy" because only that articulation secures permanent attention to gender and race as well as to class, and it constructs a concept of the enemy as a unitary complex of intersecting dominations.[29]

---

27. Ibid., 70.

28. Ibid., 74.

29. Although hooks sometimes adds "imperialist" to "white supremacist capitalist patriarchy," we may understand imperialism as one of the inexorable historical features of capitalism.

hooks has been careful to increasingly centralize issues of sexuality and transgender politics too. The most interesting chapter of *Salvation*, for instance, is on Black sexuality. hooks laments that there has never been a good historical study on Black attitudes toward homosexuality prior to desegregation, and especially because many of the people who lived in Black communities prior to racial integration in the United States can no longer be consulted for input.

hooks reassures us that she does not want to idealize Black history. Black communities had experienced so much racist violence—from slavery to lynching to economic and political deprivation—that "black communities could not expel gay folks." Because of segregation, "those communities had to come to terms with the reality of gay people in their midst."[30] Black communities instead oriented themselves as spaces of refuge for all Black people, accepting gays and lesbians both for reasons of racial solidarity and because of religious notions popular in Black communities that proclaim all of God's people as acceptable and welcome. hooks reviews a whole catalog of anecdotal evidence of early Black acceptance of gay and lesbian lives. She talks about Duke Ellington's acceptance of the openly gay Billy Strayhorn, and familial admonitions to accept and understand people in the Black community who were known to be gay or lesbian. She ties the rise of hostility to homosexuality in the Black community to the machismo of the Black liberation struggles in the 1950s and 1960s, specifically citing "Eldridge Cleaver's blatant attack on James Baldwin, whom he wanted to dethrone from his position as an authority and spokesperson for black experience."[31] (More recently, Tommy J. Curry has problematized this particular narrative in a discussion of an unpublished manuscript by Eldridge Cleaver in which Cleaver openly explores his own homosexuality. However, hooks's observation is not totally negated by Curry's research because it remains true that major Black militants of the 1960s adopted an increasingly macho and patriarchal posture.)

This has influenced expressions and affections of love in Black life in the United States today: "Fear of homosexuality has led many black adult men to withhold their love from male children and adult peers. Rooted in homophobia, this fear must be overcome if black men are to experience self-love."[32] Men who are raised to be hypermasculine, patriarchal, or homophobic are less inclined to hug and kiss other boys and men, including their own sons, brothers, and fathers, so as to avoid behaviors considered

---

30. hooks, *Salvation*, 192.
31. Ibid., 194.
32. Ibid., 204–5.

effeminate. This avoidance is a loss for all of the boys and men deprived of affection. While I think hooks is right about this, I am not convinced that such a homophobic fear of male affection is uniquely pronounced in Black communities in the United States. Homophobia runs deeply across class and racial divides.

However, hooks does map junctures in the history of Black political life that reveal a certain trajectory. Her most persuasive example is that of Louis Farrakhan, popular leader of the Nation of Islam, who hooks claims was quite intentionally popularized by a white supremacist capitalist patriarchal press.[33] hooks points out that Farrakhan "supports militarism, capitalism, imperialism, and patriarchy."[34] In other words, Farrakhan is opposed to white supremacy but was never capable of offering a healthy alternative to the problems he diagnosed. The central piece of evidence that hooks singles out to show the homophobic direction of Black politics from Cleaver to Farrakhan is the Million Man March. Farrakhan's popular and widely covered Million Man March was a celebration of Black patriarchy, "entrepreneurial spirit," and antifeminist sensibility. The event took place in Washington, D.C., in 1995 and was meant exclusively for African American men. A couple of years later there would be the Million Woman March, but hooks has long argued against this type of gendered separatism in social movements and political struggles, an argument she has strengthened in light of transgender politics. Nonetheless, Farrakhanian politics brings forward the worst elements of earlier Black liberation struggles, showing no significant development in the analysis of the problems of capitalism and gender, and further entrenching homophobic masculinities.

Yet, hooks's program—rooted in her theory of love—unfortunately does not exist in the world, ultimately amounting to the vague prescription that Black politics needs to recover and revitalize an old practice of love and commitment, reviving an activism animated by a love ethic. I am unsatisfied with hooks's overly anecdotal substantiation of her arguments and convinced by Curry's refutation of her characterization of Eldridge Cleaver (and the homophobic patriarchy of Black men). On the other hand, while I remain worried about a politics of communalism that is scarcely political, I ultimately find hooks's variegated analysis of love in different social contexts both necessary and instructive. Although hooks's books often feel far too general, they are at the same time diatribes against

---

33. Ibid., 216.
34. Ibid.

generality. hooks makes clear that good analysis requires consistent and thorough attention to race, class, and gender. If her theory suffers from some generalization, it nonetheless reveals the dangerous generalizations of other theories that are often considered more rigorous.

For example, one of the most rigorous and theoretically impressive contemporary scholars of love is Eva Illouz. In multiple studies, Illouz explores problems of love and loving within specific contexts of capitalist consumption and privatization. But it is somewhat astonishing how inattentive Illouz is to questions of race and class. Beyond this, I challenge and reject the tendency in Illouz's work to treat love as primarily romantic and sexual. This feature of her research produces a sociology of love that is insufficiently sociological. Yet in the milieu of theories of love, Illouz is the towering giant of recent years.

Whereas hooks and Fromm speak of love as a nonmarket value, Illouz is concerned with the marketization of love. For Illouz, the marketization of love is carried out through the construction of a romantic utopia that appears increasingly connected to and reliant on capitalist consumption. She traces a history according to which, "between 1900 and 1940, advertising and movies, the emerging and increasingly powerful cultural industries of the period, developed and advanced a vision of love as a utopia wherein marriage should be eternally exciting and romantic and could be if the couple participated in the realm of leisure."[35] The basic idea was that a lack of excitement in love could be addressed and even reversed through consumption, specifically by way of purchasing new experiences; paying for romantic activities such as getaways, encounters, and expensive vacations; or spending money on beachside dinners and bejeweled gifts or other surprises. Of course, participating in such consumption would only be the purview of people in privileged class positions. As a result, the many others who cannot afford to purchase utopian romance come to wonder if their love is of lesser value.

Illouz explains that a "utopia is a realm of the imagination within which social conflicts are symbolically resolved or erased through the promise and the vision of ultimate harmony, in both political and interpersonal relationships."[36] A romantic utopia would be something like a perfect unity of sexual and interpersonal gratification, full of good feeling and harmonious energy that never wanes. Even though the romantic utopia became, in the twentieth century, a commodity available for purchase

---

35. Eva Illouz, *Consuming the Romantic Utopia: Love and the Cultural Contradictions of Capitalism* (Berkeley: University of California Press, 1997), 41.

36. Ibid., 48.

through capitalist consumption, the basic notions of unity, gratification, and harmony have become the utopian vision of romantic love across class lines. Reading Illouz, it is difficult not to wonder if the vision of love from hooks and Fromm, or from other radical thinkers like Kollontai, is already subsumed by the romantic utopia of consumerism. Contrary to the romantic utopia, I claim that love is a field of conflict and disunity, a force of disturbance. Although Illouz does not treat love as something like utopia, we should beware anyone who does. Love is an effort, an ethic, a direction, a practice of relationality, but it is fraught with difficulty and failure. We cannot stop calling love by its name whenever it is hard.

While Illouz's work helps us to critically assess the origins of romantic utopian hopes and dreams, her focus on romantic love is a terrible limitation that we have already surpassed. Illouz also tracks predominantly male-female romantic relationships, generally steering clear of queer love and of broader and more socially circuitous concepts of love as relationality or as ethic and practice. When Illouz thinks of love, she thinks about the ways that the romantic utopia of monogamous relationships becomes integral to the broader utopianism of the American dream.[37] Such a way of studying love, however, is akin to speaking about water and its properties by exploring it in the confines of a glass.

Illouz's research does an excellent job, however, of exposing the extent to which our concept of romance has been produced and held hostage by capitalism. In one of her most stunning findings, Illouz showed four advertising pictures of romantic interaction to a sample of subjects. Among the pictures, the one that "was not chosen as romantic by any of the respondents" was "the only one of the four that is *not* an advertising picture."[38] Twentieth-century advertising and media representations, it would seem, have succeeded in making certain images of romance iconic to the point where we do not recognize romance in other scenes of life. Respondents would never have said that their images of romance were advertising images, and indeed, many of them even explained their selection of the most romantic photo by mentioning their unique take on romance. For example, they would say something like, "I'm sure no one would pick this photo, but in my own view romance is such and such." And yet, they were choosing images from advertising campaigns. We have long known that advertising is sophisticated enough to work subliminally. Nobody knows this more than advertisers: although everyone claims to

---

37. Ibid., 81.
38. Ibid., 103.

ignore the advertising on websites and in social media, firms continue to purchase ads, tracking positive results with incredible accuracy (including data on advertising costs per new customer acquisition). Measurable sales and tracking data show—more often than not—that the ads are not really ignored, that they work.

Thus, the question at the heart of Illouz's research is this: "How is the meaning of love affected by its incorporation within the culture of capitalism?"[39] Illouz answers this question as follows: "My own analysis confirms the Marxian claim concerning the all-pervasiveness of commodification: capitalism has implacably invaded the most private corners of our interpersonal and emotional lives. Although the market does not control the entire spectrum of romantic relationships. Most romantic practices depend on consumption, directly or indirectly, and consumerist activities have thoroughly permeated our romantic imagination."[40] This recalls what Honneth argued about the reorganization of love relations in accordance with privatization. And, although Illouz's analysis confirms Marx's, she does not follow Marx in thinking about a social or political reclamation or liberation of the thing from its commodified form. Consumerist love depends on investing romance and romantic movements in various patterns of consumption, such as the purchasing of experiences and gifts mentioned above. Illouz rightly diagnoses this commodification of love as catastrophic to our quest for healthy relationships in the world. Yet she conceptualizes no way out of such commodification; her Marxism is minimal and diagnostic.

Like hooks, Illouz acknowledges that capitalism does not affect love in exactly the same way everywhere. She points out, for example, that "working-class experiences of romance seem much less dependent on commodities."[41] This has more to do with varying abilities to pay than with rival visions of romance. Although the romantic utopia is "consumed" everywhere, Illouz nonetheless finds that working-class people are more likely to describe dinner at home, chance meetings, holding hands, and being together as romantic. Middle- to upper-middle-class respondents, in contrast, are more likely to invoke trips to Rome, cruises, or surprise holidays and exclusive rooftop dinners as the most romantic moments. While Illouz provides an often-fleeting and thin class analysis, she confirms that bourgeois romance is more "commodity-centric" than poor and working-class concepts of romance, the latter of which are more likely to

---

39. Ibid., 145.
40. Ibid., 146.
41. Ibid., 263.

provide nonmarket or noncommercial examples of romantic experience. This attests, once again, to different modalities of romantic love that rest on social differentiation. For example, Illouz reports that many poor and working-class people, when they speak about their romantic lives, tend not to mention financial difficulties. Financial difficulties are of course real and pressing for low-income people, but they are regarded as less fundamentally related to romance. More well-off people are more likely to satisfy or fulfill their romantic utopias precisely because the most idyllic romance requires *both* leisure and capital.

Like Cacioppo, Illouz's *Consuming the Romantic Utopia* adds empirical research to the theoretical analysis. But politically, both are inadequate. Illouz moves a bit closer to linking emotional and political life in her *Cold Intimacies: The Making of Emotional Capitalism*.[42] She begins there by stating: "Emotion is *not* action per se, but it is the inner energy that propels us toward an act.... Emotion can thus be defined as the 'energy-laden' side of an action.... Far from being pre-social or pre-cultural, emotions are cultural meanings and social relationships that are inseparably compressed together and it is this compression which confers on them their capacity to energize action."[43] This text can help us work through connections between feeling and action.

Emotion is something that moves something else, an energy connected to action. Emotions take their form and content as a result of the specific cultural and social contexts in which they develop, and because they are social energies, the actions they energize are already social. While love is not simply an emotion, we know that love is intimately connected to our emotional lives and thus participates in the assemblage that makes us act one way or another. This is a key point we will return to in our culminating arguments. But in *Cold Intimacies*, Illouz is not focused on the question of love. She is more interested in the relationship between capitalism and emotional life. She wants to focus on the emotions of capitalism, or what she calls "emotional capitalism."

Illouz traces the recent history of emotional capitalism to the experiments of Elton Mayo in the 1920s. "By suggesting that conflicts were not a matter of competition over scarce resources but rather resulted from tangled emotions, personality factors, and unresolved psychological conflicts, Mayo established a discursive *continuity between the family and the workplace* and in fact introduced the psychoanalytical imagination at the

---

42. Eva Illouz, *Cold Intimacies: The Making of Emotional Capitalism* (Cambridge: Polity, 2007).
43. Ibid., 2–3.

very heart of the language of economic efficiency. More than that: being a good manager increasingly meant displaying the attributes of a good psychologist: it required being able to grasp, listen to, and deal dispassionately with the complex emotional nature of social transactions in the workplace"[44] The story of Mayo, vividly recounted by Illouz, is astonishing in its significance.

Essentially, this means that the person who functions at a high level in the workplace, administering and integrating themselves fully into the workplace and serving its purposes with minimal difficulty, came to be seen as emotionally healthy, reasonable, and well-adjusted. Thus, economic efficiency was made into an indicator of rationality and psychological health, and good managers were even regarded as well-suited to serve as psychologists who could help the workers with their emotional lives. This codifies and idealizes capitalist functionality as the apex of emotional and psychological health; the designation of "good manager" or "worker" became portable. Thus, a male worker deemed well and healthy in the capitalist workplace could take himself home and regard his unemployed wife as insufficiently rational (or overly emotional), as incapable of doing what he does every day. This economic rationality was therefore a further entrenchment of the patriarchalism of the first half of the twentieth century.

You are not supposed to bring disruptive or distracting emotions into the rational high-functioning workplace, although the secret has always been that "the capitalist workplace turns out to be far less devoid of emotions than has been conventionally assumed."[45] Jealousy and competition are among the obvious emotions common in the workplace, but in the name of "team effort," well-adjusted members of the organization are expected to proclaim no such feelings toward fellow coworkers. Illouz appreciates the fact that things have evolved since the 1920s and 1930s and that the old secret about emotions at work has been an open secret for quite some time. Importantly, movements like feminism have won a certain level of recognition and affirmation of people's real and reasonable workplace disaffections.

Recognition and affirmation of workplace disaffections have not, however, solved the problems of emotional capitalism because they have instead produced a new discourse on "personality types" that are more or less suited for different kinds of work. "By making personality and

---

44. Ibid., 14–15.
45. Ibid., 24.

emotions into new forms of social classification, psychologists not only contributed to making emotional style a social currency—a capital—but also articulated a new language of selfhood to seize that capital."[46] Thus, the recognition of various emotional styles as personality types reinforces the idea that some people are just not "cut out" for some work, and those that are suited to particular work can attribute it to the type of person they are. Everyone looking for a job must learn how to market themselves as the right type. The idea that anyone can become the right type for anything expresses one of the most damaging lies of capitalist individualism. Not everyone can be a realist painter of landscapes, a philosopher, a mathematician, or a basketball player, and two people studying the same second language at the same time and place are unequally inclined to learn it at the same pace and efficiency. And we have to insist that the ones most suited for the jobs that pay the highest salaries are not worth more than the ones (say, the artists or musicians or caretakers) who work for low pay. That great artists make nothing while the perfect bureaucrat makes six figures—without any imagination or sense of purpose—is a failure of capitalism, not of the artist.

One of the most difficult terms to resist in contemporary and mainstream psychological discourse is "emotional intelligence." We think of emotional intelligence as an accurate self-understanding of one's own emotional and psychological state. For example, a person with high emotional intelligence would be said to possess a good understanding of why they feel jealousy and anger, and would know when and when not—and in what ways—to allow such feelings to affect their behavior. A person with low emotional intelligence would be said to have little to no idea of how their feelings make their behavior appropriate or not in a given context, so they may act from a jealousy that everyone can see, yet deny any feeling of jealousy. But Illouz wants us to beware of this seductive term. "Emotional intelligence is not only the kind of competence required in an economy in which the performance of the self is crucial to economic performance but also the outcome of this process of intense professionalization of psychologists who, historically, have been extraordinarily successful in claiming the monopoly over the definition and the rules of emotional life and who thus have established new criteria to capture, manage, and quantify emotional life."[47] Consider the Mayo study of the manager who functions like a workplace psychologist. We should resist

---

46. Ibid., 65.
47. Ibid., 66.

concluding that those seen as the most "high-functioning" have the highest emotional intelligence.

The most coldly calculative and functionalist behaviors within capitalist culture and society come to be seen as the most well-adjusted behaviors. A term like "emotional intelligence" adds an epistemological dimension, making the coldest of intimacies appear as if they were also the smartest expressions of human emotionality. But Illouz scarcely touches on the subject of "love" in this short study of emotional capitalism. When she does, she returns once again only to romantic love, her favorite example.[48] And here, much like Srećko Horvat, Illouz focuses on commodification in the technological and algorithmic world of Internet match-making. As she puts it, "not only is the cost-benefit cultural repertoire of the market now used in virtually all private and domestic interactions but it is also as if it has become increasingly difficult to switch from one register of action (the economic) to another (the romantic)."[49] While Illouz continues her dangerously narrow focus on romantic love in contemporary capitalist societies, she at least extends her analysis here so that romantic love appears as only one aspect of our emotional and psychological life that has been taken hostage by capitalist logics of organization.

In her next major study, *Why Love Hurts: A Sociological Explanation*, Illouz remains fixated on the romantic form of love, further exploring new fears and possibilities attending to romance.[50] Despite ongoing yet fleeting attention to gender and class, she remains nearly silent on questions of race. This is perhaps unsurprising given that she seems not to have noticed hooks's contributions to the study of love at all (and it is inexcusable to study love in any sustained way without a shred of attention to bell hooks). Although a full fifteen years separates her first major study of love, *Consuming the Romantic Utopia*, and this one from 2012, Illouz remains relatively uninterested in seriously attending to the racial stratifications most sociologists insist on, and although she addresses some diversity in romantic love, she tends nonetheless to continue to think of love in mainly heterosexual contexts.

In fact, Illouz specifies not only romantic love, but heterosexual love as her central focus: "Heterosexual romantic love contains the two most important cultural revolutions of the twentieth century: the individualization of lifestyles and the intensification of emotional life projects; and

---

48. Ibid., see especially "Part 3: Romantic Webs."
49. Ibid., 114.
50. Eva Illouz, *Why Love Hurts: A Sociological Explanation* (Cambridge: Polity, 2012).

the economization of social relationships, the pervasiveness of economic models to shape the self and its very emotions."[51] These are all problems Illouz is accusing heterosexual love relations for helping to realize and make worse, and she is bracketing same-gender love relationships for sociological and historical reasons. However, she drops the specification of "heterosexual romantic" when writing about love and mainly speaks of heterosexual romantic love as love itself.

Illouz retains and extends the premise of her earlier work on consumption. She points out that while love is often regarded as an overwhelming force beyond anyone's control, it looks more and more like just another consumer choice. Each lover chooses a beloved, the right type for him or for her, in a practice modeled on the experience of shopping. One of the keys to commodification in love relations has to do with beauty and sexualization. Illouz makes a feminist critique of how both men and women are subordinated "to the enormous economic machine fed by the beauty industry."[52] Importantly, Illouz observes how beauty and sexualization are inextricably linked to money and consumption, for example to expensive clothes, skincare products, treatments, preparations, and presentations, many of which the poor cannot afford. Because sexism kept women—for the first two hundred years of capitalism—out of work and away from income sufficient for autonomous survival, women sought heterosexual marriage as a way to preserve themselves economically, but women would have no choice but to appeal to men on the grounds of prevalent idealizations of beauty and dominant sexualizations of their bodies in order to marry a male with sufficient income.

In a chapter entitled "The Demand for Recognition," Illouz makes an argument similar to Honneth's. For Illouz, love matters and hurts because it is fundamentally about recognition. She argues "that love provides a strong anchor for recognition, the perception and constitution of one's worth, in an era where social worth is both uncertain and ongoingly negotiated."[53] Here, while I basically agree with Illouz, we must insist that love as a practice of recognition need not be theorized within the boundaries of the romantic milieu. I prefer the social theorization of love as a practice by Fromm, Honneth, and hooks, according to which romantic love appears as only one possible refuge from capitalism. Illouz sees romantic love as disfigured and commodified by capitalism, but if we think of love relations beyond the romantic, heterosexual, and monogamous

---

51. Ibid., 9.
52. Ibid., 54.
53. Ibid., 120.

relationship, we can consider other spaces of refuge, including spaces of political contestation.

Understanding love as a practice of recognition is important because it captures the ontology of love. When we are talking about individual persons properly recognized as such, and conduits of affirmation and attention that generate self-understanding and self-worth, we are talking about being-in-the-world. That is what we should be talking about, and it is an ontological subject. The question of love raises the question of our being-in-the-world and our being-beyond-capital. The ontological question is, for Illouz, connected to feminism. Fundamentally, she views feminism as a "way of conceiving of the self and its relationships to others."[54] And, because "feminist practice opposes any instrumentalization of bodies and persons," it makes for an ideal politics for challenging the commodification and marketization of love.[55] I am convinced by our study of Jenny Marx and Luxemburg, and by the writings of Kollontai, hooks, and Illouz, that any theory of love worth defending will have to be feminist.

In addition to the feminist critique of the emotional capitalism of love, Illouz calls on fantasy and imagination capable of challenging the carefully cultivated fantasies of the romantic utopia as they are sold in the global market. First, if we accept the romantic utopias of media and advertising, then every experience of love will be thwarted by the disappointment of its dissimilarity from marketed representations. Second, if we can imagine a love in *other* and *different* ways, then perhaps we can create experiences of love that do not need to be purchased. Romantic fantasies of utopia packaged and sold in our capitalist societies are fast tracks to disappointments with destructive social and psychological consequences. Needless to say, we must be careful how we think of love. While I appreciate Illouz's feminism, hers is ultimately a feminism reconciled to accept the world as it is. She concludes by saying of her own theory that it is "a sobered endorsement of modernity through love" that "does not have the fervor of utopias or of denunciations."[56] While our theory of love is and must be feminist, we have no need for a feminism that can only endorse the existing state of affairs, no matter how sober.

What is a feminism without utopias and denunciations? Illouz seems to think we can reorganize love relations against the dangerous commodification of romantic utopias without directly confronting, without denouncing, and certainly without destroying the basic realities that have

---

54. Ibid., 170.
55. Ibid., 184.
56. Ibid., 248.

organized our emotional lives, down to the sense of self, in accordance with the functioning of capitalism. This must be one of the many reasons Illouz is not a communist and asserts instead a more or less liberal mainstream feminism against the juggernaut of capital she so expertly diagnoses. Unfortunately, if Illouz thinks that her sobered endorsement of modernity is enough to address the problems she reveals, then she has not avoided utopianism at all. The most utopian position is one that believes in the promise of the existing state of affairs; a more practical position combines denunciation with imagination.

Certain conclusions can now be drawn from our engagement with hooks and Illouz. Capitalism is not the only enemy that dominates and disfigures love relations today. Capitalism preys on all nonmarket values by attempting to abolish them in their conversion to exchange value. If a value or virtue cannot be commodified and converted into exchange value, then it is denied value altogether, deemed worthless in the world of capital. Thus, for example, creative artistic production is either commodified or else it is reduced to an idiosyncratic sentimentality that can neither be measured nor assessed as a real value. Noncapitalist values only exist in things like weathered pictures of your dead father kept in your wallet—valuable to no one but you. But there are other problems love has to face.

White supremacy and patriarchy are also predatory enemies that destroy love. White supremacy devalues and dehumanizes Black people and other people of color. Their representation and their recognition within our racist societies—*societies that continue brazen stratification by race*—call for affirmation in communal and familial spaces capable of generating self-worth and confidence. Love looks differently for those who have been chronically excluded, systematically discriminated against, and expected to fail or be jailed. *Love has different work to do there.* Patriarchy also preys on love, and, as Illouz has shown, idealizations of beauty, the commodification of bodies, and economic rationality have historically singled out and done greater harm to women than to men over the past two capitalist centuries. The whole romantic utopia is subordinated to a patriarchal history in which women (though not only women)—and particularly poor, working-class women—are on the losing end of love.

All of this is to say that the pains of love, its particular deprivations and disfigurements, are not equally distributed. The worst casualties—although certainly not the only casualties—of love in a world of white supremacist capitalist patriarchy are nonwhite, poor, women, and sexual minorities.

5.2 Marginalities of Unwantedness and Madness

Important recent scholarship has shifted the focus from sexism and patriarchy to contemporary racialization that marginalizes and denies the humanity of Black boys and men with targeted brutality.

Mass incarceration is one side of the story. We can speak today of different systems of captivity and repression that give rise to revolt (see, for example, Heather Ann Thompson's *Blood in the Water* regarding the 1971 Attica Prison uprising).[57] Indeed, many scholars study how present incarceration in the United States continues and perfects systems of captivity and repression with direct lineages to slavery.[58] Angela Y. Davis argues "that racism is even more effective and more devastating today than it was during the era that produced the Civil Rights movement. This country's imprisoned population provides a dramatic example: among the more than two million people currently in prison, over seventy percent are people of color."[59] And according to Michelle Alexander: "The United States now has the highest rate of incarceration in the world, dwarfing the rates of nearly every developed country, even surpassing those in highly repressive regimes like Russia, China, and Iran. In Germany, 93 people are in prison for every 100,000 adults and children. In the United States, the rate is roughly eight times that, or 750 per 100,000. The racial dimension of mass incarceration is its most striking feature. No other country in the world imprisons so many of its racial or ethnic minorities. The United States imprisons a larger percentage of its black population than South Africa did at the height of apartheid."[60]

Tommy J. Curry's book *The Man-Not* is a remarkable study of the dehumanization of Black men. Curry explores how racism in the United States extends incarceration beyond physical prisons into the psyches of Black men:

> Black male death, despite its horror and gruesomeness, is tolerated within America. Many in our society accepted this reality as a norm, but what effect does death have on the lives, the mental concept

---

57. Heather Ann Thompson, *Blood in the Water: The Attica Prison Uprising of 1971 and Its Legacy* (New York: Pantheon Books, 2016).

58. Patrick Elliot Alexander, *From Slave Ship to Supermax: Mass Incarceration, Prisoner Abuse, and the New Neo-Slave Novel* (Philadelphia: Temple University Press, 2018).

59. Angela Y. Davis, *Abolition Democracy: Beyond Empire, Prisons, and Torture* (New York: Seven Stories, 2005), 96.

60. Alexander, *New Jim Crow*, 6.

of the self, that Black males formulate in this violent world? How do Black males regard the future in a world that is so limited by the present? Imagine a world in which any individual, who can be thought of as a victim of a Black male, has the power to define him as a criminal. This is the world many Black males find themselves imprisoned within.[61]

Notice that Curry talks about imprisonment beyond the prison itself. Black men outside of prisons are aware from a young age of the lopsided likelihood of their incarcerated bodies. This is one kind of quotidian violence occurring constantly between revolts. The word "quotidian" refers to that which occurs every day, appears to us as ordinary, or is so much a part of daily expectations that—*even though it may be awful*—it becomes mundane. This describes how much of the West looks on violence in the Muslim world. An attack in France is seen as more extraordinary than an attack in an airport in Turkey or an aerial bombardment on Yemen. This is also how much of white America sees poverty in Black cities or Black bodies in prisons: it is something to be expected *there*. The quotidian therefore conceals, often very thinly, an everyday racism, or "the normal racism." The expectation of imprisonment and brutality that Curry discusses is a quotidian feature of what I would call a kind of "carceral consciousness" in the everyday understanding of Black men, a consciousness that is acculturated from a young age, regardless of run-ins with the law.

Curry traces how Black men, because of the relative size of their penises, were once regarded by white ethnologists as ruled by their sex organs, and thus the science of ethnography claimed to have established a tendency in Black men toward rape.[62] This pseudoscientific view long held that Black men were not quite human, an idea that remains a less public but still-defining feature of racism today.

As mentioned above, Curry challenges bell hooks's narrative regarding Black masculinity in the movements of the 1950s, 1960s, and 1970s. Eldridge Cleaver, for example, the iconic image of homophobic Black masculinity, is revealed in Curry's work as a man who explored his own sexuality in an unpublished book written in prison, *The Book of Lives*.[63] Curry tells us that Cleaver was not certain if his sexual desire for a young man in prison was just the result of sexual repression and inactivity, but he

---

61. Tommy J. Curry, *The Man-Not: Race, Class, Genre, and the Dilemmas of Black Manhood* (Philadelphia: Temple University Press, 2017), 36.
62. Ibid., 53.
63. Ibid., 85.

nonetheless openly explored his desire in the book. This not only contradicts the homophobia commonly attributed to Black men but also contradicts Cleaver's own homophobia and notorious desire to rape as expressed in his actually published and widely read *Soul on Ice* (1968).[64]

But Curry's point cuts deeper than the question of Cleaver's sexuality: "In a prison, the playpen of white hedonism, the Black convict is transfigured as a physical object used within the various matrices of power directed by white desire. He is labor—physical and sexual. He exists for the enjoyment and legitimation of the white ideas created to explain his existence. He is prisoner because he is criminal."[65] The depth of this insight is essential to our study of love, although it may not be immediately obvious why. Curry explains that the Black man is envisioned by white people, dating back to the earliest ethnologists, as a nonhuman animalistic fucking machine driven to rape and, as a *post facto* rationalization of the legal punishment of Black men, also driven to crime.[66] Thus, those in prison are caricatured as dangerous criminals, and if they did not rape anyone, then they might, or they might kill you, or so the racist fear of the Black man suggests. As a result, factories packed full of young Black men function as living substantiations of a white supremacist fear of the Black man, who in the end is not regarded as a man at all. But, as Curry points out in relation to the caricature and condemnation of Cleaver as the iconic homophobic patriarch and rapist, "we cannot, as either students of history or theorists, overlook his analysis of the society that raped Black men and then murdered them as rapists."[67]

Abstractly, we could say that young Black boys and men need to be loved and need to learn how to love. This is true, as it is true across all lines of race, class, and gender. But what is the experience of love in a society that denies Black boys and men their humanity and imbues them with a carceral consciousness from a prepubescent age? Indeed, when Curry writes about young Black boys specifically, he refers to the repeated messages they often get about their "unwantedness."[68] The message of unwantedness runs also through carceral consciousness, which understands that if the rulers of society wanted Black boys, they would not so systematically put them behind bars. Whether inside prisons or outside of them, young Black men grow up understanding themselves as unwanted. As a

---

64. Ibid., 87.
65. Ibid., 91.
66. Ibid., 100–102.
67. Ibid., 103.
68. Ibid., 124.

result, any abstract appeal to love appears pathetically inadequate. Love starts to look like the privilege of the wanted, recognized, and most highly valued humanity.

All of this is of course related to the present reality of police brutality and police killings of Black boys and men in the United States, an epidemic that recently gave rise to revolts in Ferguson and Baltimore and to the Black Lives Matter movement. As Curry puts it: "This erasure that accepts the normalcy of Black male death simultaneously accepts the racist disposability of Black male life."[69] Curry insists that we recognize that the Black male personality in society today is a product of a long history of racist dehumanization, incarceration, and sexual repression, and not something as simple as a cultural tendency toward hypermasculine patriarchy that feminism can target for criticism. If we begin with a feminist critique of Black masculinity, Curry argues, then we take Black masculinity for granted. We uncritically accept the object of our criticism, as if it had not itself been produced in a particular social, political, and economic history.

One of the glaring flaws of Curry's brilliant and indispensable study is that he does not treat the history he traces as inextricably linked to capitalism. In fact, although he is not silent on the subject, he seems relatively uninterested in the problems of capitalism. I would suggest, however, that while racism can function independently of capitalism, societies governed by the logic of capital are always subordinated to the ruling interests of dominant and established powerholders, who have historically been white supremacist. Robin D. G. Kelley and Cedric Robinson (both ignored in Curry's study) have understood this point better than Curry.[70]

Prisons are labor factories, and even where they are not wholly private, for-profit companies, they have functioned and continue to function as storehouses of free labor, fields of pure profit continuing the labor stream from the economies of slavery, and in a no less racialized way. Here Angela Y. Davis does better than Curry to capture this critical continuity. And, despite other shortcomings that both Curry and I have pointed out, bell hooks also offers a better critical appreciation of the generative role that capitalism plays in racism. Although we can find neo-Nazis and white supremacists across the United States (including in the prisons) who have little to no capital at their command, the fact is that white supremacy is about power and money. Even among impoverished working-class

---

69. Ibid., 145.

70. See Robin D. G. Kelley, *Freedom Dreams: The Black Radical Imagination* (Boston: Beacon, 2002); and Cedric J. Robinson, *Black Marxism: The Making of the Black Radical Tradition* (Chapel Hill: University of North Carolina Press, 2000).

racists and imprisoned neo-Nazis, money partly motivates racist hatred of the "unworthy" Black men characterized as villains taking the precious opportunities of white people because of quota-counting liberals and wrong-headed efforts at social inclusion. In other words, racism is always connected to anxieties about opportunity, money, and power.

Despite Curry's problematic disinterest in the role of capital in the making of "the man-not" of Black boys and men, he clearly demonstrates that the sociality of Black men is unique and demands special care and attention. I am wholly convinced by his thesis, and am left here to wonder about the possibility of love in such a context of racist dehumanization. At the very least, a certain qualification is necessary regarding the limits of love as a communist power. We cannot say that love is absent among the impoverished and imprisoned mass of Black humanity. Of course there is love there. However, we cannot recommend some simple or generic practice of love. It is nothing but superficial moralizing to look at the realities revealed by writers from W. E. B. Du Bois to Angela Y. Davis, Michelle Alexander, and Tommy J. Curry and to respond by advocating love.

We have to confront the most rudimentary existential dilemma, that of Black life and death. Love may function as a power of communist relationality and activity, but only after basic life is secured, assured, and reliable enough to count on tomorrow. Yet people always speak of love at the time of death. Perhaps especially then. Love is reliably among the most common of dying words. I think it is because love prefers life to death that it enters the stage so dramatically at the time of dying. But certain forms of insecurity are too severe to provide footing for a political orientation. If I am a communist who is hit by a car, my communism will not be called on while I lay in a hospital bed in critical condition. I never feel less political than when I am lying in a speeding ambulance. My concept of society is of no significance (or should not be) to the doctors or surgeons charged with treating my injuries and bringing me back to life. My being-communist will be restored only once I am well enough to turn my attention away from immediate concerns of life and death.

To take another example, I sometimes wonder about writing political philosophy as the earth inexorably warms to a climate that human beings cannot survive. As I sit here writing about capitalism and racism, or preparing lectures on Plato and Marx, I think about the relative erasure of my concerns if fires and fatal storms and extreme temperatures spread across the planet and put me and my loved ones onto an immediate terrain of life and death. Political theory and philosophy rescue no one from hurricanes and tornadoes, and dinosaurs could not have been saved by bigger brains.

Some Marxists think that the impoverished and incarcerated mass of Black humanity should turn urgently to communism in order to find the right conduits for their disaffection. Communists always long for global resurgences of Marxism among the world's most disaffected and abused peoples. But we have to be careful here, for ideology is never as certain in the world as it seems to be within its own ideological space. People who live in the direst circumstances yet do not become political revolutionaries reveal no philosophical shortcoming, no lack of intellectual or political prowess. If they do not become revolutionaries, if they do not adopt a revolutionary point of view, we should assume that there are perfectly good reasons for that. Black people and other people of color today often live on the precipice of the worst precarity, and their situation is often as critical as life and death. Impoverished humanity living on the edge of life may speak of love and may seek to realize its powers too, but perhaps not right now, not in the ambulance. Simply put, *life itself* is more pressing than *forms of life*.

And there are of course many others who live so far on the margins of society, whether unwanted or abandoned, despised, addicted, outcast, or considered asocial or pathological. For a whole variegated strata of humanity, love may be a hopeful and prospective aspiration, but not a real and present power. We may think here of the unloved or of those who feel unlovable. To consider one such example, we shall move away from the subject of racialization and return to a particular marginality of gender and counterculture. Let us consider, for a moment, the example of Valerie Solanas.

Solanas's famous, murder-inflected *SCUM Manifesto* should not be read as the literal expression of homicidal rage that it may immediately appear to be to its most alarmed readers. Such a reactionary reading of the text is not very thoughtful. The manifesto should be read, instead, as a missive of revolt against—and as an unconventional and seemingly unafraid expression of disaffection with—the structure and culture of gender politics in postwar America. The text should be read that way because that is what it is.

Solanas lays bare her total disgust with a certain kind of woman as well as her total disgust with dominant and defining male desires and behaviors. Everyone who reads the manifesto will know men and women who do not embody or reflect the tendencies Solanas despises. And that is the key: Solanas's text wages war against certain tendencies in the gendered world of men and women. Her categorical, total, and even murderous language is what makes the manifesto unignorable, arresting, and so widely read. Solanas was repeatedly ignored and did not want to be. She wrote the manifesto in perhaps the only way that would make it visible. She had something to say, she wanted it heard, and conventional ways of speaking would have left her message inaudible. I want to engage *the actual critical content of her manifesto* instead of the stunning rage of its features. While it may be easiest to conclude that Solanas's text is full of hatred, *I claim that it expresses a hatred of the absence of love.* This is a text from and for love, a love lost in the world as she knew it. The seriousness that Solanas's manifesto deserves has never been realized, and what really needs to be done cannot be accomplished in the present text. But we shall take a step in the right direction here, taking Solanas seriously for what she has to say, for how her manifesto speaks to, exposes, and criticizes contemporary problems of social life, and placing her message in relation to the communism of love.

Solanas might have been a murderer indeed. It is true, for example, that she attempted to kill Andy Warhol, and she later said she couldn't care less if he died. Still, we should not mistake her writing for an act of murder. The manifesto is a text, and if we had to categorize it, we could call it a lesbian-anarchist and feminist utopian critique of existing society.

In her introductory essay to a recent edition of *SCUM Manifesto*, Avital Ronell encourages us to listen to the truths spoken in psychotic texts.[71] Ronell's point is that we should not overlook the text's insights for its apparent insanity. There are times when what is called "sensible" appears as insane and what is insane appears as sensible, and there are times when a psychotic rant contains a mix of hyperbole, blatant falsity, and very deep insight. Solanas was an iconic radical woman writer on the margins of US social life during the 1960s. She hated men, she hated capitalism, and she wanted a new form of value to rule the world. As Ronell puts it: "Her goal was to abolish money, the symbolic exchange of value.... [S]he wanted a more direct assessment of value. She abhorred abstract capital fluctuations; she dreaded substitutive tradeoffs. Men had created capital flow as part of an exploitative economy."[72] As an artist and writer, Solanas could not win in a world of capitalist exchange value. Who would assess the value of her work? Who could? Solanas saw herself as SCUM. She did not pit woman against man because, for her, too many women were themselves aspirants to bourgeois normalcy, with no destructive, creative, or subversive impulse against the world of male domination and sexual predation.

---

71. Valerie Solanas, *SCUM Manifesto* (London: Verso Books, 2004), 16.
72. Ibid., 26.

Solanas finds most men disgusting, self-obsessed, sexually violent, and depraved, but she also "wages war ... against the type of woman who relinquishes her capacity for domination."[73] In other words, women who accept societal assumptions of their own submission become the complacent and indispensable tools of the vilest men.

To say that Solanas was in the margins of society means that there was no welcome for her anywhere, not even on the fringes of the feminist and radical Left—not even among the anarchists could she find a reliable, hospitable home. Ronell reports that Solanas died homeless and destitute in San Francisco in 1988 after spending much of her life on the streets as a prostitute.[74] Solanas hated this world and wanted to transform it, just like the anarchists and Marxists who would not or could not take her in. Let us consider the relationship of Solanas to the topic of love.

So much of the political world as we know it was made by men, and it has grown all the more violent by those (including women) who go along with the depravity of men. Solanas indicts war as a male creation, as an expression of masculinity in the world. If a man is supposed to be tough, then war is a demonstration of the fiercest manliness. Many men and women who have no power to make war have nonetheless accepted the reasons given for war; such men and women are not SCUM. They are accomplices to everything awful.

Men make war to make money, to seize land and power from others, but money is yet another male creation devised to grow their own power. Solanas writes: "There is no human reason for money or for anyone to work more than two or three hours a week at the very most.... But there are non-human, male reasons for wanting to maintain the money system."[75] Among the reasons she discusses, Solanas cites the growing inability to deal with leisure time. People who hate themselves and have no creative or artistic inclinations cannot bear to be alone with themselves, so they prefer to be permanently at work. Money gives men a reason to always be at work, and in 1967 Solanas held that it also gave women reasons to stay home and tend to the purportedly "nonwork" spaces of their male overseers. Money is defended by men precisely as a defense of their own power and control, and this is because money gives them power and control in the world they have made. Money also gives men a purpose and a goal. Without it, many men would wonder what their life is for.

For us, the most apropos reason men love capitalism is that, according

---

73. Ibid., 29.
74. Ibid., 30–31.
75. Ibid., 39–40.

to Solanas, money functions as a substitute for love. "Unable to give love or affection, the male gives money. It makes him feel motherly. The mother gives milk; he gives bread."[76] If I cannot love you because I do not know what love means or how to do it, even if it is because I have never myself experienced it, then I may try to use money as a surrogate for love. If I buy my beloved things, the thinking goes, maybe I will not need to actively love her. And if I do not know how to love, money is a different power that can do something by other means that might take the place of real care and affection. In Solanas's view, men try to make up for deficits of love with money, so capitalism inhabits the spaces where love is absent. This appears as a consistent thesis throughout Solanas's manifesto. And when one follows that line in her text, a clear, overarching interest in love emerges.

It is easy to obscure Solanas's interest in love in *SCUM Manifesto* because that interest is subtle by comparison to the outrages that surround it. But Solanas writes consistently about love throughout the text and always invokes it as a reliably hostile antagonist to the male world of money, war, and sexual depravity. Solanas defines the "female function" as exploring, discovering, making jokes, and making music, "all with love."[77] The money approach to living is clearly distinguished from the love approach to living, and the love approach—although not practiced by all women—is ultimately a feminine approach to life. A loving approach to life cannot lead to exploitation, war, and rape. One problem with sexist and patriarchal history is that it codifies the feminine as weak or deficient, and so it is no surprise that love—understood as a feminine power—appears to men as too soft for a world governed by money power. In contrast, a woman who has not been overtaken by male society and colonized by its thinking knows that "the meaning of life is love."[78] It is perhaps for this reason that Solanas places her only hope in SCUM women who have not lost their basic instincts for love.

In a telling section of the manifesto, Solanas equates love and friendship, as if love in practice takes the form of friendship: "Love is not dependency on sex, but friendship.... [F]riendship is based upon respect, not contempt."[79] And, indeed, Solanas identifies capitalism at the heart of the problems of a sexist and loveless society: "Love can't flourish in a society based on money and meaningless work: it requires complete economic as

---

76. Ibid., 41.
77. Ibid., 47.
78. Ibid., 53.
79. Ibid., 57.

well as personal freedom, leisure time and the opportunity to engage in intensely absorbing, emotionally satisfying activities which, when shared with those you respect, lead to deep friendship."[80] This is to say that our societies are not well made to cultivate and reward freedom, free time, and the many joys of friendship. We are restricted to living within the limits of our ability to pay for the things that we want, and most of us find our leisure time colonized by work that is mostly miserable and does not define a healthy sense of self. Friendship, on the other hand, implies a form of being-together that stands in tension with self-interested and atomistic privatization.

Throughout her manifesto, Solanas imagines men's eventual sexual obsolescence. Her utopian horizon is of female-to-female friendship and queer sexuality. The problem is not, however, as dichotomous as men versus women, not only because of sexuality but also because the majority of women are not SCUM. Solanas puts it as follows:

> The conflict, therefore, is not between females and males, but between SCUM—dominant, secure, self-confident, nasty, violent, selfish, independent, proud, thrill-seeking, free-wheeling, arrogant females, who consider themselves fit to rule the universe, who have free-wheeled to the limits of this "society" and are ready to wheel on to something far beyond what it has to offer—and nice, passive, accepting, "cultivated," polite, dignified, subdued, dependent, scared, mindless, insecure, approval-seeking Daddy's girls, who can't cope with the unknown ... who have reduced their minds, thoughts, and sights to the male level. ... But SCUM is too impatient to wait for the de-brainwashing of millions of assholes.[81]

This passage is full of the characteristic fiery denunciations that make the manifesto seem like an impractical and categorical screed. But Solanas's text contains a critical point here.

Changing this world into something else is mainly a question for those who are motivated to take serious risks. Such people will of course be called "scum" or any one of its synonyms by their enemies, but they will accept the name. They will say that if the only people willing to break with existing society are scum, then we need more scum. "SCUM will become members of the unwork force, the fuck-up force; they will get jobs of

---

80. Ibid.
81. Ibid., 70–71.

various kinds and unwork. For example, SCUM salesgirls will not charge for merchandise; SCUM telephone operators will not charge for calls; SCUM office and factory workers, in addition to fucking up their work, will secretly destroy equipment. SCUM will unwork at a job until fired, then get a new job to unwork at."[82] Unworking is the activity that Solanas thinks can strike at the heart of capitalism. Solanas imagines property destruction and the overtaking of the airwaves, and she envisions male comrades in the Men's Auxiliary of SCUM, men who will diligently work to undo male power.

There is a clear activist and feminist dimension to all of this, a fact that would surprise those who misread Solanas's manifesto as nothing but a murderous diatribe. Solanas is calling for dangerous and subversive activity, high-risk activism that would only ever be undertaken by SCUM. But she does insist on engagement: "Dropping out is not the answer; fucking-up is."[83] In short, SCUM is the active and dangerous element within our societies, and it especially includes those identified as threats by men with money and power. If you are not threatening from the point of view of men with money and power, then you are not SCUM and should try harder. This is perhaps the main message of Solanas's manifesto. We need SCUM, but what does SCUM want? SCUM wants love as friendship and a feminist-anarchist unworking aimed at remaking the world.

Placing Curry and Solanas side by side is odd; the pairing demands explanation. Curry and Solanas make for a striking contrast in almost every way. Curry wants to defend Black men and even to raise them up against certain tendencies of feminist vilification. Solanas, on the other hand, is essentially silent on race and racism, but wants to attack men and especially capitalist masculinity. Curry does not take up Solanas because she is not one of the feminists who criticizes Black masculinity. Solanas, on the other hand, did not live to see Curry's work, and even if she did live long enough, I suspect she would be totally uninterested in it as one of many million academic discourses. Curry's stream of thought comes from 2017, Solanas's from the 1960s, and the two do not interact, not even conceptually. They are worlds apart.

So what are we doing here? We are talking about marginalities of unwantedness, of declared "madness," and of utter disposability. While Curry does not take up Solanas, he does take up the unpublished work of Eldridge Cleaver, no less a figure from the margins. Consider the terrain:

---

82. Ibid., 71–72.
83. Ibid., 75.

Black men, sexual and gender outcasts, nonconformist subversives, people starved of recognition and affirmation throughout their lives; Black men raised to think about the dangers of police brutality and murder, raised with a carceral consciousness; women who refuse sexualized and gendered behaviors and are locked out and cast away. What does love mean or do for a young Black boy, for an impoverished Black girl in a racist society, or for an indigent woman who wants to be an artist, who wants to overcome her dehumanizing invisibility? We find that love does not work in the same way everywhere, that it cannot be and should not be the same in every case. That race, class, gender, and sexuality matter has by now become old news. And love, despite its broad generality, is not a "one size fits all" concept. A theory of love may articulate general principles and commitments, but those must be translated and transposed into a world of stratification and marginalization.

How should we comport ourselves toward those treated as unwanted and disposable? Certainly, we may begin by thinking about their value beyond exchange value. It stands to reason that the most devalued humanity needs valuation the most, so an ethics and action of love may need to begin in the margins. This certainly means, of course, that we do not begin with the romantic relationships of heterosexual couples. The most marginalized humanity is to be found on the losing end of white supremacy, capitalism, sexism, and patriarchy.

We need not contrive an argument or a bridge between Curry and Solanas. They both express deep concern for strata of humanity that are viewed as the scum of society. However, until respective movements against their dehumanization materialize in the world, all we have (we theorists, communists, anarchists, radicals, and so on) is a philosophical discourse to bide the time. Only at the moment of a movement's materialization can we shift from philosophy to participation, although even then, philosophical discourse may be our only way to engage. When movements materialize, it is not always possible to enter with our physical bodies. And there are many good reasons that may be so. In that case, discursive activity may be our only way to help substantiate the critical content of the movements—be they prison revolts and prisoner strikes, uprisings against police brutality, or women's marches and strikes—and to join the new SCUM auxiliaries.

The present discussion recalls Kristeva's invocation of the extraterrestrial, which we discussed in chapter 4. She wrote of extraterrestrials in want of love, and argued that the severe want of love makes extraterrestrials out of us. People who are radically alienated from love in their lives feel deprived of a core feature of their humanity. Kristeva wanted to address problems of love through psychoanalysis, but she paid scant attention to the specific deprivations and estrangements of the imperialist white supremacist capitalist patriarchy (of these, she does best with patriarchy). There are other things that make people feel alien, extraterrestrial. Kristeva is one of many theorists of love who fail to address the specific stratifications of love analyzed in this chapter. Nonetheless, she understood well the uses of discourse in the absence of more direct redress. "But to trigger a discourse where his own 'emptiness' and her own 'out-of-placeness' become essential elements, indispensable 'characters' if you will, of a *work in progress*. What is at stake is turning the crisis into a *work in progress*."[84] The overarching aim of the foregoing review of the disparate works of Solanas and Curry is precisely that focus and framing. We have to turn the variegated crises of race, class, sexuality, and gender, such as they are defined at each moment, into real works in progress.

Kristeva perfectly summarized the central organizing issue that ties the diverse texts of this chapter together when she argued that "we have crises of love. Let's admit it: lacks of love.... This is being talked about on psychoanalytic couches, sought after in those marginal communities that dissent from official morality—children, women, same-sex, and finally heterosexual couples (the most shocking because the most unexpected). Until we notice that beneath the multifariousness of history, of stories, tenacious and permanent aspirations lie hidden."[85] We will not turn to psychoanalysis now, however. We have been talking instead about philosophical discourses capable of addressing real and particular crises in specific marginalized communities. We are talking about discourses capable of taking up crises in their particular contexts in order to combat the loveless reality of the unwanted and disposable, of the unassimilable scum.

The weaponization of theory is a predictable and favorite—albeit mostly failed—hope of theorists who want to see their words do battle against everything awful in the world. But when we attend to real marginalities of human unwantedness and madness, the unavoidable fact is that discourses can only do so much—*words and ideas must always inevitably wait for the impetus and intervention of events.*

---

84. Kristeva, *Tales of Love*, 380.
85. Ibid., 7.

CHAPTER 6

Liquid and Chaos

"In politics, love is a stranger, and when it intrudes upon it nothing
is being achieved except hypocrisy.... Hatred and love belong
together, and they are both destructive; you can afford them only
in the private and, as a people, only so long as you are not free."

—Hannah Arendt, "The Meaning of Love in Politics:
A Letter to James Baldwin"

"Love is the most durable power in the world."

—Martin Luther King, Jr., *A Gift of Love*

6.1 Chaotic Liquidity of Love

How to love and what love can do are now understood as questions not only of *who* loves but of the environment within which love is sought or practiced. We have explored a range of theories of love stretching back to Socrates and Spartacus, the logic of love in relation to the logic of capital, the communism of love and the love of communist women, and how race, class, sexuality, and gender interact with the demands and activities of love. It is time now to focus on the current global, economic, and technological terrains on which human bodies and subjectivities interrelate. The major themes in the social theory of the present are precarity, financial and emotional insecurity, liquidity, and chaos. In this chapter we explore not only how love is disrupted on contemporary terrains of human relationality, but also how love disrupts them. As Hannah Arendt writes to James Baldwin in the epigraph above, love cannot be defined as a calm antithesis to hatred. Love can be destructive; love can be chaotic.

The great philosopher of liquidity Zygmunt Bauman worries that love is being downgraded to mean almost any kind of the most transient and impersonal "love making."[1] Today, people want to have an experience of love without the inconvenience of waiting, without difficulty or effort. Bauman acknowledges that love can terrify with a consuming and disruptive emotionality, and thus that love is simultaneously longed for and dreaded with fear. To help us sharpen the focus, Bauman differentiates love from desire: "Desire is the wish to consume.... Love is, on the other

---

1. Zygmunt Bauman, *Liquid Love: On the Frailty of Human Bonds* (Cambridge: Polity, 2017), 5.

hand, the wish to care, and to preserve the object of the care."[2] It is a familiar distinction. As Illouz has also argued, consumption is a more fitting domain for desire than for love. Love tends toward care, not consumption.

But Bauman quickly departs from the consensus of scholars like hooks and Illouz, arguing to the contrary, "Love is a Siamese twin of power greed; neither would survive the separation. If desire wants to consume, love wants to possess."[3] This immediately raises a peculiar idea about care and possession. It is true that to properly care for my young children there is a certain inclination to possess them, to keep them close and bound by a somewhat rigid administration of their freedom, a rigidity that will be loosened with age. My children are, in a sense, *mine*, notwithstanding Kollontai's hopeful horizon for a community's sense of collective responsibility for its young children. To the extent that something in my care belongs to me, love as care implies a kind of ownership. If my children are improperly cared for, if they are neglected or abused, some of the blame must rightly target me as the one responsible for their care. How can one care for a beloved who is entirely out of their control? To what extent does love imply control, or even possession?

Bauman likens a romantic relationship to an investment, which although different than a business transaction, functions in some similar ways. "If you invest in a relationship, the profit you expect is first and foremost security," including of course financial security.[4] While Bauman worries about social relations governed by the logic of capital and his body of work makes sustained criticism of capitalism, his observations suggest a logical proximity that we have heretofore resisted. Let us consider his point: If my partner and I do not keep a spreadsheet of exchanges and rewards, is it not inevitable that an imbalance of rewards and securities reassuring one but not the other would inevitably lead to a sense of unfairness? Can anyone expect only to give and to give, to care for the other person's being and becoming, without at some point begrudging or resenting an uneven exchange? Perhaps it is too easy or maybe disingenuous to assert that love always eludes and betrays every sense of exchangeability. But if we are really talking about fairness, I think that fairness can be better likened to things other than financial investment. If I always make dinner, can I not expect that someone else—in the name of fairness—will do the dishes? Or is such a thought only possible with recourse to a capitalist imaginary? Is every possible accounting that of

2. Ibid., 9.
3. Ibid., 10.
4. Ibid., 13.

an accountant? Is it not possible to establish a noncapitalist division of labor? Unfairness in love can certainly be discussed without Bauman's lamentable analogy to financial investment. Unfairness may be a special purview of capitalism, but the former is not the private property of the latter.

In this particular context it makes less sense to speak of "ownership" than of "responsibility." With my children, once again, what varies from infancy to adulthood is not ownership but responsibility. I have a greater responsibility to care for an infant or toddler than to care for a grown son who does not need or desire my help in the same way. Indeed, as my sons grow, I frequently say, "this is your responsibility now," transferring an increasing number of my former responsibilities to them. And, while love cannot escape concerns about fairness and responsibility, these concerns should not be expressed in the language of exchange relations. True, financial reality necessarily permeates relations of love in the world. Uncertainty and insecurity in work and capital cannot avoid having an impact on relationships external to those of work and capital.

Bauman claims that family and kinship are attempts to create durability in a liquid world, where most things are moving, fluid, and temporary. Children can participate in the construction of a durable relational unit to provide security in the face of liquidity, but we cannot deny the financial colonization of such a loving relationality. As Bauman puts it:

> Children are among the most expensive purchases that average consumers are likely to make in the course of their entire lives. In purely monetary terms, children cost more than a luxurious state-of-the-art car, a round-the-world cruise, even a mansion to be proud of. Worse still, the total cost is likely to grow over the years and its volume cannot be fixed in advance nor estimated with any degree of certainty. In a world that no longer offers reliable career tracks and stable jobs, for people moving from one project to another and earning their living as they move, signing a mortgage contract with undisclosed and indefinitely long repayments means exposure to an uncharacteristically high level of risk and a prolific source of anxiety and fear.[5]

Indeed, considered in terms of both a financial and emotional rationality, the creation of a durable family unit may best be avoided. Most people cannot afford a family with children, and the anxiety and insecurity of the

---

5. Ibid., 42.

long-term endeavor may be too much to bear. For many people around the world, the family unit, which could conceivably be a resistant and durable little commune, becomes yet another risk. The outcome of this double risk is that people are both afraid to build a family and afraid to be without one.

Bauman observes that "lightness and speed" have become the virtues of consumer society today, by which he means that people now need to accumulate things without sacrificing any of their increasingly flexible mobility (liquidity).[6] We expect to be able to buy things anywhere, with no physical proximity to anyone selling anything, and we also expect that what we buy will not anchor us to any place. We want to be, and increasingly need to be, everywhere and nowhere in particular. But what is a family unit without some anchoring to place? What is a liquid family? To build a family well, and especially to promote the health and well-being of young children, the family unit requires some dedicated space and time, actual places of safety and becoming. This is, in a sense, the basic concept of home. But such a home, while it may provide durability, inevitably diminishes mobility. Inasmuch as capitalist societies are societies of flexible flows liberated from geographic rootedness, the mobility demands of present society stand in a further tension with the basic model of a home for family and kinship. Expectations of constant movement and liquidity play a role in decisions to not have a family, to not establish a home, as people often think that their lives are not stable enough for a family. Or, they have become so accustomed to liquidity that they fear and avoid all anchors, including the anchor of a family.

Of course, people have not simply abandoned family or kinship. The establishment of durable family and kinship persists because we still feel that we cannot live well without some modality of reliable being-together. The fact is that either form of life—with or without family—is a risk. Therefore, individual persons look more and more for forms of love consistent with their liquid lives, as Bauman explains: "You *stay connected*— even though you are constantly on the move, and though the invisible senders and recipients of calls and messages move as well, all following their own trajectories. Mobiles are for people on the move."[7] Mobile connectivity is the infrastructure of liquid love, of a love liberated from actual places. As Bauman puts it: "It is unimportant which place you are in, who the people are around you and what you are doing in that place filled

---

6. Ibid., 49.
7. Ibid., 59.

with those people. The difference between one place and another, one set of people within your sight and corporal reach and another, has been cancelled and made null and void."[8] There is a basic logic of separation here. "Those who stay apart, mobiles allow to get in touch. Those who get in touch, mobiles allow to stay apart."[9] Separation either way.

We are building technologies that do not counteract separation but rather assist us with it. Persons who cannot get together or be together ameliorate that separation with the aid of a technological connection; those who want to create even greater distance between themselves and others can do so by way of the same technology. According to the prevailing techno-logic, it matters less and less if you are near others because we can come together through the screens on our devices. Those who are always together can go away from each other while sitting side by side in the same physical space. Family members may pay diminishing attention to each other because, firstly, they are seduced to flee into the cognitive space available through the device's screen and, secondly, the same technology of separation reassures them that they can always make a connection no matter where they are or what they are doing. Although it is a far cry from Levinas's ideal, perhaps this liquid relationality could give rise to the love that we need, a liquid love that can counteract our alienation without abolishing our separation.

In any case, we are always trying to use the tools at our disposal to keep *communitas* together while the forms of our togetherness become increasingly liquid. And Bauman, at least, will not claim that liquid love is good enough.

> The invasion and colonization of *communitas*, the site of the moral economy, by consumer market forces constitutes the most awesome of dangers threatening the present form of human togetherness. The principal targets of the assault by the market are *producers*; in a fully conquered and colonized land, only human *consumers* would be issued residence permits.... Forms of life, and the partnerships that support them, would be available only in the shape of commodities.... [A]nything in the moral economy of the *communitas* that resists such commodification is denied relevance to the prosperity of the society of consumers; it is stripped of value in a society trained to measure values in currency and to identify them with the price

---

8. Ibid.
9. Ibid., 60.

tags carried by sellable and purchasable objects and services; and ultimately it is pressed out of public (and, it is hoped, individual) attention by being struck out of the accounts of human well-being.[10]

Bauman describes this invasion and colonization as a veritable war between healthy human togetherness and our separation, alienation, and commodification in a liquid life. Liquid love is not good enough because it simply accepts and follows the transformation of life into a web of unfixed and fluid exchange relations. The consequences are both social and political. "Human solidarity is the first casualty of the triumphs of the consumer market."[11] In this, Bauman agrees with the old thesis of critical theory from Fromm to the present.

The real challenge is that we do not know how to make a serious countermovement against these tendencies. Bauman does not know either. We can explain what is happening, but do not know how to stop it. Mobile connectivity stops and reverses nothing. It keeps a certain connectivity alive, but at the same time it erodes human solidarity in various ways. Theory can imagine and recommend possibilities and experiments, but I do not think people have yet looked closely at problems pertaining to the growing liquidity of love. I am not sure how to get there, although I am certain that the perspective that views love as apolitical or antipolitical is a key obstacle (this is Hannah Arendt's view, which I address in chapter 8). For now, let us note that there has been too much displacement of love in and by the social sciences, a displacement that derives from the sustained treatment of love as a mainly private, erotic, or romantic phenomenon—and not a term of politics or sociality. People think they can think about politics without thinking much about love. That problematic tendency remains alive and well in the contemporary theorizing of Illouz, Badiou, Horvat, and others.[12] Fromm and hooks tried to displace the love of politics with a politics of love in order to start thinking about love as a practice—and, I would add, as *a necessarily and irreducibly communist practice*. But how to move from theorization to a political practice of love has not been their purview. Perhaps we can be forgiven, then, for attempting to increase understanding while merely hoping to see events realize our ideas. Bauman reconciles the problem this way: "You cannot make this world kind and considerate to the human beings who inhabit it, and as accommodating to their dreams of dignity as you would ideally wish it

---

10. Ibid., 74–75.
11. Ibid., 76.
12. More on the problem in Alain Badiou and Srećko Horvat in chapter 7.

to be. *But you must try*."[13] I agree. We must try to do what we do not know how to do.

Bauman ultimately thinks that the answer to our problem lies in moral argument: "Loving your neighbor may require a leap of faith; the result, though, is the birth act of humanity. It is also the fateful passage from the instinct of survival to morality."[14] There is no morality intrinsic to exchange value. Loving the other, and especially some distant other elsewhere, on the basis of their basic humanity (a humanist love) may seem to cost more than it earns. Survival instincts for a capitalist world do not recommend the active respect, care, and love of one's neighbor, unless it is proven mutually profitable. But that is not a moral consideration. In this regard, Bauman sounds a bit like Kant, who argued for following moral obligation over any circumstantial concern for one's private happiness. But what might Kantian humanism or any other humanism have to do with love? Maybe humanism is the form love takes on a global or cosmopolitan scale. This is likely the answer for most (if not all) humanists and cosmopolitans, and maybe even for Marxist-humanists in a different way. However, aside from the cosmopolitan Martha Nussbaum, none of these other humanists offers sustained attention to a politics of love. I claim that love must be wrenched from the theological and romantic conceptualizations that have held it hostage, but at the same time I reject Nussbaum's belief in the basic compatibility of love and capital.

One of the key distinctions of Bauman's theory of love is that he does not believe we can address global problems with local solutions. The liquidity of life and love are globalized in a financial capitalism that has effectively normalized flexibility and mobility instead of anchored durability everywhere, from South Korea to Japan to China to France to the United States to Argentina to Singapore—indeed throughout Latin America, Europe, and Asia. Speed and liquidity are the twin modalities of global exchange, and seeking safety afforded by a durable family or community in that context is like holding on to a tree in a hurricane. For Bauman, this means that you cannot deal with global xenophobia by loving your literal neighbor. The neighbor that you claim to love may even join you in xenophobic hatred. In fact, for Bauman, the "spectre of xenophobia" is one of the ways we can see the dismantling of our togetherness on a global scale.[15] One could perhaps say the same thing about chauvinistic and nationalistic patriotisms in a world of climate change and climate crisis,

---

13. Bauman, *Liquid Love*, 83.
14. Ibid., 78.
15. Ibid., 119.

or in a world of pandemics and nuclear weaponry. We need something bigger than an anarchist *communitas* that functions like a tree of human solidarity when we are facing a hurricane that can pull it up at its roots. Love in our epoch of always-accelerating global capital conjures an image of David versus Goliath, but with none of the confidence of that story's conclusion. The fact is that capitalism is increasingly uprooting us and turning love to liquid by way of technologically aided flights from place and people. The love that we make is quite a distance from the love that we need.

There is liquid and there is chaos, but what happens when such conditions become simple expectations by way of normalization? To an extent, the normalization of chaos is the defining concern of Ulrich Beck and Elisabeth Beck-Gernsheim's *The Normal Chaos of Love*.[16] Like too many of the social scientists studying love, Beck and Beck-Gernsheim are overly focused on romantic love and family life. Their basic thesis has become somewhat familiar. Beck and Beck-Gernsheim maintain—as do others—that everyone aspires to and places their hope in love, while society increasingly generates isolated or alienated individuals in a world of globalizing separation. What they add to our discussion is a consideration of the problems of love itself, as opposed to the problems that love may potentially solve. We have tended to focus a bit one-sidedly on the latter.

Beck and Beck-Gernsheim contend that some of the ugliest and most painful aspects of love are part of love and belong to it. "Love is pleasure, trust, affection and equally their opposites—boredom, anger, habit, treason, loneliness, intimidation, despair and laughter. Love elevates your lover and transforms him/her into the source of possible pleasures where others only detect layers of fat, yesterday's stubble and verbosity."[17] To go into love, therefore, requires an understanding that some of the experience will be awful, or at least will require accepting certain failures. People can and do feel despair and loneliness while in love, and we must understand that these feelings may not be absences of love but part of it. Yet love changes the way you see the other person so that, even in boredom or anger, you can see in your beloved a hope and a possibility that others cannot see there. That one can be with their beloved and feel at the same time boredom, anger, habit, loneliness, and despair is very important. If we recall Illouz's thesis about the romantic utopia according to

---

16. Ulrich Beck and Elisabeth Beck-Gernsheim, *The Normal Chaos of Love*, trans. Mark Ritter and Jane Wiebel (Cambridge: Polity, 2004).

17. Ibid., 12–13.

which love is thought to abolish everything mundane, we see that the romantic mythology about there being no pain in love may be more harmful than an understanding of love as inclusive of pain. I agree with Beck and Beck-Gernsheim here, and I think we should imbue all romantic conceptions of love with real insights about its difficulty, chaos, and pain.

Beck and Beck-Gernsheim understand that love relations are formed largely to create vehicles made to pursue happiness and realize dreams. We come together so that we might leverage our efforts with others to live happy lives. Happiness is the basic gravitational pull of loving. However, very often the unit does not hold its initial promise and "happiness turns out to be fugitive.... [T]he space occupied by each individual in modern society makes close relationships precarious."[18] It is difficult to be together when there is a countervailing gravitational pull, pulling togetherness apart by way of separation and privatization. Beck and Beck-Gernsheim view this as a two-faced liberation, where we are expected to be totally liberated from other people yet end up liberated also from loving support and human solidarity. To be precarious is to have no confident future to count on, and human relationships that are intended to diminish precarity are themselves increasingly precarious. Recalling Bauman, we might argue it is something like treating the liquidity of one thing with the liquidity of another. How do we keep the solid unit of our precarious little communes together?

People sometimes attempt to address the precarity of their relationships by having children, which rarely solves the problem. Beck and Beck-Gernsheim agree with Bauman that there is no financial motivation or advantage to having children. The drive for children is a psychological and emotional phenomenon, which includes the hope that having children will strengthen the couple's togetherness, be a mark of real stability, signify upward mobility, or give the parents a sense of rootedness that they did not previously have. But such motivations for having children are frequently frustrated, often in ways that are catastrophic for the children. Beck and Beck-Gernsheim note that "attacks on children from members of the family are on the rise.[19]" This may well be the darkest side of the ugliness of love. Beck and Beck-Gernsheim note:

It becomes comprehensible that where there is love there is often hostility, an idea that at first seems strange, incongruous and

---

18. Ibid., 99.
19. Ibid., 138.

irritating. The two have become linked, not by coincidence but as an outcome of social change: love in conjunction with anxiously high hopes is volatile and can quickly deteriorate into bitter disappointment and cruelty. We mostly prefer to repress such insights.... Love is one of our greatest achievements, the foundation of our relationships between men and women, parents and children—but we cannot have it without its darker sides, which sometimes emerge for a second and sometimes linger for years: disappointment, bitterness, rejection and hatred. The road from heaven to hell is much shorter than most people think.[20]

It would be tempting here to say that disappointment, hatred, and cruelty cannot be properties of love at all, for they only appear in the wake of love's destruction or in the absence of love. However, we must resist that simple conclusion. The complex emotional and psychological life of human beings should not be minimized for the sake of more favorable definitions. Being-together has to be allowed a certain dynamic and dialectical range of experience and feeling if it is to be a really human togetherness. Everyone who has loved a parent, a child, a partner probably knows well that sometimes your beloved is both cause and respite from the darkness of bad feeling. Their being, if it is connected to yours in any meaningful and durable way, is part of a complex relationality that may cause terrible pain, including feelings of hatred or disappointment. Of course, such bad feeling is not everything. But we should be careful here. I am in no way suggesting that "no" means "yes" or that "bad" means "good." Rather, I am suggesting that an analysis that ignores real complexity is a bad analysis. And there is complexity here. I am already prepared to believe that my son loves me if and when it comes time for him to declare that he hates me.

Beck and Beck-Gernsheim acknowledge that we repress such insights, and it may even be necessary to do so because we must beware any rationalization of abuse that hides behind the good name of love. We know, for example, that terrible abuse is often mitigated after the fact with declarations of love. And we must not accept such declarations as a rationale for staying in an abusive situation. Children need rescuing from such situations, and we should condemn abusive relationships everywhere for everyone. So we arrive here at a difficult nuance. How can we know that a cruelty, disappointment, anger, or even hatred is part of a love that we

---

20. Ibid., 139.

want to keep and not an indication of an abuse we should abolish? I do not know how to address this important question confidently, so I will only say something tentative here. A victim of abuse may come to accept her victimization by believing that her abuser really loves her when that is not true, or may come to a position where she wrongly believes that the abuse will end. We obviously have to distinguish love from Stockholm syndrome. But one of Beck and Beck Gernsheim's most difficult messages is that we cannot ignore the dark side of love. And I agree that it is too simple to say that there can be no pain or suffering where there is love. We have to proceed cautiously here. A person who suspects abuse should be advised to engage in a critical, safe, and open conversation with another trusted person—a friend or analyst, *not the person who has something to gain from being seen as not abusive*—to help assess the nature of the relationship.

More important than their attention to the dark side of love is Beck and Beck-Gernsheim's claim that love is best understood as a religion. It is, however, a religion that is losing its power. Increasing precarity, individualism, and global capitalism have been making love into "a social hybrid of market forces and personal impulses, an ideal of love (or marriage or parenthood) which is safe, calculable and medically optimized."[21] Even excepting the abuse discussed above, love remains full of chaos and uncertainty, whereas people want less risk and more security. At the same time, individual persons have become so accustomed to their individual lives, full of routine and ritual, that adding another person to the mix often seems too difficult, despite any longing to be with someone. Until the acceleration and establishment of the neoliberal normality of the 1970s and 1980s, being alone was considered—in most of the world—a terrible fate. But in the 1970s and 1980s being alone was reconceived as a kind of freedom. In the decades since, however, new forms of life have become only more inhospitable to the love relations of previous generations. This is not to glorify those times, which should not be made into a future horizon, but rather to track some of the trends of individuation that impact the secular religion of love.

Beck and Beck-Gernsheim want to defend love in times of its growing precarity, and even in light of its darker sides of pain and despair. They work ultimately toward the conclusion that "love in all its glory, its loftiest and deepest values, its hells and heavens, in all its human and animal entirety will turn out to be one main source of satisfaction and meaning

---

21. Ibid., 141.

in life."[22] One of the key similarities between love and religion is that its failures and difficulties are not dissuasive of an overarching faith in it. This is especially true when we look at the question of marriage and family life. Beck and Beck-Gernsheim argue throughout *The Normal Chaos of Love* that while marriage and family life are disintegrating and divorce rates are sky-rocketing, remarriage rates are also skyrocketing, and longing for family seems unshaken by present challenges. These are the marks of religiosity, of a faith in a possibility that is not empirically assured or even probable. One crisis and challenge after another faces loving relationships and family life; statistically, we should not expect these institutions to deliver on their promises, or even to last. Yet Beck and Beck-Gernsheim observe that "love occupies its own different world separate from real life in the family and separate from the person whom it is supposed to help to greater happiness."[23] This means that in the face of instability, abuse, and broken hopes, there is no reason to think that people will turn away from love. People will continue to pursue it in their lives, "wishing and hoping for the ultimate in love" and adopting "a religious state of mind, which must be clearly distinguished from their behavior, or what people actually do."[24]

Love and religion need faith, and they each provide a locus of hope for happiness and meaning in life. Both love and religion also offer an escape from the rootless banality of a life defined by work and consumption. Beck and Beck-Gernsheim observe that people will follow their inclination for love even if doing so leads to a nightmare. One of the things that distinguishes love from religion is that religion seems to require a strong intergenerational education in discourses, rites, and passages, whereas love needs no churches or priests and seems to call for faith without any confidence in its customs or aims. And there is a strange dialectical power of love as "the only place where you can really get in touch with yourself and someone else. The more impersonal life around you seems, the more attractive love becomes."[25] Capitalist societies separate and individuate us into ever-sharper isolation, yet also drive us dialectically to love.

Beck and Beck-Gernsheim are aware of the important differences between love and religion, which they highlight at the end of their study. But they maintain that "love is the best ideology to counteract the perils of individualization."[26] While I agree with the spirit of their conclusion, I ar-

---

22. Ibid., 169.
23. Ibid., 173.
24. Ibid., 174.
25. Ibid., 178.
26. Ibid., 181.

gue that love is not and cannot be an ideology. Indeed, its ideologization is its obliteration (a claim that can be made equally about communism). But we can appreciate the point: the promises of love ensure and require an infinite faith, and that faith becomes more pronounced as our isolation becomes more severe.

Beck and Beck-Gernsheim shrink the metaphysical enormity of religion down to an unexciting and practical matter when they turn finally to the position of love after the destruction of its romanticization. The disappointment and boredom of being with another person whom you genuinely and deeply love, and who loves you in a comparable register, is the "realistic core" of love, of love as "loneliness for two."[27] This gray realism in Beck and Beck-Gernsheim will be a terrible disappointment to those who prefer the perpetual rapture of romanticized love; but for us, this realism is welcome. After all, the present book is not about sexual ecstasy and overjoyed infatuation, it is about forms of life that can shield us from loneliness, insecurity, exploitation, and death in a world of capitalist exchange relations. Imagine two lovers sitting together alone and possibly even disappointed. It is not an enviable scene. But what if we know that each one will spring into action for the other, that the little unit is ready for a collective action in miniature in the face of sickness or crisis? Such activity would be an extrapolation and exercise of being-together, making our love a little bit of communism within capitalism. Such a perspective should help us to understand, finally, that no communism is a utopia.

Beck and Beck-Gernsheim therefore offer a much-needed recalibration. But they also appreciate, as we do here, love's subversive power: "Love is thus also a radical form of self-government.... The mechanics of love follow a law: the law of the lawlessness of subjectivity and intimacy oriented towards personal needs, which has divested itself of all external controls and been left to its own devices."[28] In this way, when we create forms of life through love relations, we create our own territory, little autonomous zones that need not always be characterized by a permanently peaked sensuality.

In all of this, we can agree with much in Beck and Beck-Gernsheim. But we have to oppose their conclusion that love "cannot be aimed at" and that it "simply happens, strikes like lightning or dies out according to laws which are not open to individual or social control."[29] They conclude that indifference, instead of hatred, is the true opposite of love, and that

---

27. Ibid., 190.
28. Ibid., 194–95.
29. Ibid., 198.

it too can be suddenly struck down by "an attack of love."[30] Indeed, love is often a surprise and cannot be planned for or acted out with certainty. But it is possible to aim at love, to consider its logic of relationality, of being-in-the-world. It is possible, and I think even necessary, to understand love as expansive beyond romantic and familial relations and, most importantly, as necessarily (and dialectically) antagonistic to capital. These latter points cannot be substantiated within the work of Beck and Beck-Gernsheim.

Yet Bauman and Beck and Beck-Gernsheim do understand the precarious state of love in the present world of the twenty-first century. Love comes with high risk, dark sides, faith against facts, and a high probability of failure. Nonetheless, we still stubbornly and irrepressibly try to make little communes of human being-together that stand against prevailing capitalist insecurity. One could even say that we resist capitalist precarity by way of love as a form of what I have called "precarious communism."[31]

There is no certain opposition or confident antidote to the problems of the present world, whether we are thinking of alienation and loneliness or xenophobia and ecological crisis. Still, our little precarious communes activate and practice an opposite and antithetical logic within which we become micropolitical communards, equipped with a peculiar liberation theology, trying to save each other and to save ourselves.

6.2 Precarious Communes

Our little precarious communes can be bad news. They may do just as much to cut us off from others around us than to connect us to those just outside the commune's boundaries. People on the outside of the little commune may appear to people on the inside as a threat. Also, while the little communes we create may provide some refuge from the larger world and its cruelties, our little communes may do nothing to directly confront that world, leaving it essentially unchanged. Retreat into family or community spaces that happily coexist with the existing world may become just another feature of living in the world such as it is. Finally, the precarity of each little commune indicates a desperate situation; consider that, for previous generations, some kind of global commune or

---

30. Ibid.

31. See Gilman-Opalsky, *Precarious Communism* (Wivenhoe, UK: Autonomedia, 2014).

international communism was the dream, whereas we are in the position of scarcely keeping together our tiny little communes with much smaller aspirations.

We have just been discussing chaos and liquidity, and one of the foremost theorists of precarity, Franco Berardi, has something to say about these subjects: "The word *chaos* thus stands for an environment that is too complex to be decoded by the explanatory grills available to us, an environment in which flows are too quick for conscious elaboration and rational decision. The word *chaos* denotes a degree of complexity that is too dense, too intense, and too fast for our brains to decipher."[32] Chaos is connected with precarity. We perceive as chaotic any situation, environment, or flow of information that is too fast, too complex, or too overwhelming for us to process and understand with confidence. So a person may feel chaos in the morning if they wake up and face too many demands over email or if work, life, and death offer rapid and surprising changes, as in the case of sudden job loss, a new relationship, or the death of a family member. Chaos here means a debilitating confusion, an experience of being overwhelmed by information and feelings that have to be sorted out and worked through. We want to live a good life. We want to experience love. The experience of love can itself be an experience of chaos, but it is not the only source. Our world of instantaneity and high-speed information is chaotic in its modus operandi.

Audre Lorde directly connected chaos to love. She notes that the "word *erotic* comes from the Greek word *eros*, the personification of love in all its aspects—born of Chaos, and personifying creative power and harmony."[33] Lorde sees love as chaotic because it can "give us the energy to pursue genuine change within our world, rather than merely settling for a shift of characters in the same weary drama."[34] Lorde therefore understands and appreciates the disruptive power of love, since it is unsettling in ways that carry hope within the chaos. Love's disruptive power is not merely destructive, then, but also productive in its hopeful creation of new relations.

Chaos and precarity are connected to a third term, what Berardi calls sensibility, or "the ability to understand what is unspoken."[35] Sensibility is

---

32. Franco "Bifo" Berardi, *And: Phenomenology of the End: Sensibility and Connective Mutation* (South Pasadena: Semiotext(e), 2015), 218.
33. Audre Lorde, *Sister Outsider: Essays and Speeches* (Berkeley: Crossing, 2007), 55.
34. Ibid., 59.
35. Berardi, *And*, 35.

the human faculty that helps us to process and understand what is happening around us; it has to do particularly with comprehending other peoples' moods, emotions, and feelings. Sensibility can take the form of empathy, but it need not be expressed that way. For Berardi, sensibility must be understood as an active engagement with one's environment: actively paying attention, exercising careful perception and reception. Weil's old idea of attention returns once again. But attention is harder to pay now, when there is a mismatch between the "infosphere" and the "social brain." Berardi defines the infosphere as "the universe of transmitters" and the social brain as the "universe of receivers."[36] The social brain rests on human biology and cannot be reformatted as the perfect receiver to take in the mass of digital transmissions. Human neurology is highly adaptable, Berardi concedes, but it does not evolve as fast as technology, and the density and complexity of high-speed transmissions overwhelm the organic human being's receptive apparatus, causing "pathological effects: panic, over-excitement, hyperactivity, attention deficit disorders, dyslexia, information overload, and the saturation of neural circuitry."[37] To synthesize Beck and Beck-Gernsheim with Berardi, we may say that this describes the "normal chaos" of the infosphere.

But Berardi and Beck and Beck-Gernsheim do not ask the central question: *How can a human being in such a predicament as this participate in love, since the latter requires a healthy sensible capacity?*

In certain times and places, love may appear as a leisure activity meant for another world. Berardi catalogs frightening statistics on *hikikomori*, depression, debilitating anxiety, and suicide. "Suicide is the most common cause of death for those under 40 in South Korea. Most interestingly, the number of suicide deaths in South Korea doubled over the last decade, and quadrupled during the three decades of the electronic changeover, from 6.8 per 100,000 people in 1982 to 28.4 in 2011."[38] Additionally, Berardi documents how an increasing speed of life, growing competition in the labor market, and inopportunity in wages and economic security create loneliness and despair that must be understood as social phenomena connected to capitalist society and not as individual problems. Berardi observes that capitalist economists should not be consulted as much as psychologists in periods of economic crisis, because economists tend to see everything in terms of growth and competition instead of health and well-being.[39]

---

36. Ibid., 41.
37. Ibid.
38. Ibid., 110.
39. For his most incisive discussion of the limitations of economics, see Franco

Constant growth and competition are unsustainable not only from an ecological perspective but also from a psychological perspective.

The title of Berardi's book, *And*, is meant to address a conjunction between connectivity and collectivity. Connectivity does not necessitate collectivity. This is one of the reasons why our little precarious communes may not deepen connections to others outside or to a greater collective sensibility. Connectivity has to do with a sensible relationality, whereas collectivity only develops "when conscious and sensitive organisms enter into a reciprocal relation of mutual transformation, and continuous questioning and ambiguity."[40] So while connectivity may be a prerequisite for collectivity, the former does not guarantee the latter. With technology, it is easier to achieve constant connectivity without creating any enduring collectivity. Technology may be the best place to see that connectivity is not collectivity. Therefore, being connected ensures nothing in terms of love, political action, social movement, or insurrection.

Much like Raoul Vaneigem before him, Berardi turns to poetry. Poetry is composed of words yet exceeds them by evoking sensibilities. Poetry attempts not to *communicate information* but rather to *activate feeling*. Language has been held captive for too long by economistic thinking. Thus, whatever is said is expected to be carefully and objectively calculated and measured in the precise proportion that is asked for, given, or paid for. But such calculative speech fails to entice or ignite feeling. The reality is that even our connectivity can be insensible. People are often bound together for unfeeling, insensate activity. Imagine this common scene in the infospheres of our technological capitalist reality: people are sitting close together, connected to the world through screens on their handheld devices. We should hesitate to call these devices phones since they are used far more for other things than to call people for conversation. The people in this familiar scene (a room or train or office or restaurant) have never been more connected, yet those connections are scarcely based on any feeling for one another there in the scene. This is not the world in which Fromm thought about love. Berardi says that "everybody is a competitor, and the lover on Sunday night may be a competitor on Monday morning."[41] Maybe when we go home there is love waiting for us there in the family. Maybe there is love in the streets during a protest demonstration on the weekend. Maybe there is love on a playground when the banker

---

"Bifo" Berardi, *The Uprising: On Poetry and Finance* (Los Angeles: Semiotext(e), 2007).

40. Berardi, *And*, 227.

41. Franco "Bifo" Berardi, *Futurability: The Age of Impotence and the Horizon of Possibility* (London: Verso Books, 2017), 46.

or stockbroker takes time to roll in the grass with her children playing dinosaurs. But today, we have more and more connections, yet fewer made of love.

Berardi writes about slowing down as an antidote to a life of speed, density, and emotional distress. In his book *Futurability*, he finds hope in the gatherings of the retired, elderly, and aging. Toward the end of their lives, the elderly seem attracted to slowness and a bit of good *Gemeinwesen*. After a full lifetime of work that required the constant extraction of their energies, and in a culture that is accelerating so quickly that the previous version of "fast" has become the new "slow," retirement appears as an aspirational countermovement. The elderly tend to look for communities of slow attention, conversation, creativity, and care. Once we abandon the high-speed, high-energy logic of capitalist competition, "we may discover that being exhausted is not so bad.... The cult of competition must be replaced by the cult of solidarity and of sharing."[42] Berardi locates a kind of precarious communism in the little communes of the elderly and aging. He even finds a model in a recommendation made by Pope Francis to turn the church into a place where anyone can go to heal their wounds, to come with their hopelessness to find some mercy and compassion. Berardi thinks that spaces constructed for such purposes should be everywhere in our societies, open centers for care and careful attention meant to comfort the stressed-out, depressed, and anxious humanity of our capitalist world.[43] We cannot pretend that there is no despair; instead, we should take despair as our starting position and go from there.

Berardi is a communist. We communists always want to move toward some kind of *Gemeinwesen*, toward some communal being, a common being, a *Gemeinschaft* built from below. One of the problems that haunts twenty-first-century communism, however, is the possibility that community is no longer possible. How can we build community in a world of connected isolation? Our communities are precarious and tiny, and surely not enough to shield us from—let alone to reverse—global catastrophes like poverty and climate crisis. We communists are *not* communitarians. We do not seek only being-together but also active forms of being-against. We communists cannot be communitarians because we cannot abandon the hopeful possibility for a larger struggle against the present state of things. We do not want to be islands. We are also always abolitionists.

---

42. Ibid., 94–95.
43. Ibid., 98.

The fact is that community has always been problematic. We cannot say that it once was easy. It is just that the problems are different now. Peter Harrison does a good job of thinking through different communal forms of life, past and present, including tribal and indigenous forms, in *The Freedom of Things*.[44] One of the most common methods of self-defense used by tribal communities attempting to preserve their form of life from a surrounding capitalist lifeworld is to stay *disconnected* from that world of chaotic connection. Indigenous and tribal forms of life often understand the survival of their communal forms as contingent on staying outside of and autonomous from the surrounding world.[45] This would be something like *disconnection as a strategy of community*.

When we think of community, we tend to think of one of two things: First is the idea of a "primitive" or natural community, some original community from the past. Second is the idea of a future community in a changed society, a kind of ideal destination or form of being-together somewhere on the horizon. In *The Communism of Love* we have gravitated more to the second of these than to the first. But Harrison problematizes both ideas of community. He observes: "The notion of community is usually associated with something 'good' and predicated on the acceptance that if humans are not actually social animals, then circumstances have forced sociality upon us so that we must learn to live socially in the best way possible."[46] Thus, we are either destined to form communities by a biological drive or driven to form communities because they are necessary formations in the context of our societies. In any case, humans tend toward community of one kind or another. But often what we call community is not at all what we think of as a *real* or *ideal* community: "It seems that our a priori certainty of community tends to fall apart under an a posteriori scrutiny: the neighbourhood community turns out to fail to be a proper community because it is full of strangers, just as the medieval village community turns out to be a mass of competing and exploiting interests."[47] It is true that writers from Marx to Camatte have distinguished between false community and real community time and again. Harrison argues that real community has never really existed and that our faith in community has to be regarded as one of the fundamental pathologies of

---

44. Peter Harrison, *The Freedom of Things: An Ethnology of Control: How the Structure of Dependence in Modern Society Has Misinformed the Western Mind* (Fair Lawn, NJ: TSI Press, 2017).
45. Ibid., 26.
46. Ibid., 88.
47. Ibid., 91.

Western political thought. So fundamental is this pathological faith that we do not even know how to think without the concept of community. Hannah Arendt famously romanticized ancient Greek democracy in her book *The Human Condition*, but close scrutiny reveals a society that was hardly as wonderful as it may have seemed, with slavery, misogyny, fear and hatred of the barbarians, political corruption, and sophistry. The same is true of the so-called community of office workers, Black people, racists, cops, students, women, or communists. Close inspection shows *separation* where there is supposed to be *collectivity*, a weak *Gemeingeist* at best, often held together by nothing more than self-interest among strangers without any real affection, let alone love. This cynical view may well be accurate.

However, does our theory of love need a concept of community? I think we have to say yes. This yes does not mean that we should valorize any one community or any imaginable or utopian communal being. Rather, our research views love as a communizing power, and communization entails, among other things, activities of being-together. This does not mean that we need an ideal-typical notion of "community," only that we are in search of "commoning," communizing, or other tendencies of human solidarity mobilized not by exchange but by love.

Harrison invokes Pierre Bourdieu's theory of *doxa*, which refers to thoughts and beliefs that keep a group of people together. *Doxa* is, essentially, the content of a common or shared lifeway that is transmitted by a group of people across generations and keeps that group together internally by way of shared practices, customs, language, and beliefs. But *doxa* also functions as an exclusionary force because those who question it, who reject its recommended behaviors, are outsiders to the community as such. A *Gemeingeist* that holds through *doxa* pulls people together, but it also keeps other people out. And because *doxa* is no one person's sole creation and predates every community's existence in history, much of the community that each of us has experienced is accidental. In other words, our experiences with community inculcate a *doxa* that tells us how to think about community in general.

Harrison points out that the concept "of community continues to exert an insistence upon us, whether it is through remorse for the loss of community, even though ... we stand amid a plethora of communities. However community is conjured, it always seems to contain an essentially political dynamic."[48] Therefore, each person is variously in and participant

---

48. Ibid., 116.

to multiple communities, but usually these communities are like accidents of birth. One is born here or there, not by any choice of their own, and finds oneself in a Black community or Jewish community or Francophone community or the community of women or of people with disabilities, and all of these communities are there from the start, and we are just *in them*. Although they *may* be intentional or political communities, they are not *necessarily* intentional or political.

Still, we are accustomed to thinking of community in relation to political power, struggle, or liberation. And indeed this is one of the pervasive influences of Marxism, which Harrison thinks we should finally and fully confront, criticize, and leave behind. "Although there is no prospect of the ideas of community and communism disappearing from our daily and intellectual discourse, it seems appropriate nevertheless to indicate that the time might have come to abandon these concepts."[49] Harrison argues that our connection to the concept of community in political theory and everyday life has long led us astray by concealing an ideological way of thinking about being-in-the-world and politics that we seem incapable of even noticing because of the total integration of this thinking into our common sense. Harrison argues that we have long been obsessed with the idea of a community that does not and cannot exist.

In a peculiar twist, however, Harrison turns to work as a better focus than community. As he puts it: "We need to work: the anticipation of work anticipates meaning; work enables us; it defines us. Why else have I written this book? Work gives us purpose and justifies our existence. The joke is on us. If anything, this is our community, this is our communism. Impossible though it may be, it is time to stop talking of community."[50] There are many problems with this conclusion, and this is where we must make our intervention and departure.

Firstly, why would work anticipate meaning? To connect work with meaning, one has to presuppose at least two problematic premises: (1) that work is good for one's self and for others and (2) that people are doing the work they would like to do. Harrison makes his point by invoking the reasons he wrote his book. But even his work—which was surely not done for money and which is not like the work of most people (few of whom are authors)—necessarily presupposes readers who will take it up. The purpose of his work, which according to him justifies his existence, is (in this example) a published book that is meant for readers

---

49. Ibid., 130.
50. Ibid., 137.

other than him. That is why it is published and why there is more than one copy. Like any author on a similar terrain, Harrison hopes to participate in the debates that interest him, a participation that largely depends on the attention of other people. A published book presupposes a hopeful community of readers, a community that may have nothing else in common beyond the fact that they have read the same text. The thoughtful attention of other people is what every book seeks. In this way, the work hopefully presupposes a particular community. So shifting the focus from community to work neither transcends nor leaves behind the question of community.

More importantly, precious few can work as authors of books. We live in societies where our work is usually *not* what gives our lives their purpose or justification. Sometimes, work is what brings us to the brink of anxiety, despair, or suicide. And, very often, it would be healthier to do something else than the work that we must do in order to live in our societies. Many people have written well on this subject, including Franco Berardi, Harry Cleaver, Peter Fleming, and Kathi Weeks.[51] Harrison's conclusion about work generating a life of purpose is all but obliterated by the fact that, for most people, work is exactly the opposite of Harrison's description. Work in capitalist societies defines us against the purposes we might like to make of a human life. Work may colonize our existence, and usually it takes things other than work to justify a life. Work can only be understood in the community of exchange relations, and this is the context in which work is done (for the most part) in capitalist societies.

Harrison's book concludes with a discussion of indigeneity and indigenous community. He is deeply critical of capitalism yet wants to advance lines of inquiry that reject Marxian assumptions about work and community. He finds a way to do this in the example of indigenous community: "It is the consideration of the incommensurability of different ways of living that provides us with some of the theoretical tools to critically evaluate our way of life and, for those who still live a different life, the threat

---

51. See Franco "Bifo" Berardi's *The Soul at Work: From Alienation to Autonomy*, Harry Cleaver's *Rupturing the Dialectic: The Struggle against Work, Money, and Financialization*, Peter Fleming's *Resisting Work: The Corporatization of Life and Its Discontents* (Philadelphia: Temple University Press, 2014), and Kathi Weeks's *The Problem with Work: Feminism, Marxism, Antiwork Politics, and Postwork Imaginaries* (Durham: Duke University Press, 2011). Also useful here is the classic anarchist essay by Bob Black, "The Abolition of Work," which was recently republished in a volume with other important antiwork essays by Black entitled *Instead of Work* (Berkeley: Little Black Cart, 2015). There are many other good criticisms of work going back at least to Paul Lafargue's *The Right to be Lazy* (Chicago: Charles H. Kerr, 2011).

to their way of life.... The indigenous way of living and the Western way of living are not two sets of discrete knowledge interacting uneasily at a complicated cultural crossing point. They are radically different ways of occupying the land and relating to others."[52] In the end, then, Harrison does not stop talking about community. He talks about a radically different form of life, of being-together.

To those born into indigenous lifeworlds, whether in Chiapas, Mexico, the Amazonia, or in Canada, Australia, or elsewhere, their *doxa* is also an accident of birth, and while Harrison does not romanticize any indigenous way of life, he does identify indigeneity as a rival model of life to that accepted in Western Marxism and left-wing politics. We are also interested in radically different ways of living with and relating to others, but we cannot make indigenous community into a community of choice, whether we live in Australia or anywhere else. You cannot simply declare yourself a member of whatever community you like. People who want a radically different way of relating to others cannot strive for indigeneity, ancient or otherwise, because such a form of life is itself contingent on historical acculturations, inherited intergenerational valuations, and inculcations that are neither present nor pervasive around the world today. This is why I argue that it makes more sense to pursue rival logics of relationality—to the extent we are able to do that—within the lifeworlds we actually inhabit and from the raw materials of our lived experience.

And that is why we go to love. Love is not alien to our thinking, even to those who never stop to think about what it means. The fact that love, no matter how ill-defined, appears somewhere in the aspirations of human beings almost everywhere, and that love can be understood as a noncapitalist aspiration, means that we can identify at least one rival logic of relationality that would, as a politics, aim at the radical reorganization of life and society. In addition, love is also something people say that they want to realize in the world. Does this mean that people everywhere in search of love are also in search of a different world, and that we may even know more about that world than we think?

Our political argument emerges from thinking through the answer to that question. The human longing for love indicates that everybody wants more of communism than they may understand or confess. If love is not communist, it is a false form of love. Bearing that out has been our central task. If we succeed in this task, then it is ultimately unnecessary to say that we are communists or to play around with problematic

---

52. Harrison, *Freedom of Things*, 249.

concepts of community. Such ideological and romantic content would be totally dispensable to the present theory if only we could establish love as the name of a universal tendency toward a life ungoverned by money, for a human relationality that reveals the poverty and limitations of exchange value.

CHAPTER 7

Unalienation

"Though I listen to all the arguments which the most divergent systems employ to demystify, to limit, to erase, in short to depreciate love, I persist: 'I know, I know, but all the same ...' I refer the devaluations of love to a kind of obscurantist ethic, to a let's-pretend realism, against which I erect the realism of value: I counter whatever 'doesn't work' in love with the affirmation of what is worthwhile. This stubbornness is love's protest.... The world subjects every enterprise to an alternative; that of success or failure, of victory or defeat. I protest by another logic."

—Roland Barthes, *A Lover's Discourse*

"Normally, people live apart from one another. I cannot ring a stranger's doorbell and embrace whoever opens the door. The owner of merchandise can exchange wares with others, but he certainly does not embrace his customers. People can stand close to one another in a streetcar, but they do not have the right to consider the touch of another to be tender."

—Oskar Negt and Alexander Kluge, *History and Obstinacy*

7.1 Movements of Love

Love is unsafe and unpredictable, and yet these attributes do not dissuade humans from it. Alain Badiou agrees with many others that love is an antidote to the pathological pursuit of self-interest.[1] He makes a Lacanian argument against the association of love with sex, observing that very often and quite naturally, "the other's body has to be mediated, but at the end of the day, the pleasure will always be your pleasure. Sex separates, doesn't unite."[2] One can and typically does bring their own self-interest into a sexual relationship, and often the pretense of mutuality is cover for a pursuit of one's own private pleasures. As we know well, there may be no trace of love in sexual activity. Love is unsafe and unpredictable because it uproots our being, our sense of self, and marks a divergence from the established order of life. It is an irruption and interruption, inconvenient, difficult, and yet welcome.

The defining notion of love, according to Badiou, is the idea of a world seen from the perspective of two (not one): love is a way of looking at things from an enlarged point of view that includes yet expands beyond your own. Love is also an existential project in which I can "construct a world from a decentered point of view other than that of my mere impulse to survive or re-affirm my own identity."[3] This is, for example, how love is involved in the birth of a child, where a parent may at once look at the world from a newly reconstituted point of view, a point of view that tries to see things now from the perspective of the new life.

---

1. Alain Badiou, *In Praise of Love*, trans. Peter Bush (New York: New Press, 2012), 17.
2. Ibid., 18.
3. Ibid., 25.

One of the difficulties in Badiou's theory is that he simultaneously criticizes romantic conceptions of love and thinks of love mainly in the monogamous "two scene" of adult lovers.[4] Badiou challenges the romantic conception of love as a metaphysical mystery in which every emotion is set on fire and exists beyond all human understanding. I agree with Badiou's contention that we can understand love and that we can stop regarding it as a metaphysical mystery. If we think of love as important, then how can we not try to understand it? But Badiou rejects any social or political concept of love, and on that he comes close to Arendt's view. Like Arendt, he is wrong and has to be challenged. (We will address Arendt's error in chapter 8.)

Badiou defines nonsexual love by talking about friendship. Philosophers, he contends, have largely preferred friendship to love because the former is understood to be the more intellectual relation. But over time, Badiou insists, love "embraces all the positive aspects of friendship," although it encompasses the totality of the other's being.[5] What this totality means is something like this: I can be your friend with only a small part of the space and time of my being. We can meet for lunch or coffee once every several months, we may speak on the phone or stay connected through electronic applications, and my relation to you as a friend can be authentically maintained as a relation that matters to both of us. However, far more of the space and time of my being (and yours) is taken up by love. If we are in love, then much more of what we do and think and say comprises the activity of our relation. In this way, love appears as an intensification of friendship. It is friendship with more space and time, with greater attention, and with more obligation and responsibility. With love, we may speak of a nonobligatory obligation, by which I mean that you cannot oblige the other to be obligated to you, and they cannot oblige you to be obligated to them. Still, obligation emerges inevitably in the love relation and takes the form of a responsibility that wants to stay there—you cannot help but to feel obliged even in the absence of the other obliging you.

Badiou is inclined to a concept of love that moves individuals beyond their self-interested points of view, a movement that is necessary for seeing what is possible in the world, for seeing what a different world may look like. Because of this, we might expect Badiou to connect love to politics, but he rejects any politics of love:

---

4. "Two scene" is a term coined by Badiou to capture the movement from a perspective of one to a perspective of two. See Badiou, *In Praise of Love*, 29.

5. Ibid., 36.

I don't think that you can mix up love and politics. In my opinion, the "politics of love" is a meaningless expression. I think that when you begin to say "Love one another," that can lead to a kind of ethics, but not to any kind of politics. Principally because there are people in politics one doesn't love.... A real enemy is not someone you are resigned to see take power periodically because lots of people voted for him. That is a person you are annoyed to see as head of State because you would have preferred his adversary. Any you will wait your turn, for five or ten years or more. An enemy is something else: an individual you won't tolerate taking decisions on anything that impacts on yourself.[6]

It is true that Martin Luther King, Jr. and others have tried to construct a politics of love by way of admonishing people to love their enemies, but that is not the only political theory of love.[7] If discussing a politics of love means that we *have to* invoke the platitudes of a sentimental and religious discourse, then we would have to agree with Badiou. But why should love mean that you must love your enemies? Here Beck and Beck-Gernsheim's recognition of the hatred that resides within love is useful.

Why do I hate an enemy? Sometimes I hate an enemy out of my love for a friend, for another human being, and the hatred is part of a particular intolerance that Badiou would encourage in politics. I think Badiou is right to point out that we do not have real enemies in politics whenever we come up with excuses for tolerating the supposedly intolerable and accepting the unacceptable. However, maybe the absence of enemies is a deficit of love. Love in politics would suggest at least some clear commands with regard to victims of hatred, such as gays and lesbians, immigrants, transgender people, Jews, or communists. It is possible to express a hatred of the enemy grounded in love. I do not agree therefore with Badiou that a politics of love cannot be found in the hatred of an enemy. Alexander Kluge was right to observe:

Millions of families want to live and love each other and so forth, or hate each other, but together they produce the possibility for Auschwitz.... It isn't something made by women, or men, or children, or old people—it's a reality, a typical contradiction, that you do for others the contrary of what you want for yourself.... It's not simply

6. Ibid., 57–58.
7. See especially Martin Luther King, Jr.'s "Loving Your Enemies," in King, *Gift of Love*, 45–55.

emotion, but sentimentality. Which is just as cruel as industry and patriotic wars. This means that all our human emotional relations, including the family, are extremely cruel on one hand, and extremely productive on the other—they produce motivation.[8]

Kluge's point is partly that love guarantees nothing in politics, for the very best and most loving people can be full of cruelty and harm to others. The now-proverbial example of good Germans who love their families and kiss their children goodbye before going to work on the genocide is clearly on Kluge's mind. But love motivates and mobilizes political feelings and actions. Badiou's opposition is scarcely clearer than when he says: "The issue of the enemy is completely foreign to the question of love. In love, you can find hurdles ... but there are in fact, no enemies."[9]

Here, Badiou is stunningly wrong. His position is a result of the most common error in thinking about love, that of seeing hatred as alien to it. Love is not to be confused with hatred, and love does not tend toward hatred, but it cannot be categorically incompatible with any feeling. A person whose beloved is killed in Auschwitz may feel a hatred mobilized by love. Badiou also sees jealousy as wholly external to love, but if I am jealous of a lover, this does not necessarily mean that I do not love her. We might even say in certain cases that if I do not love you, then I cannot hate your enemy. We cannot and do not always feel about every perpetrator just the same way as the victim's friend or father. But we have cultivated a different line of thinking here, where love produces a motivation for the hatred of capitalism, and at the same time offers a rival logic of life.

Badiou is careful not to say that love is always peaceful. He knows it is not. He even points to a history of murders and suicides that accompany love, so he sees a proximity of love to death. In the end, his central opposition to a politics of love is that "in politics we really have to engage with our enemies," whereas enemies are foreign to love.[10] While it is true that we have to engage enemies in politics, we do not have to love them. Badiou seems to suggest that the hatred of the Nazi enemy during the Second World War was never motivated by love. Albert Camus wrote powerfully about the underground activities of love and friendship during the Nazi occupation of France, during the Wehrmacht, and there are many Jews whose hatred of the Nazi enemy was substantiated by real love for a son

8. Alexander Kluge, interviewed by Gary Indiana for *BOMB Magazine*, April 1, 1989, https://bombmagazine.org/articles/alexander-kluge/.
9. Badiou, *In Praise of Love*, 59.
10. Ibid., 61.

or a daughter or a husband or a wife or a mother or a father or a friend.[11] Today, if there is a Palestinian hatred of the Jews, we will have to confront the fact that while some such hatred is motivated by anti-Semitism, some of the hatred is also motivated by a love for a son or a daughter or a mother or a father or a place.

If Badiou wants to separate love and hatred from political *action*, we can perhaps agree with that. The fact that I hate my enemy does not mean I will stand up and fight against him. I may be afraid. I may know that acting out against an enemy would mean my death, and there may be things and people who depend on my continuing to live. So because of other considerations, I may not act at all against a political enemy—despite my love or hatred. But feeling is not cut off entirely from action, and much collective action has been motivated by feeling. It is easier to stand up against an enemy with others who will stand up together with you. In the multiplication of each individual's bravery, a collective courage can form and often has formed in history, and that bravery is not the private property of any one individual—it exceeds that of any individual. In the example of revolution, an individual person cannot enter a revolution (and there would be no revolution to join) if she were all alone. But Badiou insists on love as a movement from the position and perspective of one to a "two scene," where each of us may look at the world from a larger point of view than ours alone. In the scene with others we may find more than a point of view: we may also find the courage to confront an enemy.

It is surprising when Badiou—who rejects any politics of love—thinks about love in relation to communism. Fundamentally, the communist idea involves moving beyond the capitalist disposition of privacy and individuation, and while "the word 'communism' doesn't immediately relate to love … the word brings with it new possibilities for love."[12] Badiou is willing to consider something like a miniature communism in love. He acknowledges that "we can also say that love is communist in that sense, if one accepts, as I do, that the real subject of love is the becoming of the couple and not the mere satisfaction of the individuals that are its component parts. Yet another possible definition of love: minimal communism."[13] But we have to be cautious with Badiou's more hopeful, and seemingly political, conclusion. Notice that his original error—of constraining love to

---

11. See Albert Camus, *Resistance, Rebellion, and Death: Essays* (New York: Alfred A. Knopf, 1988).

12. Badiou, *In Praise of Love*, 73.

13. Ibid., 90.

two, or as he puts it here, to the couple—makes a comeback in this ultimate position. Although this may derive from his interests in Socrates and theater, it is nonetheless perplexing that Badiou insists on love as a movement from one to two, yet sees little sense in speaking about love at the social or political level. He expressly recognizes a certain minimal communism in love, which we have been exploring throughout this book. To move from the love of a couple to a communist movement would require something more than love. He is right about that, but we should not leave love locked up in the homes of couples. I think it can come along with us, out into the world, and I think it can and must participate in movements that surpass the limits and the lives of couples.

Happily, some other communists have recently thought about the communism of love. The most influential of these are Michael Hardt and Antonio Negri. It would be fair to say that *The Communism of Love* has been devoted in part to a full development of sparse but promising fragments in their work. In *Commonwealth*, for example, Hardt and Negri theorize the concept of the common as the starting point for thinking about a future communism. Like Silvia Federici and others, Hardt and Negri think of the common as a category that includes every single thing that should be shared as the common wealth of all people and that should not be privatized or commodified into the legal property of only those with money. There have been many criticisms of the theory of the common, since it often seems to operate abstractly, conceiving of a communism without sufficient class analysis or attention to current workers' struggles.

Arguably, talking about love does little to concretize abstract talk of the common, but Hardt and Negri do it anyway. They say: "Love provides another path for investigating the power and productivity of the common. Love is a means to escape the solitude of individualism but not, as contemporary ideology tells us, only to be isolated again in the private life of the couple or the family."[14] Already, we can see that Hardt and Negri are concerned about cutting love off from the political. Unlike Badiou, they worry about a privatization of love in the couple or family because that narrow sphere threatens to constrain love to something smaller than its aspirations and tendencies.

Hardt and Negri acknowledge that love is a subject that has largely been left to poets and considered too soft for politics. Yet they insist that "love is an essential concept for philosophy and politics, and the failure to

---

14. Michael Hardt and Antonio Negri, *Commonwealth* (Cambridge, MA: Harvard University Press, 2011), xi–xii.

interrogate and develop it is one central cause of the weakness of contemporary thought."[15]

They claim that love is at the heart of any radical and revolutionary theory, even when writers are afraid to say so. Hardt and Negri begin from the perspective of the poor, from the relation of love to poverty. They claim that among the poor especially, "solidarity, care for others, creating community, and cooperating in common projects" is essential, even to the point of being an existential necessity connected with survival.[16] Love is not, in the context of poverty, passive or spontaneous; rather, it is well tended to and consciously incorporated into the daily life of family and community. Love in a community appears as an organizational effort to create spheres of life as spaces of refuge, camaraderie, friendship, strategy, and survival.

Hardt and Negri, like Badiou, warn their readers about identitarian love, which they define as a love of the same that often takes the form of the racist love of one's own or of chauvinistic patriotism. Hardt and Negri refer to these as "corrupt forms of love" on the grounds that they do not move from one to two or more, and thus they are a love of self that excludes a love of the other.[17] Racist or nationalist proclamations of self-love are about the defense of sameness against difference, and they therefore betray the most fundamental logic of love, which constitutes a being (ontology) and an understanding (epistemology) that includes difference, that encompasses others and the unlike. People who do not know what love means often invoke it to justify their fear of other people. If such a parochial narrowing to the familiar were accepted as a form of love, it would be a shrinking love, for it necessarily entails the shrinking of affection for others, the diminishing of human solidarity. If such identitarian love were accepted as real love, this would render love an isolating and separating practice. To call such feeling love is to purge love of its powers and, worse, to invoke the amorous name as a mask to camouflage opposite tendencies. We mustn't forget our conclusion about love being compatible with feelings of hatred—but love motivates a hatred of precisely that which destroys human solidarity, diminishes affection for others unlike us, and abuses the commonwealth as a terrain for predation, competition, brazen individualism, or worse. As Hardt and Negri put it, love is best understood as "a motor of association."[18]

---

15. Ibid., 179.
16. Ibid., 180.
17. Ibid., 182.
18. Ibid., 189.

Hardt and Negri seek to establish love as a power that forges spaces of refuge from and resistance to competitive privatization. Whenever we see one group laying claim over some part of the common in order to keep it for themselves, they are either defending against imperial conquest or opposing the politics of love. The common is not a walled-off autonomous zone that is good only for the tiny subset of the population that can get to it. This is because love is not only a motor of association that "produces the common and consolidates it in society, but also an open field of battle.... [T]he power of love must also be ... a force to combat evil. Love now takes the form of indignation, disobedience, and antagonism."[19] I take this to mean that love compels us to fight against what harms us, to resist the destruction of what love defends and wants to make. In this way, Hardt and Negri clarify that love is not alien to force and that "the actions of love are themselves deployments of force."[20] But not all force is the force of love. Racists may also deploy force, and it is not out of love that they do so.

This is the best move among Hardt and Negri's fragmentary gestures toward a theory of love. They overstep Badiou's boundary that separates love from politics, and they see love as a form of engagement, or even social movement, that can be insurrectionary. The question of love *must* be a question of movements. What can or does love move? How does it move people, and what does it move people to do? What is its law of movement? What movement embodies love? What movements are deployments of love? Everything we have done thus far has set us up for these culminating inquiries, which have already been part of our journey. We have to move more resolutely now toward a consideration of revolutionary struggles and movements.

Hardt and Negri have always considered revolutionary possibilities, but they have shifted their attention most fully to the practical strategies of social, political, and revolutionary movements in *Assembly* (2017), where they think through the meaning and insights of Black Lives Matter, Occupy Wall Street, uprisings in North Africa and the Middle East, and insurrections in Argentina and Spain, with reference to a global history of revolutionary struggle. Hardt and Negri continue to challenge so-called identitarian love, but in this book they do so in light of the rise of recent right-wing movements. They maintain here, as in *Commonwealth*, that love of one's own race or nation is a corrupted love, and they add that

---

19. Ibid., 195.
20. Ibid., 196.

"behind identity lurks property."[21] What they mean here is that identity politics is often about which people have a right to which things—not only things like opportunities and money, but even things like discourses. The Left, communists included, should be cautious. We may consider demands associated with identity in intersectional ways that associate rather than separate, and we must take seriously the focus on "Black lives" in Black Lives Matter and women in the #MeToo protests. The way to distinguish the seemingly identitarian content of these movements from that in movements on the right is to consider what the movements are responding to. Are the movements about defending race and nation and deepening the exclusionary power of existing powerholders over others (as in a patriarchal or racial order)? If yes, then the movements are not movements of love. Movements of love will express the disaffections of those who have nothing or little to lose, those who are singled out and targeted by racism or sexism, those who oppose isolation and exclusion, who make movements of the common.

> The individual subject is defined by what it *has*.... Alexandra Kollontai argues that the logic of possession is so deeply ingrained that it infuses even the modern conception of love. People have no way to think of their bonds to each other except in terms of property: you are mine and I am yours. In contrast, subjectivities in the common are grounded not in possessions but in their interactions with and openness to others. Subjectivity is defined not by having but being or, better, *being-with*, acting-with, creating-with. Subjectivity itself arises from social cooperation.[22]

In this passage, Hardt and Negri sound like a newfangled Fromm. But notice that the concept of the common, and with it a necessary openness to others, distinguishes Hardt and Negri's theory as incompatible with the so-called self-love of racial identification. These distinguishing features are largely what connect their theory to communism. When people rise up together in revolts, strikes, occupations, and other forms of resistance and indignation, they invoke "the language of love and equality."[23] Love is a common refrain in revolt. Even when the movements do not speak of communism, they speak of "humanity" and "equality," and they only

---

21. Michael Hardt and Antonio Negri, *Assembly* (New York: Oxford University Press, 2017), 51.

22. Ibid., 105.

23. Ibid., 241.

speak audibly because of a certain phase of being-together that gives their revolt its being-in-the-world. In the uprising, love is enacted in more than the "two scene" of the couple.

While Hardt and Negri argue that inattention to love is the central major weakness in contemporary political thought, they themselves only attend to the question in passing, in fleeting passages in *Commonwealth* and in other assorted writings and speeches by Hardt alone. I submit *The Communism of Love* as a dedicated effort to account for the weakness that Hardt and Negri identify but do not themselves address. Other authors and books have tried to do this, but for various reasons to no avail.

One of the biggest misses has been Srećko Horvat's *The Radicality of Love*. Horvat's book is neither about love nor about radical politics, although that is its pretension. His book lightly touches on romantic and sexual relationality, and breezily alights on uprisings and rebellions, without any real effort to define love in either context or to connect his disparate themes. Horvat's misfire of a book would appear to substantiate Badiou's warning to never combine politics with love.

Horvat claims that there is a feeling in a revolt or an uprising, a feeling of deep connection to others, and that "this feeling can be described as love. Revolution is love if it wants to be worthy of its name."[24] While he insists that love cannot be reduced to solidarity, Horvat maintains that "every act of solidarity contains love."[25] Horvat's definition of love never moves beyond the level of vague generalization about a feeling of solidarity that is bigger than solidarity. He speaks of love in the Iranian Revolution, in Occupy Wall Street, in Syntagma Square, in Tahrir Square, and in the revolt of Haitian slaves, about Lenin's regard for love, Ulrike Meinhof's uses of love, and Che Guevara's love, but not what connects them, not what love is, not what it does, not what it moves or how it moves people.

Horvat discusses how the gathering spaces of revolutionaries, from the early eighteenth century on up to Khomeini's time, have been looked on as dangerous "*information centers*" that may need to be placed under surveillance and even shut down to preempt their participation in revolts.[26] Horvat is right about this, a point that was previously well documented by Jürgen Habermas in *The Structural Transformation of the Public Sphere* (1962). But Horvat confuses desire and revolutionary hope for love. There are connections between desire and love and revolution, but these are not synonyms for the same mysterious or subversive feeling. Just as you can

---

24. Srećko Horvat, *The Radicality of Love* (Malden: Polity, 2016), 6.
25. Ibid., 7.
26. Ibid., 43.

have solidarity without love, your desire may be wholly self-interested, like the sexual desire that Badiou analyzes through a Lacanian lens.

Horvat appears to take Kollontai's side over Lenin's in a discussion about the importance of sex and human sexuality. Horvat points out that "at the very beginning of every revolution, or upheaval, or protest, or occupation, you must deal with the 'human factor' (to organize things, channel energy, etc.); you can't ignore desires or libidinal investments."[27] Here Horvat is responding to Lenin's wish to postpone the discussion until more important revolutionary matters are settled first. In agreeing with the importance of human desire and libidinal investment at the start of every revolution, Horvat stresses the significance of sexual drives and human feelings, and he is right to do this. The problem is that this particular point is quite separate from any consideration of love, unless one mistakes libidinal desire for love, or for the terrain of love. Despite my criticism of Badiou's separation of politics from love, he was correct to define love as an altogether different terrain than that of libidinal desire.

But Horvat wants to establish a dialectical relationship between love (which he largely sees as libidinal and sexual desire of a romantic kind) and revolution (which he sees in a more conventional way). Following Hegel's dialectical thinking, Horvat claims that "the true radicality of love is to be found in the radicality of revolution, and the radicality of revolution is to be found in true love."[28] This expresses the basic sensibility of Horvat's entire book, and boils down to the following: Horvat is excited by revolutionary history and by new rebellions and revolts, and because he likes them, he simply asserts that they are expressions of love. Because Horvat thinks that love is a great virtue, he insists that love is always in line with radical and revolutionary politics on the left. Whatever Horvat loves he calls revolutionary, and whatever is revolutionary he calls love. Notwithstanding some kernels of insight along the way, the book offers a trite simplification that cannot help anyone interested in theorizing a more nuanced and concrete understanding of love.

While Horvat's book is mainly useful for illustrating the danger of a wrong turn, it is not without some merits. For example, he deals well (and better than others) with the compatibility of love and hate, saying that they "are not necessarily opposites, they can lead to a third instance."[29] Here I agree with Horvat that love can mobilize hatred (and other things, like indignation and defiance). And Horvat also thinks, as do I, about the

---

27. Ibid., 102.
28. Ibid., 110.
29. Ibid.

communism of love. He appreciates Badiou's idea of love as a miniature communism for two. Love is like revolution in the sense that both are interested in creating new worlds. But aside from some useful insights such as these, Horvat's main practice is that of cataloging superficial similarities between love and revolution—for example, that they both demand sacrifice.[30]

From the beginning to the end of Horvat's book, its main concern is with sex, sexual bodies, sexual freedom, and the possibility of revolutionary politics—*not love*. I suppose it is possible to think that any discussion about any of these things is also always a discussion about love, but that is not the case. The fact is that Horvat's study of love provides no sustained focus on, definition, or theory of love, and so it is not a study or book about love. Horvat's own thinking about love is, at its best, a mirror of Kollontai's thinking at around the time of the Russian Revolution, but with less sociological content. He thinks that love is an important discussion for revolutionaries and that, today more than ever, what we need is Kollontai's concept of "free love," and specifically a theory and practice of "sexual relations liberated from bourgeois possessiveness."[31] This is a peculiar conclusion to say the least. The revolutions and insurrections that Horvat writes about are not focused in any way on the subject of free love, nor do I think that they should be. And whether or not they should be, they have not been and will not be. It turns out that the concern about free sexual relations is itself a predominantly bourgeois concern. I am interested in the revolutionary history that Horvat takes up, but it does not suffice to endorse whatever we like by naming it "love."

There are movements and then there is love. Social and political movements are not about erotic or sexual love or libidinal desire, even though such things do appear within them like debris swept up in a tornado. Yes, it's all in there, and it matters what gets swept up in the passions of social movements. Yet there are many other things in the movements, including jealousy, frustration, desires for fame and influence, political manipulation, and plenty of insincerity too. Love appears in revolutionary movements like many other things that we may not endorse so easily.

Revolution is the cohesive materialization of heterogeneous anguish and hope that transforms things into something new. And love is not mainly about sex, sexual bodies, and sexual freedom, no matter how much sex, bodies, and sexual freedom are caught up within love.

---

30. Ibid., 123.
31. Ibid., 156.

We have to disentangle what Horvat equivocates and synonymizes, as we have been doing throughout this book. We have also been wanting to talk about love and revolution, but we have to do better. Insurgent forms of love show themselves in many places having little to do with sex, bodies, or sexual freedom, and while love may motivate *some* of what happens in an insurrection, it is not the necessary or defining power of any revolt. Love moves some things, but not everything. While we must endorse and defend free and open human sexualities, the nonsexual powers of love are its most important ones.

7.2 Insurgent Love

Raya Dunayevskaya reads Hegel and Marx as philosophers on quests for universality.[32] Hers is a much-contested reading, but what I appreciate most about Dunayevskaya's approach is her consistent attention to the struggles of the most oppressed people everywhere, not only in the United States but around the world. She theorizes from the bottom up and claims that the most important insights come out of revolutionary struggles. Therefore, we should study those struggles and learn from them. The revolutionary movements of women, Black Americans, and impoverished workers in the United States were always leading forces of revolutionary theory in Dunayevskaya's account. She sees the struggles of women, Black people, sexual minorities, and the disaffected poor as nodal points in a *total* struggle against the world such as it is. She sees the distinct struggles of the oppressed as part of a totality guided by humanist universality. There must first be total negation, an abolition of what exists, followed by a second negation, which indicates the moment of the positive creation of something new. As Dunayevskaya puts it: "The overthrow, what is called the first negation, is saying *No* to what is. But the second negation, the creation of the new, is harder, because you want to have entirely new human relations."[33]

Dunayevskaya knows enough about the revolutionary struggles of women to never accept Horvat's reductionist identification of love with sex. Women's struggles have aimed to transform human relations, and not merely sexual relations. Women "categorically refused to remain an appendage to the men. They wished to have not only sexual but human

---

32. Raya Dunayevskaya, *Women's Liberation and the Dialectics of Revolution: Reaching for the Future* (Atlantic Highlands, NJ: Humanities Press, 1985), 27–28.
33. Ibid., 51.

relations with them. They were out searching for a *total reorganization of society.*"[34] Thus, Dunayevskaya insists on focusing on all of human relations, including of course sexual relations, but without any reduction to the latter.

When Dunayevskaya looks at the revolt of women throughout the world, for example in strikes in Portugal and Africa, in the movement against the Vietnam War in the United States and elsewhere, she finds different yet interconnected aspirations there, including the opposition to war, workers' power, different relations in the home, equality, and opposition to patriarchy—indeed, they wanted "nothing short of the wholeness of the person."[35] This is an expression of Dunayevskaya's humanism. As the foundational Marxist-humanist in North America, Dunayevskaya could not have avoided being the target of fierce criticism, although I think that her unorthodox but important condemnation of state capitalism was the root cause of much of the animosity directed toward her theories. We should keep in mind that Dunayevskaya was an uncompromising critic of state capitalism in Russia during a time when many other leftists, including other unorthodox Marxists such as Herbert Marcuse, were more amenable to what they accepted as Soviet or Chinese communism or socialism. Dunayevskaya did not wait until it was safe to criticize those regimes from a Marxist or humanist point of view. And, as always for her, every major advance of history comes from revolts, because only revolt can "release new sensibilities, new passions, and new forces—a whole new human dimension."[36] This, the state can never do.

Notice the sequence of new sensibilities, passions, and forces. This is important. Speaking of new sensibilities, passions, and forces is not the same as speaking of love. However, any experience of love is also an experience with new sensibilities, passions, and forces. Dunayevskaya was always thinking about the human being and human relations. Therefore, it may come as a surprise to learn that she had very little to say about love. One can find fleeting attention to the subject, but nothing as sustained as we should expect to find given her concern for the whole of the human person with the totality of its sensibilities, passions, and forces. Fortunately for us, however, Dunayevskaya was asked to address the question of love very directly in a radio interview she did on WBAI in March 1984. What she said then was and remains very important.

---

34. Ibid., 32.
35. Ibid., 87.
36. Ibid., 116.

People want to have a conclusion on the question of love—what is love, whether it's physical, whether it's emotional, whether it's total, and all that sort of thing. But I don't think it's correct for us to try and solve it for others. I think that what we have to do is to create the conditions for everyone to be able to experiment with choices, in love, in the family—and I don't think we'll really have those choices until we get rid of capitalism. Capitalism tries to use everything for its power.[37]

Dunayevskaya's reply expresses reluctance to answer the question of love for others. It is perhaps this reluctance that has kept her away from the subject. Most philosophers, authors, and activists have the most to say on subjects about which they can claim some confident knowledge. Love, it would seem, was not such a subject for Dunayevskaya. However, she does recognize that there are many different planes on which love operates. Rather than saying what love is or how it works, Dunayevskaya says that we have to create the conditions that will enable people to get creative and experiment with new and different forms of human relationality. She notes that we cannot really do that in a capitalist society because capitalism instrumentalizes everything human for its own power. Every human energy and motivation is something for capital to seize.

Dunayevskaya explains her point with reference to the splitting of the atom. The possibility of splitting the atom, hypothesized by Einstein's theory of relativity, preceded actually doing it by roughly forty years because, according to Dunayevskaya, the atom was only split after capitalists saw that they could do it in the interests of their own power. So it became a catastrophic and destructive thing as opposed to something potentially liberating and useful for human life. When it comes to love, theorists like Eva Illouz have shown how the commercial interests of capital have historically and rather thoroughly seized on human aspirations for love and have created endless romantic utopias for the marketplace. This is perhaps an inevitable fate for love in a capitalist society. Indeed, from capital's perspective, what better fate than a commodity for something that everyone wants?

This is why, for Dunayevskaya, love is only able to become what it presently is within the limits of a capitalist society. In a world governed by money and ruled by the logic of capital, love will not and cannot be developed to its full and possible flourishing. We may and do love within the limits of the space and time of a life organized by capital in a world

---

37. Ibid., 180.

governed by money, but we must understand that those limits affect what we do and how we do it. The world of capital would have to be abolished for us to really see what love can do. Kollontai tried to imagine that world, but none of us has ever lived in it. So when asked about love, Dunayevskaya could only speak of the abolition of capitalism as the first part of an answer, the remainder of which would have to be worked out from there.

Dunayevskaya locates the reaching out for new sensibilities, passions, and forces inside revolt. She understands revolt as a search for new forms of life. While she treats each revolt as a distinctive instance with its own motivations and specific purposes, she sees revolt as part of striving for a world in which love can be developed along with the full and free development of the human person. "There surely is some time in everyone's life when one wants to reach for something of the future. I do not doubt that in the present historic stage women *want* to reach for that total uprooting of this sexist, racist, exploitative society. Let's begin there."[38] Yes, let's begin there. But love remains possible in the present capitalist world, as it is actually realized and experienced in every society, despite the fact that it faces different challenges in different times and places. I view love, in part, as an insurgent force inside the present capitalist world. It can be seen in real interests and efforts to uproot our sexist, racist, and exploitative society. A radical concerned with the root of things may say that love is somewhere at the root of all problems (and solutions). Elsewhere, love is uprooting.

In the language of John Holloway, we could say that love is like a crack in capitalism. It does not destroy the old and create a new world in its place, but it breaks with the logic of the present world, cracking it like a window pane, leaving the world in place yet weakening it as the crack grows or spreads. Holloway describes the crack as a space or moment for a different way of doing things: "We take the moment or space into our own hands and try to make it a place of self-determination, refusing to let money (or any other alien force) determine what we do."[39] As we have established, love relations that mean anything at all are not held together by exchange relations. Most of us, if I may assume some good fortune, have experience with such a different way of doing and relating to others. Regardless of my money or their money, there are certain people to whom I am connected by love. Money does not determine our relationality.

So, we can consider love relations as a crack in capitalist exchange relations, although Holloway, much like Dunayevskaya, is not

---

38. Ibid., 230.
39. John Holloway, *Crack Capitalism* (New York: Pluto, 2010), 21.

terribly concerned with love. Holloway talks about comradeship and alter-relationality among striking workers, and he mentions love in fleeting moments. He observes that when striking workers describe what's happening, they stress the importance of the experience, which is independent from the question of whether or not they win or lose. Workers on strike may have—and possibly for the first time in their lives—"the practical experience of a world without bosses: the creation of a world of different social relations goes beyond what was foreseen at the outbreak of the strike."[40] Most importantly, Holloway acknowledges that the "relations generated are relations of love that give the movement force and permit the participants to overcome and respect their disagreements."[41] It is, unfortunately, a case of wishful thinking to say that strikers overcome and respect their disagreements, but there is a certain love in the strike, a love that animates it, and a peculiar if temporary sense of community and solidarity. While Holloway does not single out love for sustained focus, he regards it as one necessarily anticapitalist relation that human beings can and do experience within capitalist society: "Comradeship, dignity, amorosity, love, solidarity, fraternity, friendship, ethics: all these names stand in contrast to the commodified, monetised relations of capitalism, all describe relations developed in struggles against capitalism and which can be seen as anticipating or creating a society beyond capitalism. They stand in contrast to the commodified relations of capitalism not as timeless alternatives, but as struggle-against."[42]

We call these "cracks" precisely because they do not create lasting alternatives, they do not establish new lifeworlds that we can inhabit instead of the capitalist one. Comradeship, love, solidarity, friendship, and the like are only experiences within capitalist society of noncapitalist relations. Capitalism cannot foreclose everything all the time, and we have lived experiences with breaks in its logic. This is exactly why the strike is such a good example. "Cracks break with the logic of capitalist society."[43] But they do not abolish that form of society, and if they are very small and contained, they are merely logical and minor experiential breaks, and, as such, they do not threaten capitalism in any significant way.

The central point here is to recognize that not everything that is anticapitalist is revolutionary or even potentially revolutionary. Some anticapitalist or noncapitalist relations and activities are permissible by capital

---

40. Ibid., 41.
41. Ibid.
42. Ibid., 43.
43. Ibid., 49.

and can be carried out on a small scale, at least as long as they don't threaten the overarching social logic that binds us and our daily lives together. While Holloway seems at times to want to make more out of the cracks, he points to them, including even the tiny little rebellions that don't change anything, as evidence that human dignity will persist and will not wait until capitalism is totally abolished. Anarchists sometimes speak about the same relations and activities as prefiguration, and writers like Marina Sitrin and Dario Azzellini have argued that, in the relations and activities of revolts, people experience doing democracy directly and immediately.[44] Holloway agrees with the anarchist emphasis on the importance of such experience.

Cracks are spaces and times made for what we want inside of a world that we don't want. As such, every crack is a little resistance that may show us what we're capable of. "We create the world that is killing us, and if we create it, then we can stop creating it and do something else instead."[45] I have long read Holloway as just as much a poet as a philosopher. I think he is one of the great poetic voices of theory, and his poetry moves me. But we have to confront the fact that Holloway's poetic philosophy exaggerates the emancipatory power of the cracks. It is remarkably difficult to "stop" doing what capital expects of us and to "do something else instead." Of course, everything revolutionary will be difficult, and we must never abandon an argument because its recommendations are hard to carry out. For over twenty years I have challenged students who readily recognize beautiful ideals yet immediately declare them too hard to realize. I have pointed out time and again that if we can't do hard things, we will have to give up on any concept of justice. Every great victory for women, people of color, sexual minorities, and exploited people has been hard-won, and only seemed possible when the change was underway.

But Holloway's texts would be better by way of a real confrontation with the difficulties we face. Logically, yes, we can undo everything by doing nothing. It's a remarkable and simple insight. But doing nothing can also mean dying, losing a job you hate but need for survival, or otherwise exacerbating your own pain in the very effort to relieve it. People cannot be expected to break capitalist society if they will themselves be further broken in the effort. Until people reach a point of material suffering when stopping what they're doing and doing something else is the only way to improve things—including their own lives—most people are

44. See Marina Sitrin and Dario Azzellini, *They Can't Represent Us! Reinventing Democracy from Greece to Occupy* (London: Verso Books, 2014).

45. Holloway, *Crack Capitalism*, 124.

unfortunately inclined to reproduce what they despise indefinitely into the future. The point is an important one, and it is not altogether lost on Holloway: "We are enclosed, locked in, entrapped. Enclosed by money, locked in by violence, entrapped by the logic of the social cohesion of capitalism.... The fact that we build our own prison is a source both of hope and profound depression."[46]

But this realism about the challenges we face leads to serious questions about the relationship between the cracks and revolutionary politics. If a crack in capitalism is just any experience of a rival logic to that of capitalist society, then the existing society can even claim credit for the experience as evidence of an already-existing freedom. Holloway worries about this too. We should, he claims, think of an interstitial revolution, and we should appreciate the cracks as what keep capital from the totality it desires. But we would be right to worry about isolated insubordinations, and we have to find ways to move past an acceptance of a micropolitics comprised of fleeting interruptions. Holloway therefore focuses on and insists that we study the way a crack spreads across a glass pane, how once it gets started it can move and become more dangerous in its growth.

With Holloway, we ultimately end up with a humanism not too far from that of Dunayevskaya. But Holloway makes a distinction that matters for our present study. He includes love in the process of seeding a revolutionary humanism. "Simply trying to be human, chatting to our friends, falling in love, becomes converted by the dynamic of capital, that constant turning of the screw, into an act of insubordination. And conversely: it is this trying to be human that is our revolutionary hope, the potential breakthrough of another world, another doing, another way of relating."[47]

We have been thinking about other ways of relating, of alter-relationality, throughout this book. We seek, like Holloway, to connect the alter-relationality of love and loving to revolutionary hope. But we have been a little bit less hopeful, recognizing that we may have to wait for material crises to channel love and its aspirations into social disruptions that pose a real threat to the existing state of things. Logic and hope can be well understood and convincing, yet disrupt nothing outside of heads and hearts.

Revolt is not revolution, yet it happens more frequently. A revolt might want to be revolution, and is often a real effort or a gesture in a revolutionary direction. But a revolt is not a revolution because the former does not structurally transform the world as we know it. Revolt does

---

46. Ibid., 165.
47. Ibid., 251.

other things. Revolts typically contain much real disaffection, fierce criticism, and imagination, but inadequate energy and confidence for revolution. Revolts lack the overwhelming social force and sensibility for Dunayevskaya's first negation. A revolt is an experience with or an expression of revolutionary disaffection that typically takes a nonrevolutionary form. Accordingly, I am inclined to think of love as closer to revolt than to revolution. Love is not a structural transformation, but gestures in that direction whether lovers know it or not. To better develop this point, we may need to sharpen our understanding of the relationship between love's aspirations and some of the specific hopes of revolt.

In his books and essays, Franco Berardi has closely followed all of the recent global uprisings, and he reliably sees in them a precarious, revolutionary hope. Berardi points out that recent rebels are not trying to take the state, overthrow the government, or even necessarily fight with the police or military. Understanding what they *are* doing needs some unpacking. Berardi observes that today's insurgents seem to be "looking for recomposition of the social body and re-activation of the erotic body of the general intellect.... [T]he acceleration of the infosphere ... has stressed the social psychosphere, provoking loneliness, panic, depression, dis-empathy. In the street riots cognitarians are looking for empathic rhythm.... The rebels of today are first of all performing a self-therapeutic and poetical action. They are recomposing the empathy of the bodies, rediscovering a common sphere of sensibility."[48] The decomposition of the social body refers to the individuations and withdrawals of persons from society. People feeling cut off from one another, feeling lonely and fragile, sad, and stressed out, are people in need of a recomposed social body. Recomposition is the hopeful opposite of decomposition, and it indicates an effort to revitalize confidence and hope, to be with others who share your feeling, and to confront and combat loneliness—not alone, but together. Our feeling for one another can be erotic or some other intense affection. To be empathic together, to express feelings together—this is what revolts do when they break out. A revolt is no less about collective sadness than it is about anger. Often, revolt is less about political transformations than ontological ones. Berardi assesses revolt as activities that are not planned from political agendas but rather come from despair, from sensibility, from a drive for psychosocial health and survival. I agree with Berardi's basic assessment of global revolts from roughly 2008 to 2012.

---

48. Franco "Bifo" Berardi, *Skizo-Mails*, trans. Laurie Schwartz and Alex Wildcat (Los Angeles: Errant Bodies Press / Doormats, 2012), 36–37.

Berardi draws a connection between rebels in the streets and love. He says that solidarity "has nothing to do with altruistic self-denial. In materialistic terms, solidarity is not about you; it is about me. Like love, it is not about altruism, it is about the pleasure of sharing the breath and the space of the other. Love is the ability to enjoy myself thanks to your presence, thanks to your eyes."[49] A beautiful passage, to be sure, but it should be appreciated also for its understanding of how love and solidarity with others is good for one's own self. When we speak of love, we are not speaking of charity. But we should resist the idea that love is either egoistic or altruistic. Love is both altruistic and egoistic, but at the same time it is neither. Love recombines individuals into a collective being, a one comprising many, a heterogeneous collectivity of two or more that has interests beyond any of its discrete members.

I am one of about five theorists (depending on how you count) who associates love with revolt or finds the former as part of the mobilizing and motivating content of the latter. Of those theorists who think of love as a specifically communist power, I am one of about two or three. Part of what I have been trying to address is the failure—on the part of both of these tiny clusters of theorists—to connect the disparate projects of finding love in revolt and of understanding love as a communist power. The study of the communism of love in relation to social movements and revolts distinguishes my work at the theoretical level, but politically I want to distinguish my theory of communism as nonstatist and abolitionist. I am more interested in forms of life than forms of government, and the present theory insists on the development of a total opposition to unacceptable realities. Of the tiny little band of thinkers who swim in similar waters, the one who comes closest to my position is probably George Katsiaficas in his elaborations on Marcuse's concept of eros.

A bit like Berardi, Katsiaficas understands riots, revolts, and rebellions as the activation of certain feelings of disaffection and hope, as the activation of love and solidarity. "We need to cultivate our capacities to love and to act in an efficient manner.... The eros effect is about people continuously activating their inner desire for freedom, which is the greatest force for liberation on our planet."[50] The "eros effect" refers to the seemingly contagious geographic spreading of human feeling that one can witness in the passionate expressions of social and political movements

---

49. Ibid., 113.
50. George Katsiaficas, *Spontaneous Combustion: The Eros Effect and Global Revolution*, ed. Jason Del Gandio and AK Thompson (Albany: State University of New York Press, 2017), 30.

and global uprisings of all kinds. Eros is what makes us human, what distinguishes us from machines. "The capacity of human beings to love is what keeps us from death.... Machines don't need to love."[51] Here Katsiaficas echoes the humanism of his teacher and friend, Marcuse, but also that of Dunayevskaya (also a friend and interlocutor of Marcuse's) and Holloway too, as discussed above. Like Berardi, Katsiaficas also associates love with solidarity. "When the eros effect is activated, humans' love for and solidarity with each other suddenly replace previously dominant values and norms."[52] When the eros effect is activated in an uprising or revolt, it is much like a crack in the capitalist hegemony, and, indeed, Holloway and Katsiaficas have a similar appreciation for the importance of little things.

Katsiaficas closely studied the Gwangju Uprising, which refers to a popular rebellion in Gwangju city in South Korea in May 1980. While the exact number may never be known, well over one hundred people were killed in the uprising when citizens of Gwangju dared an armed insurrection, breaking into police stations.[53] University students protesting the government were beaten, shot, and killed by soldiers. But Gwangju is largely regarded as a democratic movement against the government of South Korea, after the assassination of President Park Chung-hee in 1979. The end of Park's rule of almost two decades led to social and political instability. Similarly minded social movements were suppressed while Park was in power, so after his assassination they rose up in full expression at a moment that seemed ripe for creating something new. The uprising raged against Park's martial law and called for democratization, better wages, and a free press wherein the government could be criticized. Government troops were deployed against the uprisings, the latter of which included students and professors, as well as some sympathetic local politicians. Authorities declared the uprisings a communist rebellion instigated by Marxist students and supportive rioters. Katsiaficas cites Choi Jungwoon, a Korean social scientist, who "concluded that Gwangju citizens had crystallized an 'absolute community' in which all were equal and united by love."[54] Katsiaficas points out that as maligned as the uprising was by

---

51. Ibid., 35.
52. Ibid., 38.
53. Indeed, reporting on deaths related to the Gwangju Uprising have varied widely and wildly, from roughly one hundred killed up to six hundred or more. Katsiaficas discusses this difficulty and context well in his *Asia's Unknown Uprisings, Volume 1: South Korean Social Movements in the 20th Century* (Oakland: PM Press, 2012), 214–15.
54. Katsiaficas, *Spontaneous Combustion*, 42.

Korean authorities, it was, according to Choi, the creation of real (albeit temporary) community based on love and solidarity.

But love is not enough to make temporary community into permanent reality. Katsiaficas asks: "Can we simply will ourselves to remain in love? If the eros effect were continually activated, we would have passed from the real of prehistory to a world in which human beings for the first time are able to determine for themselves the type of society in which they wish to live."[55] Obviously, we cannot will ourselves to stay in love, and the eros effect cannot be continuously activated, not even in the little community comprised by two lovers. We cannot keep our affection going in energetic movements indefinitely. Human energy can be exhausted and recharged variously for different causes, but not "kept on" for a lifetime. Movements come and go, and the sad fact is that they often leave the world much as it was before they began.

For this reason, neither Katsiaficas nor I claim that love is a surefire solution to our problems. It is, however, *an essential part of what we need to address our problems*, and we need to understand love for the power that it is. I call it a communist power. Katsiaficas does not. That is a mistake, because in eluding the communism of love Katsiaficas eludes the necessarily contestatory relationship and rival logic of love to capital, and the irreducibly antagonistic relationship of love to capitalist exchange value. Despite this critical limitation, Katsiaficas understands much of what we need now to transition to our final chapter: "Love binds us together, gives us the courage to make history, to stare down our fears, and to act decisively. Love makes our blood sparkle with courage, makes us willing to take risks and gives us the nerve to be resolute. Love gives us senses more powerful than touching, smelling, tasting, seeing, and hearing. Unlike the cute and flighty eros of ancient times, our erotic impulses are at the center of everything humans have produced, and thus an essential aid in the fight for a better world."[56] Love appears in the final analysis, then, as a power that generates togetherness and courage. The courage is a courage to act in the name of what we deserve and demand, and this togetherness is expressed through forms of collective action, including but not limited to revolts and rebellions. Love makes commitments. Some commitments are difficult to make, not only for lack of courage but from indecision. Love often enters the scene as the substance that gives us the confidence to make commitments we wouldn't make without it. The

---

55. Ibid., 50.
56. Ibid., 69.

key is to grasp that while all of this is true in the love relationship of two or of four or of five or more in a family, it applies no less to larger social formations of being-together, beyond the family and its commitments. But to see this broader applicability outside of and beyond the family, we have to learn how to see the practice of love in moments of riot, revolt, and insurrection. Katsiaficas and others we have engaged in this chapter can help us to do that.

But to finally break with the other theories and theorists, let us be done with concealing the communism of love. Let us fully embrace the ever-present communism of love explored throughout this book. Let us reject any ideological refusal to see the clarity of love as a communist power, whether that resistance comes from liberals, conservatives, or even from those anarchists who (much like their conservative enemies) refuse to see communism outside of the state.

We have had to unpack the communism of love, but not for me or my thesis, and certainly not for communists. It is for the sake of everyone else that the irreducible communism of love must finally be made visible in its fundamental incontrovertibility. This is precisely because everyone is someone who aspires to love, who wants to give it or get it, to experience it, to live it, to know it, to be changed for the better by it. Love is not the private property of anyone, and least of all of the communists who have mostly ignored love as a soft and vaporous feeling unfit for materialism or militancy! For so many communists, love has been nothing but a private affection or idealist residue of religion or of secular, spiritual humanism. But that love has not been the purview of communists or communist theory does not mean that love itself is not a communist power. It can be nothing but, and those who aspire to love—which is to say most everyone everywhere—must finally see the communism of their aspiration. Why? Because only in so doing can we understand the relation of love to all of the other relations that surround us and govern our everyday lives. Only in so doing can we finally see that love has to be a counterpower to capital in order to be worthy of its name. It is therefore time to finally say not only what love can do, but what it is for and against.

CHAPTER 8

Conclusion: For and against

"The community of lovers—no matter if the lovers want it or not, enjoy it or not ... has as its ultimate goal the destruction of society. There where an episodic community takes shape between two beings who are made or who are not made for each other, a war machine is set up or, to say it more clearly, the possibility of a disaster carrying within itself, be it in infinitesimal doses, the menace of universal annihilation."

–Maurice Blanchot, *The Unavowable Community*

"Nearly everywhere ... instead of thinking, one merely takes sides: for or against. Such a choice replaces the activity of the mind. This is an intellectual leprosy; it originated in the political world and then spread through the land; contaminating all forms of thinking."

–Simone Weil, *On the Abolition of all Political Parties*

This chapter's epigraph from Simone Weil serves as a critical caution to us now. Any unthinking and uncritical taking of sides is a victory for one ideology or another, which rarely is the outcome of philosophical inquiry. Ideology relieves us of the burden of having to think—which admittedly can be difficult—and seeks instead to provide us the comfort, convenience, and stubborn confidence of a fixed position. But on the subject of love, we face a somewhat opposite problem. Love has generally been opposed *both* to thinking and to politics. Love, we are often told, is beyond all politics and should not be shrunk down to anything political. And love is commonly held to be more about ineffable feeling than thought. These bad ideas have contaminated discussions of love for too long, and we have tried to repudiate them in the present study. Love is a power, and for that reason we cannot sequester it from all politics or keep it trapped in theological and mystical privacy. Love is not a neutral power that agrees with everything. But love lives precariously in a world that vacillates between not knowing what it is and subjecting it to the values of capital.

Unfortunately for us, Hannah Arendt—who is not known for bad arguments—is on the other side of this debate. Arendt had a certain idea about love, which we must confront and overcome. In *The Human Condition*, Arendt wrote: "Because of its inherent worldlessness, love can only become false and perverted when it is used for political purposes such as the change or salvation of the world."[1] We should understand what Arendt means by the worldlessness of love. Arendt viewed the human world as a field of separation, as the terrain or environment that relates us as

---

1. Hannah Arendt, *The Human Condition* (Chicago: University of Chicago Press, 1958), 52.

separate, individual beings with private interests. On this premise, Arendt viewed politics as the most worldly affair possible because politics more than anything else is a field of separation. From that point of view, love appears as a tendency opposed to all of the dominant and defining worldly tendencies—it wants to connect us instead of separate us. This is its worldlessness. Arendt says it this way: "Love, by reason of its passion, destroys the in-between which relates us to and separates us from others."[2] Thus, against the worldly tendencies of separation, love functions as an abolitionist force, destroying the in-between and bringing people together. While I would quibble over Arendt's insistence on the necessary worldly tendency of human separation, as well as on her apparent rejection of dispassionate love, those are not my major disagreements here. My major disagreement with Arendt is over the conclusion that she draws.

Before going further, we should appreciate that not everything in Arendt's consideration of love is objectionable. She identifies the connective tissue of loving and rightly condemns the separation and isolation of contemporary privatization (which she views, once again rightly, as privation in the human condition). Arendt even identifies the widespread everyday "loneliness" of mass society, in The Origins of Totalitarianism, as a critical precondition of "totalitarian domination."[3] But none of that erases the fact that, according to Arendt, because love appears as an otherworldly or worldless force, and because politics is the most worldly of all earthly forces, love must be antipolitical. "Love, by its very nature, is unworldly, and it is for this reason rather than its rarity that it is not only apolitical but antipolitical, perhaps the most powerful of all antipolitical human forces."[4] This is the wrong conclusion.

This last claim of Arendt's is already refuted by her preceding claim about love as an abolitionist force destroying the in-between that separates us from others. The two claims appear on the same page of The Human Condition, and Arendt is not guilty of any oversight. Rather, she sees the two claims as consistent. To the contrary, I argue that the destruction of the in-between that relates and separates us is indeed political, but this position requires that we define the political differently than Arendt does. Following Marx, we find another way to speak of the in-between that separates us, which involves alienation, individuation, privatization, and competition. From that point of view, our relation to and separation from others is clearly political and economic and ultimately cultural too, as our

---

2. Ibid., 242.
3. Arendt, Origins of Totalitarianism, 478.
4. Arendt, Human Condition, 242.

worldly separation is a necessary feature of the capitalist division of labor. To say that love destroys the in-between that separates us from others, as Arendt does, and yet to insist that this abolition of the in-between is antipolitical is a mistake we can attribute to a dangerously defined conception of the political. Any idea of the political that excludes the conditions of our own disassociation—*or the abolition of those conditions*—is an idea of the political that we must reject. That is precisely what we have done in this book.

Perhaps love appears apolitical or antipolitical also because no one is against it. Or so it seems. But is love against anything or anyone? Does it not still sound peculiar to think of love as a force of negation, even after all these pages? We are all for love, but what is love for? Love cannot be made into a synonym for anything we like or may like to praise. When love was praised in Plato's *Symposium*, and when Badiou wrote *In Praise of Love*, we must remember that every effort to praise love in those works tried to say both what love is and what it is not. But if we don't take up love as a power, as a political concept, capital will continue to do with it whatever it pleases, for its own purposes. As Dunayevskaya correctly observed: "Capitalism tries to use everything for its power."[5] And as Illouz has demonstrated, capital has and will continue to make love into a word and idea for itself, just as it has so effectively done with other concepts such as democracy, freedom, and value.

Against capital, theorists such as Cornelius Castoriadis, Angela Y. Davis, Marina Sitrin, Jacques Rancière, and Jürgen Habermas have tried to tell us what democracy really means, just as others, including a long list of anticapitalists from Marxism, anarchism, and critical theory, have tried to tell us what freedom and value really are. Theory is full of confrontations with and deconstructions of the false forms of so many keywords and concepts. We must do the same for love. We cannot leave important matters to be decided by those who would use love to sell commodities, a particular form of life, or to defend identitarian racism or nationalism as if these were healthy instances of "self-love."

We can affirm the basic claim of Oskar Negt and Alexander Kluge: "Love politics is the field of experience in which humans are able to test their intimate conduct and at the same time their power of political judgment."[6] Negt and Kluge also understand the disposition of capitalist

---

5. Dunayevskaya, *Women's Liberation*, 180.

6. Oskar Negt and Alexander Kluge, *History and Obstinacy*, trans. Richard Langston with Cyrus Shahan, Martin Brady, Helen Hughes, and Joel Golb (New York: Zone Books, 2014), 341.

societies wherein "the realism of values is read economically: Is a thing or a service worth the money I pay for it? In this context, raising children, love relationships, the work of mourning, and joy are all 'unproductive labor.'"[7] But we have shown that capitalism does not leave such "unproductive labors" alone, as it appropriates family, love, and the whole range of human feeling as instruments of production, reproduction, and consumption. Negt and Kluge are right, however, about the noneconomic values of the most meaningful aspects of a human life. Nonetheless, the logic of capital does not stop at the boundary of homes and families, where children are the most expensive investment of a lifetime and economic pressures put love to its test. Capital even rules over the proceedings and aftereffects of death, as in how to pay for death and dying or what to do about the money. We have always been talking about love politics not only as a field of experience but also as a battlefield on which we must fight wars of maneuver and wars of position.

8.1 Love Against / Against Love

1. Love is against the isolation of the human person. As Arendt has said, tendencies that pull us apart are contrary to love. Many things that are not love also bring us together, from family gatherings and ceremonies to office parties, meetings, and airplanes. Not all forms of togetherness come from love. It is perhaps more reliable to find love by way of what it opposes, in what it resists, in how it breaks certain laws of our being-in-the-world. Alain Badiou writes: "Love is then itself exposed in its function of resistance to the law of being."[8] Wherever love is active, being is affected. Bodies in proximity are not evidence of the absence of isolation. The presence of physical bodies together on a train or plane, for example, does not indicate being present with others. Among such "false presences" one can find any number of technologically mediated forms of togetherness. We have not denied that isolation can be mediated to some extent through technology. But, technologically mediated sociality often abets isolation behind a pretense (a screen) of combatting it. We must think about love in order to know the difference between isolation and togetherness.

2. Love resists its common reduction to sex. Tendencies to view love in that narrow frame are tendencies against love. Active practices and

7. Ibid., 347.
8. Alain Badiou, *Conditions*, trans. Steven Corcoran (London: Bloomsbury, 2017), 187.

experiences of love move against that reduction, as can be seen in the loving nonsexual relationality of family, friends, and comrades. We have consistently recognized that sexual activity can be and is included in love relations, but so many people who crave love, to fall in love, to possess love, mistakenly think that the locus of love is in the sexual relationship. Hardt and Negri observe: "The modern concept of love is almost exclusively limited to the bourgeois couple and the claustrophobic confines of the nuclear family. Love has become a strictly private affair. We need a more generous and more unrestrained conception of love.... This does not mean you cannot love your spouse, your mother, and your child. It only means that your love does not end there, that love serves as the basis for our political projects in common and the construction of a new society. Without this love, we are nothing."[9]

Bodies matter, and so do bodily pleasures that we pursue in the private spaces of our lives. However, the fetishization of a mainly monogamous, heterosexual, and religious model of sexual togetherness invariably miniaturizes love to make it fit with a narrow strand of human relationality. Those of us who have actively loved other people know that love does not abide by such limits or laws, and this transgressive fact is telling. Instead of trying to contain love by way of conventions about sexuality and sexual activity, we should understand and confront the potentially terrifying and ungovernable nature of love in the human world.

3. Love works against the privatization and commodification of life and relationships, and, in that way, it always expresses a certain communism. Tendencies to convert every aspect of life into a salable commodity fit for exchange are tendencies in tension with love. As discussed in chapter 3, this is one of the most significant facts that has made communist inattention to love so anomalous. That inattention can be explained, but the explanations are no excuse. Even those hostile to communist ideas, if they have experienced love, have some sense of communist relations. Even anticommunists would be offended if their friends or lovers or parents or children demanded payment to remain their friends or lovers or parents or children. Money organizes life and governs us, but it is not a totality.

The communists who have best understood the communism of love have been women. This has nothing to do with any essentialist claim about cisgender women, but rather is a feature of the long historical socialization of women toward care for others. The labor of care has been unpaid,

---

9. Michael Hardt and Antonio Negri, *Multitude: War and Democracy in the Age of Empire* (New York: Penguin Books, 2004), 351–52.

and capital cannot value it appropriately because the value of care super-sedes exchange value. This point has been well argued by Silvia Federici, Selma James, Leopoldina Fortunati, and others. However, understanding that the work of caregiving has been sexualized, feminized, exploited, and denied by capital helps to explain why people like Jenny Marx, Rosa Lux-emburg, and Alexandra Kollontai, among other radical women, have been so keen to see the communism of care. Of course, so-called women's work *should* be paid for with a better approximation of its social value. And we should stress that even outside capitalist exchange value, taking care of the sick, elderly, children, and the most vulnerable members of society would remain of utmost importance. A long history of taking care of each other attests to a primitive yet still-necessary communism. It is perhaps not surprising that Luxemburg understood long before her male comrades the importance of sharpening our regard for everything that suffers.

4. Love can be the most important counterpower against psychosocial sicknesses. Anything within the social, economic, and political setting of life that diminishes our ability to have healthy relationships with other human beings, to develop a robust sense of our own worth, is contrary to loving others and ourselves. Psychosocial maladies such as depression and anxiety and panic disorders are not totally incompatible with loving, but they run in opposite directions. The epidemic loneliness and depression we have studied in this book, growing anxiety, social withdrawal, precari-ty, fear, ruthless competition, and maladaptive permutations like *karoshi*, *otaku*, and *hikikomori* are all characteristic features of life in our contem-porary capitalist societies.

Martin Luther King, Jr., wrote about the relationship of fear and anx-iety to love. He held that "Love casts out fear. This truth is not without a bearing on our personal anxieties."[10] When white people look at Black people and are afraid of them, King argued, they are filled with anxiety. Fear and anxiety also characterize a life of economic insecurity, uncertain-ty during times of war and displacement, rampant racist violence, and police brutality; they may also come from feelings of jealousy and low self-confidence. We cannot abolish all fear and anxiety with love. I am entirely unpersuaded by King's idea that we can erase hatred through pro-fessing love. What is a profession of love, we should ask, where there is no real feeling to substantiate it? There may be no real love for the cop who beats you, and why should there be? Love is elsewhere and doing other things, and only where it is being acted out in the world as a praxis does

---

10. King, *Gift of Love*, 120–21.

it counteract destructive tendencies within our society. This explains why many theorists of love, from Fromm to hooks, have advocated a love ethic in practice, which takes the form of an activist life that hopes, at least in part, to counteract any number of fears, anxieties, and insecurities.

5. Love acts against the complex hierarchies of white supremacy, nationalist imperialism, and sexism, as well as their normalization in society and politics. White supremacy, nationalism, and sexism, even in their most subtle and least detectable forms, have to be understood as antagonists to love, even though they often hide behind invocations of self-love or the love of one's own. We cannot call these hierarchies love because of their irreducibly narcissistic core, which is often expressed as hostility to or disregard of others unlike them. Capitalism, in the way that it structures wealth as power, is also a hierarchy, but it is not the only one. We must beware of other hierarchical tendencies in politics and populist movements that endorse narcissistic declarations of hatred and fear as self-love. Such attentiveness, however, cannot come only from surveilling our enemies, for it also requires listening deeply to Black men and women, people of color, women of all identities, and sexual minorities, including those participating in new transgender movements. Existing hierarchies from white supremacy to patriarchy regard the points of view of such groups with little hospitality or concern. But these are often matters of life and death and therefore demand serious attention and real understanding.

Huey P. Newton wrote about what he called "revolutionary suicide" in order to capture the sense of wanting to live only with hope and dignity and therefore being willing to die in the struggle for a life worth living. Revolutionary suicide is about understanding the risk of death in the struggle for life. Black people take great risks whenever they attempt to directly confront and oppose any problem of white supremacist society. White supremacist societies are set up to police disaffected Black people and to incarcerate a wildly disproportionate subset of populations of color. When Black people stand up to declare that Black Lives Matter, when they become ungovernable with indignation in the face of police brutality, they are—quite unlike white people in the same society—risking imprisonment, death, or both. Newton understood this well.

> I do not think that life will change for the better without an assault on the Establishment, which goes on exploiting the wretched of the earth. This belief lies at the heart of revolutionary suicide. Thus it is better to oppose the forces that drive me to self-murder than to endure them. Although I risk the likelihood of death, there is at least

the possibility, if not the probability, of changing intolerable conditions.... Revolutionary suicide does not mean that I and my comrades have a death wish; it means just the opposite.[11]

The critical insight here is to recognize that, for the despised and marginalized among us, one risks death by demanding a life of hope and dignity.

Sometimes women, transgender people, sexual minorities, Black people, and others keep quiet and stay hidden in the margins not because it affirms dignity but because becoming visible and audible in a world that doesn't want to see or hear them is dangerous. We always have to look at and listen to the margins because only there can we can note what's missing in the body text, what the dominant story leaves out. The activity of love works against marginalizing hierarchy, but we have to nurture the connective tissue of human relations with something that precedes solidarity: *attention*. Pay attention to the locked up, left out, vilified, and marginalized. Attention is the precursor to real concern, understanding, and action.

6. Love works against insecurity by establishing other securities. Economic crises deepen our precariousness and undermine our confidence in a life of meaningful work. High-speed and growing expectations for total flexibility turn connections to liquid, making so many things that were fixed for previous generations into constant flows. In the midst of a liquid and often chaotic life, love can still be both insurance and an assurance that at least something will hold. It is decreasingly the case that a parent's money can effectively come to the aid of their child. So family love must strive for a nonmonetary security. Following Zygmunt Bauman, we must think not only of our security and the security of our loved ones, but also of the precarious state of immigrants and refugees who flee one instability only to arrive at another. What can love do there? Active love in the world seeks to mitigate insecurity and diminish precarity. Therefore, love is most needed in precisely those places where people are most vulnerable, where people live the most insecure lives. This is yet another reason—if another were needed—that love cannot be conceived of as the terrain of bourgeois romance. In the romantic conception of bourgeois society, to think of love is to think of one's own life. But the greatest demands on love should come first from the lives of the most vulnerable and insecure.

7. Love is opposed to alienation and to the passivity that comes from depoliticization. Wherever people accept their isolation and do nothing to

---

11. Huey P. Newton, *Revolutionary Suicide* (New York: Penguin Books, 2009), 3.

express their disaffection, that alienation and passivity is hostile to love because it only grows the in-between that separates us, that renders us inactive and invisible. This is why it is a mistake to care only about the results of every revolt. In the face of every uprising, liberals and conservatives only want to know how policies and political institutions have been changed. We have to resist such quantitative assessments and look instead for an insurgent love, not only for what it accomplishes in politics and policy but because it counteracts alienation and passivity.

In the present theory, love is not only creative and kind, for it is also oppositional, antagonistic, and against so much in the world as we know it. Although it sounds perhaps too idealistic, I ultimately endorse Simone Weil's claim that "all that is highest in a human life, every effort of thought, every effort of love, has a corrosive action on the established order."[12] This is one of the main reasons we need to see love activated in politics: not only for what we want, but to mobilize activity against what we do not want. This is how love participates in what Dunayevskaya calls the first negation.

Yet we are also for love because of what love is for.

8.2 Love For / For Love

1. Love is for the *Gemeinwesen*. When we are motivated to come together because the togetherness itself helps us to realize our being-in-the-world and deepens our existential connection to others—especially to others unlike us—we are motivated to expand our humanity beyond the purview of an isolated self. This means expanding being-in-the-world, communalizing or communizing being. Communist being-in-the-world is difficult to achieve in the world such as it is. I may want to see my colleagues, comrades, and friends, but there are other things I need to do, and in the world such as it is, those other things are often done best without my colleagues, comrades, and friends. Yes, I can imagine a different world, one in which my work, the caretaking of my children, my attention to my partner, my maintenance of a household, and my active connection to the lives of others in a small circle of family could all be done well or better without having to be cut off from colleagues, comrades, and friends. But in the capitalist lifeworld, everything is monetized, especially time, and

---

12. Simone Weil, *Oppression and Liberty*, trans. Arthur Wills and John Petrie (London: Routledge, 2001), 137.

efficiency and functionality are laws at the heart of capital. As Marx and Camatte understood so well, the *Gemeinwesen* was one of the first casualties of capital, but love seeks its recomposition, restoration, and renewal.

2. Love aims for the supersession of sex. This is to say that every durable being-together that supersedes sexual bodily pleasure is for love. We live in societies that valorize youth, youthful beauty, speed, energy, and stamina. Every romantic reduction of love to sexual relations depicts uncontrollable passion for the other's body and being, for an erotic explosion that is sustained over time. But real explosions do not work like that. Explosions are periodic, and we would do better to call the nonsexual sustenance between people love, because love continues to keep people together—even those who are romantically *in love*—after sexual activity dies down or fails, or in the wake of an unhealthy body. We have considered the widespread recognition of love in the nonsexual relations of family and friends, and yet so much of the literature studied in this book, and so much of the common discourse on love, thinks first to the romantic and sexual activity of bodily pleasures. That is to be included, of course, but we must learn to think first of love as a mode of relationality that increases, revitalizes, or reconstructs some *Gemeinwesen*, even the *Gemeinwesen* whose sociality has yet to be determined.

3. Love makes value beyond exchange value. When people and experiences and activities and events are valued for reasons other than their exchangeability, that is a valuation for love. Have you played drums that no one has heard? Have you been moved by or made a painting that no one has paid for? Have you cherished a moment or experience with another human being, outside of work and money, in a public park, holding hands with affection, awed by the leaves falling from trees? Have you loved an animal, deeply appreciated a bird or a cat or even marveled at the world of an insect, perhaps as Rosa Luxemburg did for her beloved Mimi and other creatures? Luxemburg's affection for Mimi, like care for an infant child, could potentially be monetized, but that would be irrelevant to its value. *We are talking about the value of other valuations.* If I am playing the drums and get to a space of deep feeling and listening, of complex nonlinguistic interaction with another musician, a scientist may explain the experience in a demystified way. But the real value of the experience is a noncapitalist value, a value beyond and even against exchange value, like that of the picture of my father in my wallet or a note from my son in my pocket. We have to recognize and defend such valuations whenever we love something or someone that we do not pay for. In short, love is for values that exceed capitalist valuation.

Maurice Blanchot observed that real community only forms in the burdens we have in common, and that real community breaks with exchange relations. The life of a community, he argues, is the life "of the inexchangeable—of that which ruins exchange. Exchange always goes by the law of stability."[13] Blanchot means that the community and the people who comprise it come together not from some stable state of affairs, but rather from instability on a field of disproportionately shared burdens. A community and the individuals that comprise it are mutable and subject to change and in various stages of becoming. Exchange presupposes stability, equality, and fixity, for without those features in the basic structure, no exchange could be even. But real community forms out of the relative absence of stability, equality, and fixity, and wants to become something other than a set of exchange relations. The relations that comprise a community can be understood and appreciated, but not forced into the immutable measurements of exchangeability.

Hardt and Negri connect Blanchot's observations on community to love, proclaiming: "Become different than you are! These singularities, act in common and thus form ... a new race or, rather, a new humanity. When love is conceived politically, then, this creation of a new humanity is the ultimate act of love."[14] I agree, but the creation of any new humanity is up against a far greater challenge than acting on behalf of a new conception of love. Any new conception of love will need to draw on its very old—indeed ancient—incompatibility with capitalist exchange relations, meaning that we need less attention to constructing a new idea of love than to unpacking and understanding love as a basic human aspiration traceable in global histories.

4. Love is for health, yours and mine. When we think of the health of other people, for the sake of the well-being of the social body, of the family, and the world, we think from the position of love. Love is not as necessary as water. We can live for a long time without love, but doing so is bad for us. We have created ways to try to stay sane and to ameliorate our isolation and despair, but these are often inadequate surrogates, avatars of friendship and family, maintained through the single-stranded interactions of technological relationality.

People usually do not cry out from the darkness of despair and loneliness that what they need is love, unless they are listening to a song or reading poetry. A demand for love seems vague and insufficient. But it

---

13. Blanchot, *Writing of the Disaster*, 87.
14. Hardt and Negri, *Multitude*, 356.

is time, if it is not too late, to consider in concrete ways the actual relationship between a world in which love is difficult and all of the new maladies and pathologies of panic, anxiety, depression, and so on. One concretizing question: What would a healthcare system look like if it were made by love? Even policymakers can ask that question, and if it begins vague, it can be made concrete through consideration. But policymakers are not reading this book, and they will never read it (remember its title). Beyond policy, love means disconnecting from toxic and abusive relationships within one's own family, including even from one's own sister or mother or father or brother. Health and well-being rely on connections but may sometimes require disconnections too. An unhealthy world is full of sick, narcissistic people with no sense of what love means. Those people have children, and those children often get healthy only after making certain disconnections and other new connections. Thinking about love and human health puts us in a good place from which to concretely take up these issues.

5. Love is for radical equality and communist inclusion, against the exclusive hierarchies of white supremacy, nationalism, and sexism, all of which are concerned with defending unequal and exclusive powers. Here love appears as an abolitionist force. If, for example, we love Black men and women, both in principle and practice, and if we look at others in other countries as our sisters and brothers, and if we confront histories of sexism and racism that continue up to the present, then the practice of love takes humanist form through argument and counteractive relationalities. That is, love makes a case for the abolition of racialized hierarchy and patriarchy in both thought and action.

Humanism is for love because humanism advocates ethical obligation to and responsive regard for others than ourselves, others than "our own kind." No humanism is limited to those just like us, to only "our own kind." To be clear, I am not posing radical equality as a denial of difference, and I am not posing radical inclusion as inattention to unequal needs. I agree with Marx on the question of equality, as he took it up in *Critique of the Gotha Programme*.[15] Rather, we need to raze racist, sexist, and imperialist logics to the ground, we need to see their total decimation in both argument and feeling, which can be cultivated in various ways and places. It seems to me that the real destruction of racist, sexist, and imperialist thinking would result in a basic humanism. Love does not advocate

---

15. See Marx's discussion of equality as a system of unequal rights, particularly in part I, point 3, in *Critique of the Gotha Programme* (New York: International Publishers, 2002).

CONCLUSION: FOR AND AGAINST | 313

accepting the unacceptable or tolerating the intolerable, and love may even give rise to armed insurrection and violence in a conflict with an enemy (history is replete with examples). This means that love's humanism is not unwaveringly pacifist.

6. Love is for the creation of precarious little communes, which are increasingly necessary in a liquid world defined by chaos and insecurity. Our little communes are for love, for the sustenance of meaningful connections in a world of single-stranded interaction and general disconnection. Little communes of community centers, publishers and authors, activists, artists, musicians, forums, families with or without children, workers on strike, and other groups of joyfully gathering people give us experience with a certain *Gemeinwesen* and counteract feelings of isolation in practices of a different relationality.

In May 2017, I went on strike with my faculty colleagues. We gathered daily outside of the university. Many did not join us. Many who have vocally supported unions for their entire lives did not join us. Many who said they were supportive did not join us. I will never forget who did and who did not join the strike, and I especially remember the students who stood up with courage and shouted at the chancellor's window. The strike was not the creation of a real community, and it was not communist in any easily discernible sense. Many of the most active participants were liberals and Democrats, and many went to the line with fear and trepidation, mustering the courage to refute the usual defamations about striking workers, which in the case of professors is that they don't care about their students.

But the point I want to convey is about the logic of the strike. Workers on strike are not a family per se (although in some cases they may be), and there is no security in going on strike. In our case, we were docked pay for each day of the strike, and many younger colleagues wondered how their participation might impact their tenure and promotions. I worried about my students who would be graduating in the weeks to come, and how the strike might impact them and their state of mind. One could say that our strike was motivated by money because we demanded a contract that stipulated some increases in pay and other similar provisions. But this is not what motivated and mobilized the strike. More generally, it is not usually what motivates and mobilizes other strikes. The idea that workers could not possibly have any interests beyond wages and income is one of the greatest—and stupidest—lies of capitalist mythology. In our case (and each case is different), we wanted the power to check an increasingly unilateral and top-down administration that had proven able to decide our lives at the university. We wanted the so-called "fifth floor" administration to have its power curbed, its will thwarted where and when necessary, and its self-interest hobbled, because we did not like what they did with unchecked power (which sometimes included increasing pay, usually their own!).

But the strike was a little precarious commune, motivated by a different logic than the logic of profit. A family keeps together in a somewhat similar way, but a good family endures for longer than a strike. Some precarious communes, like a strike, make little stands against a world of insecurity, and even if they don't make any lasting communism, they matter. They do not change everything, but they change *some* things. The enlargement of the little precarious commune is a little bit of communism, and in the case of strikes and occupations, we see a little communism that does not necessarily rely on the activity of communists. If we remain materialists who want more than ideological opposition—that is, if we are carrying on a certain Marxism—then we have to accept the noncommunist content of communist experiences and experiments that change relations and challenge relations of power. Merleau-Ponty's maxim is largely true: "It is impossible to be an anti-Communist and it is not possible to be a Communist."[16] For example, most of the world's lovers would denounce communism yet seek communism in their healthiest relations and activities, in their own little communes. For Merleau-Ponty, it was impossible to be a communist only insofar as communists would have to reject what was passing for "communism" in 1947.

But there is always some love in the practice of communist forms of life and activity, whether those forms are short-term or long-term. As in the strike, there is always something there about the power and necessity of an oppositional gathering that follows a rival logic.

7. At a social level, love seeks the abolition of alienation. People want love because they expect it to counteract alienation, whether that is a sexual alienation, alienation at work while doing estranged labor, or alienation in a family of neglect or abuse. Also, meaningful social relations can generate, over time, the love relations that matter in our lives. I have written about movements—social, political, and cultural—but also about insurgency, revolt, and insurrection. Like the strike, the romantic love of lovers, or the bookstore gathering of activists for regular discussion of texts, revolt offers a being-together that is—in between specific demands

---

16. Maurice Merleau-Ponty, *Humanism and Terror: An Essay on the Communist Problem*, trans. John O'Neill (Boston: Beacon, 1969), xxi.

and motivations—trying to gather a pool of feeling for others, and for another world. It does not make any sense to claim that every movement or insurgency is connected or committed to a concept of love. That cannot be reconciled with what insurrectionists themselves say they are doing: they do not always speak of love. We must consult what insurgents say, and we must start from there. We cannot generalize about an amorphous "love movement" in every instance of revolt. That is the kind of ideologizing we have opposed from the start.

Alienation in present societies of capitalist technology is debilitating, at a crisis point, and the single-stranded connections of our technological togetherness are not turning things around. Technologies of relationality are mostly—though not entirely—taking us further down the road of loneliness and isolation, and into pseudosocial surrogates of the *Gemeinwesen*. When people rise up—as they always have and will—they rise up for specific reasons as in a strike or an occupation or a demonstration or civil disobedience or armed rebellion. But something else happens there too, inside the space of collective action. An experience with a form of togetherness becomes part of the event and of the memory of the event. The social or political movement communicates to each participant that they are not totally alone, that they can act against their alienation.

We have discussed loneliness within the loving family because we know it is there, even alongside love. Feelings of alienation at work say nothing about the presence of love in the home, so one may feel alienated in both modes of life. One cannot simply decide to activate love against their daily reality, because love needs other people (this is perhaps its core virtue). But we know the difference between love relations and exchange relations, and even capitalists who defend the latter demand the former in their lives. Love relations practice a communist being-in-the-world that approaches universality, if we may still allow ourselves to think about the universal. According to Badiou: "In our world, love is the guardian of the universality of the true."[17] Love is an experience, an event, and a practice that keeps us from forgetting that there are some things about a human life (not only in our biology) that are true for everyone everywhere.

Readers of my work know well that when I say "communism" I never mean to refer to an institutional-political administration of social and economic affairs. The communism I speak of is always about forms of life, not forms of government. The communism I speak of aims at revolutionary transformations of life, including and especially the creative production

---

17. Badiou, *Conditions*, 190.

of new forms of life. While the communism I speak of is a social—and not primarily *political*—movement, the basic structures of legal order and politics are always implicated. Insurrectionary upheavals that confront the legal order and its limitations and purposes as established by capitalist power are movements that understand their own incommensurability with the existing state of things.

Readers of this book should not underestimate the significance of its conclusions, however tentative those may be. We have gravitated toward philosophies of love that have helped us to critically explore the specific questions of this project. We have generally not attended to others. To take one obvious example: Martha Nussbaum, one of the most influential philosophers of our time, wrote a philosophy of love too, *Political Emotions: Why Love Matters for Justice* (2013). But in this major 450-page study, Nussbaum is almost totally silent on the incommensurability of love relations with capitalist exchange relations. She thinks that Marx has nothing to contribute to her inquiry, mentioning him once in passing and without significance to her central questions. Aside from a single chapter that confronts questions of love in the context of inequality and resource distribution, Nussbaum gives little attention to the political economy of love. She assumes that we can pursue a politics of love within the limits of existing political economy, and she assumes that a politics of love will lead to increasing justice, the latter being fully compatible with the capitalist organization of life.[18]

True, Nussbaum wants to change our societies. She observes that "all love has aspects of the ideal, and political love no less than parental or personal love. When we love people, we want to be good to them, and this typically means being better than we sometimes, even usually, are. Personal love, like political love, is threatened by narrowness, partiality, and narcissism, and love therefore involves a continual struggle."[19] But whereas the struggle we imagine follows Marx, Fromm, hooks, and a history of revolts and rebellions, Nussbaum follows Abraham Lincoln, Jawaharlal Nehru, and Martin Luther King, Jr., instead (and I note that King's socialism appears irrelevant to her). Whereas Nussbaum assumes that the existing basic structure of liberal capitalist society is not a problem and that our problems can be adequately addressed within its boundaries, I

---

18. See Martha Nussbaum, *Political Emotions: Why Love Matters for Justice* (Cambridge, MA: Harvard University Press, 2013), esp. chaps. 5 and 11. On her basic faith in the full compatibility of justice with capitalism, Nussbaum agrees with John Rawls, another major American liberal philosopher of the late twentieth century.

19. Nussbaum, *Political Emotions*, 384.

have argued that love inexorably suggests a structural transformation of capitalist society, a passage only possible through revolutionary movements and revolts aimed at radically different forms of life, toward a sociality ungoverned by money or exchange relations. Whereas we find capitalism and its social logic hostile to relations of love, for Nussbaum the main problems are inadequate compassion and political conservatism.

Certain conclusions of the present study, which have been substantiated along the way, must now be plainly stated. What is called "love" by the best thinkers who have approached the subject is the beating heart of communism. The love that we have been theorizing tends toward communism in every meaningful way, even if only in miniature. The love that we have been theorizing, which is neither a commodity nor a private property nor a corrupt "love" of only one's self or one's "own kind," tends toward a humanizing sociality, toward the *Gemeinwesen* in and against a world of alienation. If we would speak of a politics of love, we would have to speak of a politics of insurgency against the order of exchange. Whether or not readers have been fully convinced by my arguments, the human aspiration for love is as close as we may ever get to a universal communist aspiration. Maybe today, then, a person's real communist sensibility is evidence of a figurative heart. A simple notion, in the end: no communism, no heart.

What we are after, and what we must strive to participate in, contribute to, and create—in *word, friendship,* and *revolt*—are real experiences of love as a communist power. What is the particular practice this implies? Most immediately and concretely, we can point out, illustrate, and otherwise show the communism of love wherever, whenever, and however we are able to show it. The world is full of lovers and those who are looking for love, and it is not as full of communists. Does the multifarious humanity of the world understand the irreducible communism of the basic aspiration to love? Do they grasp the organic and necessarily communist content of the being-in-the-world that they live for? If not, we may act in the world as midwives for the birth of that understanding. But, we cannot create movements all alone or whenever and wherever we want to. Most times, you can only have an effect within your own little lifeworld, and you can only touch fragments of your cause as the larger world that encircles you seems indifferent to your existence or point of view. But we also know that movements in *word, friendship,* and *revolt* are happening and will continue to happen, sometimes when we least expect them and with people we could have never guessed we'd know.

Marx often spoke of "real knowledge" as opposed to false knowledge (ideology), and he juxtaposed real value (for example, personal worth) to exchange value and real "numberless indefeasible" freedoms to free trade.[20] Today, however, we must beware all discourses of "authenticity," especially since that mutable term has become a distinguishing mark of quality for commodities in the marketplace. Yet despite any healthy suspicion of claims to authenticity, it remains both possible and necessary to distinguish communism from its vilified form as spectacle during the Cold War, just as it is necessary to distinguish real capitalism from its mythological and false form of promised, inevitable prosperity. You may have also heard that the anarchists never really called for total chaos and violence, as it was mainly the anarchists' most Hobbesian enemies who insisted we'd have nothing but murder and mayhem without a strong government to repress our vile human nature. Distinctions such as these matter. In a similar way, it is time to fully realize the fact that love—if love means anything at all—is antithetical to the logic of capital. Exchange relations maintained and ruled by money cannot be associated with love any more than upward mobility should be associated with capitalism, Stalin should be associated with communism, or chaos should be associated with anarchy. No, all of these associations are demonstrably false and dangerous too, and we must break those false associations in defense of the actual meaning of things.

We must break any association of love with capital for the sake of association itself. And if we do not see the communism of love, that is only because we do not think enough about love. Additionally, we must look for real opportunities to participate in the experimentation, theorization, imagination, and realization of new ways of being, new forms of *being-against*, new forms of *being-for*, new forms of *being-with*.

As Simone Weil wrote: "One can only steer towards an ideal. The ideal is just as unattainable as the dream, but differs from the dream in that it concerns reality; it enables one, as a mathematical limit, to grade situations, whether real or realizable, in an order of value from least to greatest."[21] Above all, it is necessary to retrieve and rethink value in a society designed to eliminate all values but one. We have to allow ourselves to imagine what could come from extrapolating what we know from our own experiences of love in the little communes that make our lives worth living.

---

20. See Karl Marx, *German Ideology* and *Communist Manifesto* in Kamenka, *Portable Marx*, 170 and 206, respectively.

21. Weil, *Oppression and Liberty*, 79–80.

Index